T0169106

JFK –
FROM PARKLAND
TO BETHESDA

The Ultimate Kennedy Assassination Compendium

VINCENT MICHAEL PALAMARA

JFK – FROM PARKLAND TO BETHESDA: The Ultimate Kennedy Assassination Compendium
Copyright © 2015 Vincent Michael Palamara. All Rights Reserved.

Published by:
Trine Day LLC
PO Box 577
Walterville, OR 97489
1-800-556-2012
www.TrineDay.com
publisher@trineday.net

Library of Congress Control Number: 2015951109

Palamara, Vincent Michael
JFK – FROM PARKLAND TO BETHESDA: The Ultimate Kennedy Assassination Compendium —1st ed.
p. cm.

Epub (ISBN-13)   978-1-63424-028-4
Kindle (ISBN-13)   978-1-63424-029-1
Print (ISBN-13)   978-1-63424-027-7
1. Kennedy, John F. – (John Fitzgerald), – 1917-1963 – Assassination. 2. United States. – Secret Service – Officials and employees – Biography. 3. United States. – Secret Service – History – 20th century. I. Title

First Edition
10 9 8 7 6 5 4 3 2 1

Printed in the USA
Distribution to the Trade by:
Independent Publishers Group (IPG)
814 North Franklin Street
Chicago, Illinois 60610
312.337.0747
wwpgbook.com

"...Secret Service men literally seized the body from local officials at Parkland Hospital, who were demanding that an autopsy be performed in accordance with Texas law. If the law had been observed, there might have been no controversy, and the Bethesda doctors, and the FBI and the Secret Service would have escaped the heavy responsibility they now bear. Sadly and ironically, the report of the autopsy performed on the murdered Oswald in Dallas is a model of clarity and precision alongside the sloppy, ambiguous and incomplete record of the autopsy President Kennedy received...the President's body remains the object of obscene speculation, and the country suffers needless, disruptive controversy. As matters stand, no single element of the (Warren) Commission's version of the assassination is more suspect than the official account of the President's autopsy."

–*The Saturday Evening Post*
January 14, 1967

CONTENTS

INTRODUCTION

I. PARKLAND HOSPITAL – THE DOCTORS, NURSES, AND SUNDRY OTHER PEOPLE WHO WERE IN SOME WAY CONNECTED TO THE EMERGENCY TREATMENT OF PRESIDENT KENNEDY IN DALLAS, TEXAS ON NOVEMBER 22, 1963:

LIMOUSINE, WINDSHIELD, SKULL FRAGMENT

INCLUDES FELLOW AGENTS GEORGE HICKEY, JOHN JOE HOWLETT, JAMES

Contents

Rowley, Floyd Boring, Paul Paterni, Charles Taylor, Richard Keiser, Donald Brett, Harry Geiglein, Abraham Bolden, Gerald Behn, Morgan Gies, John Marshall, Ernest Aragon, Elmer Moore, Gilbert Paraschos, Martin Kennedy, Frank Hancock, Claude Davis, Victor Gonzalez, John Simpson, Robert Bouck, And Prs Photographers James K. Fox & Howard K. Norton; C-130 Crew Members: Capt. Roland Thomason, Wayne Schake, Vincent Gullo, Hershal Woosley, David Conn, Stephen Bening, And Frank Roberson; Chief Petty Oficers William Martinell And Thomas Mills; Newsman Richard Dudman And Frank Cormier; Dpd Motorcycle Officer H.r. Freeman; Spectators Evalea Glanges And Carl Renas; White House Policeman J.w. Edwards, J.c. Rowe, Snyder, Rubenstal, Burke, And Edmunds; And Fbi Agents Orrin Bartlett, Charles Killian, Cortlandt Cunningham, Robert Frazier, And Walter Thomas; Charles Brehm, And Seymour Weitzman

Contents

II. DALLAS, PARKLAND, AND BETHESDA:

{INTERLUDE}

INC. FELLOW AGENTS RICHARD JOHNSEN, DAVID GRANT, SAMUEL SULLIMAN, AND ERNEST OLSSON. PLUS: DARRELL TOMLINSON, RONNY FULLER, NATHAN POOL, AND GOVERNOR AND MRS. JOHN CONNALLY

III. BETHESDA – THE DOCTORS, TECHNICIANS, AND OTHER SUNDRY PEOPLE WHO WERE CONNECTED in some way to the autopsy of President Kennedy at the National Naval Medical Center in Bethesda, Maryland on November 22, 1963:

Contents

IV. Miscellaneous:

Contents

V. VARIOUS MOTORCADE OCCUPANTS:

SMELL OF GUNPOWDER, SMOKE

INCLUDES TOM DILLARD, DPD EARLE BROWN, MRS. ELIZABETH CABELL, CONGRESSMAN RAY ROBERTS, MRS. DONALD BAKER, SENATOR RALPH YARBOROUGH, DPD B.J. MARTIN, DPD JOE M. SMITH, BEVERLY OLIVER, JAMES L. SIMMONS, RICHARD DODD, SAM HOLLAND, LEE BOWERS, NOLAN POTTER, CLEMON JOHNSON, AUSTIN MILLER, THOMAS MURPHY, WALTER WINBORN, FRANK REILLY, JEAN HILL, W.W. MABRA, AND ED HOFFMAN

MISSED SHOT/ PAVEMENT, MANHOLE COVER/ TURF

INC. ROYCE SKELTON, JACK FRANZEN, MRS. FRANZEN, SECRET SERVICE AGENT WARREN TAYLOR, JAMES TAGUE, DPD J.W. FOSTER, HUGH BETZNER, WAYNE AND EDNA HARTMAN, CLEMON EARL JOHNSON, HARRY CABLUCK, DPD D.V. HARKNESS, DPD CARL DAY, ROGER CRAIG, AND BUDDY WALTHERS

BACK WOUND

VI. MISC. EYEWITNESSES:

Contents

VARIOUS SOURCES USED, SPECIAL THANKS, AUTHOR INTERVIEWS, CORRESPONDENCE LISTING

INTRODUCTION

T he medical evidence in the assassination of JFK is, without question, the biggest and most daunting area of the case to study, bar none. This is also an avenue of the case that can be both compelling and frustrating for these very same reasons, as there are literally hundreds of books, thousands of articles, and perhaps millions of documents to peruse on the subject from numerous authors, reporters, the National Archives, the Warren Commission, the House Select Committee on Assassinations (HSCA), and the Assassination Records Review Board (ARRB), just to name the major repositories of related statements, testimony and reports. When one factors in the Internet and the potential for repetition from authors citing the same or similar primary sources, one can become lost in a literal quagmire of data, to say the least.

Hence, the reason for this book.

That said, please do not look at this work as (just) "a book", per se, but a roadmap – a GPS, so to speak – through miles and miles of literary jungle. In short, the ultimate JFK assassination medical evidence compendium, a truly unique endeavor in the gigantic morass of the Kennedy murder literary world. Want to know what every medical evidence related witness had to say or write about the wounds of President Kennedy and other related, vitally important items? This is THE source for current students and future historians to delve into.

My first book, Survivor's Guilt: The Secret Service and the Failure to Protect President Kennedy , took over 20 years to research and write, as it was my goal to present the most detailed and comprehensive look at the JFK agent detail in every respect related to November 22, 1963. In the middle of that project (starting in 1998, to be exact), I began a side project on my other major obsession with regard to the JFK assassination – the medical evidence and the statements by the Parkland doctors, Bethesda witnesses, and all other related sundry and vital persons. Thus was born JFK – From Parkland to Bethesda: The Ultimate Kennedy Assassination

Compendium: my vision of what the penultimate encyclopedia/ dictionary on the JFK assassination medical evidence would look like. This one "only" took a little over 15 years to refine and complete. I hope you find it both fascinating and useful.

Vince Palamara
December 29, 2014

I

PARKLAND HOSPITAL

1) Dr. William Kemp "High Pockets" Clark – Chief Neurosurgeon:

a. WR 516-518/ 17 H 1-3 / CE 392 [undated summary; see also 21 H 150-152: Clark's 11/23/63 report to Admiral Burkley with the verbatim summary. In addition, see *Assassination Science*, pp. 416-418: this is an FBI report dated 11/25/63 which includes the verbatim summary to Burkley from 11/23/63]: "...in the occipital region of the skull..."; "There was a large wound in the right occipito parietal region..."; "Both cerebral and cerebellar tissue were extruding from the wound.";

b. WR 524-525/ 17 H 9-10 /CE 392: handwritten report 11/22/63---"The President was bleeding profusely from the back of the head. There was a large (3 x 3 cm) remnant of cerebral tissue present... there was a smaller amount of cerebellar tissue present also"; "There was a large wound beginning in the right occiput extending into the parietal region..."

c. Parkland Press conference, 11/22/63, 3:16 PM CST [*Assassination Science*, pp. 427]: "A missile had gone in or out of the back of his head... the back of his head... I was busy with his head wound... The head wound could have been either the exit wound from the neck or it could have been a tangential wound, as it was simply a large, gaping loss of tissue."

d. *New York Times*, 11/24/63---"Dr. Kemp Clark... said that there were two wounds, a traumatic wound in the back of the head and a small entrance wound below the Adam's apple... He said the [head] wound was 'large with a considerable loss of tissue'" (the same day, *The Los Angeles Times* reported that "The occipito parietal, which is a part of the back of the head, had a huge flap.");

e. AP article, 11/26/63---"...said in Dallas today that a bullet did much massive damage at the right rear of the President's head... A missile had (come or gone) out the back of his head..."

f. *Washington Evening Star*, 11/27/63---"Clark... said in Dallas yesterday that a bullet did such massive damage at the right rear of the President's head that attending surgeons could not tell whether it had entered or come out of the head there."

g. *New York Times*, 11/27/63: article by John Herbers---"...Clark, who pronounced Mr. Kennedy dead, said one struck him at about the necktie knot. 'It ranged downward in his chest and did not exit', the surgeon said. The second he called

1

a 'tangential wound' caused by a bullet that struck the 'right back of his head'";

h.   CBS, NBC, the BBC, and *L'Express* quoted Dr. Clark as saying that the bullet had entered Kennedy's neck from in front and entered the chest [see 6 H 21-30 and "*Killing The Truth*", p. 718];

i.   January 1964 Texas State Journal of Medicine article "*Three Patients at Parkland*", pp. 60-74 [pages 63-64](see "*Assassination Science*", p. 399)---repeats the gist of his 11/22/63 report contents: "Two external wounds, one in the lower third of the anterior neck, the other in the occipital region of the skull, were noted. Through the head wound, blood and brain were extruding...he noted a ragged wound of the trachea immediately below the larynx...Dr. Clark noted that the President had bled profusely from the back of the head. There was a large (3 by 3 cm.) amount of cerebral tissue present on the cart. There was a smaller amount of cerebellar tissue present also...Because of the likelihood of mediastinal injury, anterior chest tubes were placed in both pleural spaces...There was a large wound beginning in the right occiput extending into the parietal region. Much of the right posterior skull, at brief examination, appeared gone.... Both cerebral and cerebellar tissue were extruding from the wound.";

j.   6 H 20, 26, and 29/ testimony---"I then examined the wound in the back of the President's head. This was a large, gaping wound in the right posterior part, with cerebral and cerebellar tissue being damaged and exposed."; "...the loss of cerebellar tissue...The loss of the right occipital [lobe]...";"...in the right occipital region of the President's skull, from which considerable blood loss had occurred which stained the back of his head..."; other WC references: WR 53-55, 90, 526, 529; 2 H 39, 81; 3 H 360, 369, 371-376, 381; 6 H 4, 9-13, 40-41, 47-49, 55, 61-62, 64, 67, 70, 74, 81, 114, 141, 145, 148-149; 17 H 11, 14; 20 H 5; 21 H 150-152, 153, 155, 231, 241, 258, 262, 263, 265, 267

k.   11/9/66 interview by David Lifton ("*Best Evidence*" [hereafter known as "*BE*"], pp. 300-301)---nothing specific about wounds;

l.   "*Resident and Staff Physician*", May 1972 issue, p. 60: article by Dr. John K. Lattimer entitled "Observations Based on A Review of the Autopsy Photographs, X-Rays, and Related Materials of the Late President John F. Kennedy"---"... some other explanation seemed more likely for the President's major sideways lurch to the left, with its slight backwards component. It seemed to the author, after consultation with neurosurgeon Kemp Clark, who had declared the President dead, that the prime speculative possibility would be the opisthotonos-like reaction of the body, often seen immediately after acute, severe cerebral injuries, because of the massive downward discharge of nerve impulses.";

m.   "*JFK: Conspiracy of Silence*" by Dr. Charles Crenshaw (1992), page 87---nickname "High Pockets" [*NOTE: all references for this work can also be found, albeit on a different page, in Crenshaw's updated work entitled "Trauma Room One" (2001)*];

n.   "*Killing The Truth*", p. 702---"Although I [Livingstone] had no interview, Dr. Kemp Clark passed a verbal message to me in his outer office that the picture of the back of the head was inaccurate."

o. 1/5/94, 1/20/94, and 1/28/94 interviews with David Naro [see COPA 1994 abstract]: "The lower right occipital region of the head was blown out and I saw cerebellum. In my opinion, the wound was an exit wound...a large hole in the back of the President's head...blown out";

p. [Unanswered letter from Vince Palamara 1998]

q. "Murder In Dealey Plaza" by James Fetzer (2000), pages 56, 63, 68, 177, 179, 193-197, 199, 240, 259, 298

r. "JFK Absolute Proof" by Robert Groden (2013), page 153: Clark is pictured with a nice summary of his statements

2) Dr. Malcolm Oliver "Mac" Perry, Attending Surgeon (deceased 12/5/2009):

a. WR 521-522/ 17 H 6-7/ CE392: report written 11/22/63---"A large wound of the right posterior cranium...";

b. Parkland press conference, 11/22/63 [see "Assassination Science", pp. 419-427; silent film clip used in "Reasonable Doubt" video (1988), "20/20" (4/92), etc.]---"There was an entrance wound in the neck...It appeared to be coming at him... The wound appeared to be an entrance wound in the front of the throat; yes, that is correct. The exit wound, I don't know. It could have been the head or there could have been a second wound of the head." (Apparently, based off this conference, the Associated Press dispatch on 11/22/63 stated that Dr. Perry "said the entrance wound was in the front of the head," while all the AP wires for this day stated that JFK had a large hole in the "back" of his head.);

c. UPI report published in the "New York World Telegram & Sun", 11/22/63 (see also the 11/23/63 "San Francisco Chronicle" [Groden's "The Killing of a President" [hereafter known as TKOAP], p. 76]): "There was an entrance wound below his Adam's apple. There was another wound in the back of his head."

d. Filmed interview by Bob Welch, WBAP-TV/ NBC (Texas News), 11/23/63 [available on the video "Kennedy In Texas" (1984) and, in edited form, on "The Two Kennedys" (1976)]---"He had a severe, lethal wound"; "There was a neck wound anteriorly and a large wound of his head in the right posterior area."; "passage of the bullet through the neck"; "chest tubes were put in place"; mentions the presence of Drs. Seldin and Bashour [this was the second conference that weekend---21 H 265: "this was a final conference to give reporters who had missed earlier conferences a chance to hear from (the) medical team and to answer their questions."];

e. 22 H 832: reprint of article from "New York Herald Tribune", 11/23/63---"... Dr. Malcolm Perry...said he saw two wounds---one below the Adam's apple, the other at the back of the head. He said he did not know if two bullets were involved. It is possible, he said, that the neck wound was the entrance and the other the exit of the missile."

f. "New York Times", 11/23/63: article written by Tom Wicker (rode in the Dallas motorcade): "Mr. Kennedy was hit by a bullet in the throat, below the Adam's apple…This wound had the appearance of a bullet's entry. Mr. Kennedy also had a massive, gaping wound in the back and on the right side of the head… A missile had gone in and out the back of his head causing external lacerations and loss of brain tissue."[see also "*Seeds of Doubt: Some Questions About the Assassination*" by Jack Minnis and Staughton Lynd, 12/63: they quote from this article, as well];

g. "*Los Angeles Times*", 11/24/63: article by Jimmy Breslin---"The incision had to be made below the bullet wound."; "There was a mediastinal wound…in connection with the bullet hole in the *chest.*"[Emphasis added: see reference "j)" below; also, the "*New York Herald Tribune*" for 12/19/63 stated, "…the first bullet lodged in Kennedy's lung."];

h. "*Dallas Times Herald*", 11/24/63 [see p. 35 of Jesse Curry's 1969 book entitled "*JFK Assassination File*"] Perry said that JFK "was dead for all practical purposes when he arrived in the emergency room…It was obvious he never knew what hit him."; "Staff doctors at Parkland Hospital in Dallas said only that the sniper's bullet pierced the mid-section of the front part of his neck and emerged from the top of his skull. The White House sources said they understood that one bullet hit Kennedy in the neck area. He bent forward, turned his head and was struck in the skull by the second bullet."

i. "*Boston Globe*", 11/24/63: article by Herbert Black [see also "*Cover-Up*" by Stewart Galanor, p. 30]: Dr. Perry said he observed an exit wound "despite the fact the assassin shot from above down onto the President."

j. "*New York Times*", 11/28/63---Perry saw the gaping wound in the President's skull, and he knew that it was mortal. ""He said he believed the President had two wounds---a massive one in the back of the head and a small, circular wound in the neck.";

k. "*The Saturday Evening Post*", 12/14/63, article by Jimmy Breslin entitled "*A Death in Emergency Room No. One*"---he observed damage to the cerebellum; "There was a mediastinal wound in connection with the bullet hole in the *throat.*"[emphasis added: compare to reference "g)" above]; the President's clothing included a "T-shirt".[the 11/30/63 "*New York Times*" mentioned an "undershirt"];

l. January 1964 Texas State Journal of Medicine article "*Three Patients at Parkland*", p. 62---repeats the gist of his 11/22/63 report: "A small wound was noted in the midline of the neck, in the lower third anteriorly. It was exuding blood slowly. A large wound of the right posterior cranium was noted, exposing severely lacerated brain."

m. 6 H 9, 11, and 15 / testimony (3/25/64)---"I noted there was a large wound of the right posterior parietal area in the head exposing lacerated brain...a large avulsive injury of the right occipitoparietal area in which both scalp and portions of skull were absent…"; the throat wound was "between 3 and 5 mm in size.";

n. 3 H 368 and 372 / testimony (3/30/64)---" …there was a large avulsive wound on the right posterior cranium…";"I noted a large avulsive wound of the right parietal occipital area…"; other WC references: WR 53-54, 89-91, 517, 518,

519, 523, 524, 525, 526, 529, 536-537, 539; 1 H 162; 2 H 39, 41, 361-363 [Humes: "Doctor Perry told me that before he enlarged it to make the tracheotomy wound it was a 'few millimeters in diameter.'"], 367-368, 371-373; 3 H 360, 363; 6 H 2-5, 20-23, 29, 31-33, 35, 37-38, 40-41, 44, 47, 52-54, 56, 59, 64, 69-73, 76, 79-80, 83, 114, 141, 145, 149; 17 H 2-4, 8-11, 14, 21-22, 29, 31, 39; 20 H 333; 21 H 151-152, 185-186, 205, 265;

o. 10/27/66: interview with David Lifton ["BE", pages 238 and 706]---Perry's tracheostomy incision through the existing wound was "2-3 cm";

p. Part 2 of "*CBS News Inquiry: The Warren Report*" 6/26/67 (Eddie Barker interview)-""I noted a wound when I came into the room, which was of the right posterior portion of the head..."; "[JFK] had been previously started on intravenous fluids and blood, and given hydrocortisone by Dr. Carrico; and assisted respiration was in progress."

q. "*JFK Assassination File*" by DPD Chief Jesse Curry (1969), page 34---"As Dr. Perry took charge he sized up the situation. A small neat wound was in the throat. The back of the head was massively damaged and blood from this wound covered the floor and the aluminum hospital cart. Dr. Perry examined the throat wound and assessed it as the entrance wound...at the time Dr. Perry insisted that the President was shot from the front----entering at the throat and exiting out the back of the head.";

r. 1-11-78, (audiotaped) interview with HSCA's Andrew Purdy (7 HSCA 292-293; 302; 312 re: neck)---"Dr. Perry...believed the head wound was located on the 'occipital parietal' region of the skull and that the right posterior aspect of the skull was missing..."; "...the parietal occipital head wound was largely avulsive and there was visible brain tissue in the macard and some cerebellum seen..."; "I thought it [the neck wound] looked like an entrance wound because it was so small."

s. 1979 interview with Robert Groden ["BE", p. 706; Groden's "TKOAP", p. 77 (includes photo of Perry)]---photos of neck and head wound not as he remembered them to be: his trach was "neater", and not the "larger, expanded" one seen in the pictures. Also, the head wound more closely matched the Dr. McClelland drawing in "*Six Seconds in Dallas*"; "When interviewed in 1979, he still maintained that the bullet had entered the President's throat from the front..."

t. 1979 interview by Jeff Price, "*Baltimore Sun*," 11/18/79 entitled "*The Bullets Also Destroyed Our Confidence*" [as reported in "*High Treason*", p. 47 (Berkley edition) and "*Killing The Truth*", p. 702]---the official autopsy picture of the back of the skull was not accurate and did not show the head wound as he saw it: "Earlier this year, during an investigation by the Sun, one doctor [Perry] who had been given access to copies of the [autopsy] photos said the president's head wounds in the pictures were not consistent with what he recalled seeing that day 16 years ago.";

u. 8/10/79 interview by Harry Livingstone ("*High Treason 2*", p. 121 and "*Killing The Truth*", p. 118)---"My whole credibility as a trauma surgeon was at stake...I COULDN'T have made a mistake like that [re: entrance wound allegedly being an exit wound]. It destroys my integrity if I don't know an entrance wound from an exit wound!"; "he has told me often enough that what he said in 1963 stands.";

v. Letter to Livingstone 12/21/81 ("*High Treason 2*", p. 121): "I've never verified nor challenged the accuracy of any photos.";

w. 8/29/89 letter to Joanne Braun ("*The Third Decade*", March 1991): "There was no incision or indentation [in the right forehead]…One of the problems was that there was so much damage to the skull and the scalp that the entire scalp and hair were displaced, sagging slightly forward and to the side, and of course this made it appear that there was something really there. You must recognize that the parietal occipital bone was shattered and parts of it were missing which allowed the scalp to be displaced anteriorly."

x. 6/14/91 interview with Livingstone ("*High Treason 2*", p. 572)---photo of neck accurate but distended due to the flexion of the neck;

y. Photo in "*JFK: Conspiracy of Silence*" by Dr. Crenshaw;

z. Interview with Dr. Robert Artwohl---said the throat wound was an entrance wound;

aa. 5/19/92 press conference, as reported in the 5/20/92 "*New York Times*": article by Dr. Lawrence K. Altman entitled "*Doctors Affirm Kennedy Autopsy Report*"---*five doctors who attended JFK at Parkland* maintained that they observed nothing to contradict the findings of two pathologist who performed the autopsy [see "*The Man Who Knew Too Much*" by Dick Russell (1992), p. 787, footnote 22];

ab. JAMA May 27, 1992: "*JFK's Death, Part II, Dallas Mds Recall Their Memories*" [includes a photo of Perry]: "made a…large incision" and the autopsy photos are "very compatible" with the way he left the incision; Re: Crenshaw: ""I do not remember even seeing him in the room". [!]; JAMA articles:

ac. 4/2/92 interview with Gerald Posner for "*Case Closed*", p. 312---"…like everyone else, I saw it back there. It [the head wound] was in the occipital/ parietal area." BUT "I did not see any cerebellum" (!?)

ad. 11/6/96 letter to researcher Russ McLean [provided to the author]---friendly but did not want to answer questions: "My sworn testimony is in the public record in detail, and I have no new information…There are 26 volumes of the Warren Report, and although one might disagree with the conclusions, there are many facts presented… Most of the participants are dead, and the rest of us have no new information."

ae. Interview with Wallace Milam [referred to at Copa 1994]---wouldn't comment on any possible change in throat wound as seen in photos;

af. 5/2/94 letter to Brad Parker [see "*The Dealey Plaza Echo*", July 1997 issue; letter provided to the author from Parker]: "No one, except Dr. Kemp Clark, carefully examined the head wound. Dr. McClelland arrived after I called for help, and he assisted me in the tracheostomy. He was rather busy during this time."

ag. 5/16/94 follow-up letter to Brad Parker [letter provided to the author from

Parker]---"Recollection immediately after an event is likely to be more accurate (although often wrong) than when made 30 years later... [Dr. Crenshaw] did not examine the wounds in my presence, and his opinions are not supported by anyone involved in our work. I don't remember his even being in the room." [!];

ah. Interview with Gary Aguilar---nothing much gained [e-mail to Palamara, 8/20/98];

ai. 1998 AUDIO-taped interview with Mark Oakes ("*Eyewitness Video Tape III*"): Regarding the throat wound: "It was small, like an entrance wound" (said this four times) but "they took it out of context... It offended me-I never changed my mind: it DID look small, like an entrance wound, but it wasn't" (!);

aj. 8/27/98 Joint ARRB deposition 1998 (w/ Jones, McClelland, Baxter, and Peters [see Fetzer's "*Murder in Dealey Plaza*" and "*Trauma Room One*" by Dr. Charles Crenshaw (2001), pages 206-207, 258]);

ak. 8/26/98 letter to Vince Palamara---"I did not inspect the head wound---I was much too busy. The only person who carefully evaluated the head wound was Dr. Kemp Clark, Chief of Neurosurgery (no one could be better qualified). His testimony (and mine) is in the Warren Report. His findings are consistent with those described by Dr. Hume[s] et al during the autopsy."; "Since I made the tracheostomy incision through the anterior neck wound few people saw it. I was in a hurry and did not take time to wipe the blood off, so no accurate measurements were taken."; Do you believe the official story in every respect? "I have met only one person (Gerald Posner) who has read and studied the 26 Volume Warren Report. I haven't, and can't comment on its contents."

al. "*Murder In Dealey Plaza*" by James Fetzer (2000), pages 10, 56, 63, 97, 115, 150, 176, 190, 192-197, 199, 240, 247, 256, 257, 270, 274, 274, 289, 296, 298, 301

am. "*JFK Absolute Proof*" by Robert Groden (2013), pages 86, 146 and 153: Perry is pictured with a nice summary of his statements

3) Dr. Robert Nelson McClelland, Attending Surgeon:

a. WR 526-527 / 17 H 11-12 / CE 392: report written 11/22/63---"...a massive gunshot wound of the head with a fragment wound of the trachea...The cause of death was due to massive head and brain injury from a gunshot wound of the left temple."

b. "*St. Louis Post-Dispatch*", 12/1/63---"This [the neck wound] did appear to be an entrance wound."[*Another important "St. Louis Post-Dispatch" article, dated 12/18/63: "Secret Service Gets Revision of Kennedy Wound-after visit by agents, doctors say shot was from rear."-"[The Secret Service] obtained a reversal of their original view that the bullet in his neck entered from the front. The investigators did so by showing the surgeons a document described as an autopsy report from the United States Naval Hospital at Bethesda. The surgeons changed their original view to conform with the report they were shown." One of the agents may very well have been SA Elmer Moore. RIF#180-10109-10310 is a 6/1/77 HSCA interview tran-*

script of graduate student James Gouchenaur and his 1970 conversation with Moore, who told him that he felt remorse for the way he (Moore) had badgered Dr. Perry into changing his testimony to the effect that there was not, after all, an entrance wound in the front of the president's neck! (See 2 H 39, 41; 6 H 36-37; and "*Best Evidence*", pages 156, 166-167, 196 and 286); *SEE ALSO* CD 379; 3 H 363, 364 and 6 H 6, 7 (Carrico); 3 H 387 and 6 H 17 (Perry); 6 H 27 (Clark); 6 H 57 (Jones); 6 H 44 (Baxter); 6 H 50-51 (Jenkins); 6 H 63 (Bashour); 6 H 75 (Giesecke)

c. Article by Richard Dudman in "*The New Republic*", 12/21/63 ["*Assassination Science*", p. 167]: "Dr. Robert McClelland... told me afterward that they still believed it [the neck wound] to be an entry wound."

d. January 1964 Texas State Journal of Medicine article "*Three Patients at Parkland*", p. 63---repeats the gist of his 11/22/63 report, but with one change"...a massive gunshot wound of the head with a fragment wound of the trachea...massive head and brain injury from a gunshot wound of the *right side of the head*." [Emphasis added; Brad Parker has learned that this article, "*Three Patients at Parkland*", while based on the original reports made by the Parkland doctors, incorporated subtle changes which he was told were made by none other than Dr. Marion Jenkins!]];

e. 6 H 33-34, 35, 37 / testimony---"...I could very closely examine the head wound, and I noted that the right posterior portion of the skull had been extremely blasted...probably a third or so, at least, of the brain tissue, posterior cerebral tissue and some of the cerebellar tissue had been blasted out..."; "...there was definitely a piece of cerebellum that extruded from the wound..."; "...the loss of cerebral and cerebellar tissues were so great...massive head injuries with loss of large amounts of cerebral and cerebellar tissues..."; "The initial impression that we had was that perhaps the wound in the neck, the anterior part of the neck, was an entrance wound and that it had perhaps taken a trajectory off the anterior vertebral body and again into the skull itself, exiting out the back, to produce the massive injury in the head.";

f. Other WC references: WR 53-54, 56, 517, 524, 529, 535-537; 2 H 39; 3 H 361, 369-371, 377-378, 384-385; 6 H 4, 11-12, 20, 23, 25, 41, 47, 55, 64, 69, 71, 73, 80, 106, 110, 114, 149; 17 H 2, 9, 14, 20-22; 20 H 6; 21 H 151, 186, 196;

g. "*Six Seconds In Dallas*", p. 140 (also pictured in "*High Treason*")---approved this drawing which shows the right-rear of the skull blasted open;

h. [TWO: Lifton interviewed McClelland on 11/9/66 *and* CFTR radio Canada interviewed the doctor in 1976 but previous WC references were used in regard to the head wound on these occasions];

i. "*Speak-Up America: JFK Assassination Inquiry*" NBC 1980;

j. "*The Men Who Killed Kennedy*", 1988---"It would be a jagged wound that involved the half of the right side of the back of the head. My initial impression was that it probably was an exit wound, so it was a very large wound." McClelland drew a picture for the camera demonstrating this right-rear wound; "Almost a fifth or perhaps even a quarter of the right back part of the head in this area had been blasted out along with probably most of the brain tissue in that area…I would estimate that about 20 percent to 25 percent of the entire brain was missing."

k. *"High Treason"*, p. 42,

l. *"The Baltimore Sun"* article by Steve Parks, 11/18/79, and

m. *"The Boston Globe"* article by Ben Bradlee Jr., 6/21/81: the right-rear skull defect drawing used in Thompson's book is accurate and what McClelland "vividly" remembers;

n. *"Nova"*, 11/15/88 (see still photo in *"Killing The Truth"*)---before AND after viewing the official photos, McClelland places his hand on the right rear area of his head where he saw the wound on JFK and "speculates" that a large flap of skin is obscuring the large wound in the official photos;

o. *"JFK: An Unsolved Murder"*, KRON, 11/18/88 (Included in *"JFK: The Case For Conspiracy"* video by Robert Groden; see still photo in *"Assassination Science"*, p. 43)---demonstrates the right rear of the skull being blasted and the cerebellum protruding from the wound;

p. TWO: A)*"Conspiracy"* by Anthony Summers (paperback, 1989), pp. 484-486 (interviewed McClelland in 1989)---"I don't think they were trying to cover up the fact that there was a large hole…but that's what they were doing…they were covering up that great defect in the back and lateral part of the head by pulling that loose scalp flap up. You can see the hand pulling the scalp forward [in the autopsy photo; this is what McClelland said, more or less, on *"Nova"*]"; "Dr. McClelland says the 'great defect in the back' IS visible on some photographs amongst the FULL set of some fifty pictures he saw at the National Archives"; B) 8/29/89 letter to Joanne Braun (*"The Third Decade"*, March 1991)---sees nothing to be concerned about re: the incision(s) that appear in the official autopsy photos;

q. *"Inside Edition"*, June 1989---McClelland "says the x-rays do not show the same injuries to the President's head that he saw in the emergency room…I think he was shot from the front…" [See *"Conspiracy"*, pp. 485-486];

r. *"Hard Copy"*, 5/21/90: interviewed by David Lifton---more of the same, and does not agree with the official x-rays/ photos: "are not consistent with what I saw";

s. 4/91 Livingstone video (see *"High Treason 2"* photo section and Chapter 14; see also p. 118 of *"Killing The Truth"* [photo of himself also appears in *"JFK: Conspiracy of Silence"* by Dr. Crenshaw]);

t. Livingstone interviews of 7/79, 12/28/88, and 10/6/91 as sourced in *"High Treason 2"* (1992);

u. Portrayed by actor Joseph Nadell in the Oliver Stone movie *"JFK"* (1991) [see *"JFK: The Book of the Film"* (1992), p. 156---references 6 H 33, as well as a *1991 interview of McClelland by Robert Groden*]: "…almost a fifth or perhaps a quarter of the back of the head-this area here (*he indicates his head*)-had been blasted out along with the brain tissue there. The exit hole in the rear of his head was about 120 mm. across. There was also a large piece of skull attached to a flap of scalp in the right temporal area."

v.   "*The Jim Garrison Tapes*" video 1992---similar to previous interviews: "in the back part of the head" [indicates both the location and the size];

w.   4/29/92 interview with Livingstone ("*Killing the Truth*", p. 103)---Knew that LBJ had called 11/24/63 and spoke to Crenshaw;

x.   JAMA 1992 [Includes a photo of McClelland]--- "Robert McClelland, MD, is a respected surgeon who assisted in the last steps of the tracheostomy on President Kennedy. Interviewed in Dallas, he told this reporter that he maintains a "strong opinion" that the fatal head wound came from the front. Pressed on his reasons, he says, "After I saw the Zapruder film in 1969, I became convinced that the backward lurch of the head had to have come from a shot from the front. Unlike Crenshaw, I do not believe that one can tell the direction from which the bullet came simply by looking at the head wound, as I did, but the wound I observed did appear consistent with a shot from the front. That observation is secondary to my viewing of the Zapruder film, which convinced me that the shots were from the front."

y.   9/10/92: interview by Brad Parker (see the Spring 1997 issue of "*Kennedy Assassination Chronicles*" in its entirety; see also "*The Dealey Plaza Echo*", July 1997 issue, as well as Parker's Lancer 1997 paper entitled "*The Subjective Degree of Medical Certainty*")---"Well, it was probably really larger than that [Carrico's 7 centimeters]. I would say that it was more like ten centimeters: the whole right posterior part of the head"; "...the bullet hit from the front, and hit him tangentially in the side of the head, and probably the bullet---it entered somewhere near the front part of the wound that I saw, and blew out part of the skull, and then continued out the back of [the] head at the posterior edge of that wound."; "...there was definitely a piece of cerebellum that extruded from the wound as I stood there holding the retractor while the tracheostomy was being performed."; described the 1992 JAMA article as a "travesty"; [see also "*Fair Play*", issue #16]

z.   Letter to Dr. Gary Aguilar;

aa. 3/9/92 interview with Gerald Posner for "*Case Closed*", p. 312---"I saw a piece of cerebellum fall out on the stretcher";

ab. New interview for Groden's "*JFK: The Case For Conspiracy*" video 1993 (see page 87 of Groden's "TKOAP");

ac. 1/24/94 letter/ drawing to Brad Parker---"Brad, the drawing below is an exact copy, in regard to location and dimensions, of the drawing I made for Josiah Thompson in 1966. [See "*Six Seconds in Dallas*", p. 140] ";

ad. 8/27/98 Joint ARRB deposition (w/ Perry, Jones, Baxter, and Peters) [see "*Trauma Room One*" by Dr. Charles Crenshaw (2001), pages 206-207, 258];

ae. 9/98 letter to Vince Palamara (written on photocopies of two pages from "Six Seconds in Dallas", Includes his drawing on page 140!)---"The Zapruder film causes me to believe the wound I drew below is an exit wound in the back of the head, not because of what can be seen about the wound per se on the film (I saw this much better on my direct inspection), but because the shot from the front propelled the President's head & body violently backward and to his left-a bullet from behind could not do this in defiance of the laws of physics & motion ("jet effect" of brain is untenable). [Regarding his drawing: arrow drawn pointing towards the right rear defect] Right posterior, probable exit wound. [Arrow pointing to an upside down "L"-shaped dotted line he drew directly above the defect, in the middle]. Fractured parietal bone protruding up thru scalp accounted for whitish "flap" over the ear in Zapruder film. I looked directly into the wound from a distance of about 18 inches for over 10 uninterrupted minutes and thus saw the wound better than any of the other medical witnesses. I clearly saw cerebellar tissue as well as cerebral tissue." [His emphasis]; also, Dr. McClelland underlined "posterior portion"(Jones [6 H 56]), "right occipitoparietal"(Perry [6 H 11]), "back of the skull" and "right side of his head had been blown off" (Baxter [6 H 40-41]) from Thompson's quoting of various colleagues of his. From his own WC testimony [6 H 33], he underlined "very closely," "right posterior," "parietal bone," "protruded up through the scalp," and "cerebellar."

af. *"The Secret KGB Files On The JFK Assassination"* DVD (2000)---short interview with McClelland;

ag. *"Murder In Dealey Plaza"* by James Fetzer (2000), pages 56, 63, 150, 152, 174, 176, 178, 190, 192, 197, 199, 233, 239, 248, 249, 252, 259, 293, 298, 416, 448

ah. *"JFK Absolute Proof"* by Robert Groden (2013): see page 151- Dr. McClelland is pictured with a nice summary of his statements

ai. *"The Kennedy Half Century"* by Larry Sabato (2013): pictured, interviewed

4) Dr. Marion Thomas "Pepper" Jenkins, Chief Anesthesiologist (deceased 11/22/94):

a. WR 529-530 / 17 H 14-15 / CE 392: report addressed to Administrator C.J. Price dated 11/22/63 (the verbatim, retyped report, this time addressed to Dean A.J. Gill, can be found at 20 H 252-253)---" a great laceration on the right side of the head (temporal and occipital), causing a great defect in the skull plate so that there was herniation and laceration of great areas of the brain, even to the extent that the cerebellum had protruded from the wound."[See also p. 35 of Jesse Curry's 1969 book entitled *"JFK Assassination File"*];

b. January 1964 Texas State Journal of Medicine article *"Three Patients at Parkland"*, pp. 64-65---repeats the gist of his 11/22/63 report, but with an added bit of information: "...there was also obvious tracheal and chest damage...There was a great laceration on the right side of the head (temporal and occipital), causing a great defect in the skull plate so that there was herniation and laceration of great areas of the brain, even to the extent that part of the *right* cerebellum had protruded from the wound. There were also fragmented sections of brain on the drapes of the emergency room cart." [Emphasis added; Brad Parker has learned that this article, *"Three Patients at Parkland"*, while based on the original reports

11

made by the Parkland doctors, incorporated subtle changes which he was told were made by none other than Dr. Marion Jenkins!]]; ALSO: pp. 72-74 re: Oswald---"Dr. Jenkins recalls that the following physicians were members of the resuscitation team: Drs. Jenkins and Akin…Drs. Gerry Gustafson, Dale Coln, and Charles Crenshaw, all residents in surgery, who were prepared to introduce cannulae into the veins via cutdowns or percutaneous puncture…three members of the staff were performing venous cutdowns, one in each lower extremity and one in the left forearm. These were performed by Drs. Coln, Crenshaw, and Gustafson."

c. 6 H 48 and 51 / testimony---""Part of the brain was herniated; I really think part of the cerebellum, as I recognized it, was herniated from the wound…"; "…the wound with the exploded area of the scalp, as I interpreted it being exploded, I would interpret it being a wound of exit…"; "…I thought there was a wound on the left temporal area, right in the hairline and right above the zygomatic process."

d. Other WC references: WR 53-54, 517, 520, 536-537; 3 H 363, 370-371, 381-382, 384, 386; 4 H 148; 6 H 9, 11, 20, 23-24, 32, 40, 52-53, 55, 60-61, 64, 67, 69-71, 74-76, 79-80, 114, 141, 149; 17 H 2, 5, 21-22; 20 H 5, 333; 21 H 151, 164, 167, 182, 194, 227, 241, 253, 265;

e. 11/10/77 HSCA interview conducted by Andrew Purdy (7 HSCA 285-7)---He (Dr. Jenkins) "…was positioned at the head of the table so he had one of the closest views of the head wound…believes he was '…the only one who knew the extent of the head wound.'…Regarding the head wound, Dr. Jenkins said that only one segment of bone was blown out---it was a segment of occipital or temporal bone. He noted that a portion of the cerebellum (lower rear brain) was hanging out from a hole in the right-rear of the head."

f. 11/24/78 "American Medical News"---JFK "…had part of his head blown away and part of his cerebellum was hanging out";

g. "High Treason", p. 46 (based off a 1979 interview with Jenkins; "The Continuing Inquiry", 10/80; author's tape-JFK Library): "Dr. Jenkins stared at the official picture for a long time and then said: "No, not like that. Not like that. You want to know what it really looked like?"; "Well, that picture doesn't look like it from the back." Jenkins continually demonstrated on his head and Livingstone's where the large exit wound was, in the rear and slightly to the side…"You could tell at this point with your fingers that it was scored out, that the edges were blasted out."

h. "Killing The Truth", p. 711 (based off a 10/8/90 interview): "…right at the occipital area. It was higher. One of the things I don't understand is that this would not have been low enough to have gotten into the cerebellum."

i. THE GENESIS OF JENKIN'S RETREAT? ---"Best Evidence", pp. 704-705 (based off a Jan. 1983 interview)---"Jenkins now said that whatever the Warren Report said was correct, and whatever the photographs showed was fine with him." (?!);

j. *"Nova"* 11/15/88 (see still photo in *"Killing The Truth"* and in *"Assassination Science"*, p. 43)---before seeing the official photos, Jenkins places his hand between the right rear and the right side of his head; waffles on the cerebellum, among other things, after seeing the official photos;

k. *"JFK: An Unsolved Murder"*, KRON, 11/18/88 (Included in *"JFK: The Case for Conspiracy"*)---"it still looks like cerebellum, but obviously it's not": more waffling;

l. *"Miami Herald"* article by Martin Merzer, 11/20/88---"Inside the vessel formed by [Jackie's] hands, Jenkins saw a clump of Kennedy's brain matter. The president's wife had been holding this for many, many minutes. It is a memory that brings long pauses to Jenkins' conversation. 'She didn't... say anything,' Jenkins says. 'She...just nudged me and handed it to me...I guess it ended up in her hand sometime during what happened in the car. I...handed it to a nurse. It was a horrible scene...It was good that she got rid of it.'

m. *"JFK"* 1991---plays a doctor with a small speaking role and was a technical advisor! [See *"JFK: The Book of the Film"* (1992), p. 590. Also, on page 10, *referencing an April 1991 interview with Jenkins*, there appears this note: "Contrary to popular rumor...Mrs. Kennedy was not trying to escape the crossfire, but apparently retrieving a fragment of BONE and brain tissue on the trunk of the car. She turned the FRAGMENT over to Dr. Marion Jenkins at Parkland Hospital". (Emphasis added)] ;

n. JAMA 1992 [Includes a photo of Jenkins]---"Crenshaw's conclusions are dead wrong" (!?); the autopsy photos are "very compatible" with the trach incision he saw [!];

o. 8/18/92 interview with Brad Parker---"... there was a chunk of bone, the size of the palm of your hand, that was blown out in his right temporoparietal area ... I did talk about the cerebellum extruding from the wound, and that was wrong "(!?)'

p. 3/10/92 interview with Gerald Posner for *"Case Closed"*, pp. 311-312---"I never did say occipital" (!?);

q. Dallas Forum, 6/4/92 (see *"Killing The Truth"*, p. 41, 118, 172-178)---saw an entry wound on JFK's neck; would let their 1963 observations stand ;

r. *"20/20"* 11/12/93---nothing specific about the wounds;

s. *"New York Times"*, 11/23/94---obituary;

t. *"Murder In Dealey Plaza"* by James Fetzer (2000), pages 56, 63, 152, 176, 179, 190, 191, 193, 197, 199, 218, 233, 240, 259, 298, 301

u. *"JFK Absolute Proof"* by Robert Groden (2013): see page 153- Dr. Jenkins is pictured with a nice summary of his statements

5) Dr. Charles James "Jim" Carrico, Resident Surgeon (deceased 7/25/2002):

a. WR 519-520 / 17 H 4-5 / CE 392: handwritten report dated 11/22/63---"[the skull] wound had avulsed the calvarium and shredded brain tissue present with profuse oozing…attempts to control slow oozing from cerebral and cerebellar tissue via packs instituted…."; "small penetrating wound of ent. neck";

b. January 1964 Texas State Journal of Medicine article "*Three Patients at Parkland*", p. 61---repeats the gist of his 11/22/63 report, but with an added bit of information: a "…wound (which) had caused avulsion of the *occipitoparietal calvarium*…", rather than his original description [above] of simply a "…wound (which) had avulsed the calvarium…" [Brad Parker has learned that this article, "*Three Patients at Parkland*", while based on the original reports made by the Parkland doctors, incorporated subtle changes which he was told were made by none other than Dr. Marion Jenkins!];

c. 6 H 3 and 6/ testimony (3/25/64)---"There seemed to be a 4-5 cm. area of avulsion of the scalp and the skull was fragmented and bleeding cerebral and cerebellar tissue…The [skull] wound that I saw was a large gaping wound, located in the right occipitoparietal area. I would estimate to be about 5 to 7 cm. in size, more or less circular, with avulsions of the calvarium and scalp tissue. As I stated before, I believe there was shredded macerated cerebral and cerebellar tissues both in the wounds and on the fragments of the skull attached to the dura."; throat wound: "probably a 4 to 7 mm wound" and had "no jagged edges or stellate lacerations";

d. 3 H 361 / testimony (3/30/64)---"This [skull wound] was a 5-by 71-cm [sic] defect in the posterior skull, the occipital region. There was an absence of the calvarium or skull in this area, with shredded tissue, brain tissue present..";

e. other WC references: WR 53-54, 56, 89, 91, 517, 526, 529; 2 H 362; 3 H 367-370, 372-373, 376-378, 381; 6 H 8-11, 20, 29, 32, 35, 40-41, 46-48, 52-53, 58-59, 64, 69, 73-74, 80, 83, 114, 136, 140-141, 145, 149; 17 H 2, 11, 14; 21 H 151;

f. 11/8/66 interview by Lifton---the trach incision was "between two and three centimeters";

g. 7 HSCA 266-280 [see esp. pages 268 and 278]: 1/11/78 (audiotaped) interview---"The head wound was a much larger wound than the neck wound. It is 5 by 7 cm., two and a half by three inches, ragged, had blood and hair all around it, located in the part of the parietal-occipital region…a fairly large wound in the right side of the head, in the parietal, occipital area. One could see blood and brains, both cerebellum and cerebrum fragments in that wound.";

h. "*The Boston Globe*" 1981 [see "*High Treason*", pp.50-51]---Dr. Carrico "made such contradictory statements to the Globe that it would be inaccurate to count him as supporting the [autopsy] picture…Dr. Carrico was not interviewed by the Globe, but he wrote them two contradictory letters.";

i. "*JFK: An Unsolved Murder*", KRON, 11/18/88 (repeated in "*JFK: The Case for Conspiracy*": see still photo on page 87 of Groden's "TKOAP" and "*Assassination Science*", p. 43): places his hand directly on the right rear portion of his head!

j. photo in "*JFK: Conspiracy of Silence*" by Dr. Crenshaw;

k. JAMA 1992 [Includes a photo of Carrico]---Regarding the autopsy photos of the neck wound and what he himself observed: "They're the same"; "Nothing we observed contradicts the autopsy findings that the bullets were fired from above and behind with a high-velocity rifle" (?!);

l.   Dallas Forum, 6/4/92---same as Jenkins above;

m.   Brad Parker interview, 7/7/92---"a very large wound in the top of the President's head...you can read what I said in the medical---in our emergency room reports, which were in Texas Medicine." Ironically, the article cites the 11/22/63 report above!;

n.   3/8/92 interview with Gerald Posner for "*Case Closed*", p. 311---"we saw a large hole in the right side of his head. I don't believe we saw any occipital bone. It was not there. It was parietal bone. And if we said otherwise, we were mistaken." (!?);

o.   3/94 letter to Brad Parker---"with the President lying on his back, the wound was visible without moving his head...";

p.   [unanswered letter from Vince Palamara 1998]

q.   "*Murder In Dealey Plaza*" by James Fetzer (2000), pages 61-62, 150, 174, 176, 178, 180, 193-194, 197, 199, 240, 298, 301

r.   "*JFK Absolute Proof*" by Robert Groden (2013): see page 152- Dr. Carrico is pictured with a nice summary of his statements

s.   *Parkland* movie (2013): portrayed by actor Zac Efron

6) Dr. Ronald Coy Jones, Chief Resident Surgeon:

a.   6 H 53-54, 56 / testimony (3/24/64)---"...he had a large wound in the right posterior side of the head...There was large defect in the back side of the head as the President lay on the cart with what appeared to be some brain hanging out of this wound with multiple pieces of skull noted with the brain..."; "what appeared to be an exit wound in the posterior portion of the skull...the only speculation that I could have as far as to how this could occur with a single wound would be that it would enter the anterior neck and possibly strike a vertebral body and then change its course and exit in the region of the posterior portion of the head."; "The hole [in the throat] was very small and relatively clean cut, as you would see in a bullet that is entering rather than exiting from a patient.";

b.   20 H 333: handwritten report dated 11/23/63---"...severe skull and brain injury was noted as well as a small hole in anterior midline of neck thought to be a bullet entrance wound...air was bubbling through the neck wound.";

c.   other WC references: WR 53-54, 517, 526, 536-537; 2 H 39; 3 H 360, 363, 366-367, 370, 376, 383, 384-385, 390; 6 H 4, 8, 10-11, 20, 27, 40-41, 46, 64, 69-70, 149; 17 H 2, 11, 21-22; 21 H 151, 186, 227

d.   11/10/66 interview with Lifton---gave Lifton a description of the trach incision that agreed with Humes ("BE", p. 273). More importantly, Jones said :" The whole back side of his head was blown off, and there were fragments of skull hanging out...it appeared to be more on the right side than on the left side..." (p. 317n);

e. *"Speak-Up America: JFK Assassination Inquiry"* NBC 1980;

f. Jan. 1983 reinterview with Lifton ("BE", p. 705)---"If you brought him in here today, I'd still say he was shot from the front.";

g. *"High Treason"*, p. 43 (re: *Boston Globe* article 6/21/81): "Dr. Jones viewed the official picture shown to him by the Globe team and stated that the wound was not the same as what he saw in 1963. He outlined with his finger a large hole in the very back of the head. He said that the McClelland drawing was "close"";e H

h. *"JFK: An Unsolved Murder"*, KRON, 11/18/88 (repeated in *"JFK: The Case for Conspiracy"*---see page 86 of Groden's "TKOAP")---places hand on the back of his head and also says there was no damage to the face;

i. 1989 letter to Joanne Braun (*"The Third Decade"*, March 1991)---did not see the V-shaped feature at Parkland;

j. *"High Treason 2"*, pp. 106-107 and *"Killing the Truth"*, p. 717---"Dr. Jones stated that it was emphatically a wound of entrance to Harrison E. Livingstone which was filmed by Al Fisher."(4/5/91);

k. photo in *"JFK: Conspiracy of Silence"* by Dr. Crenshaw;

l. 6/19/92 interview by Brad Parker—"[M]y original impression was that some-one had probably come up at close range, with a pistol or something, and shot him in the neck, and then it exited in the back of the head... [j]ust looking over the head, all I saw was a lot of matted hair with blood and maybe some fragments of tissue out on the table... My impression was that it was a fairly large wound... I didn't think that there was any large wound---I didn't appreciate any wound, any-way, in the right temporal area or the right side of the upper part of the head, you know---in front of the ear say, or anything like that... a lot of that injury was on the down side with him flat on the table... [JFK's throat wound] "compatible with an entrance wound... I would stand by my original impression.";

m. 8/10/92 interview by Brad Parker---"seeing what I saw, I would say he was shot from the front";

n. 4/14/92 interview with Gerald Posner for *"Case Closed"*, p. 306---"large side wound, with blood and tissue that extended toward the rear, from what you could tell of the mess that was there... The neck wound could have been either an entrance or an exit.";

o. 3/4/94 letter to Brad Parker---the McClelland drawing indicates the "general" location of the wound, "but certainly not with as defined edges as shown in this description... perhaps only indicates the skin involvement but not the true de-struction of the skull and brain."; [see also *"Fair Play"*, issue #9]

p. *"Biography: Lee Harvey Oswald"* A&E 1995---doesn't say much due to editing: "We had an opportunity to look at the head wound and see the massive injury that he had sustained." [unlike Dr. Perry's later "recollections" that they did not get a good look at the head wound];

q. 8/27/98 Joint ARRB deposition (w/ McClelland, Perry, Baxter, and Peters) [see *"Trauma Room One"* by Dr. Charles Crenshaw (2001), pages 206-207, 258];

r.   10/13/98 letter to Vince Palamara----"I recently testified on August 27, 1998 before the Assassination Review Panel regarding several issues including these that you ask. I was located on the left side of President Kennedy, the region of his left chest, where I inserted the left chest tube and did a cut down on the left arm to place an IV line. As a result I did not have clear view of the backside of the head wound. President Kennedy had very thick dark hair that covered the injured area. In my opinion it was in the occipital area in the back of the head. Because the scalp partially covered the wound I cannot give an exact size of the defect in the skull. There was no obvious injury to the face. The wound in the neck was very small, perhaps no larger than 1/4 of an inch and the wound in the back of the head was much larger. It was for this reason that I initially thought that the injury to the neck was an entrance wound. During the time the President was at Parkland Hospital the physicians did not roll him over after he was pronounced dead and thus did not appreciate the wound in the back which was discovered at autopsy."[emphasis added];

s.   s) *"Murder in Dealey Plaza"* by James Fetzer (2000), pages 56, 60, 90, 174, 177, 179, 192, 199, 240, 247, 249

t.   t) Presentation at JFK Lancer conference, 2000

u.   u) *"JFK Absolute Proof"* by Robert Groden (2013): see page 151- Dr. Jones is pictured with a nice summary of his statements

7) Dr. Gene Coleman Akin, Resident Anesthesiologist [a.k.a. Solomon Ben Israel]:

a.   6 H 65 and 67 / testimony---"The back of the right occipitalparietal portion of his head was shattered, with brain substance extruding."; "I assume the right occiptalparietal region was the exit, so to speak, that he had probably been hit on the other side of the head, or at least tangentially in the back of the head ..."; "this [the neck wound] must have been an entrance wound ...";

b.   other WC references: WR 53, 529, 536; 6 H 70, 73, 76, 79-80; 17 H 14, 21; 20 H 5;

c.   January 1964 Texas State Journal of Medicine article *"Three Patients at Parkland"*, pages 64, 72, and 73---"Dr. Gene Akin, a resident in anesthesiology, and Dr. Giesecke connected a cardioscope to determine cardiac activity."; involved in treatment of Oswald, as well;

d.   *"High Treason"*, pp. 44-45 (*"The Boston Globe"*, 6/21/81): "Akin reaffirmed this [his WC testimony] to the Globe team and basically did not accept the official picture. On seeing the sketch, he said, "Well in my judgment at the time, what I saw was more parietal. But on the basis of this sketch, if this is what Bob McClelland saw, then it's more occipital." Akin further said that Dr. Kemp Clark saw the entry wound in the temple.";

e.   6/28/84 FBI Memorandum, SA Udo H. Specht to SAC, Dallas, re: interviews with Akin (RIF#124-10158-10449)---"On 6/18/84, the writer and SA DOUG DAVIS interviewed an individual who stated he was formerly Dr. GENE COLE-

MAN AKIN, the senior resident anesthesiologist at Parkland Hospital, Dallas, Texas. AKIN stated that he was on duty at the hospital on 11/22/63 when President KENNEDY was brought in the emergency room. AKIN stated that the FBI interviewed him during the 1963-1964 period concerning any of the observations he made on 11/22/63. AKIN stated that the "historic accident" of being present in the emergency room on 11/22/63 changed his whole life in a negative way. He feels that the governments on both a federal and state level have harassed him since that time. He stated that he quit practicing medicine in 1979 or 1980 and that DEA took his narcotics license away. He has never recouped the money it cost him to practice medicine because of government interference with his own destiny and self-initiative. He has been on welfare since 1980 and feels it is now the government's obligation to take care of him. He claims that his sister had him committed to Terrell State Hospital and he was incarcerated in that institution from March 9 through May 25, 1984. He stated that it took him that long to convince the doctors that he was not a "nut." AKIN is in the hospital for heart by-pass surgery on 6/20/84 and he has also been diagnosed as having renal cancer. AKIN also stated that he had his name changed to SOLOMON BEN ISRAEL and he was interviewed in Room 439, St. PAUL's HOSPITAL, Dallas, Texas. AKIN ranted and raved about government injustice and conspiracies against him and behaved in a general aberrant manner. His mannerism in communicating, in the opinion of the writer, gave him or the information he was trying to relate no credibility whatsoever. The writer attempted to listen to him for over one hour. AKIN made efforts to contact the Dallas news media in order to tell his story, but apparently received very little favorable response. The writer made efforts to get AKIN to tell his story. AKIN kept ranting and raving about items from the right to the left of the political spectrum. AKIN did finally say that *when he saw President KENNEDY in the emergency room on 11/22/63, he thought he saw a bullet entrance wound on the President's forehead. The President was covered with blood in the head area and the back of his head was blown wide open. AKIN feels that his observation as to the possible entrance wound on the President's forehead is significant and that he did not mention this item when he was interviewed in 1963-1964 because he did not want to be killed by any conspirators. AKIN stated that if this entrance wound was not documented in the Presidential autopsy, then plastic surgery was probably conducted to cover this up.* AKIN made available a cassette tape recording of items he recorded himself during the past few days. The tape recording was reviewed by the writer and contained no information whatsoever concerning AKIN's comments about the assassination of President KENNEDY. [redaction: at least one paragraph] At 1:45 pm, 6/28/84, AKIN telephonically contacted the writer and stated that he checked himself out [of] St. Paul's hospital to [be] re-evaluated as to what to do about his medical condition. He stated that he was calling from the Dallas County Jail and that he had been arrested on 6/26/84. He was unspecific as to why he was arrested, but he indicated that it was some type of fraud charge and alcohol might have been an issue also. He wanted the writer to get him out of Jail and that it was all the FBI's fault that his troubles are continuing. AKIN became extremely verbally abusive and the writer terminated the call. [redaction: at least a few sentences; end]" (*emphasis added in italics*) [for important information on SA Specht, see *"JFK: Breaking The Silence"* by Bill Sloan, pages 40-44: Specht said that he "was assigned to be a kind of custodian of the files pertaining to the Kennedy case", and was the official media spokesman for the Dallas FBI office from 1978 to 1990; in fact, as Sloan writes, he "personally wrote the memorandum that formally closed the Kennedy case from that office's point of view in 1983"!];

f.   [unanswered letter from Vince Palamara 1998]

g.   *"Murder In Dealey Plaza"* by James Fetzer (2000), pages 56, 60, 150, 180, 197, 199, 240, 249, 252, 298

8) Dr. Paul Conrad Peters, Urologist (deceased 12/26/2002)

a.   6 H 70-71 / testimony---"It was pointed out that an examination of the brain had been done...we saw the wound of entry in the throat and noted the large occipital wound...";"...I noticed that there was a large defect in the occiput... It seemed to me that in the right occipitalparietal area that there was a large defect.";

b.   other WC references: WR 53-54, 517, 526, 529; 2 H 39; 3 H 370-371; 6 H 4, 10-11, 16, 20, 32, 34, 47, 54, 114, 141; 17 H 2, 11, 14; 20 H 333; 21 H 151;

c.   11/12/66 interview with Lifton ("BE", pages 317 and 324)---" a hole in the occiput...exited through the back of the head..."; "I'd be willing to swear that the wound was in the occiput, you know. I could see the occiputal lobes clearly, and so I know it was that far back, on the skull. I could look inside the skull, and I thought it looked like cerebellum was injured, or missing, because the occipital lobes seemed to rest almost on the foramen magnum...the cerebellum and brainstem, might have been injured, or missing.";

d.   Letter to Harry Livingstone dated 8/7/79 (*"High Treason"*, p. 44 and photo section; see also *"Killing Kennedy"*, p. 392): "There was a large hole in the back of the head through which one could see the brain." Peters also marked an "x" where McClelland drew the defect to be: the right-rear of the skull; "[Peters] reconfirmed this in long phone conversations, and in talks with fellow researcher Gary Mack, Ben Bradlee of the Globe, and others.";

e.   letter to Wallace Milam dated 4/14/80 ("BE", p. 557)---"...The only wound I saw on President Kennedy's head was in the occipitoparietal area on the right side.";

f.   *"Killing The Truth"*, p. 684 (*"The Boston Globe"*, 6/21/81): "Dr. Peters told reporters that the large defect was in both the occipital and parietal area of the head. When shown the official picture, he stated: "I don't think it's consistent with what I saw." He said of the McClelland drawing, "It's not too far off. It's a large wound, and that's what we saw at the time.';

g.   Jan. 1983 reinterview by Lifton ("BE", p. 705)---"now, shown the autopsy photos...he reacted with considerable surprise. He told me he could have sworn the wound was at the back of the head.";

h.   *"High Treason"*, p. 459 (interview 12/28/88): scalp in the back "badly torn...I'm sure part of it was missing."

i. *"The Men Who Killed Kennedy"*, 1988---"I could see that he had a large about 7 cm. opening in the right occipital parietal area. A considerable portion of the brain was missing there, and the occipital cortex, the back portion of the brain, was lying down near the opening of the wound.";

j. *"Nova"*, 11/15/88 (see still photo in *"Killing The Truth"*): places hand on right rear part of the skull; waffles after seeing photos, allegedly for the first time (!); "I would have to say, honestly, in looking at these photos, they're pretty much as I remember President Kennedy at the time, EXCEPT FOR THAT LITTLE INCISION THAT SEEMS TO BE COMING DOWN IN THE PARIETAL AREA [outlining it on his right temple]. IN LOOKING AT THE PHOTO-GRAPHS I COULD ENVISION THAT AN INCISION MIGHT HAVE BEEN MADE IN ORDER TO PULL THE SCALP BACK TO EXPOSE THIS BONE TO MAKE A PHOTOGRAPH OF THAT AREA (emphasis added).";

k. 8/25/89 letter to Joanne Braun (*"The Third Decade"*, March 1991): [referring to his *"Nova"* commentary cited above]"It appeared to me, in reviewing the photos, that the incision was very sharp, as if cut by a knife, and I thought at the time that the prosecutor might have made it to enhance the removal of the brain and contents. I suppose it could have been an extension of the tear from the wound, but I did not notice it at the time we operated on President Kennedy.";

l. Portrayed by actor I.D. Brickman in the Oliver Stone movie *"JFK"* (1991) [see *"JFK: The Book of the Film"* (1992), p. 155];

m. *"High Treason 2"*, p. 108 (Livingstone interview 10/10/91)---throat wound photos are accurate;

n. 3/10/92 interview by Posner in '*Case Closed"*, p. 311---"... I now believe the head wound is more forward than I first placed it. More to the side than the rear.";

o. 4/2/92 speech delivered to the *"Who Killed JFK?"* meeting in Centreville, Mississippi---"The wound was occipital-parietal... I saw about a 7 centimeter hole in the occiput..."

p. Dallas Forum 6/4/92----entrance wound in neck; stand by original reports; "This was only [!] a 7-cm. hole in the occipital parietal area, which I saw.";(*"Killing The Truth"*, p. 118, 175);

q. San Francisco, CA Urologists meeting attended by Drs. Aguilar and Peters in 1992---demonstrated the wound on a human head as being in the top rear portion of the skull: the right rear corner;

r. *"JFK: The Case For Conspiracy"* video 1993 (see Groden's "TKOAP", p.87 ---"occipital-parietal";

s. 3/4/94 letter to Brad Parker (*"Kennedy Assassination Chronicles"*, 6/95)---"I have not changed my opinion since I saw it [the head wound]... It involved the upper portion of the occipital and most of the parietal bone... the wound, I still maintain, was occipitoparietal... It was a 7 cm. wound... we could see a considerable portion of the brain was missing and that there was a large hole in the occipitoparietal area…encompassing the outer portion of the occipital area and part of the parietal area of the skull. I have not changed my mind. The review of the autopsy findings at the National Archives 25 years after the injury merely reinforces my statement, which I gave to the Warren Commission. I told them there was a large 7 cm. (at least) hole in the occipitoparietal region.";

t.   "*Killing Kennedy*" by H.E.L., p. 393: 4/17/95 letter to Livingstone---"…large hole in the occipitoparietal area, estimated about 7 cm., on the right side…I did think the cerebellum was injured at the time.";

u.   "*JFK/ Deep Politics Quarterly*" journal, 1/97: interview by Russ McLean and Brian Edwards conducted on 11/2/96 [see also *"Fair Play"*, issue #16]: "…I stepped up and looked at the President's head and saw a 7 centimeter hole in the occipital parietal on the right portion of the head…we thought the bullet had gone in through his throat and come out the back of his head. A big wound of exit, and a small wound of entry…you've probably seen pictures where the wound is turned back and you can see a huge hole there in the head…If you could pull this flap of skin away, you'd see a huge hole in the head…";

v.   ARRB joint deposition (w/ McClelland, Baxter, Jones, and Perry) [see "*Trauma Room One*" by Dr. Charles Crenshaw (2001), pages 206-207, 258]

w.   10/98 letter to Vince Palamara---"The wound was occipito-parietal about 7 cm in diameter as I recall. Subsequent X-rays at Bethesda show much more fragmentation of the skull than was observable at the time through the intact scalp. Peters also drew two depictions of the wound to JFK's head, a side and rear view. In both, the head wound is depicted at the top-rear of the head, nowhere near the front. Peters also drew the back wound well down on the right shoulder.;

x.   "*Murder In Dealey Plaza*" by James Fetzer (2000), pages 56, 61, 174, 180, 192, 197, 199, 233, 240, 247, 298

y.   "*JFK Absolute Proof*" by Robert Groden (2013): see page 151- Dr. Peters is pictured with a nice summary of his statements

9) Dr. Charles A. Crenshaw, Resident Surgeon (deceased 11/15/2001):

a.   "*Conspiracy of Silence*" (1992), p. 86 (and throughout [Includes photos of himself]) [later renamed "*Trauma Room One*" (2001) and "*JFK Has Been Shot*" (2013)]: "His entire right cerebral hemisphere appeared to be gone. It looked like a crater---an empty cavity…From the damage I saw, there was no doubt in my mind that the bullet had entered his head through the front, and as it surgically passed through his cranium, the missile obliterated part of the temporal and all the parietal and occipital lobes before it lacerated the cerebellum."; [p. 79] "I also identified a small opening about the diameter of a pencil at the midline of his throat to be an entry bullet hole. There was no doubt in my mind about that wound.";

b.   "*High Treason 2*", pp. 110-115 and 549 (interviews of 7/12/80 [90?] and 9/21/91)---"…it was in the parietal-occipital area"; thinks the body was tampered with at Bethesda;

c.   WC references to his presence on 11/22/63: 6 H 40 (Baxter), 6 H 31-32 (Mc-

Clelland), 6 H 80-81 (Salyer), 6 H 141 (Henchcliffe), 6 H 60 (Curtis)+15 H 761: index;

d. Completely overlooked WC reference to his presence on 11/24/63: 21 H 265(report by Parkland Administrator Charles Price)---"Dr. Charles Crenshaw was in the corridor and said they had been alerted. He said, 'You're not going to put him [Oswald] in the same room the President was in, are you?' [I] told him I surely was glad he had thought of it and by all means, not to.";

e. January 1964 "*Texas State Journal of Medicine*" article entitled "*Three Patients at Parkland*", p. 72---"Dr. Jenkins recalls that the following physicians were members of the resuscitation team: Drs. Jenkins and Akin...Drs. Gerry Gustafson, Dale Coln, and *Charles Crenshaw*, all residents in surgery, who were prepared to introduce cannulae into the veins via cutdowns or percutaneous puncture... three members of the staff were performing venous cutdowns, one in each lower extremity and one in the left forearm. These were performed by Drs. Coln, *Crenshaw, and Gustafson.*" [emphasis added; Brad Parker has learned that this article, "*Three Patients at Parkland*", while based on the original reports made by the Parkland doctors, incorporated subtle changes which he was told were made by none other than Dr. Marion Jenkins!];

f. Geraldo's "*Now It Can Be Told*", 4/2/92 (excerpt included on James Fetzer's video "*JFK: The Assassination, The Cover-Up, and Beyond*", 1994; see p. 93 of Michael; Benson's "*Who's Who on the JFK Assassination*")---JFK shot from the front; demonstrates wounds; ALSO: on the same program, G. Robert Blakey of the HSCA makes the claim that they did talk to Crenshaw but he "was not the best witness" (?);

g. "*20/20*", 4/92 (see still photo in "*Assassination Science*", p. 43)---right rear exit wound, entrance wound in the throat;

h. "*JFK- The Final Analysis*", 4/15/92 (also a home video)---via phone call, says the same basic info. as above;

i. Letter to Livingstone re: 4/30/92 Dallas Press conference [unable to attend] (part of press kit)---"There were two wounds to the President that we observed at parkland. The first was a small and neat entrance wound to the throat, across which Dr. Malcolm Perry made an incision to put in a trach tube. The second wound was much more obvious. This wound, to the right rear side of his head, obliterated part of the parietal, part of the temporal, and all of the occipital area. This resulted in a gaping hole, the size of a baseball, in the back of the head, and the cerebellum was hanging on a thread of tissue outside the wound. The front of his head and the facial features were unmarred. The so-called "official" autopsy photos I have seen do not reflect the wounds we saw at Parkland. I believe then, as I do now, that President Kennedy was shot from the front---not once, but twice.";

j. First Midwest Symposium, Chicago, Il, 6/92---entrance wound in the neck; "parietal occipital area...obvious exit wound"; "We did three cutdowns---I did the one on the right leg."; also says that the photos are not correct: "autopsy picture no longer has the hole"; gives a presentation, including parts that back up his claim that LBJ phoned Parkland on 11/24/63;

k. 7/22/92 FBI interview of Crenshaw (FBI file # 89A-DL-60165-99 and 100)-
    --"(Dr. Crenshaw said that) The head wound was located at the back of the
    President's head and was the approximate size of Doctor CRENSHAW's fist.
    It extended from the approximate center of the skull in the back to just behind
    the right ear, utilizing a left to right orientation and from a position a couple of
    inches above the right ear to the approximate middle of the right ear utilizing
    a top to bottom orientation."; "(Crenshaw's) description which indicates that
    the wound extended from the hairline back behind the ear and to the back of
    the head was 'poorly worded [in the book].' The correct description indicates
    that the wound was located entirely at the rear of the head behind the right ear.";

l. A.S.K. conference, 10/92;

m. extensive talks with Gary Aguilar (Included on audio tape);

n. "The West Texas Connection"/ Texas News, 5/93;

o. Interview/ conversations with Dr. Cyril Wecht ("Cause of Death" by Cyril Wecht
    with Mark Curriden and Benjamin Wecht, p. 71)---"Take my good friend Dr.
    Charles Crenshaw...He looked at Jack Kennedy's body that day. He saw the
    gunshot wound to the front of the neck, and he says unequivocally it was an
    entrance wound.";

p. "JFK: The Case For Conspiracy" 1993 (see Groden's "TKOAP", p. 86);

q. "Triangle of Fire" by Bob Goodman (1993), pp. 67-68;

r. 4/19/95 interview with Brad Parker ("Kennedy Assassination Chronicles",
    9/95)---"According to Dr. Crenshaw, the Secret Service's briefing of the Dallas
    doctors as to the official autopsy findings on November 29 [1963] ended virtu-
    ally all talk among the doctors regarding the assassination";

s. "Biography: Lee Harvey Oswald", A&E, 11/21/95---doesn't say much due to ed-
    iting!

t. nice blurb on the back jacket of Walt Brown's "Treachery in Dallas" (1995);

u. "The Search For Lee Harvey Oswald" by Robert Groden (1995), pp. 202-204---re:
    last moments of Oswald's life;

v. nice blurb on the back cover of Dr. William Truels' book "Breach of Faith" (1996);

w. Plano East Conference, 2/19-2/23/96;

x. Liverpool, England/ Dallas '63 conference , Summer 1996;

y. Press Kit Handout at COPA 1996 (in absentia) [see "Fair Play", issue #13];

z. "The Warren Omission" by Walt Brown (1996), page v---Crenshaw "has also
    been a faithful and tireless friend throughout this work";

aa. "Assassination Science", pp. 37-60; 61-83; 414-415: drawings;

ab. ARRB deposition 1998;

ac. 8/26/98 letter to Vince Palamara (Including drawings ---What is your best esti-
     mate (in cm.) of the wound to President Kennedy's head and exactly where was
     it located at? "1) Wound---2 3/4 or 2.75 inches with 2.54 cm/inch---6.985appx.

7 cm's---2) Wound in right rear of head---behind ear--occipital-parietal portion of head---see pictures p. 67-68 Robert J. Groden's book *The Killing of a President*---shows the physician's showing where the wound was in the head.";

ad. *"Murder In Dealey Plaza"* by James Fetzer (2000), pages 15, 56, 61-63, 133, 174-178, 190, 196, 199, 211, 213, 240, 249, 252, 256, 257, 259, 289, 297, 421

ae. *"The Men Who Killed Kennedy"* (2003), parts 7 & 9 DVD

af. *"J. Edgar Hoover: The Father Of The Cold War"* by R. Andrew Kiel (2000), page 284

ag. *"JFK Absolute Proof"* by Robert Groden (2013): see page 151- Dr. Crenshaw is pictured with a nice summary of his statements

10) Dr. Charles Rufus Baxter, Attending Surgeon (deceased 3/10/2005):

a. WR 523 / 17 H 8 / CE392---handwritten report dated 11/22/63----"…the right temporal and occipital bones were missing and the brain was lying on the table, with [extensive?] maceration and contusion… *[see below*]*";

b. January 1964 *"Texas State Journal of Medicine"* article *"Three Patients at Parkland"*, p. 63---repeats the gist of his 11/22/63 report, but with an added bit of information: "portions of the right temporal and occipital bones were missing and *some of* the brain was lying on the table. *The rest of the brain* was extensively macerated and contused." [emphasis added; Brad Parker has learned that this article, *"Three Patients at Parkland"*, while based on the original reports made by the Parkland doctors, incorporated subtle changes which he was told were made by none other than Dr. Marion Jenkins!];

c. 6 H 40, 41, 42 (re: neck) and 44 / testimony (3/24/64)---"There was a large gaping wound in the skull…literally the right side of his head had been blown off. With this and the observation that the cerebellum was present…"; *asked to read his 11/22/63 report for the record:*"…the right temporal and PARIETAL bones were missing [emphasis added]"- a change was made!; throat wound: "4 to 5 mm in widest diameter…it was a very small wound. And, it was directly in the midline…this would more resemble a wound of entry...[but]…I think that the wound could well represent either exit or entry wound.";

d. other WC references: WR 53-54, 56, 517, 524, 526, 529, 535; 2 H 39; 3 H 363, 369, 371, 374; 6 H 2, 4, 10-12, 16, 20, 23-24, 32-33, 35, 47, 54-55, 59, 64, 69-73, 79-80, 83, 106, 110, 141, 145, 149; 17 H 2, 9, 11, 14, 20; 20 H 6, 333; 21 H 151, 241

e. 11/8/66 interview with David Lifton ("BE", p. 272)---trach incision was an inch and a half;

f. *"High Treason"*, p. 45 (*"The Continuing Inquiry"*, 10/80 [based off a 1979 taped interview]): "It was a large gaping wound in the occipital area." He thought the wound was tangential and rejected the official picture. The wound in the neck was "no more than a pinpoint. It was made by a small caliber weapon. And it was an entry wound.";

g. "*High Treason*", p. 45 and 459 ("*The Boston Globe*", 6/21/81 [see also "*Killing Kennedy*", pp. 303-304]): did not fully support the official picture; Baxter quotes Dr. Clark as saying, "My God, the whole back of his head is shot off." Baxter said that he could not see the large hole because it was in the very back of the head and it could not be seen without picking up the head. Regarding the right parietal wound: "It was such a benign wound that we thought it was an entry wound.";

h. 10/10/91 interview with Livingstone ("*High Treason 2*", p. 106)---re: chest drainage tubes;

i. "20/20", 4/92---the neck wound could have been an entrance or an exit wound; confirmed that he did instill an edict of silence;

j. JAMA 1992 [Includes a photo of Baxter]---The autopsy photos of the neck wound are "very compatible" with what he saw; now did not recall Crenshaw being present in Trauma Room One and ridiculed the notion that Crenshaw received a call from LBJ on 11/24/63 as if the call was FOR Crenshaw personally!;

k. Dallas Forum 6/4/92 (see "*Killing The Truth*", p. 172, 177-178, 718)---"Looking at that hole, one would have to---and my immediate thought was that this was an entry wound because it was SO SMALL.";

l. "*JFK: Breaking The Silence*" (1993) by Bill Sloan, p. 92---"Although Baxter... declined to be interviewed for this book, Baxter did issue a brief comment in October 1992 through the school's public information office in which he described the throat wound as being "very small" and looking as though "it might have come from a handgun.";

m. 3/12/92 interview with Gerald Posner for "*Case Closed*", p. 312 and 314---"I never even saw the back of his head. The wound was on the right side, not the back." (!?); repeats that he doesn't remember Crenshaw being in Trauma Room One;

n. "*Breach of Faith*" (1996) by Dr. William Truels, p. 12---"I asked Dr. Baxter about the Kennedy assassination... He told me that no one had the heart to lift Kennedy up and look at his back. But he described a huge hole in the back right of Kennedy's head. This wound sounded more like an exit wound to me, but Dr. Baxter would not speculate about the matter.";

o. 8/27/98 Joint ARRB deposition (w/ McClelland, Perry, Jones, and Peters) [see "*Trauma Room One*" by Dr. Charles Crenshaw (2001), pages 206-207, 258];

p. [unanswered letter from Vince Palamara 1998]

q. "*Murder In Dealey Plaza*" by James Fetzer (2000), pages 56, 60, 150, 176-181, 190, 192, 197, 199, 240, 297, 298

r. "*JFK Absolute Proof*" by Robert Groden (2013): see page 153- Dr. Baxter is pictured with a nice summary of his statements

11) Dr. Robert G. Grossman, Resident Neurosurgeon:

a. "*High Treason*", pages 30, 36, 51, 53, 459 ("*The Boston Globe*", June 21, 1981-notes placed in JFK Library [see also "*Killing Kennedy*", pp. 303-304, "*Between The Sig-*

nal and the Noise" by Roger Bruce Feinman (1993) and Groden's "TKOAP", p. 181])---saw two separate head wounds: a large defect in the parietal area above the right ear, as well as "a large [albeit smaller than the first wound described], separate wound, located squarely in the occiput."; "…described a large hole squarely in the occiput, far too large for a bullet entry wound…"; *Grossman*: "It was clear to me…that the right parietal bone had been lifted up by a bullet which had exited."; noticed the skin flap near the right temple; Dr. Clark picked up the back of the head to demonstrate the wound;

b.   6 H 81 (Salyer)---confirms Grossman's presence in Trauma Room One;

c.   ARRB interview 3/21/97 [see James Fetzer's "*Murder in Dealey Plaza*", p. 193, 199,201,240]

d.   [unanswered letter from Vince Palamara 1998]

e.   "*Murder In Dealey Plaza*" by James Fetzer (2000), pages 193, 199, 201, 240

f.   "*Trauma Room One*" by Dr. Charles Crenshaw (2001), pages 201, 207, 276-277

g.   Duquesne University 40th Anniversary Conference presentation, 11/03, Pittsburgh, PA

h.   "*JFK Absolute Proof*" by Robert Groden (2013): see page 153- Dr. Grossman is pictured with a nice summary of his statements

12) Dr. Richard Brooks Dulany, Resident Surgeon [Dulaney]:

a.   6 H 114 /testimony (3/25/64)---"…he had a large head wound—that was the first thing I noticed." Arlen Specter did not have him elaborate on any details.;

b.   Other WC references: WR 56, 529; 3 H 358, 384; 6 H 2, 11, 46, 52-53, 69, 73-74; 17 H 14; 21 H 241;

c.   "*High Treason*", pages 43, 46, 460, and 489 ("*The Boston Globe*", 6/21/81 [see also "*Killing Kennedy*", page 303]): "The copy of the autopsy photo was shown to him by the Globe and he stated that it was not accurate. When shown the official picture, he said that there was a "definite conflict" and "that's not the way I remember it."**; "Somebody lifted up his head and showed me the back of his head. We couldn't see much until they picked up his head. I was standing beside him. The wound was on the back of his head. On the back side … the whole back-side was gone … it was a big gaping wound."; **"The tape and summary of Dulaney is in the JFK Library, and I have since talked with him, verifying this.";

d.   "*Nova*", 11/15/88 (see still photo in "*Killing The Truth*")---demonstrates the right rear of the head as missing;

e.   "*High Treason 2*", pp. 107-108, 296 (based off interviews in July 1979 and 4/3/91 [Included on unreleased video])- "It included the occipital region, but was also parietal…I didn't see any damage to the face."; disputed the back-of-the-head photo;

f.   "*JFK: The Case For Conspiracy*" video (see Groden's "TKOAP", p. 87)---top-rear of the head; disputed photo;

g.   *"Case Closed"*, p. 310n---Posner mentions the *"Nova"* program (above);

h.   *"Murder in Dealey Plaza"* by James Fetzer (2000), pages 193, 199, 233, 240, 247

i.   *"JFK Absolute Proof"* by Robert Groden (2013): see page 151- Dr. Dulany is pictured with a nice summary of his statements

13) Dr. Adolph Hartung "Buddy" Giesecke, Jr., Anesthesiologist (deceased 12/24/2011):

a.   20 H 5-7: 11/25/63 report re: care of Gov. Connally;

b.   6 H 74 / testimony---"..I noticed that he had a very large cranial wound, with loss of brain substance, and it seemed most of the bleeding was coming from the cranial wound...from the vertex to the left ear, and from the browline to the occiput on the left-hand side of the head the cranium was entirely missing.";

c.   Other WC references: WR 53-54, 517, 529, 531, 533, 535; 3 H 370, 384; 4 H 103; 6 H 11, 23-24, 46-47, 64, 76, 78-79, 84, 114, 122; 17 H 2, 14, 16, 18, 20; 21 H 151;

d.   January 1964 *"Texas State Journal of Medicine"* article entitled *"Three Patients at Parkland"*, pp.69-71---"Dr. Giesecke had learned from Dr. Jenkins that the President had been shot. He went to Trauma Room 1 to assist with the President, but was soon called to attend Governor Connally in Operating Room No. 5 in the main operating suite on the second floor where the Governor had been taken." Nothing is said about Giesecke's statements re: JFK's wounds, and only his treatment of Connally is described. [Brad Parker has learned that this article, *"Three Patients at Parkland"*, while based on the original reports made by the Parkland doctors, incorporated subtle changes which he was told were made by none other than Dr. Marion Jenkins!]

e.   *"High Treason"*, pages 30, 46-49, 231 (*"The Continuing Inquiry"*, 10/80; author's 1979 interview tape-JFK Library; *"The Boston Globe"*, 6/21/81; letter to Livingstone, 4/1/81 [see also *"Killing Kennedy"*, p. 304]): "..we shined a light in the cranial vault there, and noticed a large amount of brain missing."; Livingstone: "Was this [the back of the head depicted in the official picture] blown out?" Giesecke: "Yes. It was missing."; "From what I saw, I think that's [the McClelland drawing] a reasonable representation."; confirmed to the Globe that the back of the head was missing; "in doing so (pulling down the flap), the underlying bony defect is obscured.";

f.   1989 letter to Joanne Braun (*"The Third Decade"*, March 1991)---did not see the V-shaped feature at Parkland;

g.   3/5/92 interview with Gerald Posner for *"Case Closed"*, 309 and 311---erred in his original testimony when he described the wound as more occipital (?!); "Lifton spent six hours with me trying to get me to say the wounds were like he wanted them."---funny, Lifton doesn't reference any interview at all in his book!;

h.   interview with Gary Aguilar;

   i.   3/94 letter to Brad Parker [see *"Fair Play"*, issue #20]---"Dr. Adolph Giesecke also got a copy of the McClelland sketch from Parker, with a request for comment. Dr. Giesecke said that while he no longer had a clear memory of the wounds, he would agree with the findings of Gerald Posner." [!];

   j.   9/98 letter to Vince Palamara---"I did not examine the President's head and should never have said anything about the wounds. (I testified to the Warren Commission that the wound was on the left side. That was obviously wrong)...I hope you become convinced that there was only one gunman, Oswald, and all entry wounds were from the rear." [!] Ironically, Giesecke included with his letter a photocopy of the "Three Patients At Parkland" article that includes medical information that greatly contradicts this view.;

   k.   *"Murder In Dealey Plaza"* by James Fetzer (2000), pages 56, 152, 199, 239, 240, 247, 259, 298

   l.   *"JFK Absolute Proof"* by Robert Groden (2013): see page 153- Dr. Giesecke is pictured with a nice summary of his statements

14) Dr. Fouad A. Bashour, Chief Cardiologist (deceased 1/1/2003):

   a.   WR 528 / 17 H 13 / CE392: handwritten report dated 11/22/63---very brief report that doesn't mention the wounds;

   b.   6 H 61-62 /testimony---"...the head wound was massive...": no details were elicited during Bashour's brief testimony;

   c.   other WC references: WR 53-54, 518, 537; 3 H 360, 371; 6 H 4, 11, 20, 32, 40, 64, 145, 149; 17 H 3, 22; 20 H 5; 21 H 152;

   d.   January 1964 *"Texas State Journal of Medicine"* article *"Three Patients at Parkland"*, p. 63---repeats the gist of his brief 11/22/63 report;

   e.   *"High Treason"*, p. 45 (*"The Continuing Inquiry"*, 10/80; see also *"Conspiracy"*, p. 481)---"He was most insistent that the official picture was not representative of the wounds, and he continually laid his hand both on the back of Livinsgtone's head and his own to show where the large hole was. "Why do they cover it up?" he repeated numerous times. "This is not the way it was!" he kept repeating, shaking his head no.";

   f.   Val Imm, the society columnist for the "Dallas Times Herald" (Imm's society page was called "Imm-Prints" and appeared in the "Living" section of the paper), was also the future wife of Bashour (see the July 1998 issue of *"JFK/ Deep Politics Quarterly"* journal: article by Walt Brown);

   g.   [unanswered letter from Vince Palamara]

   h.   *"Murder In Dealey Plaza"* by James Fetzer (2000), pages 56, 177, 199, 240

   i.   *"JFK Absolute Proof"* by Robert Groden (2013): see page 154- a nice summary of his statements

15) Dr. Kenneth Everett Salyer, Resident Surgeon:

a. 6 H 81 /testimony---"…he did have some sucking wound of some type on his neck…";"…(JFK) had a wound of his right temporal region…I came in on the left side of him and noticed that his major wound seemed to be in his right temporal area, at least from the point of view that I could see him, and other than that---nothing other than he did have a gaping scalp wound---cranial wound.";

b. other WC reference: 6 H 32;

c. 1989 letter to Joanne Braun ("*The Third Decade*", March 1991)---did not see the V-shaped feature at Parkland;

d. photo in "*JFK: Conspiracy of Silence*" by Dr. Crenshaw;

e. "*Who's Who in the JFK Assassination*" by Michael Benson (1993), p. 407;

f. "*Who Killed JFK: The Final Chapter?*" CBS 11/19/93---"the right side of his head is blown off, he has a wound of his neck [points to front of throat]";

g. "*JFK: The Case For Conspiracy*" video (see also Groden's "TKOAP", p. 87): "This wound extended into the parietal area."; thought one of the autopsy photos was tampered with [the one on page 82 of "TKOAP"]: "You know, there's something wrong with it. I'll leave it at that. I mean----this thing has been---something, you know, happened to this…This is not right. No. See, this has been doctored here. This is lying open. See, the way you have him here---the way they've got him here is---skin flaps have been cut or altered or pushed up or changed, and this isn't the way he looked. This was---he looked---this was wide open with brain here. This is scalp pushed back and it's all distorted."; sees two "rounded, beveled" wounds, right next to each other, in the autopsy photo that shows the cranium empty [the one on the top part of page 81 in Groden's "TKOAP"];

h. Interview with Dr. Gary Aguilar---"Salyer reported…that the wound was right sided but extended both posterior to and anterior to the ear. He repeated a claim made to Robert Groden [see video above] that the photograph appeared to have been tampered with.";

i. 2/94 letter to Brad Parker---commenting on Dr. McClelland's drawing: "This shows back of head. The main injury was temporoparietal (sic).";

j. [unanswered letter from Vince Palamara 1998]

k. "*Murder in Dealey Plaza*" by James Fetzer (2000), pages 174, 199, 240

l. "*JFK Absolute Proof*" by Robert Groden (2013): see page 152- Dr. Salyer is pictured with a nice summary of his statements

16) Nurse Patricia B. "Trish" Hutton (Gustafson):

a. 21 H 216: report of activities on 11/22/63---"Mr. Kennedy was bleeding profusely from a wound in the back of his head…A doctor asked me to place a pressure dressing on the head wound. This was no use, however, because of the massive opening on the back of the head.";

b. other WC references: 6 H 46-47, 146, 151;21 H 215, 242;

c. 1/8/83 interview by David Lifton ("BE", p. 706)---"The large throat wound shown in the photographs was not the tracheotomy incision that she saw in the emergency room on November 22,1963 ("It doesn't look like any that I've taken part in, let me put it that way.") and the head wound was at the back, not as shown in the pictures. "I was standing behind him when I was putting pressure on the head," she said, "and it was right in front of me. It wasn't around the side and up on top." Shown the large hole on the forward right hand side depicted in the x-rays, she exclaimed: "No way!";

d. "High Treason", p.43 and 459-460 ("The Boston Globe", 6/21/81 [see also "Killing The Truth", pages 652 and 702]): "She was asked to put a pressure bandage on the head wound. "I tried to do so but there was really nothing to put a pressure bandage on. It was too massive. So he told me just to leave it be. "She said the large wound was at "the back of the head." "Definitely in the back?" she was asked. "Yes." She strongly rejects the official picture. "; "She said the wound was low on the head, and about the size of a fist.";

e. 9/1/98 letter to Vince Palamara---"Because I have not discussed those two specific points publicly [size of head wound/ where it was located] I will have to leave it that way. If you read my E. Room statement from the Warren Commission it will indicate the wound was very large and I am sorry but I can't elaborate further. I do hope the public and you keep on with your research." [emphasis added; she HAS discussed these points publicly(see above), and her WC report goes against official history!];

f. 9/98 letter to Vince Palamara (in 'response' to my follow-up letter where I attempted to get her to at least endorse her prior statements)---"Sorry I only answered your 1rst letter to let you know I had received it-but I can't go into any more details-Sincerely, Trish Gustafson" [!];

g. "Murder In Dealey Plaza" by James Fetzer (2000), pages 60, 199

h. "JFK Absolute Proof" by Robert Groden (2013): see page 154- a nice summary of her statements

17) Chief Supervising Nurse Doris Mae Nelson (deceased 10/3/83):

a. 21 H 155: 11/25/63 affidavit re: Record of Death;

b. 20 H 640-643 /21 H 241-244: report of activities [see also Manchester, p. 673];

c. 6 H 145 /testimony---"...I could look and see [JFK] and tell that it was him... mainly his head [part she saw]": Specter did not ask nor did she volunteer info. regarding the head wound;

d. other WC references: 6 H 40, 52-53, 83, 116, 119, 137-139, 149, 152; 18 H 795-796, 798-799; 21 H 158, 159, 161, 180, 182, 188, 194, 202, 204, 207, 208-209, 211, 216, 219, 220, 222, 223, 224, 226, 228, 247, 255, 256, 259, 260, 261, 263;

e. 12/82 interview with David Lifton ("BE", p. 704)---"Doris Nelson told me the

tracheotomy was not the one she remembered: "Looks a little large to me...
[it] shouldn't be that big... It wasn't any 7-8 cm. [It was] just wide enough to get
the trach tube in."; "She looked at [the official autopsy photos of the back of the
head] and shook her head from side to side ... she remembered a large wound
there.";

f. *"A Hero For Our Time"* by Ralph Martin (1983), p. 519---"The operating room
nurse [unnamed; quite possibly Nelson] later told her high school friend how
difficult it was to remove his back brace..."

g. *"High Treason"*, pp. 43-44, 454 (*"The Boston Globe"*, 6/21/81 [see also *"Killing
the Truth"*, p. 702]): "Nurse Nelson drew a picture of the head wound, mostly
in the parietal area, but well towards the rear of the head. Her drawing conflicts
strongly with the official autopsy photograph. When she saw that picture she
said immediately, "It's not true... There wasn't even hair back there. It was blown
away. All that area (on the back of the head) was blown out.";

h. *"High Treason 2"*, pp. 103-105---"All I saw was missing skull and brains on the
back of his head... it was right there, in the right rear. In the right rear!";

i. deceased 10/3/83 [as per Louis Sproesser]

j. *"JFK: Conspiracy of Silence"*, p. 81;

k. [unanswered letter from Vince Palamara to Nelson's family 1998]

l. *"Murder in Dealey Plaza"* by James Fetzer (2000), pages 56, 61, 199

m. *"JFK Absolute Proof"* by Robert Groden (2013): see page 153- Doris Nelson is
pictured with a nice summary of her statements

18) Nurse Audrey N. Bell [and Elizabeth L. Wright-Good]:

a. 6 H 52 (Jones);

b. other WC references: WR 536; 17 H 21, 841; 20 H 333; 21 H 172, 187, 246,
248; 24 H 260 [see also *"Cover-Up"* by Gary Shaw and Larry Ray Harris (1976),
pp. 159-160, and *"Bloody Treason"* by Noel Twyman, pp. 112-113]; *21 H 193-
202: 12/11/63 report from Elizabeth L. Wright[Good]Director, Nursing Service to
C.J. Price* [Mrs. Wright-Good is the widow of O.P. Wright, Parkland Hospital
security chief. *Wallace Milam interview her on 6/23/93 and Mark Oakes did the
same on video in Oct. 11, 1994*---besides her belief, shared by her husband, that
the shots had to have come from more than one direction, she showed Oakes
on camera an unfired .38 special, WCC revolver bullet which she said was THE
bullet that her husband had attempted in vain to give to "an FBI agent"! She
showed the bullet to Henry Wade, which is backed up by *Oakes videotaped interview with Wade in May 1992*[although, as Oakes and Good acknowledge, Wade
got her name wrong] and, to a lesser extent, *Wright's mention of Wade at 21 H 196.*
Also, at 21 H 198: "Mr. Wright had somewhere down the line asked me if I could
ascertain the path of the bullet-or bullets-determine the path, and FIND OUT
WHERE THE INSTRUMENT OF INJURY ACTUALLY WAS" (emphasis
added).If this weren't enough, DPD Patrick Dean was married to the daughter

of O.P. Wright by a previous marriage (thanks to Wallace Milam for his help in providing transcripts)]---mentions Bell [21 H 194-197, 200, 201, 202];

c.   January 1964 Texas State Journal of Medicine article "*Three Patients at Parkland*", p. 74---Oswald's treatment: "The bullet which was palpable in the right posterior axillary line was removed and sent out by the operating room supervisor, Miss Audrey Bell, to be turned over to the legal authorities.";

d.   *Dallas Morning News* article by Earl Golz, 4/1/77 ("BE", pp. 558-559; Groden's "TKOAP", p. 128)---saw four or five bullet fragments taken from Gov. Connally's wrist, which is more metal than could have come from CE399;

e.   3/12/77 (audio-taped) interview with the HSCA (RIF#180-10090-10264)---she describes in detail how she placed approximately "four or five" Connally bullet fragments in a one-ounce medicine glass, then sealed it in a carefully labeled "foreign body" envelope before handing it to Secret Service agent Forrest Sorrels.;

f.   other HSCA references: 7 HSCA 156 and 392;

g.   1978 interview with Anthony Summers (see "*Conspiracy*", p. 546; see also "*A Complete Book of Facts*" by Duffy and Ricci, pp. 62-63, "TKOAP", p. 128, and "*Who Killed JFK?*" by Carl Oglesby, p. 32): "Bell...has caused concern with her recent remark that "the smallest [bullet fragment] was the size of the striking end of a match and the largest at least twice that big. I have seen the picture of the magic bullet, and I can't see how it could be the bullet from which the fragments I saw came.";

h.   12/82 interview by David Lifton ("BE", p. 704)---"The wound she saw was so localized at the rear that, from her position on the right hand side, with Kennedy lying face up, she couldn't see ANY damage...Perry pointed to the back of the President's head." Re: trach photo: "Looks like somebody has enlarged it...You don't make trachs that big. Not if you've got as much experience as Perry has.";

i.   "*High Treason*", pages 73, 453, 456---re: fragments mentioned above plus KRON show below;

j.   "*Nova*", 11/15/88---described the throat wound as one of entrance; said that there was no surgery done on the President at Parkland;

k.   "*JFK: An Unsolved Murder*", KRON, 11/18/88 (repeated in "*JFK: The Case For Conspiracy*" 1993 video---see Groden's "TKOAP", 87)---"There was a massive wound at the back of his head[demonstrating]"; throat wound was an entrance wound;

l.   unreleased 4/91 Livingstone video: see below

m.   "*High Treason 2*", photo section+many (see esp. Chapter 14), inc.80, 122, 317, 331-332 (interviews of 4/91, 5/1/91, 8/17/91, 9/22/91, 10/10/91, and 10/27/91---c)-h) in detail;

n.   A.S.K. conference, Dallas, Texas, 11/91 (see "*Assassination Science*", p. 392)---see c)-d) above;

o.   "*JFK-Conspiracy of Silence*" (1992) by Dr. Charles Crenshaw, p. 123---Crenshaw witnessed bullet fragments being handed to Bell;

p. *"Case Closed"*, p. 286---mentioned re: preparing the trauma room: see a) above;

q. New interview included in *"JFK: The Case for Conspiracy"*---denounces official photo; wound at the right rear of head: "back of the head ... Oh, yes, there was a big hole there."

r. [unanswered letter from Vince Palamara 1998]

s. *"Murder In Dealey Plaza"* by James Fetzer (2000), pages 174, 179, 256 (Wright: 93)

t. *"JFK Absolute Proof"* by Robert Groden (2013): see page 152- Bell is pictured with a nice summary of her statements

19) Nurse Diana Hamilton Bowron:

a. 19 H 167-170: 11/23/63 newspaper articles---"There was a gaping wound in the back of his head."; [On page 296 of Walt Brown's *"Treachery in Dallas"*, the author stated that Bowron "forfeited much credibility by telling that Parkland Doctors "tried massaging his heart manually", citing *"Killing The Truth"*, p. 180. However, this was based off Bowron Exhibit 4, 19 H 170, not something attributed to her circa 1993. In addition, not only does Dr. Crenshaw state that Dr. Perry "began closed-chest cardiac massage on the President"(*"JFK: Conspiracy of Silence"*, p. 88), Dr. Perry himself confirms this (6 H 9), as does Dr. Clark (6 H 20).];

b. 21 H 203-204: Bowron's report to Elizabeth Wright---nothing specific about the nature of the wounds;

c. 6 H 136 / testimony (3/24/64)---"... I saw the condition of his head ... The back of his head ... Well, it was very bad---you know ... I just saw one large hole.";

d. other WC references: 3 H 359; 6 H 2, 40, 46, 52-53, 146, 151; 21 H 226, 230, 239, 242, 243;

e. *"Killing The Truth"*, Chapter 6 and photo section (drawings/ notations)—"Well, to me it was an exit hole ... I assumed and I still do that that was an exit wound ... There was very little brain left"; denounced the photos; saw a hole well down on JFK's back (interviewed by Livingstone 1/8/93, 3/15/93, 5/2/93. Corresponded with Livingstone 4/25/93 and 5/11/93); [p. 718] "... the entry wound in his throat ... looked like an entry wound."; [interestingly, Bowron said nothing about noticing a back wound during her Warren Commission testimony (6 H 136: Specter- "Did you notice any other wound on the President's body?" Bowron-"No, sir.".), or, for that matter, in any of her pre-Livingstone statements.];

f. *"Murder In Dealey Plaza"* by James Fetzer (2000), pages 59, 61, 150, 199, 278

g. *"JFK Absolute Proof"* by Robert Groden (2013): see page 152- Bowron is pictured with a nice summary of her statements

20) Dr. William Midgett, Ob-Gyn Resident:

a. 6 H 135-136 (Bowron), 21 H 213 (Lozano)---confirm Midgett's presence and duties;

b. *"JFK-Conspiracy of Silence"* (1992), p. 74---same;

c. 4/16/92 interview with Gerald Posner for *"Case Closed"*, 287, 310-311---"...it was more parietal than occipital---that much I could see.";

d. 2/8/93 interview with Wallace Milam [transcript provided to author]---"Midgett saw one wound---in the head. He called it "right parietal area" and said it was behind the ear. He estimated it as being 6 cm in diameter. A piece of skull was missing and there was an absence of brain (Midgett called it "a hole" where the brain had been). Midgett said, "The brain was all over the car.";

e. *"Murder In Dealey Plaza"* by James Fetzer (2000), page 199

f. *"JFK Absolute Proof"* by Robert Groden (2013): see page 154- a nice summary of his statements

21) Dr. Don Teel Curtis, Resident Oral Surgeon:

a. WC references : WR 53, 66; 3 H 359-360 (Carrico); 6 H 2,4 (Carrico again); 6 H 11(Perry);6 H 40 (Baxter); 6 H 53 (Jones); 20 H 5 (Giesecke's report re: Connally);

b. 6 H 60 / testimony---"...I went around to the right side of [JFK] and saw the head wound...fragments of bone and a gross injury to the cranial contents, with copious amounts of hemorrhage.": no specific details on orientation and the like where elicited from Curtis;

c. 9/8/89 letter to Joanne Braun (*"The Third Decade"*, March 1991)---did not see the V-shaped feature at Parkland;

d. 10/25/94 letter from Curtis to Brad Parker---"The drawing by Dr. Robert McClelland is essentially my recollection of the wound suffered by John F. Kennedy.";

e. 12/22/94 interview with Brad Parker---had no interest in discussing the assassination;

f. 9/30/98 letter to Vince Palamara---"1. The wound involving the right posterior lateral surface of the skull appeared to me to be an exit wound or a tangential entrance wound. 2. I am unaware as to the details of the "official story" therefore I am unable to comment on my interpretation.";

g. *"Murder In Dealey Plaza"* by James Fetzer (2000), pages 56, 62, 247

h. *"JFK Absolute Proof"* by Robert Groden (2013): see page 153- Dr. Curtis is pictured with a nice summary of his statements

i. [12/6/63 *"Life* magazine" article by Paul Mandel: "the 8 mm. film shows the President turning his body far around to the right as he waves to someone in the crowd. His throat is exposed---towards the sniper's nest---just before he clutches it." (Reproduced in "Reasonable Doubt" by Henry Hurt)]

22) Donna Willie:

a. *"High Treason"*, p.456 (based off article by Nicole Levicoff of the *"Jenkintown*

[PA] Times Chronicle")---"the President had a wound in his throat that the Commission said was an exit wound or was made from a tracheotomy... the entry wound is always small, and the exit wound is much larger. I saw the entry wound in the front of the President's neck. I know he was shot from the front, and I couldn't understand why that wasn't released.";

b. "Who's Who in the JFK Assassination" by Michael Benson (1993), p. 482;

c. [unanswered letter from Vince Palamara 1998]

23) Dr. Philip Earle Williams:

a. "High Treason 2", photo section+ pp. 287, 294, 301-302, 308-312 (interviewed 4/6/91 and 5/10/92)---"Certainly the President's cerebellum was severely damaged and "swinging in the breeze", as it was described by Dr. Philip Williams"; "The bone in the back of President Kennedy's head was missing"; disputes the x-rays; "Dr. Williams, a young intern at the time, was asked to bring something to wrap the body in and brought a "plastic mattress cover---whitish-gray"... Dr. Williams said he "thought it had elastic around it. Form-fitting." He gave it to Pat Hutton, and didn't know for sure if it was used." Corroborating William's memory, Doris Nelson mentions in her report [21 H 242] that "I sent Mrs. Hutton to the 2nd floor to obtain a plastic mattress cover", while Pat Hutton herself wrote in her report [21 H 216] that "... I then left at the request of the supervisor [Nelson] to get a plastic cover to line the coffin.";

b. 21 H 215 (Nurse Bertha Lozano's report)---"Then the president's body was escorted out. The crowd vanished, and then I felt so confused that I just had to leave the desk for a few minutes. I later went to the dining room with Pat Hutton AND A DR. WILLIAMS and had coffee and afterwards, went home (emphasis added)";

c. "Killing The Truth", p. 103 and 584---Knew that LBJ called 11/24/63 and spoke to Crenshaw [see below];

d. "Assassination Science", p. 41: chapter by Charles Crenshaw (re: New York Times article 5/27/92): supports the fact that LBJ called the operating room on 11/24/63: "I heard the statement in the operating room... I have said this for years."

e. "JFK Absolute Proof" by Robert Groden (2013): see page 154- a nice summary of his statements

24) Nurse Margaret M. Hinchliffe (Hood) [Hinchcliffe; Henchcliffe]:

a. 21 H 239-240: report of activities for 11/22/63 [see also "The Death of a President" by William Manchester, p. 671]---nothing specific related to the wounds;

b. 6 H 141 and 143 /testimony---"... his head was very bloody..."; "... a little hole in the middle of his neck ... About as big as the end of my little finger... An entrance bullet hole---it looked to me like... I have never seen an exit bullet hole---I don't remember seeing one that looked like that."; "... it was just a small wound and wasn't jagged like most of the exit bullet wounds that I have seen.";

c. other WC references: 6 H 40, 46, 52-53, 136-139, 146, 152; 21 H 203, 242;

d. *"High Treason"*, pages 45, 68-69,454 (*"The Boston Globe"*, 6/21/81 [see also *"Killing the Truth"*, p. 702]): "Interviewed by reporters in 1981, she drew a picture of the large wound on a model of a skull. She sketched a gaping hole in the occipital region, which extended only slightly into the parietal area, thereby rejecting out of hand the official picture. She also insisted the President had an "entry" wound in his throat.";

e. present at the 6/4/92 Dallas Forum but not allowed to speak (see *"Killing The Truth"*, p. 172);

f. 6/25/93 interview with Wallace Milam [transcript provided to the author]---"After Kennedy died and doctors left, she and Diana Bowron washed the body... Face was cleaned by wiping [no wounds seen]. Piece of plastic was put over head wound in back of head. Did not cover face and front part of head. Purpose was to keep head from bleeding on casket interior...Hinchliffe remembers a plastic sheet [not necessarily a mattress liner], no body bag...Hinchliffe and Bowron washed off the back also... Hinchliffe says she did not see any back wound, but could not rule out that there may have been one."; "Throat wound---Definitely an entrance wound. Resented Arlen Specter trying to get her to say it might be an exit wound. Tracheotomy incision---Didn't know if it was made through or below the bullet wound. Described incision as "just a normal trach incision." Head wound---In very back of head. She put her hand back there. Everything was missing---bone, scalp, hair. She made the size of the wound about the circumference of a tea glass... Autopsy photos---She said that Crenshaw had sent her a copy of his book with the autopsy photos in it. She thought he was sending them to her to get her to verify them. She said the autopsy photos were nothing like what she saw. She referred particularly to the back of the head being intact, when she saw it to have been blown out."[all comments in brackets and emphasis via transcript];

g. [unanswered letter form Vince Palamara 1998]

h. *"Murder In Dealey Plaza"* by James Fetzer (2000), pages 61, 62, 256

i. *"JFK Absolute Proof"* by Robert Groden (2013): see page 154- a nice summary of her statements

25) Dr. Jackie Hansen Hunt, Anesthesiologist-only woman M.D.:

a. 6 H 76-79 / testimony---was blocked from seeing the wounds;

b. other WC references: WR 53, 517, 529; 3 H 371; 6 H 40,46,64,73; 17 H 2, 14; 20 H 5-6; 21 H 151;

c. January 1964 Texas State Journal of Medicine article *"Three Patients at Parkland"*, pages 63 and 70---present for JFK's treatment, as well as Connally's;

d. *"High Treason"*, p. 52 (*"The Continuing Inquiry"*, 10/80; author's tape-JFK Library): "...Livingstone showed her the [official autopsy] picture in 1979 and she instantly denounced it. She did not see the back of the head because she was standing directly over the President, but she insisted that the back part of the head was blown out and rejected the official picture. "That's he way it was described to me," she said, saying that the back of the head was gone. Had the large defect been anywhere else, she would have seen it and described it. Dr. Akin said that if you looked directly down on Kennedy, you could not see the large hole. Therefore, Dr. Hunt's testimony is significant. Dr. Hunt responded to Livingstone's question: "so, the exit wound would be in the occipital-parietal area?" "Yeah, uh-huh. It would be somewhere on the right posterior part of it…" She pointed to the sketch from Six Seconds In Dallas: "That's the way it was described to me. I went around this way and got the equipment connected and started---but I saw the man's face like so, and I never---the exit wound was on the other side---and what was back there, I don't know. That is the way it was described to me, " she said, pointing to the sketch showing the large hole in the back of the head. "I did not see that. I did not see this part of his head. That would have been here," she said, and put the palm of her hand on the back of Livingstone's head. She did this before Livingstone showed her the sketch from Thompson.";

e. 2/13/93 interview with Brad Parker---Hunt did not see the back of JFK's head, and did not observe any head injury as she stood above the president from the left side of the table. She further clarified that she observed no injury whatsoever to the temporoparietal region of either the left or right side;

f. 4/13/93 letter to Brad Parker---"The [McClelland] drawing agrees with my statement [in *"High Treason"*]"somewhere on the right posterior area of the head" and that is still my statement."

g. [unanswered letter from Vince Palamara 1998]

h. *"Murder In Dealey Plaza"* by James Fetzer (2000), pages 56, 240, 247, 298

i. *"JFK Absolute Proof"* by Robert Groden (2013): see page 154 – a nice summary of her statements

26) Dr. Martin G. White, Resident Surgeon:

a. 6 H 82-83 /testimony---" I saw the wound in his head…": unfortunately, he did not get specific, nor was he asked to by Specter;

b. other WC references: 3 H 359-360, 363; 6 H 2,4,114;

c. 1989 letter to Joanne Braun (*"The Third Decade"*, March 1991)---did not see the V-shaped feature at Parkland;

d. [unanswered letter from Vince Palamara 1998]

27) Doctor/ Admiral George Gregory Burkley, Physician to the President (deceased 1/2/1991):

a. 22 H 93-97: 11/27/63 report of his activities surrounding the assassination of JFK [see also *"The Death of a President"* by William Manchester, p. 670]---(22 H 94 and 97)"[at Parkland]It was evident that death was imminent and that he was in a hopeless condition."; [at Bethesda]"… his appearance in the casket gave no evidence of the injury he had received.": perhaps because the wound was in the BACK of the head? ;

b. 11/22/63 Press Conference by Asst. WH Press sec. Mac Kilduff (please see *"Best Evidence"*, pp. 330-331 and photo 28 [Kilduff Press Conference, 11/22/63, Transcript 1327B-LBJ Library; USSS RIF# 154-10002-10194]: "Dr. Burkley told me, it is a simple matter, Tom, of a bullet right through the head": he then points to his right temple! Question: "can you say where the bullet entered his head, Mac?" "It is my understanding that it entered in the temple, the right temple."; "They [the shots] came from the right side." [see Thomas Atkins' film clip as shown in *"The Men Who Killed Kennedy"*, *"The Jim Garrison Tapes"* video 1992, *"JFK: The Case for Conspiracy"* video 1993, *"High Treason 2"*, p. 290, Groden's "TKOAP", p. 59; "POTP", p. 408] This information was repeated by Chet Huntley on NBC that day: ""President Kennedy, we are now informed, was shot in the right temple. 'It was a simple matter of a bullet right through the head,' said Dr. George Burkley, the White House medical officer." [NBC video, 11/22/63, 1:47 p.m. CST; clip repeated in Prof. James Fetzer's video *"JFK: The Assassination, The Cover-Up, and Beyond"*];

c. Air Force One, 11/22/63---in Cecil Stoughton photos and can be heard on AF1 radio transcripts re: arrangements for transport of JFK's remains;

d. Autopsy descriptive (face) sheet, 11/22/63---back wound well down below the neck (verified by Dr. Burkley);

e. Certificate of Death, signed 11/23/63 [see *"Cover-Up"* by Stewart Galanor, p. 128]—"a second wound occurred in the posterior back at about the level of the third thoracic vertebra."; "The wound was shattering in type causing a fragmentation of the skull and evulsion of THREE particles of the skull at time of the impact, with resulting maceration of the right hemisphere of the brain (emphasis added)";

f. other WC references: WR 46, 53, 55, 545; 2 H 91 (bullet was still in Connally [see reference pertaining to Kellerman, below]), 98-99, 143; 3 H 363; 6 H 20,27,69 (Peters: indicated that Burkley asked that JFK be given steroids),148; 7 H 450, 452, 466, 469; 16 H 988;18 H 726, 728, 743, 744, 756, 757, 785, 795, 814;

g. 4/10/64, 4/14/64, 4/23/64, 3/3/65, and 7/11/65 interviews with William Manchester (*"The Death of a President"*, numerous, included p. 297): "Roy Kellerman had been the first agent to scent trouble. Shortly before the coffin arrived, Roy had been standing with Dr. Burkley in the nurse's station, hanging onto the [SAIC of WHD Gerald] Behn line..." [these same men would later converse on AF1]; According to the 5/31/87 issue of Paul Hoch's newsletter *"Echoes of Conspiracy"* (vol. 9, No. 1), Manchester told Hoch that "at that time [1964-1965] Dr. Burkley said he did not believe in a conspiracy theory, and was emphatic on that point.";

h. 4/22/65 and 4/26/65 letters of transmittal of materials to Mrs. Evelyn Lincoln and the National Archives;

i. Oral History, 10/17/67, JFK Library (see *"Reasonable Doubt"*, p. 49)---When asked by the interviewer if he agrees with the Warren Report "on the number of bullets that entered the President's body", Burkley said "I would not care to be quoted on that.";

j. 11/19/67 interview with David Lifton ("BE", pp. 401-402)---Burkley refused to discuss the matter;

k. RIF#180-10087-10092---the smaller fragment of skull found by Seymour Weitzman (7 H 107) was forwarded to Dr. Burkley [p. 213 of *"Murder From Within"*---Postal Inspector Harry Holmes told Newcomb and Adams that he himself found a piece of JFK's skull which he went on to discard!];

l. HSCA Rec. #7310080 Agency File # 004864---the Harper fragment, found by Billy Harper on 11/23/63, was forwarded to Dr. Burkley after inspection by the FBI (also, representatives from Dr. Burkley's office were involved in intercepting Kinney's call to Burkley from the C-130 re: the large, back-of-the-head fragment he found while in flight AND in the limo inspection where more fragments were found);

m. HSCA RIF#180-10116-0052 (originated from WC)---"11/27/63 5:15 p.m. Just received a small Neman [sic] Markus box about 2 1/2" x 3 1/2" containing material which had been discussed previously with them. A letter of the full report will be made. This material will be deposited with the Commanding Officer of the Bethesda Naval Hospital for subsequent retention with other material of similar nature. Material was received in the presence of Dr. James M. Young and me. The contact with the FBI was Roy Jevous at Code 175 x 353.

/s/ GGBurkley [sic]

G. G. Burkley, M.D.

Received from Robert I. Bouck, Special Agent in Charge, U. S. Secret Service, specimen of bone that appears to be from a skull, turned over to Secret Service by **David Burros**. It was apparently found on the parkway near the scene of the assassination (marked Fragment No. 2 for identification).

Both above described specimens to be turned over to Naval Hospital by Dr. Burkley for examination, analysis, and retention until other disposition is directed.

/s/ George G. Burkley

G. G. Burkley, M.D."

n. 1/11/69 *"New York Times"*---Burkley remained LBJ's personal physician from 12:30 p.m., 11/22/63, until Johnson retired in Jan. 1969;

o. THREE :AGENCY: HSCA
ORIGINATOR: HSCA [RIF#180-10086-10295]
FROM: RICHARD SPRAGUE

TO: FILE
MEMORANDUM

March 18, 1977

TO : FILE

FROM : RICHARD A. SPRAGUE

William F. Illig, an attorney from Erie, Pa., contacted me in Philadelphia this date, advising me that he represents Dr. George G. Burkley, Vice Admiral, U.S.Navy retired, who had been the personal physician for presidents Kennedy and Johnson.

Mr. Illig stated that he had a luncheon meeting with his client, Dr. Burkley, this date to take up some tax matters. Dr. Burkley advised him that although he, Burkley, had signed the death certificate of President Kennedy in Dallas, he had never been interviewed and that he has information in the Kennedy assassination indicating that others besides Oswald must have participated.

Illig advised me that his client is a very quiet, unassuming person, not wanting any publicity whatsoever, but he, Illig, was calling me with his client's consent and that his client would talk to me in Washington.; ALSO: the HSCA interviewed Burkley on 8/17/77 (RIF#180-10093-10429): he indicated that he had possession of the brain and the tissue sections of every major organ at the White House and that he took them to the National Archives; he gave the Harper Fragment to the FBI, and the other three skull fragments that were used to reconstruct the defect in the skull at the autopsy were NOT saved---he believed that they were put back in with the body.; said the autopsy doctors didn't section the brain, and that if it had been done, it might be possible to prove whether or not there were two bullets. While he thought there was only one bullet, he conceded the possibility of two! The HSCA also initiated an outside contact report (1/16/78) and *an affidavit* (11/21/78 [rough draft] and 11/28/78) [7 HSCA 20 and 34, notes 82, 48, and 47; RIF#180-10104-10271]: *"There was no difference in the nature of the wounds I saw at Parkland Hospital and those I observed at the autopsy at Bethesda Naval Hospital... I supervised the autopsy and directed the fixation and retention of the brain for future study of the course of the bullet or bullets.";* ALSO: 7 HSCA 13: "Both Dr. Humes and Dr. Burkley informed the Committee that these fragments were placed back in the skull of the President.";

p. *"Reasonable Doubt",* p. 49 (1982 interview by Henry Hurt+letters of 10/6/82 and 10/14/82)---believed that President Kennedy's assassination was the result of a conspiracy;

q. According to the 5/31/87 issue of Paul Hoch's newsletter *"Echoes of Conspiracy"* (vol. 9, No. 1), "Dr. Burkley recently told a relative of his that he did think that Oswald must have been part of a conspiracy, because the way he and his family lived and traveled was indicative of financial support.";

r. *"The Way We Were"* (1988) by Robert MacNeil, p. 198---"I was there [at Parkland] probably within three to five minutes of the time the president arrived. I went immediately to the table on which he was being treated, and saw for all intents and purposes life did not exist.";

s. Deceased, 1/2/91;

t. Roger Bruce Feinman at the second Midwest Symposium (4/93 [on video]), Feinman's book *"Between The Signal and the Noise"* (1993), and Kathleen Cunningham at Copa 1994 [on video]---re: the Burkley throat wound ignorance story;

u. November 1993 *"Fourth Decade"*: article by Richard Bartholomew---re: the late arrival at Parkland of Dr. Burkley;

v. May 1995 *"Fourth Decade"*: article by Jim Folliard (see p.202 of *"Killing Kennedy"* by H.E.L.)---extensively explores Burkley's role in autopsy control;

w. 1/13/97 contact with *Nancy Denlea*, Burkley's daughter, by the ARRB's Doug Horne-her father told her that he was very upset that the WC never called him to testify. Also, her father once showed her photographs of JFK's brain, and proudly said that it was her father who had ensured that the brain was saved.;

x. 8/98 *LancerLINE* story (see Chapter 7 of the *ARRB's Final Report*)---"An example of the cold paper trail comes from Admiral George Burkley, who was President Kennedy's military physician and the only medical doctor who was present both during emergency treatment at Parkland Memorial Hospital and at the autopsy at Bethesda Naval Hospital. In the late 1970's, at the time of the HSCA's investigation, Dr. Burkley, through his attorney, suggested that he might have some additional information about the autopsy. Because Dr. Burkley is now deceased, the Review Board sought additional information both from his former lawyer's firm and from Dr. Burkley's family. None agreed to supply any additional information.";

y. *"Murder In Dealey Plaza"* by James Fetzer (2000), pages x, 10, 13, 61-62, 96, 112, 116, 249, 252, 253, 269, 271-279, 286, 291, 304, 308, 441, 436-437, 446-447

z. *"JFK Absolute Proof"* by Robert Groden (2013): see page 153- Dr. Burkely is pictured with a nice summary of his statements (see also page 86)

28) Orderly David Sanders:

a. 21 H 224: report on activities for 11/22/63---washed off the President's face and helped place him in the casket; nothing on the nature of the wounds;

b. other WC references: 6 H 117, 137, 142, 151;21 H 203, 239, 242;

29) Dr. Donald W. Seldin, Chief Internist:

a. WC references by others present: WR 528; 3 H 371; 6 H 11,32,60-61,64; 17 H 13; 20 H 5; 21 H 184-185, 258, 263;

b. Mentioned by Dr. Perry on 11/23/63 on WBAP/ NBC Texas News film above;

c. January 1964 Texas State Journal of Medicine article *"Three Patients at Parkland"*, p. 63---"[Bashour] and Dr. Donald Seldin, professor and chairman of the Department of Internal Medicine, went to the emergency room. Upon examination, they found that the President had no pulsations, no heart beats, no blood pressure.";

d. 1/14/93 interview with Brad Parker---believes he was not called by the WC because he had nothing of value to add to the investigation

e.   8/27/98 letter to Vince Palamara---"The bullet struck the President in the forehead and literally exploded in his skull, so that the entire frontal, parietal and temporal bones were shattered...I believe that the official story is accurate in all details.";

f.   "*Murder in Dealey Plaza*" by James Fetzer (2000), page249

30) Dr. William H. Zedlitz, Resident Surgeon [Zedelitz]:

a.   WC reference: 6 H 83;

b.   11/4/98 letter to Vince Palamara--- "Dear Mr. Palamara,

I received your letter concerning my participation in the emergency treatment of President John F. Kennedy at Parkland Hospital on Nov. 22, 1963. At the time, I was a 2nd year general surgery resident at Parkland Hospital and had just finished an operation and was starting to dictate the operative report when I heard the page operator page Dr. Tom Shires (chairman of the Department of General Surgery) to the emergency room.

Since Dr. Shires was not in town at that time I proceeded to the ER to see what the problem was. As I stepped off the elevator, a man in a suit with a gun asked me if I was a doctor. I replied that I was, and he directed me to trauma room #1. I noticed at that point that the ER was entirely empty of patients (they had been transported to another area by the Secret Service). When I entered the trauma room I was surprised to see two of our staff physicians (Dr. Charles Baxter and Dr. Malcolm Perry) and one of the 3rd year surgery residents (Dr. James Carrico) already there. Dr. Carrico had inserted an endotracheal tube into the President and was trying to ventilate him with oxygen. At first glance the president seemed to be in extremely serious condition as he was not responding to any of the stimuli around him, and obviously had a massive head injury to the right occipito-parietal area (right posterior-lateral) of his cranium. This area was a mass of bloody tissue with multiple skin, hair, and bony fragments matted together with blood and brain tissue and covered an area approximately ten by twelve centimeters in diameter. His left eye also seemed to be bulging from his eyesocket. At this point, Dr. Carrico indicated that he was unable to effectively ventilate the patient via the endotracheal tube. Dr. Baxter and Perry immediately began to perform a tracheostomy. Prior to making the incision, it was noted that a small (5mm to 7mm) hole in the front of the neck below the thyroid cartilage was present. This was in the exact location where the tracheostomy was to be performed. Dr. Baxter and Perry decided to do the procedure by extending the transverse incision on either side of this hole so that the tracheostomy tube ended up being inserted in the site of the former hole. I trust this answers your questions regarding the location of the head injury and the appearance of the neck prior to the tracheostomy.

Sincerely,

William H. Zedlitz, M.D., FACS"

c.   "*Murder in Dealey Plaza*" by James Fetzer (2000), page 405

d. Presented at the JFK Lancer conference, Nov. 2003

e. *"JFK Absolute Proof"* by Robert Groden (2013): see page 151- Dr. Zedlitz is pictured with a nice summary of his statements

31) Surgeon David Stewart:

a. 12/11/81 letter to Livingstone (*"High Treason"*, pp. 51-52 , *"High Treason 2"*, p. 107, and *"Killing The Truth"*, p. 652)---"there was never any controversy concerning the wounds between the doctors in attendance. I was with them either separately or in groups on many occasions over a long period of time...Concerning [the official photo of the back of the head], there is no way the wound described to me by Dr. Perry and others could be the wound shown in the picture. The massive destructive wound could not remotely be pulled together well enough to give a normal contour to the head that is present in this picture.";

b. *"New Lebanon, Tennessee, Democrat"*, 3/30/67 ,

c. 4/10/67 *"The Joe Dolan Show"*, KNEW radio, Oakland, CA and

d. *"Post Mortem"*, pp. 60-61---Dolan said he was particularly concerned with the "statement about the shot" that killed JFK "coming from the front." Dr. Stewart said, "Yes, sir. This was the finding of all the physicians who were in attendance. There was a small wound in the left front of the President's head and there was a quite massive wound of exit at the right backside of the head and it was felt by all of the physicians at the time to be a wound of entry which went in the front.";

e. *"Probable Cause Australia"*, Issue #3: Lifton article---Dr. Perry told Stewart not long after that November weekend that "I left the [neck] wound inviolate."

f. *"Murder In Dealey Plaza"* by James Fetzer (2000), pages 249, 252, 297

g. *"JFK Absolute Proof"* by Robert Groden (2013): see page 154- a nice summary of his statements

32) *Justice of the Peace Theran Ward (deceased 12/21/2000):*

a. WC reference: 15 H 509; 21 H 163, 262;

b. 9/21/64 interview with William Manchester;

c. 10/28/91 interview with Livingstone (*"High Treason 2"*, p. 83)---"it's not safe" to talk about the case; authorized the removal of the body on 11/22/63;

d. Signed AND unsigned Death certificates: [signed] depicted in Crenshaw's *"JFK: Conspiracy of Silence"* (1992), [unsigned] Groden's *"TKOAP"*, p. 73, and [both]*"Assassination Science"*, pp. 428-429 [see also Manchester, p. 675, as well as Fetzer's video *"JFK: The Assassination, The Cover-Up, and Beyond"* 1994 and the back cover of the 10/98 issue of *"JFK/ Deep Politics Quarterly"*]---both state "held inquest, November 22, 1963", one is signed by Ward and autopsy is checked "yes" in both! [Interestingly, the *"Washington Evening Star"* for 11/26/63 reported that "The White House...declined to say whether an autopsy was performed on the body of John F. Kennedy." (!)]; [both] Cause of Death: "Multiple gunshot wounds of the head and neck."; [unsigned] Findings by the Justice: "Two gunshot wounds (1) Near the center of the body and just above the right shoulder. (2) One inch to the right center of the back of the head."; [unsigned] "Shot BY AN UNKNOWN ASSASSIN with high powered rifle" (emphasis added); [signed] "Shot by a high powered rifle";

e. *"The Killing of a President"* (1993), p. 88---photo [from video outtakes?] of Ward pointing toward the rear of the head to show where the skull wound was: "[I t was] right back here."

f. *"Murder in Dealey Plaza"* by James Fetzer (2000), pages 83, 96

g. *"JFK Absolute Proof"* by Robert Groden (2013): see page 152- Ward is pictured with a nice summary of his statements

33) Dr. Joe D. "Jody" Goldstrich:

a. *"JFK: Breaking The Silence"* (1993) by Bill Sloan, Chapter 4: pp. 84-97[Includes a photo]---"The first thing I saw was JFK lying on his back on an operating table...I didn't have a clear view of the back of his head, but I have a vague recollection of seeing a portion of his brain exposed...It [the neck wound] was a small, almost perfectly round---somewhere between the size of a nickel and a quarter [?]---and it was right in the middle of the front of his neck, just below the Adam's apple...the wound was exactly the right size and exactly the right spot to accommodate a tracheostomy tube."; disturbed by the photos of JFK's neck at autopsy: "The whole front of his neck was wide open...It had simply been fileted."; "...I realized how impossible it would have been for the neck wound I saw to have been an exit wound...";

b. *"Murder in Dealey Plaza"* by James Fetzer (2000), pages 240, 257, 405

34) First Lady Jackie Bouvier Kennedy (Onassis) (deceased 5/19/94):

a. 5 H 180 / testimony [*see also "Murder From Within" by Fred Newcomb and Perry Adams (1974), pp. 138-139*]---"And just as I turned and looked at him, I could see a piece of his skull *sort of wedge-shaped like that,* and I remember it was flesh colored *with little ridges at the top.* I remember thinking he just looked as if he had a slight headache. And I just remember seeing that. No blood or anything. And then he sort of did this [indicating], put his hand to his forehead and fell in my lap... [Reference to wounds deleted]"---!;

b. 4/11/72 declassified testimony excerpts (as reproduced in *"Post Mortem"* by *Harold Weisberg, pp. 380-381* [Groden quotes this in the program *"JFK: An Unsolved Murder"*, KRON, 11/18/88, which was repeated in *"JFK: The Case for Conspiracy"* video 1993, as well as *"TKOAP"*, p. 38): *"I was trying to hold his hair on. But from the front there was nothing. I suppose there must have been. But from the back you could see, you know, you were trying to hold his hair on, and his skull on..";*

c. other WC references: numerous;

d. 11/29/63 interview with writer Theodore H. White: his notes released 5/26/95 [wrote "*The Making of the President 1960*" , the "Camelot" article for the 12/6/63 "*Life*" magazine, and his own memoirs entitled "*In Search of History*", among others]---RE: the motorcade/ the assassination: "They were gunning the motorcycles; there were these little backfires; there was one noise like that; I thought it was a backfire. Then next I saw Connally grabbing his arms and saying 'no no no no,' with his fist beating---then Jack turned and I turned---all I remember was a blue gray building up ahead; then Jack turned back, so neatly; his last expression was so neat; he had his hand out, I could see a piece of his skull coming off; it was flesh colored not white---he was holding out his hand---and I can see this perfectly clean piece detaching itself from his head; then he slumped in my lap...Then Clint Hill, he loved us, he was the first man in the car...we all lay down in the car and I kept saying 'Jack, Jack, Jack' and someone was yelling 'he's dead he's dead.' All the ride to the hospital I kept bending over him saying 'Jack, Jack can you hear me, I love you Jack.' I kept holding the top of his head down trying to keep the...that long ride to the hospital...these big Texas interns kept saying 'Mrs. Kennedy you come with us,' they wanted to take me away from him. Dave Powers came running to me, my legs my hands wee covered with his brains...when Dave Powers saw this he burst out weeping. From here down" (here Mrs. Kennedy made a gesture about the level of the forehead above the eyes) "his head was so beautiful. I'd tried to hold the top of his head down, maybe I could keep it in...I knew he was dead..."[exactly as written];

e. 4/7/64, 5/4/64, 5/7/64, 5/8/64, and 7/20/64 interviews with William Manchester ("*The Death of a President*", numerous; see esp. p. 443): "*Time* (December 6, 1963) reported that "The casket was never to be opened because the President had been deeply disfigured." This was wholly untrue. Neither wound had damaged the President's face. His features, intact when his wife examined them at Parkland, had been treated with cosmetics, and this was what gave offense. Her impressions of Sunday morning, when she next saw him, are chronologically out of place here. Yet one of them is pertinent: "It wasn't' Jack. It was like something you would see at Madame Toussaud's." [On page 678 of "*The Day Kennedy Was Shot*" by Jim Bishop, Jackie's reaction is much the same: "It isn't Jack."];

f. deceased 5/19/94;

g. "*Killing Kennedy*" by H.E.L., pages 22 and 30 [see also "*Killing The Truth*", p. 652]---claims that, regarding the autopsy photos of the back of JFK's head, "my information that the photograph is fraudulent came from Jacqueline Kennedy through her staff in 1979 and from representatives of the Kennedy family"; "'This isn't the way it was!' This is what Jacqueline Kennedy Onassis told me through her staff..." [?!];

h. "*JFK Absolute Proof*" by Robert Groden (2013): see page 150- Jackie is pictured with a nice summary of her statements

35) OR Assistant Supervisor Jane Carolyn Wester:

a. 6 H 121 / testimony (see also "*High Treason 2*", p. 79)---"I received a phone call from the emergency room asking us to set up for a craniotomy."; Specter: "What doctors were in attendance of Governor Connally at that time." "...Dr. Ray, I believe, was there..."[this is the only reference to "Dr. Ray"];

b.   other WC references---6 H 124, 126;

c.   *"Who's Who in the JFK Assassination"* by Michael Benson (1993), p. 476;

36) Head Nurse Ruth Jeanette Standridge:

a.   6 H 118-119 / testimony---saw JFK on a stretcher cart in the emergency room while the orderlies were cleaning up the room: "...they were trying to protect his head with a sheet---it was wrapped around his head.";

b.   21 H 227-228: report of activities 11/24/63 re: LHO;

c.   other WC references: 6 H 83, 123, 137, 147, 152; 21 H 154, 182, 208, 215, 217, 220, 221, 222-223, 224, 241, 243;

d.   [unanswered letter from Vince Palamara 1998]

37) Aide Era Lumpkin:

a.   21 H 208-209: report of activities 11/22/63 [see also Manchester, p. 672]---nothing specific on nature of the wounds;

b.   other WC references: 6 H 151; 21 H 217;

38) Nurse Bertha L. Lozano:

a.   21 H 213-215: report of activities 11/22-11/24/63 [see also *"The Death of a President"* by William Manchester, p. 672]---"...obtained a carriage from Booth #5, with the help of Dr. Bill Midgett who helped me roll it out to the entrance."; SEPARATE from JFK and Connally: "A technician came to the desk and asked me to expect a private patient who was bleeding...Blood technicians came to ask me who "Mr. X" was who did not have an E.R. number. Hematology also came with the same problem and was told the same thing.";

b.   other WC references: 6 H 151; 21 H 209, 217-218, 222, 226, 227, 244, 246;

c.   [unanswered letter from Vince Palamara 1998]

39) Aide Shirley Randall:

a.   21 H 217-219: report of activities 11/22/63 [see also *"The Death of a President"* by William Manchester, p. 674]---"But I still didn't want to believe that anything had happened to our President. I wanted to think that something instead had happened to the "Secret Servicemen""; "I asked some man---I don't know who he was---if there was any more hurt before a policeman and I took the carriage in that I had; he said that he didn't think so. He asked me if I would get someone to come and wash the blood out of the car. I said that I would, but was so excited and nervous I forgot about the car.";

b.   other WC references: 6 H 151; 21 H 209;

40) Aide Rosa M. Majors:

a.   21 H 220-221: report of activities 11/22/63 [see also "*The Death of a President*" by William Manchester, p. 672]---nothing of any major importance;

b.   other WC references: 6 H 117, 151; 21 H 208, 217, 228;

41) Orderly Tommy Dunn:

a.   21 H 225: report of activities 11/22/63---helped unload the limousine of JFK and Connally but says nothing concerning the wounds;

b.   other WC references: 6 H 152; 21 H 220;

42) Orderly Joe Richards:

a.   21 H 226: report of activities 11/22/63---shortly after helping place Connally on a stretcher: "Then someone asked me to get a bucket of water; I did.";

b.   other WC references: 6 H 152; 21 H 203, 213;

43) Charles D. Gerloff, Security Officer:

a.   21 H 237: report to O.P. Wright dated 11/28/63---JFK and Connally were wheeled past him but he did not describe the wounds (if he indeed even saw them in the first place);

b.   other WC references: 21 H 229, 232, 233;

44) Administrator Charles Jack Price:

a.   21 H 254-264: report on activities 11/22/63---(21 H 259) [see also Manchester, pp. 673] "While talking with Mrs. [Doris] Nelson, one of the Secret service men who had been bruised or had a minor injury came to me and asked if there were another way out of the building. I told him there was a tunnel exit and that if he would come with me, I would walk it off for him. We walked to inspect the tunnel, then returned to the surgery area of the Emergency room."; (21 H 260-261)"...another Secret Service man grabbed me by the arm and asked if I knew an alternate route the Johnsons could use for an exit. I told him I had walked out an alternate route with another agent a few minutes ago and that if he would come with me, I would show him ...The Secret Service agent and I "ran" the alternate route, then when we got back to the Emergency Room area, he asked me to show him where the Johnsons were...but the Johnsons were gone... About that time another agent came in the door and said, "My God, they've gone." Both men left hurriedly.";

b. 21 H 265-267: report on activities 11/23 and 11/24/63---(21 H 265) "Pet[er N. Geilich] and I took off for the Emergency Room. When we got down there, DR. CHARLES CRENSHAW was in the corridor and said they had been alerted. He said, "You're not going to put him [LHO] in the same room the President was in, are you?" Told him I surely was glad he had thought of it and by all means, not to (emphasis added).";

c. 6 H 148-152 /testimony (3/25/64)---basically just identifies the Price Exhibits (21 H 150-269);

d. other WC references: 6 H 23, 27, 47, 50, 73, 147;7 H 158; 19 H 492; 21 H 150-269 [exhibits]; 24 H 38;

e. 9/21/64 and 2/22/65 interviews with William Manchester [also letter to Manchester dated 2/24/65: see "The Death of a President" by William Manchester, p. 674];

45) Chief of Security O.P. "Pokie" Wright (husband of Elizabeth Wright) [deceased]:

a. 21 H 229-332: report of activities 11/22/63---NOTHING about CE399!; (21 H 230) JFK's watch: Nurse Diana Bowron to Wright to Secret Service agent Roger Warner [misspelled "Warren"] on 11/26/63;

b. 24 H 412 / CE2011---"He advised he could not positively identify C1 as being the same bullet which was found on November 22, 1963." (Chief Rowley and SA Johnsen both "could not identify this bullet", while Darrell Tomlinson "cannot positively identify the bullet");

c. other WC references: WR 516; 6 H 119, 139, 152; 17 H 1; 21 H 153, 190, 195, 197, 198, 199, 200, 203-204, 233, 236, 237, 238, 242, 245, 246-247, 256, 261;

d. 1966 interview with Josiah Thompson ("Six Seconds in Dallas" [see p. 365 of "Crossfire" by Jim Marrs])---picked a pointed-tipped bullet shape as more like the bullet discovered at Parkland Hospital. Wright rejected round-nosed bullet shapes similar to CE399;

e. Part 4 of "CBS News Inquiry: The Warren Report" 6/28/67 [see also "Post Mortem", p. 46]---"...I got hold of a Secret Service man and THEY[sic?] didn't seem to be interested in coming and looking at the bullet in the position it was in then. So I went back to the area where Mr. Tomlinson was and picked up the bullet and put it in my pocket, and I carried it some 30 or 40 minutes. And I gave it to a Secret Service man that was guarding the main door into the emergency room...";

46) Elizabeth L. Wright (Good), Director, Nursing Service:

a. 21 H 198: page from lengthy/ 10-page (21 H 193-202) 12/11/63 report on activities 11/22-11/24/63 [see also Manchester, p. 675]---"Mr. Wright had somewhere down the line asked me if I could ascertain the path of the bullet---or bullets---determine the path, and find out where the instrument of injury actually was." (!);

b.   other WC references: 6 H 151; 21 H 231, 242, 243;

c.   6/23/93 interview with Wallace Milam and

d.   Oct. 11, 1994 videotaped interview with Mark Oakes [*see Audrey Bell above*];

e.   [unanswered letter from Vince Palamara 1998]

47) Nurse Bertha Farrington,
48) Pediatric Resident John D. Nelson
49) Chief of Surgical Pathology Vernon "Vernie" A. Stembridge, and
50) Resident Pathologist Sidney C. Stewart – all four from Brad Parker's (and Dr. Charles Crenshaw's) listing of those present at Parkland Hospital:

-**Bertha Farrington:**[unanswered letter from Vince Palamara 1998]

-**Dr. John Nelson:** [unanswered letters (2) form Vince Palamara 1998]

-**Sidney Stewart**: 21 H 174; 26 H 521;"*JFK: Conspiracy of Silence*", pp. 98-99;

-**Vernon Stembridge**: 11/30/63 surgical pathology report-see 7 HSCA 151-152, 158, 242; "*JFK: Conspiracy of Silence*", pp. 98-99; [unanswered letter from Vince Palamara 1998]

51) Dallas County Medical Examiner, Dr. Earl Forrest Rose:

a.   WC references: 21 H 163, 174, 189, 231, 244, 262; 7 H 158 and 26 H 161 (2/25/64 FBI report of interview)---re: LHO;

b.   26 H 521-524 / CE 3002:*Autopsy report on LHO*;

c.   J.D. Tippit autopsy/ report [see "*With Malice: Lee Harvey Oswald and the Murder of Officer J.D. Tippit*" by Dale K. Myers, pp.419-439; see also the Jan. 1997 issue of "*JFK/ Deep Politics Quarterly*", as well as Prof. James Fetzer's video "*JFK: The Assassination, The Cover-Up, and Beyond*" 1994]---as with the autopsy report on LHO, makes an interesting contrast with the one done on President Kennedy;

d.   12/9/63 interview with Secret Service agent Edward E. Moore (U.S.S.S.#-CO2-34,030 [see "*With Malice: Lee Harvey Oswald and the Murder of Officer J.D. Tippit*" by Dale K. Myers, pp. 435-436]);

e.   3/13/64 interview with the FBI (RIF#124-10037-10243 [see also "*With Malice: Lee Harvey Oswald and the Murder of Officer J.D. Tippit*" by Dale K. Myers (1998), pp. 495-496]);

f.   (3/16/64 and) 3/19/64 interview (s) with the FBI (see also "*With Malice: Lee Harvey Oswald and the Murder of Officer J.D. Tippit*" by Dale K. Myers, pages 236,

239, 438, 439, 638, and 639);

g. 9/21/64 interview with William Manchester (*"Death of a President"*, pp. 297-305, 319, 634)---wanted to conduct the autopsy at Parkland Hospital as per Texas law;

h. served on HSCA Forensic Pathology Panel---(i.e. 7 HSCA 115)--- "One panel member, Dr. Rose, wishes to emphasize the view of the majority of the panel (all except Dr. Wecht) that the absence of injury on the inferior surface of the brain offers incontrovertible evidence that the wound in the President's head is not in the location described in the autopsy report.";

i. 3/11/83 attempted interview with Dale K. Myers (*"With Malice: Lee Harvey Oswald and the Murder of Officer J.D. Tippit"*, page 638): "Dr. Earl F. Rose was contacted in 1983, but declined to be interviewed, citing "unkind things" said about his role in previous years."

j. 1991 interview for *"Mortal Error"* (1992), p. 228---nothing of substance;

k. 7/27/91 interview with Livingstone (*"High Treason 2"*, p. 82 and 85)---denied that any kind of autopsy occurred at Parkland Hospital;

l. Portrayed by actor Harold Herthum in the 1991 Oliver Stone movie *"JFK"* (see *"JFK: The Book of the Film"*, pages 156 and 584);

m. JAMA 1992 [Includes a photo of Rose](see *"Killing Kennedy"*, p. 28)---still feels strongly that the autopsy should have been performed in Dallas;

n. 9/4/98 letter to Vince Palamara---"At the time of the assassination of President Kennedy there were no federal laws on the matter of an assassination of the President or the Vice President. The state laws dealt with this crime. Therefore the Texas laws on homicide were controlling regarding the assassination---in other words, the Texas authorities had control and jurisdiction over this crime of murder. Had there been a trial it would have been in Texas under the Texas Rules of Criminal Procedure. The United States has since passed laws giving jurisdiction over the threat of or the murder of a President or Vice President to the federal authorities. Of course passing a law after the crime has been committed does not make the law retroactive so a person can be tried under the newly passed law."[see also *"J. Edgar Hoover: The Father Of The Cold War"* by R. Andrew Kiel (2000), page 180];

o. *"Murder in Dealey Plaza"* by James Fetzer (2000), pages 96, 176, 232

p. *"J. Edgar Hoover: The Father of The Cold War"* by R. Andrew Kiel (2000), page 180

52) Fort Worth Star-Telegram Photographer Jarrold Cabluck,
53) Priest Thomas Cain,
54) Priest Oscar L. Huber [deceased 1975] (administered the last rites), and
55) Priest James Thompson [deceased]: all four are non-medical people listed as present on Brad Parker's Parkland Hospital attendance chart.--

-Cabluck: 11/4/85 interview with Richard Trask in *"Pictures of the Pain"*,

Chapter 14 (pp. 325-357): "I ended up being in Trauma One for about 10 seconds. As a young kid mesmerized or petrified, I didn't do anything. I was in there very briefly and the Secret Service threw me out…I made shots of a policeman carrying plasma in there…"; [unanswered letter from Vince Palamara 1998];

-**Cain:** 9/21/64 interview with William Manchester [see also "*The Death of a President*", p. 670: notes re: 11/22/63];

-**Huber:** WR 55, 7 H 489, 21 H 159, 160, 195, 233: WC references for Huber. Huber was interviewed 11/24/63 on WFAA and 11/25/63 on WBAP/ Texas News (see "*Kennedy in Texas*" video 1984). The 11/24/63 "*Philadelphia Sunday Bulletin*" reported that Father Huber said that JFK had a terrible wound over his left eye [see "*Best Evidence*", p. 46, and "*Who's Who in the JFK Assassination*", p. 202]; 8/26/64 and 9/20/64 interviews with William Manchester ("*The Death of a President*", numerous, including p. 216)---performed the sign of the cross on JFK's forehead, evidently still intact; interviewed by Jim Bishop ("*The Day Kennedy Was Shot*", p. 684); "*The (Denver) Register*", 12/8/63: article by Huber entitled "*President Kennedy's Final Hours*"; JFK Library Oral History1964; photo of Huber: p. 23 of "*JFK: For a New Generation*" by Conover Hunt; "*Four Days In November*" (1964, David Wolper): including part of his WFAA interview;

-**Thompson:** WC references: 21 H 160; 8/28/64 interview with William Manchester

56) Undertaker Vernon B."Pegg" O'Neal,
57) Asst. Undertaker Dennis "Peanuts" McGuire, and
58) Asst. Undertaker Aubrey "Al" L. Rike: employees of the O'Neal Funeral Home.

-**O'Neal [deceased]:**

a. references (Including to ambulance and funeral home: WR 516; 2 H 142; 13 H 91,94-96,239-240, 242; 17 H 1; 21 H 162, 230, 236, 242, 262;

b. 9/25/64 interview with William Manchester ("*The Death of a President*", pages 168, 291-292, 294, 300, 302, 305, 306, 308, 320, 329, 381, 383, 634-635);

-**McGuire [deceased]:**

a. 11/22/63 interview (with Aubrey Rike)on WFAA/ ABC---talks about picking up the epileptic seizure victim and the Secret Service taking the ambulance;

b. "*Four Days in November*" (1964, David Wolper): small excerpt from his WFAA interview but captioned as his partner "Aubrey Rike"!

c. "*Best Evidence*", p. 674---mentions him along with Rike (see below);

d. *"High Treason"*, p. 449---along with Rike, wrapped JFK's body in a rubber sheet before closing the coffin at Parkland;

-Rike:

a. CD 1245/ FBI report of 5/28/64 interview with Rike [see the back of the 3/90 issue of *"The Third Decade"* for a copy]: tells of the epileptic seizure incident; "Rike stated he was advised by a Secret Service Agent at Parkland Hospital that his ambulance was not to be moved because they might need it to move the President to another location. Rike stated he cleared the hospital at 3:00 p.m. and returned to Oneal Incorporated, Funeral Directors.";

b. Interview (with Dennis McGuire) on WFAA/ ABC on 11/22/63 [referenced in Jan Stevens' article in the Jan-March 1992 *"The Third Decade"* journal]: the Secret Service took the hearse away and "they left us just standing there.";

c. *"Ambulance Driver sees Kennedy, Governor Connally brought to hospital."* Dallas: *United Press International*, 11/24/63;

d. 21 H 242 (Nurse Doris Nelson's report)---'After Mr. O'Neal, and some of the boys who work with him (only one of whose name I knew-Audrey Riker [sic]) placed the President in the casket, and closed it.";

e. *"Four Days In November"* film, 1964 (1988 video)---see McGuire above;

f. *"The Day Kennedy Was Shot"* by Jim Bishop, p. 297---"Audrey Riker [sic], who worked for Oneal, ran up to the driver's side of the ambulance and said: "Meet you at the mortuary," and [Secret Service agent and driver of the hearse Andy] Berger nodded: "Yes, sir."";

g. 3/11/80 telephone interview with David Lifton (*"Best Evidence"*, pages 600 and 674) and

h. *"Best Evidence: The Research Video"* ([Oct.] 1980/ 1990 [clips repeated in *"The Fifth Estate-Who Killed JFK?"* 1983, "Nova" 11/15/88 ,*"Dispatches: The Day The Dream Died"* 11/16/88 London, and *"A Current Affair"* 9/4/90] ---"[JFK] still dripping quite a bit of blood from the wound in the back of his head [motioning]"; Tells about the experience of placing JFK's body into the casket; Rike emphatically denied that they used a body bag;

i. *"The Men Who Killed Kennedy"* (1988 [1991/1995])---more on his experiences, including the struggle with the casket at Parkland with the Secret Service and Dr. Earl Rose; includes a period film depicting Rike driving the hearse;

j. *"JFK: An Unsolved Murder"*, KRON, 11/18/88 ---similar in content to the *"Best Evidence"* video but no less interesting;

k. *"Crossfire"* (1989) by Jim Marrs, pp. 42-43;

l. 2 episodes of *"Hard Copy"*: 5/9/90 and 5/14/90 (including Paul O'Connor)---also similar, albeit brief, in content, Rike places his hand behind his head to describe where the jagged edge of bone/ the wound was;

m. 8/28/91 interview with Joel Wagoner (*"The Third Decade"*, Jan-March 1992 issue): re: his FBI interview: "They shoved me around, forced me into a chair...

They threatened me, told me they could kick my ass. I was scared to death when I left...";

n. TWO: A.S.K. conference, Dallas, Texas, 11/14/91---mentioned 6 to 8 false ambulance calls in the Dealey Plaza area in the 2 or 3 weeks prior to 11/22/63; talked about the epileptic seizure victim/ incident (Jerry Belknap); felt a jagged wound edge at the back of the head, as well as brain matter; said that some of the autopsy photos show what he saw but others do not; INTERVIEW with Jerry Rose at the conference (see "*The Third Decade*", Jan-March issue, pp. 45-46)---inconsistencies re: the epileptic seizure and departure to Love Field;

o. "*JFK: The Book of the Film*", p. 8: Rike, as a technical adviser to "JFK" (but not one of those, like Dr. Marion Jenkins, who was credited at the end of the film), told Oliver Stone and co. about the false alarms to Dealey Plaza prior to 11/22/63;

p. 4/6/91 [unreleased film], 6/10/91, and 8/15/91 interviews with Livingstone ("*High Treason 2*", photo section+pages 80, 81, 89, 112, 114-119, 130-131, 238, 271, 275, 297, 305-308, 312, and 527 [re: "JFK"])---"I know the back of the head was gone"'

q. "*The Search for the Truth*" video 1992 AIC;

r. 11/92 interview with Noel Twyman ("*Bloody Treason*", p. 867);

s. outtakes from Groden's video?---see photo on p. 88 of "TKOAP": "You could feel the sharp edges of the bone at the edge of the hole in the back of his head."

t. Acknowledgments, "*The Search For Lee Harvey Oswald*" by Robert Groden (1995);

Interviews with Walt Brown: April 1996 "*JFK/ Deep Politics Quarterly*" Journal. "Rike helped put JFK in the expensive coffin [which would later be returned to Texas and serve as the burial place for someone else...], and in the process noted a great deal of blood, a jagged hole, and the ability to feel brain material--all when holding the back of the President's head.";

u. *11/22/97 video interview by Vince Palamara (Includes a segment with Rike and Brad Parker), Dallas, Texas, at JFK Lancer conference[see reference on p. 18 of "Kennedy Assassination Chronicles" journal, Vol. 3, No. 4, Winter 1997]---the most detailed interview on video: covers a lot of what he said before (in print/ on previous programs) but with more insights; including him placing his hand three times to the right rear of his head to show where the wound was located at: "I could feel the brain and the jagged edge... yeah, it [the back of the head] was gone... almost in the middle of the back of the head; on the side a little bit. "Regarding the autopsy photos, Rike believes they "pulled [the] hair back over" the wound; "didn't notice the bullet wound in the shoulder"; throat wound: "thought it was an exit wound"; witnessed the episode where the FBI agent was knocked to the floor with a punch while trying to enter Trauma Room One; said that, regarding the ambulance false alarms ("bogus calls... in that vicinity") being tied into the assassination, "that was the FBI's theory"!;*

v. "*Murder In Dealey Plaza*" by James Fetzer (2000), pages 27, 174

w. Presentations at JFK Lancer conferences in 2002 and 2004

x. *"JFK Absolute Proof"* by Robert Groden (2013): see page 152- Rike is pictured with a nice summary of his statements

59) Scripps-Howard reporter Seth Kantor [deceased 8/17/93]
(Saw Jack Ruby at Parkland [see also Wilma Tice and Roy Stamps]):

a. 20 H 353: Kantor's notepad for 11/22/63---"intered [sic] right temple";

b. 15 H 71-96 / testimony---saw "a great deposit of blood" on the ground to the right of JFK's limo;

c. other WC references: WR 335-336; 7 H 480; 12 H 29; 15 H 457; 25 H 236-237;

d. *"The Fifth Estate-Dallas and after"* 1977 CBC/ Canada;

e. *"Who Was Jack Ruby?"/ "The Ruby Cover-Up"* by Seth Kantor (1978/ 1992);

f. HSCA Report, pp. 158-159;

g. *"On Trial: Lee Harvey Oswald"* 1986 Showtime;

h. *"Crimes of the Century"* program 1988;

i. *"The Men Who Killed Kennedy"* 1988;

j. 3/19/93 letter to Todd Wayne Vaughan;

k. *"Who Killed JFK: The Final Chapter?"* (11/19/93) CBS;

60) Texas State Highway Patrolman Hurchel D. Jacks
(Drove LBJ's car in motorcade)[**deceased 12/19/95**]:

a. 18 H 801: 11/28/63 report re: 11/22/63---"Before the President's body was covered it appeared that the bullet had struck him above the right ear or near the temple.";

b. other WC references: WR 46; 2 H 69, 147; 5 H 562; 17 H 607; 18 H 766, 768, 778;

c. Part 2 of *"CBS News Inquiry: The Warren Report"* 6/26/67;

d. 9/20/64 interview with William Manchester;

e. 8/31/98 letter to Vince Palamara from Bobbie Jacks, Hurchels' widow---"Yes, he did observe Kennedy's wounds at Parkland Hospital and he guarded Kennedy's car to make sure that no photos were taken. He did not seem to think that there was a conspiracy. He accepted the Warren Commission report as factual---I don't think this issue will ever be put to rest."[emphasis added];

61) Secret Service agent Samuel A. Kinney
(Driver of the Secret Service follow-up car in the motorcade) [deceased 7/21/97]
AND related information regarding the presidential limousine/ evidence within:

a. 18 H 732: report dated 11/22/63---"... it appeared he had been shot because he slumped to the left. Immediately he sat up again. At this time the second shot was fired and I observed hair flying from the right side of his head.";

b. 18 H 730-731: report dated 11/30/63---"I saw the President lean toward the left and appeared to have grabbed his chest with his right hand. There was a second pause and then two more shots were heard ... I saw one shot strike the President in the right side of the head [doesn't indicate front or back]";

c. other WC references: 2 H 68, 86, 96, 134; 17 H 607, 608, 615, 625, 626, 630; 18 H 678, 679, 722, 724, 726, 734, 739, 741, 751, 752, 758, 761, 762, 763, 764, 765,

d. CD 80: Secret Service report dated 11/27/63 re: limousine inspection at White House garage---[interlude:]

e. 2/19/65 interview with William Manchester;

* * *

Interlude: regarding Kinney and the limousine

PRESIDENTIAL LIMOUSINE (1961 MODIFIED STRETCH LINCOLN CONTINENTAL, SS-100-X) AND SECRET SERVICE FOLLOW-UP CAR (1956 CADILLAC CONVERTIBLE, SS-679-X, A.KA. "THE QUEEN MARY"):

11/22/63 UP TO/INC. PARKLAND HOSPITAL-

SS-100-X: DRIVEN BY SA WILLIAM R. GREER;

SS-679-X: DRIVEN BY SA SAMUEL A. KINNEY;

PARKLAND HOSPITAL TO LOVE FIELD/ C-130 CARGO PLANE:
Kinney places bubbletop and fabric top on SS-100-X with the help of a DPD motorcycle officer; SA Hickey assists;
Kinney given permission to drive the cars back to Love Field by ASAIC (#3) Roy H. Kellerman-

SS-100-X: DRIVEN BY SA GEORGE W. HICKEY, JR. WITH DALLAS SA JOHN JOE HOWLETT BESIDE HIM
[Hickey would go on to drive the SS-679-X during the May 1964 WC reenactments, while Howlett participated in the WC's TSBD stairway reenactment; Howlett: 11/26/97 letter to Vince Palamara---re: his career with the Secret Service]

SS-679-X: DRIVEN BY SA SAMUEL A. KINNEY

C-130;

KINNEY, HICKEY, SS-100-X. SS-679-X, + THE 76TH AIR TRANSPORT
SQUADRON FROM CHARLESTON (S.C.) AIR FORCE BASE:
CAPT. ROLAND H. THOMASON (PILOT) [18 H 730 (Kinney); CD80];
WAYNE E. SCHAKE;
[Schake: unanswered letter from Vince Palamara 1998]
VINCENT J. GULLO, Jr.;
[Gullo: 8/27/98 letter to Vince Palamara---I wrote "Sam [Kinney] told me
that a) he found the piece of the right rear of President Kennedy's skull on
the C-130 while en route back to AAFB after the tragedy and b) that one of
you guys got sick from seeing the rear of the limousine with all the blood
and gore…do you remember any of these specific events?" Gullo responded:
"…I am totally familiar with the facts as you outline them…This was a bench
mark in my life and I have shared my thoughts on this incident with few indi-
viduals---mostly federal agents. I am sure you can understand my reluctance
to entertain your questions given the sensitivity of the matter even to this
date."(emphasis added); Gullo did not respond to my follow-up letter; see
also "The Great Zapruder Film Hoax" by James Fetzer (2003)]
HERSHAL R. WOOSLEY;
[Woosley: unanswered letter from Vince Palamara 1998]
DAVID J. CONN;
STEPHEN A. BENING;
FRANK E. ROBERSON
[other names via Sam Kinney/copy of flight manifest---also found in CD 3 ex-
hibits-LBJ Library. This manifest was also referred to in George Hickey's report
dated 11/30/63 (18 H 761, 764) but was not included in the volumes]
(Kinney finds the back part of JFK's skull lying in the rear of the car and puts
in a phone patch to Dr. Burkley aboard Air Force One hours before "official"
limousine inspection)

CARS ARRIVED AT ANDREWS AFB AT 8:00 P.M.;
[Sorrels: 1/28/92 and 9/27/92 interviews with Vince Palamara; deceased,
11/6/93; Rowley: 9/27/92 interview with Vince Palamara; deceased, 11/92;
Boring: 9/22/93 and 3/4/94 interviews with Vince Palamara; 11/22/97 letter to Vince Palamara; Paterni: deceased 1984]

CARS ARRIVE AT WHITE HOUSE GARAGE AT 9:00 P.M.:
KINNEY DROVE SS-100-X BACK TO GARAGE WITH WFO (Washing-
ton Field Office) AND FORMER LBJ AGENT CHARLES E. TAYLOR, JR.
BESIDE HIM;
HICKEY DROVE SS-679-X BACK TO GARAGE WITH WFO SA'S
RICHARD "DICK" E. KEISER AND DONALD F. BRETT BESIDE HIM

"OFFICIAL" LIMOUSINE INSPECTION BEGINS AT 10:10 P.M.:

BORING, PATERNI, KINNEY+ REPRESENTATIVES FROM DR. BURKLEY'S OFFICE (PART OF THE WH MEDICAL STAFF):
CHIEF PETTY OFFICER WILLIAM MARTINELL;
CHIEF PETTY OFFICER THOMAS G. "TOMMY" MILLS

WINDSHIELD

ALSO: TAYLOR., IN HIS REPORT TO WFO SAIC HARRY W. GEI-GLEIN [CD80], NOTES THAT HE SAW A "SMALL HOLE" IN THE WINDSHIELD OF SS-100-X (TAYLOR WAS THERE FROM 9:00 P.M. UNTIL 12 MID)

OTHERS WHO SAW/ KNEW OF HOLE:

CHICAGO SA ABRAHAM W. BOLDEN, SR- 9/16/93 interview with Vince Palamara;
DPD OFFICERS STAVIS ELLIS AND H.R. FREEMAN (outriders in motorcade)- CFTR RADIO INTERVIEW, 1976; "NO MORE SILENCE" BY LARRY SNEED (1998), PP. 147-148;
[Ellis: 9/8/98 letter to Vince Palamara---"Yes, I did see a hole in the limousine windshield at Parkland Hospital. I did not see the bone fragment. The officer on the escort with me said there was one fragment, approximately 6 or 7 inches around.";]
NEWSMEN RICHARD DUDMAN AND the AP's FRANK CORMIER-ST. LOUIS POST-DISPATCH, 12/1/63; for Cormier, see "Seeds of Doubt: Some Questions About The Assassination" by Jack Minnis and Staughton Lynd, 12/63, p. 4, "Killing The Truth", p. 64, and 17 H 614[Cormier also appears on the video "Air Force One: The Planes and the Presidents"]
SPECTATORS EVALEA GLANGES AND CARL RENAS- "JFK CONSPIRACY OF SILENCE", PP. 105-107, 110 [Glanges: correspondence with Vince Palamara+ "The Men Who Killed Kennedy" (2003) DVD (Glanges is now deceased); Renas: unanswered letters to Vince Palamara, 1997 and 1998];
TWO DIFFERENT UNIDENTIFIED CALLERS: TO THE "JIM BO-HANNON" RADIO SHOW (Doug Weldon, as verified via e-mails to Vince Palamara, 1998), 11/22/93, AND TO "LARRY KING" TV SHOW, JANUARY 1992 (caller unknown)
[see new limousine windshield photos in "High Treason III" (1998), as well as the TWO different photos that comprise CE 350 and 351: 16 H 946-947].

OTHERS WHO NOTED THINGS OF SIGNIFICANCE:

[SEE "MORE BORING DETAILS", 11/95 "The Fourth Decade"]
SAIC GERALD A. BEHN- SKULL FOUND IN REAR SEAT (FBI/S&O

INTERVIEW, 11/27/63)[Behn: 9/27/92 interviews (3) by Vince Palamara; deceased 4/93];

GREER- CLAIMED TO NOT NOTICE WINDSHIELD DAMAGE AND CHROME DENTING RIGHT IN FRONT OF HIM UNTIL AN UNNAMED AGENT POINTED IT OUT TO HIM ON 11/23/63 (2H122);

KELLERMAN- FELT WINDSHIELD ON 11/27/63, BUT IT "FEELS SMOOTH TODAY", 3/9/64 (2H89); SKULL IN REAR SEAT (2H85); FRAGMENTS (2H90);

WH GARAGE SAIC MORGAN L. GIES[deceased]- "*THE DAY KENNEDY WAS SHOT*" BY JIM BISHOP, P. 511, 1992 EDITION;

CLINTON J. HILL- BACK OF SKULL IN REAR SEAT (2H141);

SKULL FRAGMENT

SEE DPD MOTORCADE MOTORCYCLE OFFICERS STAVIS ELLIS, BOBBY JOE DALE, JAMES W. COURSON, AND H.B. McCLAIN, AS WELL AS FBI AGENTS JAMES W. SIBERT AND VINCENT E. DRAIN, BELOW (SEE ALSO DEPUTY SHERIFFS SEYMOUR WEITZMAN, JACK FAULKNER AND AL MADDOX, AS WELL AS CHARLES BREHM, DPD JOE CODY AND POSTAL INSPECTOR HARY HOLMES, ALSO BELOW)

WHP (White House Police/ Uniformed Division of Secret Service) ON SECURITY:

J.W. EDWARDS;

J.C. ROWE;

[fnu] SNYDER (FROM 3:25 P.M. TO 11:25 P.M.);

[fnu] RUBENSTAL (FROM 12:30 P.M. TO 11:00 P.M.);

SGT. [fnu] BURKE (7:25 A.M. TO 11:00 P.M.);

[fnu] EDMUNDS (11:25 P.M. TO 7:25 A.M.)

WFO AGENTS ON SECURITY:

KEISER (9:00 P.M. TO 12 MID) [Later, became SAIC of WHD, Nixon-Carter];

BRETT (9:00 P.M. TO 12 MID);

GILBERT J. PARASCHOS (11/23: 12:01 A.M. TO 8:00 A.M.);

MARTIN J. KENNEDY (11/23: 12:01 A.M. TO 8:00 A.M.);

FRANK HANCOCK (11/23: 8:00 A.M. TO 12 NOON);

CLAUDE E. DAVIS, JR (11/23: 8:00 A.M. TO 5:00 P.M.) [originally from Charlotte, N.C. office; temporarily assigned to Dallas office 12/23/63 to 2/2/64 (41 days)];

VICTOR J. GONZALEZ (11/23: 12:00 P.M. TO 5:00 P.M.);

JOHN R. SIMPSON (11/23: 4:00 P.M. TO 5:00 P.M.) [Later, SAIC of

WHD, Carter era; Director of Secret Service, 1981 to 1992; appears on the 1995 video "*Inside the Secret Service*"]

FBI INSPECTION BEGINS AT 1:00 A.M. 11/23/63:

[SEE 5H71]

ORRIN H. BARTLETT (1:05 A.M. TO 1:55 A.M)- DROVE LIMO OUT OF THE GARAGE BIN A FEW FEET;

CHARLES L. KILLIAN (1:05 A.M. TO 4:35 A.M.);

CORTLANDT CUNNINGHAM (SAME AS ABOVE);

[9/14/98 letter to Vince Palamara---Re: my two questions concerning a possible hole in the windshield and the skull fragments: "I am sorry but I am presently in no position to answer your questions. However, it is suggested that you contact a library where the multi-volume record of The President's Commission on the Assassination of President Kennedy can be found. These volumes set forth all of the testimonies of the witnesses who appeared before the Commission. Also, I have been told that my testimonies before the Commission can be found on the internet." (!)]

ROBERT A. FRAZIER (SAME AS ABOVE);

WALTER E. THOMAS (SAME AS ABOVE)

PRS SAIC ROBERT I. BOUCK- CONTACTED BY GONZALEZ; BY REQUEST, MISC. DEBRIS ON REAR FLOOR OF LIMO SENT TO WFO;

[Bouck appears on the 3/97 A&E program "Investigative Reports: The Secret White House Tapes"; 4 H 294-299, 300-317 / testimony; other WC references: WR 429. 432-433. 440, 458; 4 H 347; 5 H 464, 466, 581; 6/25/76 JFK Library Oral History; RIF#180-10097-10141: 9/6/77 interview with the HSCA's Jim Kelly and Andy Purdy---"Bouck said he believes some of the photographs and x-rays were received later but...";approval to see materials-Rowley;

"Prior to the transfer [April, 1965], Bouck said the materials had only been seen '... about twice...'-1) to WC :

"... believes Tom Kelley may have been present during the inspection by the WC representative who he believes was '... possibly the general counsel or a staff attorney [SPECTER?!?!]";

2):Bouck believes the other time the material was viewed was '... rather early, when someone from SS and possibly MR. KELLEY looked to see what was in there.; transfer accomplished by Bouck and Kelley in Bouck's car-GEORGE DALTON may have been present; "Regarding the photographs Bouck first said that they were '...all processed when I got them[?!?!]"; James Fox- his photographer at the White House; "Bouck said that to his knowledge none of the material was sent to the family or destroyed. "Bouck said '... it seemed to me a PORTION of the brain was preserved."; *9/27/92 interview with Vince Palamara*; 12/95 interview with Seymour Hersh for "*The Dark Side of Camelot*"; 5/2/96 ARRB interview---"He stated items of President Kennedy's clothing, such as the shirt, etc. were received at the same time as the autopsy materials. He said that the autopsy materials were received all at the same time, and included several little cans containing the brain and other biological materials. He said some of these cans or 'round canisters' had material which 'sloshed' inside; two of the canisters were about 4"X5" or so in size, and that one might have been labeled as brain matter. He said that he had a four-drawer lock-file safe which was fireproof and had a combination lock on each drawer...Mr. Bouck stated that his personal opinion was that although Lee Harvey Oswald was the assassin, he did feel that there was a conspiracy." (emphasis added; Bouck is in good company: John Marshall, Sam Kinney, Roy Kellerman, Bill Greer, Maurice Martineau, Abraham Bolden, John Norris, and DNC advance man Marty Underwood felt the same way!); "I'm pretty sure Dr. Burkley was the one who asked for the photos and that he suggested Anacostia...Yes, it was Burkley, I believe. We didn't use Bethesda because Burkley would have suggested the Navy lab at Anacostia." Bouck remembered showing the autopsy photos to WC staffers, probably Specter (see above) and Rankin.; "Jeremy Gunn recounted a story involving the opinion of a former CIA employee who had stated that President Kennedy was not very popular with many Secret Service agents, and asked Mr. Bouck to comment on that allegation. Mr. Bouck stated that he did not feel that was true..."; (from 7/31/98 staff report)---"Memories, of course, fade over time. A very important figure in the chain-of- custody on the autopsy materials, and the living person who perhaps more than any other would have been able to resolve some of the lingering questions related to the disposition of the original autopsy materials, is Robert Bouck of the Secret Service. At the time he was interviewed he was quite elderly and little able to remember the important details.";]

PRS PHOTOGRAPHERS JAMES K. "JACK" FOX AND HOWARD K. NORTON (HAD BEEN IN AUSTIN ON 11/22)- PHOTOGRAPHED SS-100-X AT 4:00 P.M. ON 11/23/63 [*Mark Crouch Re: Fox (deceased 1987): 1/28/92 and 9/23/92 interviews with Vince Palamara;*]

[*end of interlude*]

* * *

f.   RIF # 180-10078-10493:HSCA summary of an interview with Sam Kinney conducted on 2/26/78. In regard to the shooting sequence, Sam said the following:
      "SA Kinney immediately recognized the first sound as that of gunfire, realizing that it was a "shot from over our right shoulder" which hit the President IN THE THROAT. The President, his movement (in Kinney's opinion) affected by the brace he wore, fell toward "Jackie", who "after catching him, set him back up."

SA Kinney commented on Mrs. Kennedy's influence on the position of the President by remarking that the SS preferred not to have persons riding in jump seats with the President. The writer understood this remark to mean the President might have had room to be pushed to the floor.

"While Jackie was setting him back up, Connally turns right, then left then pow, pow. THE SECOND SHOT" (hit Connally and) "left Connally's back open." "THE THIRD SHOT HIT THE PRESIDENT." As the third shot landed, SA Kinney was able to see "hair coming up." At this point he hit the siren on the follow-up car." (emphasis added); "Inside the aircraft [the C-130 transport plane] during flight, the loading sergeant, who had been in the rear compartment where the cars were stored, entered the forward cabin and said, "I can't stand to be back there." SA Kinney gave him his seat and returned to the rear compartment. At this point he discovered in the Presidential limousine (1) a skull fragment under the jump seat where Connally had been seated, and (2) a bullet fragment in the front seat between the driver's and passenger's seat. He remarked that the bullet fragment "looked like it had hit the windshield frame above the windshield." SA Kinney put on a radio patch to *Presidential Physician Admiral Burkley* to inform him that he had discovered the skull fragment. *Chief Petty Officer Tommy Mills*, an aide to Burkley, received the message. SA Kinney then announced that he was going to go directly to the White House non-stop. The Washington Field Office learned of this and sent 6 or 7 Park police to escort SA Kinney to the White House Garage. In the garage they were met by FBI agents.""";

g. *"Mortal Error"* (1992), pp. 252-253 (letter to St. Martin's Publishers from 1991 or 1992 and Publisher's call to Kinney in response)---"I was driving the car at the time and I can assure you that there was not a gun fired from the U.S.S.S. follow-up car."; "The HSCA did send two men in 1978 to interview him, but he did not know what happened to their report or transcript [recently released; see above for excerpts]";

h. 10/19/92, 3/5/94, and 4/15/94 interviews with Vince Palamara---Sam told me twice that he saw the back of JFK's head come off immediately when the fatal shot struck the President's head (Kinney was watching Kennedy's head-and the rear bumper of the limousine-as a normal part of his duty to maintain a five-foot distance between the follow-up car and JFK's limo, something he did hundreds of times before). Sam told me "it was the right rear-I saw that part blow out." Kinney added that his windshield and left arm were hit with blood and brain matter immediately after the head shot.

Once at Parkland Hospital, Kinney helped remove the President from the back seat of the limousine along with Clint Hill, Roy Kellerman, and Dave Powers, thereby receiving an extremely vivid, close-up look at the wound on JFK's head. "His brain was blown out," Sam said, " there was nothing left !" I pressed further, to which Sam added: "There was brain matter all over the place...he had no brains left in his head."

So far, pretty valuable information, right? Well, there's more: Kinney and fellow agent George W. Hickey, Jr., both members of the White House Garage Detail (chauffeurs), drove the follow-up car and the limousine respectively back to Love Field for boarding onto the C-130 transport plane. Once the cars were loaded on board and properly secured to the floor of the plane, the C-130 took off for Washington with Kinney, Hickey, and the following members of the 76th Air Transport Squadron from the Charleston, S.C. Air Force Base: Capt. Roland Thomason, Wayne Schake, Vincent Gullo, Hershal Woosley, David Conn, Stephen Bening, and Frank Roberson [these names are revealed for the first time via Sam's copy of the flight manifest]. However, it was Kinney alone who made a most valuable discovery: he found the piece of the back of JFK's head lying in the rear seat of the bloody limousine, exactly were Clint Hill told the Warren Commission he saw the "right rear" piece at (2H141; fellow agents Roy Kellerman [2H85] and Jerry Behn[Sibert & O'Neill interview, 11/27/63] confirm this fact)! Sam told me it was "clean as a pin" and that it resembled a "flowerpot" or "clay pot" piece. Kinney added: "It was a big piece-half his head was gone." When I pressed him on this point and asked him if he was sure of the skull piece's orientation, he said " I don't know what else it could have been but the back of his head."

Realizing the obvious significance of this find (made several hours BEFORE the "official" limousine inspection instigated by ASAIC FLOYD BORING), Kinney put in a phone patch to Admiral George Burkley (unfortunately, like many other events, this radio traffic no longer exists on the heavily edited Air Force One radio tapes that are available at the present time [I wonder why?]). Kinney had the piece in his suit pocket during his talk with Burkley and during the flight back to Washington. Upon landing at Andrew Air Force Base, Burkley got a hold of the skull piece Kinney had (it is important to note that Sam did NOT attend the autopsy and, when pressed on exactly HOW Burkley obtained the fragment, Sam constantly changed the subject, the ONLY time he was ever less than frank with me). For what it's worth, Sam said that Dr. Burkley was a "good friend" of his: "I even have his picture on my wall along with the President's[JFK's] and Harry S. Truman, and I thought as highly of him as I did those gentlemen." When asked about the controversy Burkley has caused concerning the autopsy, Sam said "well, you have to give orders to people...they(?) were very hard on Dr. Burkley."

Sam told me, in somewhat of an understatement, " All of these books are always wondering about this incredible missing part- I've had the answer all these years but nobody's called me" (meaning the WC, the FBI, private investigators, etc. As Sam told the author of the dreadful "Mortal Error"["I tried to squelch that book", Sam said], the HSCA DID send two investigators to his door...). Why, then, did Sam Kinney tell me about this? Well, it's not just because I asked: Sam tried to tell NBC's "Today" show about the same thing during Sam's only (first and LAST) television interview on 11/22/93, but his lengthy interview was edited down to some harmless soundbites about John-John's salute (Sam was one of two people who taught JFK's son to do this on the Veteran's Day right before the assassination) and other human-interest topics. Kinney, who believes there was a conspiracy (although he also believes Oswald was the lone shooter), wanted his story told, even if it was told to a relative unknown like me without the reward of money, fame, and prestige, all things Sam has little or no desire to obtain at the age of 68. As for the shooting itself on Elm Street, Kinney was ada-mant to me, on three different occasions, that he "saw all three shots hit" and that "the second shot hit Connally and he agrees with me." Sam added that there were NO missed shots that day- he spoke to Connally about this during 1963-1964 and Connally agreed with him ("Very gracious guy, the Governor", Sam said. " I told him 'I'm the one who called you a son-of-a-bitch' and he said 'I wondered who that was'"-this was said by Sam to Connally as he tried to get the Governor out of the way in order to get JFK out of the limousine on 11/22/63)!

The significance of all of this speaks volumes in and of itself. However, in re-gard to the back-of-the-head skull fragment Kinney found in the rear of the lim-ousine, there is a definitive chain of possession on it, as Dr. Robertson confirmed for me: the Nix and Zapruder films show it, spectator Charles Brehm* saw it, Agent Clint Hill observed it in the rear of the limousine on the way to Parkland, Agent Sam Kinney had it on the C-130, SAIC Gerald Behn(who I spoke to) confirmed its location to the FBI agents who attended the autopsy, and Agent Roy Kellerman did the same thing for Arlen Specter of the Warren Commission. [*Brehm appears on the following programs: NBC 11/22/63 (familiar newsreel interview); Mark Lane "Rush To Judgment" film 1967 (clip repeated in Lane's "Two Men In Dallas" video); Part 4 of "CBS News Inquiry: The Warren Report" 6/28/67; "On Trial: Lee Harvey Oswald" 1986 Showtime; "JFK: That Day In November" 11/22/88; "The Men Who Killed Kennedy" 1991;and Mark Oakes' Eyewitness video 1991; see also the book "No More Silence" by Larry Sneed (1998), pp. 63-64; "JFK Absolute Proof" by Robert Groden (2013): see page 150- Brehm is pictured with a nice summary of his statements]

In my opinion, something is definitely amiss with the handling and chain of possession of the OTHER skull fragments discovered between 11/22 and 11/23/63:

    1) the "Harper fragment" (11/23/63);

    2) the THREE pieces of skull found by none other than ASAIC FLOYD BORING during the "official" Secret Service limousine inspection late on 11/22/63(CD 80. p.3), four hours before the FBI did the same- this is separate from the finding made by Kinney;

    3) the small piece found by Seymour Weitzman (7H107[Part 1 of "CBS News Inquiry: The Warren Report" 6/25/67]);

    4) Postal Inspector Harry D. Holmes ("Murder From Within" by Fred Newcomb and Perry Adams, p. 213)--- "A postal inspector [Holmes] picked up a piece of skull from the Elm St. pavement. He said it was as "...big as the end of my finger..." Furthermore, it was one of many: "...there was just pieces of skull and bone and corruption all over the place..." He later discarded it.[!!!]";

    5) Deputy Sheriff Jack Faulkner (see below);

    6)DPD Joe Cody (see below);

Roy Kellerman told HSCA investigators that he only remembered ONE skull fragment being examined at the autopsy, and was only told of TWO by ASA-IC FLOYD BORING (Memo: Jim Kelly and Andy Purdy-interviews with Roy H. Kellerman, 8/24-8/25/77)! Since both Dr. Burkley and Floyd Boring were involved in the chain of possession and handling of the above fragments (including, at least Dr. Burkley, the fragment found by Kinney on the C-130), the disappearance and possible manipulation/ "switching" of fragments at the autopsy leads back to them...

a. *"Today"* show, 11/22/93 NBC: Kinney's first and last television interview (brief/ edited): "[after the first shot] I saw the President grab his neck [indicating]. Then there were two following shots: pow, pow.";

b. 11/20/97 letter to Palamara from Hazel Kinney---Sam passed away 7/21/97;

c. k) "Murder In Dealey Plaza" by James Fetzer (2000), pages 19, 20, 24, 26, 62, 121, 159, 160-163, 166-169, 343, 429

d. l) "J. Edgar Hoover: The Father of the Cold War" by R. Andrew Kiel (2000), page 291, 304-305

e. m) "JFK Absolute Proof" by Robert Groden (2013): see page 154- a nice summary of his statements

* * *

62) Joe Henry Rich :Texas Highway Patrolman (drove V.P. SS follow-up car):

a. 18 H 800: report dated 11/28/63: "...I did see them get Governor Connally out of the car and also take the President out of the car."---nothing specific on wounds;

b. WC references: 17 H 608; 18 H 777-778;

c. 1970's interview with Fred Newcomb for *"Murder From Within"* (1974), p. 71 [see also *"Killing Kennedy"* by H.E.L., p. 152]: "...the motorcade came to a stop momentarily.";

d. [unanswered letter from Vince Palamara 1998]

e. e) *"Murder In Dealey Plaza"* by James Fetzer (2000), pages 121, 172

63) Milton T. Wright, Jr. :Texas Highway Patrolman(driver of Mayor Cabell's car):

a. 18 H 802: report dated 11/28/63---"At the hospital we unloaded the Governor first and then the President. Then we were instructed to keep the news media away from the car."---nothing specific about the wounds;

b. 8/28/98 letter to Vince Palamara---"...I do recall helping to move the President from the car to the stretcher. As I recall about a 1/4 [quarter] of his head was missing, mostly to the left of the back of the head. I believe he died instantly from the wound I saw. I don't believe in the conspiracy or more that [sic] one gun theory. This is why. As we were turning in front of the book depositor [sic], the first shot was fired. When the second shot was fired I believed that it came from the book building. I stopped and was looking at the building when the 3rd shot was fired. I did not see the rifle because I was too close to the building and the shooter was inside the building. If you read the Warren Report you probably saw that Mrs. Cabell stated she saw the rifle being pulled back into the building after the 3rd shot. That was impossible because of our position and she was riding in the left rear after the 1st shot. She slid down in the seat with her back to the building. I gave an affidavit to the Secret Service [see reference "a)" above] but my testimony was not usable. Mrs. Cabell was flown to Washington to testify. That's how her husband got to be a Congressman." [emphasis added];

c. 9/3/98 e-mail to Vince Palamara---"As I recall, prior to the President arriving at the airport we were already staged on the tarmac. I do not recall what position I was in at that time but it was not #1[the number taped to his car's windshield]. At the last minute there was a lot of shuffling and I ended up in the 5th vehicle. My vehicle was the last to leave downtown after the shooting because the police set up a road block behind my car. On your 2nd question[asking for more clarity/ specifics], the wound was left ear to back of head, generally." [emphasis added; see also "J. Edgar Hoover: The Father Of The Cold War" by R. Andrew Kiel (2000), page 302];

d. "J. Edgar Hoover: The Father Of The Cold War" by R. Andrew Kiel (2000), page 302

e. "JFK Absolute Proof" by Robert Groden (2013): see page 154- a nice summary of his statements

64) Parkland Assistant Administrator Steve Landregan:

a. 21 H 158-175: report of activities 11/22-11/24/63 [see also Manchester, p. 672]---nothing about JFK's wounds;

b. Other WC references: 3 H 374; 6 H 5,12, 22, 24, 150; 21 H 179, 180, 181, 184, 185, 186, 191, 194, 195, 197, 198, 205, 209, 218, 226, 227, 255, 257, 258, 259, 261, 266, 267;

c. 9/21/64 interview with William Manchester;

d. "Who's Who in the JFK Assassination" by Michael Benson (1993), pp. 245-246;

e. [unanswered letter from Vince Palamara 1998]

65) Assistant Administrator Robert G. Holcomb:

a. 18 H 245-250: report of activities11/22-11/24/63 [see also Manchester, p. 671]---"...the first of two stretchers rolled by me. The first, I believe, was Governor Connally and the second was president Kennedy.": nothing about the wounds;

b. other WC reference: 6 H 152; 21 H 166, 174, 175, 190, 194, 214, 229, 251, 254, 255, 267;

66)-67) Presidential aides David F. Powers and Kenneth Patrick O'Don-nell (both rode in Secret Service follow-up car)[**deceased 3/27/98 and 9/9/77, respectively**]:

    a.   7 H 472-474: Affidavit dated 5/18/64---"…the first shot went off…I noticed then that the President moved quite far to his left after the shot from the extreme right hand side where he had been sitting. There was a second shot and Governor Connally disappeared from sight and then there was a third shot which took off the top of the President's head and had the sickening sound of a grapefruit splattering against the side of a wall. The total time between the first and third shots was about 5 or 6 seconds. My first impression was that the shots came from the right and overhead, but I also had a fleeting impression that the noise appeared to come from the front in the area of the triple overpass. This may have resulted from my feeling, when I looked forward toward the overpass, that we might have ridden into an ambush…Upon arriving at the emergency entrance, I raced over to where President Kennedy lay and Special Agent Hill and I, along with Special Agent Kellerman, placed him on a stretcher. The three of us and Special Agent Greer pushed him into the emergency area.";

    b.   WC references: 2 H 68; 7 H 446-447, 450, 452, 454-455, 466-469, 471;

    c.   4/8/64, 8/10/64, 10/21/64, 3/17/65, and 5/24/65 interviews with William Manchester ("*The Death of a President*", numerous) [see also p. 673: handwritten notes];

    d.   Powers and O'Donnell: both did a JFK Library Oral History in 1969;

    e.   Interviewed for Ralph Martin's "*A Hero For Our Time*" (1983): see esp. pages 519 and 545---Powers appears strongly to be the source for the following sentence: "The third shot tore off the top back half of his head "and we could see the hair and all the stuff go right up in the air", an aide said.";

    f.   "*High Treason*", p. 423 and Groden's "TKOAP", p. 205 (referring to O'Neill's 1987 book "*Man of the House*", p.211); "*Larry King Live*", 1/20/92 (interview with O'Neill); "*Beyond JFK: The Question of Conspiracy*" video (1992-O'Neill)--Powers (and Kenneth P. O'Donnell[deceased]) told Tip O'Neill that the shots came from the grassy knoll [for his part, O'Donnell said "my reaction in part is reconstruction---is that they came from the right rear."[7 H 468; see also "*Who's Who in the JFK Assassination*" by Michael Benson (1993), p. 321]);

    g.   6/23/87 interview with Livingstone ("*High Treason*", p. 40)---disputes Lifton's theory;

    h.   7/20/87 "*Boston Herald*"---"we'll never know for sure what happened."

    i.   "*JFK: That Day in November*", 11/22/88, NBC---JFK's eyes were open when he helped lift him out of the limo;

    j.   "*JFK: The Day The Nation Cried*", 1988---the most detailed (albeit brief) account of the shooting by him on video---does not leave room for a missed shot;

    k.   *CBS with Charles Kuralt*, 11/22/88---re: Greer's remorse over assassination and, if Greer had sped up/ reacted properly, JFK would still be alive;

l. *"JFK-A Time Remembered"* 1988;

m. 3/28/89 letter to Trask (*"Pictures of the Pain"*, pp. 368-369)---would not allow access to his film;

n. letter to Joel Wagoner dated 7/31/91 (*"The Third Decade"*, Jan-March 1992 issue)---did speak to Livingstone once but did not grant an "interview", per se;

o. letter to Vince Palamara dated 9/10/93 ---JFK did not order agents off his limo and disputes a statement in Bishop's book;

p. 1996 interview with the ARRB's Tom Samoluk---Powers agreed with my take on the Secret Service!;

q. CNN 11/22/96 interview re: his film (also shown on *"Oprah"*);

r. *"Murder in Dealey Plaza"* by James Fetzer (2000), pages 21, 26, 27, 38, 67, 80, 83, 84, 96, 97, 102, 126, 160, 168, 170, 225

s. *"J. Edgar Hoover: The Father of the Cold War"* by R. Andrew Kiel (2000), page 305

t. t) *"JFK Absolute Proof"* by Robert Groden (2013): see page 154- Powers is pictured with a nice summary of his statements

68) Fort Worth Newsman Roy Stamps:

a. *"Crossfire"*, pp. 362 [re: wounds], 366-367; *"JFK: Conspiracy of Silence"*, p. 108; *"The People Vs. Lee Harvey Oswald"* by Walt Brown, pp. 505-506 [re: wounds]; article *"The Head Shot From The Front"* (1996) by Michael T. Griffith [re: wounds]: like Kantor (and Tice), saw Ruby at Parkland. Also, regarding JFK's head wound, he said: "I rushed up and saw Kennedy lying in the car on his side. His foot was hanging over the side of the car. The back of his head was gone.";

b. [unanswered letter from Vince Palamara 1998]

c. *"JFK Absolute Proof"* by Robert Groden (2013): see page 154 a nice summary of his statements

69) Wilma May Tice:

a. 25 H 216-218; 224-227:, 564-565: FBI reports dated 6/27/64, 7/22/64, and 7/23/64, as well as

b. 15 H 388-396 / testimony---saw someone she believed to be Jack Ruby at Parkland: this person called "Jack" was either Ruby or his twin brother;

c. other WC references---25 H 285-287; 21 H 670;

d. UNEDITED Mark Lane *"Rush To Judgment"* film 1967;

70) Asst. Press Secretary Malcolm Kilduff (deceased):

a. see reference "b)"to Dr. Burkley, above;

b. WC references: WR 57, 335; 2 H 98; 5 H 566; 6 H 21; 7 H 451, 466; 15 H 76-79, 81, 89-90, 457-458; 21 H 159-160, 179-180;

c. 5/2/64 and 5/19/65 interviews with William Manchester ("*The Death of a President*", numerous);

d. "*The Day Kennedy Was Shot*", by Jim Bishop, p. 684 (and throughout);

e. 12/15/76 meeting with the HSCA's Robert Tanenbaum (RIF#180-10084-10398)---"He had film which he will supply to us." [?];

f. 8/14/78 Outside contact report with the HSCA's Dawne Miller (RIF# 180-10082-10079): "He's available if needed… Announced JFK's death at the hospital."

g. "*JFK: That Day In November*", NBC, 11/22/88;

h. "*Time*" magazine, 11/28/88: article by Hugh Sidney, p. 45, re: Kilduff, on 11/22/63: "I saw that man's head." He sobbed. "I couldn't believe it. I nearly died. Oh, my God. Oh, my God.";

i. "*High Treason 2*", pp. 443-450: 4/17/91 interview with Harry Livingstone—"… it [the head wound] was clearly in the left side of his head… I do not accept the so-called 'Magic' Bullet Theory… No, I can't buy that one… I have [sic] been swimming with Connally in the pool at the White House, and I saw a clean scar in his back… I talked to Connally about it several times, and his feeling on that and mine are precisely the same [this squares with what Sam Kinney told me and what Connally himself insisted on for years]… It was a very short period of time between the second and third shot… the left part of his forehead looked like---when I got over to the car---looked like two pounds of ground beef… the left part of his forehead… They found that piece of skull, over by the curb, either later that afternoon or the following morning, with hair on it.";

j. '*Today*', NBC, 11/22/93 [behind Kilduff is a copy of "*Best Evidence*"!];

k. three interviews, beginning in Feb. 1995, with Seymour Hersh for "*The Dark Side of Camelot*";

l. [unanswered letters from Vince Palamara 1997/ 1998]

m. "*Murder In Dealey Plaza*" by James Fetzer (2000), pages xii, 84, 98, 249, 252

n. "*JFK Absolute Proof*" by Robert Groden (2013): see page 178- Kilduff is pictured with a nice summary of his statements

71) UPI White House Reporter Merriman Smith [deceased 4/13/70: self-inflicted gunshot wound to the head]:

a. UPI story, 11/23/63 (see "*Four Days*", UPI, p. 32)---'The President's car, possibly as much as 150 or 200 yards ahead, seemed to falter briefly… [at Parkland] I ran to the side of the bubbletop [the limousine]. The President was face down on the back seat… I could not see the President's wound. But I could see blood splattered around the interior of the rear seat and a dark stain spreading down the right side of the President's dark gray suit...the bloody scene in the rear of the car...;"

b.   WC references: 15 H 75-76; 17 H 614; 18 H 781 ["Mariam Smith"];

c.   4/14/64 interview with William Manchester ("*The Death of a President*", numerous);

d.   "*Best Evidence*", p. 45 [see reference "b)" Burkley, above];

e.   "*The Third Decade*", July 1992 issue, pp. 19-20: article by Louis Sproesser;

72-75) Drs. Jack C. Harper, A.B. Cairns, and Gerard Noteboom, Methodist Hospital (re: the Harper fragment, found 11/23/63 by Dr. Harper's nephew William Allen "Billy" Harper, a medical student):

a.   8/17/77 interviews of Harper and Cairns with the HSCA (RIF#180-10093-10429) [see also pp. 261-262 of "*Killing Kennedy*" by H.E.L.]---"Dr. Harper said the consensus of the doctors who viewed the skull fragment was that it was part of the occipital region...Dr. A.B. Cairns...said the piece of skull fragment came from an area approximately two and a half to three inches above the spine area. He said it had the markings of a piece of skull fragment from the lower occipital area, specifically: suture and inner markings where blood vessels run around the base of the skull.";

b.   CD 5, pp. 150-151, CD 1269 and FBI 89-43-479 (11/25/63)---Billy Harper, after finding the skull fragment and taking it to Drs. Harper and Cairns, spoke to FBI agent James Anderton, who notified the Secret Service and was then immediately instructed by SAIC of PRS Robert Bouck to send the fragment to the White House "AND NO PUBLICITY WHATSOEVER", wrote Agent Anderton;

c.   FBI lab sheets, 11/27/63; FBI 62-109060; FBI 62-109060-60, p. 2 [see "*Best Evidence*", p. 503]---the fragment was personally delivered to Dr. Burkley. Burkley said it should be delivered to him "so that in the event this bone piece is from President Kennedy's head it can be enclosed in the autopsy reports." However, the fragment was NOT given to the autopsy doctors, nor was it mentioned at the autopsy;

d.   CD 1395, p. 50/ FBI interview of Cairns+ pages 46 and 44---"Dr. Cairns stated the bone specimen looked like it came from the occipital region of the skull."; The doctors made 12 photographs of it at Methodist Hospital; a woman wrote RFK in June 1964 and told him that in Dallas she had seen snapshots, taken at a hospital, of JFK's head!; RFK forwarded this letter to the WC and J. Lee Rankin's assistant, Howard Willens, immediately requested the FBI to investigate the matter.;

e.   7 H 25, 123, 228-230, 245-248---the HSCA believed the Harper fragment came from the upper middle third of the parietal area;

f.   Noteboom: "*Best Evidence*", p. 504 (1972 interview with Robert P. Smith [7/20/72 letter from Smith to Lifton])---"also saw the bone and held the same opinion [as Harper and Cairns]";

g. Noteboom: 8/25/98 letter to Vince Palamara---"Re: Skull fragment, JFK. My best estimate of the fragment was that it was occipital. I took 35mm transparency slides, which were turned over to the FBI.";

h. Noteboom: interview with Millicent Cranor 1998---confirms his same opinion;

i. "*Mortal Error*", p. 169; Groden's "TKOAP", pages 34 and 83; "*JFK: The Case For Conspiracy*" video 1993; "*Bloody Treason*" by Noel Twyman, p. 222; CD 1269a [in the author's collection]----photos of the Harper fragment; Dr. Randy Robertson, at COPA 1996, showed slides of X-rays of the Harper fragment that the FBI took;

j. Article by Joseph N. Riley, Ph.D, in the April 1996 issue of "*JFK/ Deep Politics Quarterly*" journal entitled "*Anatomy of the Harper Fragment*".

k. 9/15/98 letter from William A. Harper to Vince Palamara---"Your letter to my uncle Dr. Jack C. Harper has been forwarded to me for response. My uncle told me that the fragment I found was from the occipital area of the skull. I have seen drawings in various publications that would indicate that it belonged to this region. With regard to the question of the existence [of] photographs, it is my understanding that my uncle gave his pictures to an assassination investigative agency.";

l. "*Murder In Dealey Plaza*" by James Fetzer (2000), pages 41, 226-227, 248, 279-282, 293, 297

m. "*JFK Absolute Proof*" by Robert Groden (2013): see page 159, 173

76) Dr. Lito Porto:

a. "*High Treason*", p. 460---"The first doctor to see what he said was a bullet entry wound near the left temple was Dr. Leto (sic) Porto."[only reference to Dr. Lito Porto];

b. 8/31/98 letter to Vince Palamara from Dr. Boris Porto, Lito's son---"Vince, Lito is my father! Call me and I'll give you info.-Boris";

c. 9/6/98 call to Dr. Boris Porto from Vince Palamara;

d. 9/8/98 call from Dr. Boris Porto to Vince Palamara (relaying info. from his father)- His father said that "he needs to keep his mouth quiet" but referred me to Drs. Charlie Baxter and Jim Carrico; Boris: "he was there…he was the neurosurgery chief resident, the first one to come out of that program"---Kemp Clark was "overseeing my father";

e. "*Murder In Dealey Plaza*" by James Fetzer (2000), page 259

77) Ulah McCoy, Chief Clerk, Admitting Office, Parkland:

a. a) 21 H 154: 11/25/63 affidavit re: blank Record of Death, presumably for JFK;

b. b) other WC reference: 6 H 149;

78) Peter N. Geilich, Administrative Assistant:

a. 21 H 176-189: 11/26/63 report of activities11/22-11/24/63 [see also *"The Death of a President"* by William Manchester, p. 671]: "I got a good look at the Governor who looked to me as though he were dead." Nothing about JFK's wounds, though;

b. other WC reference: 6 H 151; 21 H 170, 171, 173, 190, 227, 242, 243, 246, 248, 257, 263, 265, 266, 267;

79) Robert Dutton, Administrative Assistant:

a. 21 H 190: report of activities 11/22 and 11/24/63---nothing about the wounds;

b. other WC reference: 6 H 151; 21 H 187-189, 228, 243, 248, 250, 265, 267;

80) Carol Reddick, Administrative Aide:

a. 21 H 191-192: 12/2/63 report---"Mrs. [Evelyn]Lincoln, personal secretary to the President, asked to be taken to the Emergency Room to contact two of the security officers. I took her there and asked Mrs. Beck to assist her."; nothing about the wounds;

b. other WC reference: 6 H 151; 21 H 166, 168, 248, 266;

81) Nurse Sally Lennon:

a. 21 H 205; report of activities 11/22-11/24/63---not on duty 11/22/63;

b. other WC reference: 6 H 151; 21 H 171, 223;

c. *"That Day In Dallas"* by Richard Trask (1998), p. 126 [possibly the woman in photo on page 127];

82) C. Watkins, R.N.:

a. 21 H 206: report of activities 11/22-11/23/63---not on duty 11/22/63;

b. other WC reference: 6 H 151; 21 H 210;

83) Nurse Faye Dean Shelby:

a. a)21 H 207: report of activities 11/22-11/23/63---"About 12.45, I went [to] Major Surgery to see if I could help but was turned around by Miss Nelson... about 2.15. Then I went back to Major Surgery to help clean up for about 15 minutes.";

b. b) other WC reference: 6 H 151;

84) Aide Jean Tarrant:

a.   a) 21 H 210: report of activities for 11/23-11/24/63;

b.   b) other WC reference: 6 H 151;

85) Aide Frances Scott:

a.   21 H 211:report of activities for 11/22/63---"I'm glad I didn't see very much because I do not think I could have taken it.";

b.   other WC reference: 6 H 151; 21 H 209;

86) Orderly Willie Haywood:

a.   21 H 212: report of activities 11/24/63;

b.   other WC reference: 6 H 151;

87) Ward Clerk Jill Pomeroy:

a.   21 H 222-223: report of activities 11/24/63;

b.   other WC reference: 6 H 151; 21 H 215, 221, 227;

88) Joe H. Shankles, Security Officer:

a.   21 H 233-235: 12/1/63 report of activities 11/22-11/24/63---"Mr. Wright placed me in the corridor between the Emergency desk and Emergency entrance...Father Huber arrived and I escorted him to the Emergency desk at Check Point Three where he was ushered immediately into Emergency by members of the hospital staff. At about 2:00 p.m., we received word to clear a passageway through the emergency corridor of all personnel and within a few minutes the casket bearing President Kennedy's body was escorted out by Secret Service Agents and placed in a hearse. This was done quietly and without any incidents.";

b.   other WC references: 21 H 229, 231, 232, 237, 238;

89) L.G. Moore, Security Officer:

a.   21 H 236: report of activities 11/22-11/24/63---"A casket was brought to the hospital by Oneal Funeral Home, and it was taken into the room where the body of the late President was. Later when they brought the casket out, we assisted in helping them get it into the hearse, and they drove off.";

b.   other WC references: 21 H 229, 231, 232, 234;

90) Henry N. Locklin, Security Officer:

a. a)21 H 238: report of activities 11/22/63---"On Friday, November 22, 1963, I was instructed to keep all unauthorized persons off the second floor, where the Governor of the State of Texas was being treated for gun shot wounds.";

b. b) other WC references: 21 H 231-233;

91)-95) Dr. Charles Francis Gregory (operated on Gov. Connally)[deceased April 1976], Dr. William Osborne, Dr. John Parker, Nurse [fnu] Rutherford, and Nurse Pat Schrader:

a. Gregory: WR533-534 / 17 H 18-19 /21 H 268-269: 11/22/63 Operative Record---assistants: **Drs. William Osborne,**[see also WR 56; 6 H 97, 110; 20 H 6; January 1964 Texas State Journal of Medicine article *"Three Patients at Parkland"*, pages 70 and 72 re: treatment of Connally and Oswald; Crenshaw, p. 123; 9/3/98 letter to Vince Palamara---"...I do recollect taking multiple fragments of mohair fiber from Governor Connally's wrist, and I am sure that we must have taken a few bullet fragments out also. One bullet fragment had gone all the way through his wrist and lodged in his right thigh. The wrist wound of course occurred after the bullet had traveled through his chest and caused more extensive damage to his lung. As far as any theory about a single bullet, I guess theoretically it could have evolved from a single bullet, however it is also quite possible, maybe even probable that there was more than one bullet fired, and maybe even one from the grassy knoll[, this of course is all speculation and there are many very fanciful conclusions that Chuck Crenshaw draws in his book, and I would take most of those with a grain of salt if I were you."], **John Parker,**[see WR 56; 6 H 97, 110] and Adolph Giesecke [*see above*]; **Nurses: Miss [fnu] Rutherford and Pat Schrader**[*Rutherford*: see 4 H 126; 17 H 841; Groden's "TKOAP", p. 127; *Schrader*: see WR 535, 536; 4 H 126; 17 H 20-21, 841; Crenshaw, p. 49; Groden's "TKOAP", p. 127;]

b. Gregory: 4 H 117-129 and 6 H 95-104 / testimony;

c. Gregory: other WC references: WR 56, 93, 95, 532, 535; 3 H 383, 389; 4 H 108-109, 112-113, 138-139; 5 H 78-79, 81, 87, 96, 142; 6 H 88-90, 92, 109-110, 150, 152; 17 H 17, 20, 841; 20 H 6; 21 H 198-199;

d. Gregory: 11/30/63 FBI interview of Gregory re: Connally bullet fragments [7 HSCA 155-156];

e. Gregory: January 1964 *"Texas State Journal of Medicine"* article entitled *"Three Patients at Parkland"*, pages 67 and 69 re: Connally;

f. Gregory: *"JFK: The Dead Witnesses"* by Craig Roberts and John Armstrong (1995), pp. 126-128;

96) Dr. Robert Roeder Shaw (operated on Gov. Connally)[deceased]:

a. 17 H 336-337, 346: body diagrams [see also photo 16B in *"Best Evidence"* and photos in *"High Treason"*; see also 6 H 112: Dr. Shires said the Secret Service prepared the original charts];

b.   4 H 101-117 and 6 H 83-95 / testimony---doubted that CE399 caused the Connally wrist wound [4 H 113-114; see also pages 73 and 90 of *"Best Evidence"* and numerous references in *"Post Mortem"*];

c.   other WC references: WR 56, 92-93, 531, 532; 3 H 383, 389; 4 H 118, 122, 126-127, 136-139, 148; 5 H 78-79, 85, 96, 142, 154; 6 H 23-24, 69, 96-97, 100-103, 105, 109-111, 115, 117; 17 H 16-17; 20 H 6; 21 H 165, 170, 176, 196;

d.   11/22/63 WFAA/ ABC video--- Press Conference 7:00 CST "The bullet is in the leg...it hasn't been removed...it will be removed before he goes to the recovery room"(?!)- what about CE399(the stretcher bullet) that entered the record around FIVE hours earlier?;

e.   NBC, 11/22/63 [repeated in Mark Lane *"Rush To Judgment"* film 1967, *"The Two Kennedys"* 1976, *"JFK: The Day the Dream Died"* 1988, etc.];

f.   AP dispatch/ *"The Atlanta Constitution"*, 11/23/63: quotes Dr. Shaw---"[The Governor] seems to have been struck by just one bullet...We know the wound of entrance was along the right shoulder. He was shot from above...[the bullet] entered the back of his chest and moved outward...It emerged from his chest and struck his wrist and thigh...The bullet is still in his leg." [see reference "d)" above];

g.   11/27/63 *"New York Herald-Tribune"*: article by Martin Steadman---a bullet had entered the front of JFK's throat and "coursed downward into his lung [and] was removed in the Bethesda Naval Hospital where the autopsy was performed."

h.   11/29/63 *"Houston Post"*---"The assassin was behind him [JFK], yet the bullet entered at the front of his neck. Mr. Kennedy must have turned to his left to talk to Mrs. Kennedy or to wave to someone.";

i.   January 1964 Texas State Journal of Medicine article entitled *"Three Patients at Parkland"*, pp. 65-67 re: Conally---"the wound of entrance was approximately 3 cm. in its longest diameter";

j.   11/9/77 interview with the HSCA's Andy Purdy and Mark Flanagan (7 HSCA 323-331) [see drawing on p. 126 of Groden's *"TKOAP"*];

k.   1978 interview with Anthony Summers (see *"Conspiracy"*, pages 36 and 540): "Dr. Robert Shaw...has never been satisfied that the "magic bullet" caused all his patient's injuries."

l.   Interviewed for *"Reasonable Doubt"* video 1988;

m.   Interviewed for *"Nova"*, 11/15/88;

n.   3/11/92 interview with Gerald Posner (*"Case Closed"*, pp. 293-294);

o.   6/4/92 Dallas Forum (*"The Dallas Morning News"*, 6/5/92; see also *"Killing The Truth"*, pp. 80-81, 172-173)---"...the wound he saw on Connally's back was not that of a tumbling bullet or of a bullet that had struck anything else before striking Connally. He insisted that it was a clean, round wound of entry---very small."; Shaw also said that only a fragment entered Connally's thigh, and not a whole bullet, as he implied on 11/22/63 (see above).;

p.   Interviewed for *"JFK: The Case for Conspiracy"* video 1993;

97) Dr. George Thomas Shires (operated on Gov. Connally and, later, on Oswald):

a.   21 H 252-253: statement re: Oswald 11/24/63 [see also *"The Death of a President"* by William Manchester, p. 674];

b.   6 H 104-113 / testimony---did not think JFK and Connally were struck by the same bullet;

c.   other WC references: WR 56, 532, 535-537; 3 H 363-364, 367, 376, 380, 383-386, 389; 4 H 111, 139; 6 H 6, 8, 17, 23-24, 45, 52, 88, 91, 150; 17 H 17, 20-22, 29; 20 H 6; 21 H 170, 172, 173, 174, 185-186, 198-199, 263, 265, 267;

d.   11/24/63 WFAA/ ABC—re: statement on Oswald's condition;

e.   January 1964 "Texas State Journal of Medicine" entitled *"Three Patients at Parkland"*, pages 69, 71, and 72 re: Connally and Oswald;

f.   *"Medical Times"*, November 1974 issue: article by Gary Lattimer, Dr. John K. Lattimer, and Jon Lattimer entitled "The Kennedy-Connally One Bullet Theory" (p. 56): 5/6/74 letter from Shires to Lattimer "verifying that the metallic fragment was located more distally on the Governor's leg than the wound of entry into the skin of his upper leg, and that the metallic fragment was *not* removed.";

g.   1/9/78 interview with the HSCA (7 HSCA 158-159; 332-347);

h.   picture in *"JFK: Conspiracy of Silence"* by Dr. Crenshaw;

i.   *"Dallas Morning News"*, 4/9/92—refused to confirm or deny Dr. Crenshaw's claim that LBJ called Parkland on 11/24/63;

98) Henrietta Magnolia Ross, Operating room technician:

a.   6 H 123-124 / testimony---re: "the stretcher cart on which Governor Connally was transported while in the hospital";

b.   other WC references: 6 H 123, 126;

c.   *"Who's Who in the JFK Assassination"* by Michael Benson (1993), p. 388;

99) Orderly R.J. Jimison:

a.   6 H 125-128 / testimony---did not see JFK but helped transport Connally by carriage to the operating table;

b.   other WC references: 6 H 122, 124;

c.   *"The Day Kennedy Was Shot"* by Jim Bishop, p. 241;

d. *"Who's Who in the JFK Assassination"* by Michael Benson, p.219;

100) Phyllis Bartlett, Chief Telephone Operator (1954-1968):

a. *"The Death of a President"*, pages 178 and 669: referring to her report of activities, 11/22-11/24/63 [not in WC Volumes];

b. *"The Day Kennedy Was Shot"*, p. 191—obviously referencing:

c. 21 H 241 (report of Doris Nelson)and 21 H 254 (Price);

d. *"The Dallas Morning News"*, 7/15/92 (see also *"Assassination Science"*, p. 41)---"There very definitely was a phone call from a man with a loud voice, who identified himself as Lyndon Johnson, and he was connected to the operating room phone during Oswald's surgery.";

e. *"JFK: Breaking The Silence"* by Bill Sloan (1993), p. 185---Hugh Huggins/ Howell: "I talked to some of the doctors and nurses at Parkland [on 11/22/63 and again on 11/25/63], and I talked to Phyllis Bartlett, the chief telephone operator at the hospital, about a call she had allegedly received from Lyndon Johnson while Oswald was in surgery after being shot by Ruby... Bartlett confirmed hat she'd spoken to a man with a loud voice who identified himself as Johnson." [see Hugh Huggins/ Howell, below];

f. March 1993 interview with Bill Sloan (*"JFK: Breaking the Silence"*, p. 185): "... Ms. Bartlett...recalled conversing at the time of the assassination with a man fitting Hugh Howell's description. "My little office was overflowing with as many as fifty people at once back then," she said, "but I do remember talking to a short man with a crewcut who identified himself in that capacity [CIA], and I do believe he said his name was Howell.";

g. g) *"The Men Who Killed Kennedy"* (2003) DVD

101) Evelyn Lincoln, JFK's secretary [deceased 5/11/95]:

a. WC references: 2 H 98; 7 H 466, 470; 21 H 191, 259;

b. 4/3/4, 4/4/64, 4/15/64, and 5/15/64 interviews with William Manchester (*"The Death of a President"*, many) [see also p. 672];

c. Her book *"My Twelve Years With Kennedy"* (1965);

d. Her book *"Kennedy & Johnson"* (1968);

e. 7/5/78 interview with the HSCA and

f. 10/16/78 affidavit to HSCA: see 7 HSCA 27--- "The committee contacted Lincoln to determine what happened to the materials in item No. 9, the missing materials, following their documented transfer to her in April 1965. She informed the committee of an interview and subsequent affidavit that Burkley and Bouck brought her some materials in the spring of 1965 that Dr. Burkley identified as being related to the autopsy of the President. (60) She recalled that these materials arrived in a box or boxes, and that within 1 day she obtained a flat trunk or footlocker from the Archives personnel to which she transferred the materials. (61) She added that these materials were kept in a security room in her office in the National Archives.";

g. interviewed for Ralph Martin's "*A Hero For Our Time*" (1983);

h. JFK Library Oral History, 1990;

i. numerous TV appearances, including *CBS News* (11/22/88), "*Today*" (1/11/89) NBC, and "*Today*" (11/22/93) NBC;

j. 4/21/91 interview with Harry Livingstone for "*High Treason 2*", pp. 435-437--- "...I remember coming into Parkland Hospital, and Dr. Burkley telling me that he [JFK] had gone, and Jackie was sitting outside of the place where he was being kept---they were doing the autopsy or whatever they were doing, and I went up to her and tried to console her."; "I never looked at any of that [the autopsy materials]. Nothing. I kept it, and then Bobby [Kennedy] moved it into another room. It was all sealed up. I never saw any of it...I had no access to it."; "It was a conspiracy. There was no doubt about that...J. Edgar Hoover was involved in it.";

k. "*Bloody Treason*" by Noel Twyman, p. 831 and

l. "*Assassination Science*" by James Fetzer, p. 372: 10/7/94 letter to Richard Duncan---"As for the assassination is concerned [sic] it is my belief that there was a conspiracy because there were those that disliked him and felt the only way to get rid of him was to assassinate him. These five conspirators , in my opinion, were Lyndon B. Johnson, J. Edgar Hoover, the Mafia, the CIA, and the Cubans in Florida. The House Intelligence Committee investigation, also, came to the conclusion that there was a conspiracy."[Lincoln conveyed the same thoughts to Anthony Summers: see "*The Fourth Decade*" journal, May 1998 issue, p. 14];

m. three interviews with Seymour Hersh, beginning in March 1994, for "*The Dark Side of Camelot*";

n. n) "*Murder In Dealey Plaza*" by James Fetzer (2000), pages 98, 100

102) Mrs. [fnu] Deibel:

a. 21 H 161;

103) Norris Uzee:

a. 21 H 166, 167, 196;

104) Comptroller Bob Struwe:

a. 21 H 160, 166, 170, 181, 246-250;

105) Edward Maher, Chairman, Board of Managers:

    a.   21 H 163, 166, 181, 190, 191, 260, 266;

106) Dr. Luther Holcomb:

    a.   21 H 164;

107) Paul Crall:

    a.   21 H 166, 168, 169;

108) Fayetta "Faye" Gannon:

    a.   21 H 168, 175, 191-192, 220, 245, 247-248, 254, 266;

109) Mrs. [fnu] Lively:

    a.   21 H 167-168, 194, 198, 228;

110) Mrs. Katie Huber:

    a.   21 H 168, 175, 198, 199, 249;

111) Dr. James "Red" Duke (operated on Connally):

    a.   WR 531; 4 H 103; 6 H 78, 84, 110, 117; 17 H 16; 20 H 6; 21 H 170, 199, 208;

    b.   January 1964 Texas State Journal of Medicine article "*Three Patients at Parkland*", p. 70 re: treatment of Connally;

    c.   HSCA references: 7 HSCA 325;

    d.   picture in "*JFK: Conspiracy of Silence*" by Dr. Crenshaw;

    e.   [unanswered letter from Vince Palamara 1998]

    f.   "*Murder In Dealey Plaza*" by James Fetzer (2000), page 67

    g.   "*JFK Absolute Proof*" by Robert Groden (2013): see page 153- Dr. Duke is pictured with this statement: "Although Dr. Duke has never made a public statement about the head wounds, he has told several friends and others about the "Massive exit wound in the rear of the President's head."

112) Dr. Donald E. Jackson:

    a.   21 H 171, 205, 215;

b. 9/8/98 letter to Vince Palamara---"Regarding your first question, the resuscitation of Lee Harvey Oswald was carried out in the trauma room in the Parkland Hospital Emergency Room. I was present when he was brought into the room and participated directly in his resuscitation. There were several strangers who were present in the corridors and in the immediate area. I assume that some of them were law enforcement individuals or part of the news media, which had been in abundance in Parkland Hospital since the assassination. I have no information which would directly link any of these individuals to the Secret Service. I am also not sure of what evidence Dr. Crenshaw has reviewed which might lead him to such a conclusion. I am encouraged that historians such as yourself are continuing an investigation into this important event. *I continue to be dissatisfied with the explanation of the Warren Commission. The reason for my skepticism is linked to discrepancies in descriptions of the Kennedy wounds between the Parkland Emergency Room and the autopsy findings. Drs. McClelland, Perry, and Jenkins gave accurate descriptions of the wounds as they saw them in the Emergency Room. The descriptions in Washington were radically different.* In addition, Dr. McClelland and several other colleagues went to Washington and reviewed the findings with the medical authorities. It seemed at that time, that they then reversed themselves on the findings that they had described in Dallas. I do not question their veracity but I am confused by this discrepancy. It is possible that there is a simple explanation that I am not aware of."[emphasis added; see also "J. Edgar Hoover: The Father Of The Cold War" by R. Andrew Kiel (2000), pages 288-289];

c. "*J. Edgar Hoover: The Father Of The Cold War*" by R. Andrew Kiel (2000), pages 288-289

113) Mrs. Billie Martinets, Associate Nursing Supervisor:

a. 21 H 176, 177;

b. 9/8/98 letter to Vince Palamara---"The information you have from the Warren Commission refers to a meeting at Woodlawn Hospital, which was the old Parkland Hospital and housed chest medicine, long-term care rehab and psychiatric patients. Pete Geilich and I were at a meeting and making administrative and nursing rounds. Discussion of hospital refers to Woodlawn, not Parkland. Woodlawn was approximately four to five (4 to 5) miles from Parkland. Pete Geilich had seen the news report on T.V. and rushed to tell us. I was told to stay on the Woodlawn campus, which I did. The Dallas Police picked up Dr. Robert Shaw, thoracic surgeon from our Woodlawn campus to take him to Parkland to attend to Governor John Connally of Texas.";

114) Dr. C.A. LeMaistre:

a. 21 H 176;

115) Mrs. Ruth McLaughlin, operator:

a. 21 H 176;

116) John Willis, Purchasing Agent:

    a.   21 H 178, 190, 228;

117) Mrs. Faye Storey:

    a.   21 H 179, 180;

118) Dr. Carter Pannill:

    a.   21 H 181, 263, 265;

119) Chaplain/ Dr. Ken Pepper:

    a.   21 H 187-189, 195, 258;

120) Chaplain [fnu] Davis:

    a.   21 H 189;

121) Mrs. Sara Miller, Nursing Supervisor, Out-Patient Clinic:

    a.   21 H 193;

122) Mrs. Luella Owens:

    a.   a) 21 H 193;

123) Mrs. Virginia Reid, Asst. Dir. Of Nursing Service:

    a.   21 H 193;

124) Miss [fnu] Beck:

    a.   21 H 194, 196, 199, 242, 243;

125) Miss Myrtle Drake:

    a.   21 H 194;

126) Mrs. [fnu] Curtiss:

    a.   21 H 197, 198;

127) Mrs. [fnu] Fitzgerald, second floor supervisor:

    a.   21 H 197, 200;

128) Nurse Eleanor Molden:

    a.   21 H 199;

129) Mrs. Carolyn Rogers, Asst. Dir. Of Nursing Service:

    a.   21 H 199-200;

130) Mr. [fnu] Jones:

    a.   21 H 200;

131) Mary Nell:

    a.   21 H 200;

132) Miss Madeleine Magin, assignment desk:

    a.   21 H 200;

133) Miss [fnu] Stravapolous, Head Nurse:

    a.   21 H 201

134) Miss [fnu] Palmer:

    a.   21 H 202;

135) [fnu] Holse, Admitting Orderly:

    a.   21 H 249;

136) Dr. Gerry Gustafson:

    a.   6 H 124; 21 H 205;

    b.   January 1964 Texas State Journal of Medicine article *"Three Patients at Parkland"*, p. 72 re: treatment of LHO;

    c.   photo in *"JFK: Conspiracy of Silence"* by Dr. Crenshaw; see also p. 179;

d. *"That Day In Dallas"* by Richard Trask (1998), pages 126-127 (photo: back to elevator, facing camera; glasses);

137) Miss [fnu] King:

a. WR 531; 17 H 16; 21 H 215, 227;

138) Dr. [fnu] McGaw:

a. 21 H 215;

139) Dr. J. Garvey:

a. 21 H 215;

140) Miss Sally Settles, R.N.:

a. 21 H 222, 223;

141) Mr. [fnu] Davis, engineer:

a. 21 H 223, 245, 256;

142) Jose Reyse:

a. 21 H 223;

143) Mrs. [fnu] Davenport:

a. 21 H 229;

144) Mr. [fnu] Watson:

a. 21 H 229;

145) Mrs. [fnu] Lewis, Supervisor, Housekeeping Dept.:

a. 21 H 229;

146) Mrs. [fnu] Ellis:

a. 21 H 242;

147) Mrs. [fnu] Berger:

    a.   21 H 242;

148) Mrs. [fnu] Scroggins, Social Service:

    a.   21 H 245;

149) Dr. [fnu] Guy:

    a.   a) 21 H 246, 262;

150) [fnu] Geddis:

    a.   21 H 267;

151) Dr. David Mebane (worked on Connally):

    a.   *"JFK: Conspiracy of Silence"*, p. 94;

    b.   4 H 103; 6 H 84;

    c.   c) *"Murder In Dealey Plaza"* by James Fetzer (2000), page 67

152) Dr. James Boland (worked on Connally):

    a.   *"JFK: Conspiracy of Silence"*, p. 123;

    b.   WR 531, 3 H 384; 4 H 103; 6 H 110; 17 H 16; 20 H 6;

    c.   January 1964 Texas State Journal of Medicine article *"Three Patients at Parkland"*, p. 70 re: treatment of Connally;

    d.   HSCA references: 7 HSCA 325;

153) Dr. Ralph Don [David?] Patman (worked on Connally):

    a.   *"JFK: Conspiracy of Silence"*, p. 123;

    b.   WC references: WR 56, 535; 6 H 106, 110; 17 H 20;

154) Dr. Dale Coln:

    a.   *"JFK: Conspiracy of Silence"*, pages 179 and 182;

    b.   January 1964 Texas State Journal of Medicine article *"Three Patients at Parkland"*, p. 72 re: involvement in treatment of LHO;

    c.   [unanswered letter from Vince Palamara 1998]

155) Dr. William Risk:

a. *"JFK: Conspiracy of Silence"*, p. 183;

b. 3 H 384;

c. January 1964 Texas State Journal of Medicine article *"Three Patients at Parkland"*, pages 72 and 73 re: involvement in treatment of LHO;

d. *"The Search For Lee Harvey Oswald"* by Robert Groden (1995), p. 202;

e. 9/8/98 letter to Vince Palamara---"It was rather long ago that I was in the operating room at Parkland during Oswald's surgery. As you might imagine, there was really no time to think about who was there or much of anything else. I was given the job of recording all the units of blood we had to use on him...if I recall correctly, we literally "pumped" 22 units of blood through Oswald...and it was rather literally "through" him because we could not keep up with his loss due to extensive damage done by the bullet. Therefore, I do not know whether a Secret Service agent was actually in the operating room or not...sorry. As far as a conspiracy or not, I only know what most Americans know, and that is what we have been told of the facts. However, as a physician, I have the feeling there was more than one "shooter" and more than one bullet involved because of the nature of the wounds. I would suggest that, if you have not already done so, you get a copy of an article from the Journal of the Texas Medical Association, January 1964, entitled "Three Patients at Parkland." This article is a MEDICAL version of those days. The wounds described there, to me, suggest entrance and exit wounds which differ from the "one bullet theory."...Sorry I can't be of more help." [emphasis added];

156) Nurse [fnu] Burkett:

a. WR 531, 536; 17 H 16, 21;

157) Nurse [fnu] Oliver:

a. WR 535; 17 H 20;

158) Nurse [fnu] Deming:

a. WR 535; 17 H 20;

159) Nurse [fnu] Johnson:

a. WR 531; 17 H 16;

160) Nurse [fnu] Lunsford:

a. WR 536; 17 H 21;

161) Nurse [fnu] Simpson:

a.   WR 536; 17 H 21;

162) Dr. Curtis Spier (worked on Oswald):

a.   WR 536; 17 H 21;

b.   January 1964 Texas State Journal of Medicine article "*Three Patients at Parkland*", p. 73---"Dr. Curtis Spier, fellow in anesthesiology, canulated a vein in [LHO's] right forearm to aid in fluid replacement."

c.   [unanswered letter from Vince Palamara 1998]

163) Dr. A.J. Gill, Dean, Southwest Medical School:

a.   6 H 50; 20 H 7, 252-253;

164) Dr. Deuon Baker:

a.   20 H 6;

165) Orderly Joe Mata:

a.   20 H 5;

166) Charles Harbison, Texas State Trooper:

a.   1983 interview with Henry Hurt ("*Reasonable Doubt*", p. 66): "Harbison was standing guard at the door to the operating room when a nurse [apparently Audrey Bell] ... handed him the [Connally] fragments. Harbison told the author, "I immediately turned around and handed them to somebody else. And who that somebody else was, I'll never know.";

b.   "*The Dallas Morning News*", 4/3/77; interviewed by DMN reporter Earl Golz in Sept. 1977 (as reported in "*Conspiracy*" by Anthony Summers, p. 546, "*Who Killed JFK?*" by Carl Oglesby, p. 32, "*A Complete Book of Facts*" by Duffy and Ricci, p. 209, and "*Who's Who in the JFK Assassination*" by Michael Benson, p. 170): "he had turned over to the FBI three additional bullet fragments that fell from Connally's leg [according to Summers' account, they were GIVEN to Harbison by somebody, maybe a doctor]when he helped move Connally to another hospital room three or four days after the shooting.";

167) Ken Raley, a reserve policeman/ medical technologist:

a.   8/16/91 and 9/30/91 interviews with Harry Livingstone for "*High Treason 2*" (pages 82 and 572): "Ken Raley told me that there "definitely was a post", and that Justice of the Peace Theran Ward authorized the examination... He says that he had a copy of the report, signed by four or five "pathologists". He told me that he tried to obtain this paper again---which he at one time possessed and has now lost... Raley says that they tried to trace the bullet tracks and examined the brain.";

168)-169) Hugh Huggins (aka Hugh Howell), Marine/ undercover CIA agent, 4/55 to 10/65, and Colonel William C. Bishop [deceased 7/92], CIA contract agent:

a. 1993 interview (s) with Bill Sloan for "*JFK: Breaking the Silence*" (1993), Chapter 9, pp. 175-189 [Includes photo of Huggins circa 1962]: claims, among other things, to have been at both Parkland and Bethesda on 11/22/63: "I distinctly saw an entry wound in the left temple. To my knowledge, only two other people beside myself have admitted to seeing this wound. It was assumed to be a blood clot by the doctors at Parkland, but it was an entry wound, and it could not have been fired from the rear. The bullet from this wound exited the right side of the president's head, blowing out a section of skull and obscuring the entry wound of a second bullet that struck him from the right front almost simultaneously. There were two large, separate holes in the upper right side of the head, separated by about three-quarters of an inch of bone matter and skin tissue. The wound in the throat, although greatly enlarged by a tracheostomy, was also an entry wound. All the wounds had a puffy, torn appearance as though they had been probed prior to the autopsy. There was also an entry wound high in the back, between the neck and the shoulder. It had penetrated approximately the depth of one finger joint---I actually put my small finger into the hole---then made a forty-five degree turn to the left. To my knowledge, this bullet never left the body."[!]; 11/25/63: "I talked to some of the doctors and nurses at Parkland, and I talked to Phyllis Bartlett, the chief telephone operator at the hospital, about a call she had allegedly received from Lyndon Johnson while Oswald was in surgery after being shot by Ruby... Bartlett confirmed hat she'd spoken to a man with a loud voice who identified himself as Johnson.";

b. March 1993 interview with Bill Sloan ("*JFK: Breaking the Silence*", p. 185): "... Ms. Bartlett... recalled conversing at the time of the assassination with a man fitting Hugh Howell's description. "My little office was overflowing with as many as fifty people at once back then," she said, "but I do remember talking to a short man with a crewcut who identified himself in that capacity [CIA], and I do believe he said his name was Howell.";

c. 18 H 795: Secret Service agent Andy Berger (who would go on to drive the hearse containing JFK's body out of Parkland) reported of meeting the following persons at Parkland Hospital shortly after the assassination:

   1. FBI agent Vincent Drain (sent via Hoover! [*see below*]), the same agent who would go on to accompany Agent Lawson during the transfer of critical assassination evidence later on that weekend;

2. "a doctor friend of (Drain)" ;

3. c. an *"unidentified CIA agent"* who had <u>credentials</u> *(like the FBI man sent by Hoover, how could the CIA agent get to the Dallas hospital so soon after the murder?)*;see Bill Sloan's "Breaking the Silence", pp. 181-185]

4. d. an "unidentified FBI agent" [J. Doyle Williams-*see below*]who did <u>not</u> have credentials.;

d. 5/8/90 interview of **Colonel William C. Bishop [deceased 7/92], CIA contract agent**, by Dick Russell (*"The Man Who Knew Too Much"*, numerous--see esp. pages 570-571 [see also *"Who's Who in the JFK Assassination"* by Michael Benson (1993), pp. 40-41])-"Over at Dallas' Parkland Hospital ... another military man was standing in the doorway to Trauma Room 1. This was Colonel William Bishop, who had been working for months with the anti-Castro Cuban exiles on behalf of the CIA. "I had been in Palm Beach at the Berkeley Hotel," Bishop told me in 1990, "when I received a phone call telling me to be in Dallas on the morning of November 21. I wasn't the only Army officer called, that's all I can say about that. I was flown to Dallas by military aircraft and checked into a Holiday Inn, at which time I received instructions that I was to make sure the press had proper credentials at the Trade Mart when Kennedy came to speak the next afternoon. I was in position and waiting for his arrival, when I heard over a squad car parked at the curb that shots had been fired in Dealey Plaza. *I commandeered a police car and ordered the driver to take me directly to Parkland Hospital. With the ID I had, that was not a problem. There the Secret Service instructed me to secure the area outside the Trauma Room and make myself available to the First Lady or medical staff."* [emphasis added---sounds a lot like Huggins' story!];

e. *"Murder in Dealey Plaza"* by James Fetzer (2000), pages 68, 259, 404

170) Nurse "J.D.", from San Angelo, Texas:

a. Page 69 of Abigail ("Dear Abby") Van Buren's 1993 book entitled *"Where were you when President Kennedy was Shot?"* [all writers were shielded with anonymity via initials]---"When Kennedy was shot, I was at Parkland---a student nurse. I heard all the department chiefs being paged. I saw all the press buses arriving; watched the E.R. grow crowded; saw Jackie in her bloodstained pink suit. Thirty years later, I find it hard to believe I was there.";

171) Mrs. Anne Ferguson, switchboard operator:

a. *"The Death of a President"*, pages 162 and 670: report of activities, 11/22/63 [not in the WC Volumes];

172) Dr. Jack Reynolds, Administrator:

a. 11/29/63 FBI report re: Connally x-rays [see pages 505-506 of *"Post Mortem"*];

b. 11/9/77 interview with the HSCA (7 HSCA 159-162; 319-321)---radiologist who conducted the x-raying of the wounds of Governor Connally: submitted 9 Reports of Diagnostic X-ray Consultation pertaining to the examination of these x-rays, 11/22-12/4/63;

173) Lawrence F. "Larry" O'Brien, Special Assistant to the President[deceased 1990]

(rode in Congressman's car #1 in the motorcade; also at Bethesda Naval Hospital, but on the 17th floor with Jackie and RFK):

a. WC references: WR 59; 7 H 446, 452-455, 475;

b. 7 H 457-472 / testimony;

c. 5/4/64 and 6/4/64 interviews with William Manchester ("*The Death of a President*", many);

d. "*The Day Kennedy Was Shot*" by Jim Bishop (many);

e. His book entitled "*No Final Victories: A Life in Politics from John F. Kennedy to Watergate*" (1974) [see also "*Reflections on JFK's Assassination*" by John B. Jovich (1988), pages 35 and 37]: At Parkland Hospital: "It was chaotic, doctors, nurses running in and out. Medical equipment being wheeled into the room. *At one point Jackie and I stepped into the adjoining room where the President's body lay. All I recall is I thought he looked as he always had.*" (emphasis added); from AAFB to Bethesda: rode in the car directly behind the grey Navy ambulance (fellow passengers: O'Donnell and Powers) and in front of O'Neill's car, which was two cars behind the ambulance;

f. 7 HSCA 32: regarding missing autopsy materials;

g. Interviewed for Ralph Martin's "*A Hero For Our Time*" (1983);

h. JFK Library Oral History, 1985, 1987 (conducted by the LBJ Library);

i. Numerous TV programs, including "*JFK: A Time Remembered*" and "*JFK: The Day The Nation Cried*", both from 1988;

j. deceased 1990;

174) Dr. Doyle Rogers, an intern:

a. 5/29/91 interview with Harry Livingstone ("*High Treason 2*", p. 54): "an intern and was present at Parkland Hospital when President Kennedy was brought there. He then entered the Navy to do his residency, and came to know some of the autopsy doctors. Rogers knew Jack Ruby... rather well."; believed that JFK had Pott's disease;

175) Dr. Harlan Pollock, anesthesiology resident:

a. January 1964 Texas State Journal of Medicine article "*Three Patients at Parkland*",

p. 73: "The [Oswald] operating team consisted of Drs. Shires, McClelland, Perry, and Jones. The anesthesia team consisted of Drs. Akin, Jenkins, and Dr. Harlan Pollock, resident on anesthesiology.";

II

DALLAS, PARKLAND, AND BETHESDA

176) Secret Service Agent William R. Greer [deceased 2/85]
(the driver of the presidential limousine)[and CE 399]:

a. 18 H 723: report of activities on 11/22/63---nothing about wounds to JFK specifically;

b. FBI (Sibert & O'Neill) interview of Greer, 11/22/63 (RIF#124-10012-10239);

c. RIF#180-10090-10263: 11/23/63 PRS document, Greer to SAIC Robert Bouck, re: inventory of JFK's clothing---no mention of a t-shirt [2 H 125: "there was no undershirt"] or Seymour Hersh's extravagant back brace, either: just "sacro-iliac bandages" [2 H 125: "a corset-type brace, maybe 6 inches wide, he wore it around his, down low around his, haunches, a little lower than the waist, probably, just probably below his belt he wore it there."]!;

d. FBI (Sibert & O'Neill) interview of Greer, 11/27/63 (RIF#180-10004-10466)---"GREER recalls helping take the President's stretcher into the emergency operating room. It is his recollection that the President was breathing when removed from the vehicle and transported into this room."; the agents record his complete physical description for the record!;

e. 2 H 124 and 127/ testimony (3/9/64)---"His head was all shot, this whole part was all a matter of blood like he had been hit." Specter: "Indicating the top and right rear side of the head?" Greer: "Yes, sir; it looked like that was all blown off."; "...they [the autopsy doctors]saw this hole in the right shoulder or back of the head, and in the back...this wound was in the back...they took a lot of X-rays, we looked at them and couldn't find any trace of any bullet anywhere in the X-rays at all, nothing showed on the X-rays where this bullet or lead could have gone...in the soft part of the shoulder...I believe the doctors probed to see if they could find that there was a bullet there...I questioned one of the doctors in there about that, and when we found out that they had found a bullet in Dallas, I questioned the doctor about it and he said if they were using pressure on the chest that it could very well have been, come back out, where it went in at, that is what they said at the time...I hadn't heard anything like that, any traces of it going on through" [see below];

f.   3/12/64 memo, Specter to Rankin re: interview of FBI agents' Sibert & O'Neill (regarding Greer and Kellerman) [see *"Post Mortem"*, pp. 537-538]---the FBI men were certain that Greer DID state that he turned around and saw JFK hit, something Greer would go on to deny;

g.   other WC references: WR 2,4,45,49-50,53; 2 H 62, 68, 74-76, 78, 86, 92, 94, 97, 99, 104, 141; 3 H 220; 4 H 130, 133-134; 5 H 67; 7 H 473; 17 H 607, 614, 615; 18 H 678, 722, 724-727, 728-729, 731, 733, 739, 740, 742, 744-745, 757, 762, 810-811, 814, and 815: "ASAIC Kellerman and SA Greer assumed responsibility for President Kennedy's personal effects and the photographic records made of the autopsy.";

h.   11/19/64 interview with William Manchester (*"The Death of a President"*, numerous, including pages 304, 307, and 671 [see also RIF#180-10116-10119 for Manchester's complete transcript])---Greer returned to the trauma room first, then Dr. Burkley;

i.   interviewed by Jim Bishop (*"The Day Kennedy Was Shot"*, p. 684);

j.   11/20/67 and 1/18/71 interviews with David Lifton (*"Best Evidence"*, pages 401 and 448): JFK's head "looked like a hard boiled egg with the top chopped off."

k.   1970 interview with Walt Brown (*"Treachery in Dallas"*, pp. 50-51): "I...ask[ed] if he could have slowed the vehicle either in the act of looking back or because his perception of the threat was from the front. He told me that he had asked himself that same question many times, and he had no answer for me. He did not deny the possibility.";

l.   2 telephonic interviews conducted by Fred Newcomb and Perry Adams for *"Murder from Within"* (1974 [letter from Fred Newcomb to Palamara 1/21/92]): the authors believed he fired the fatal head shot; page 139: "...my back was covered with it [debris from JFK's head]."

m.   TWO:RIF#180-10099-10491: 2/28/78 HSCA interview---"When the doctors pronounced President Kennedy dead Greer was handed the President's clothing, wallet and WATCH, which he took back to Washington...A few days later he returned Kennedy's WATCH and wallet to Ken O'Donnell (emphasis added)": contradicted by the accounts of O.P. Wright (21 H 230), Nurse Diana Bowron (21 H 203-204), and Inspector Thomas Kelley of the Secret Service (12/10/63 report to Chief Rowley and PRS)---JFK's watch, recently a news item in and of itself, was given to Dallas Secret Service agent Roger C. Warner [misspelled "Warren"] on 11/26/63 (21 H 230)!; "He was puzzled about the single bullet (399) theory. He could not see how one bullet could have caused both Kennedy and Connally such extensive wounds."; "Greer recalls Kellerman going to a telephone and talking to someone about a bullet found in Dallas. The doctors turned Kennedy over and found the bullet hole in his shoulder. He indicated a point on his right shoulder, which approximated the spot. He said one of the doctors inserted a metal probe in Kennedy's back, which only went in a short way. Greer says he asked the doctor if the bullet in [the] back could have worked itself out during heart message. The doctors continued to take x-rays, looking for lead, but they couldn't find where the bullet went.";

Interlude re: CE 399

1)CE2011-O.P. Wright, **Darrell C. "D.C."** **Tomlinson**, Chief James J. Rowley, and **SA Richard E Johnsen** could NOT identify CE399 as the bullet they all allegedly handled on 11/22/63("over-the-counter" references: *"JFK-Conspiracy of Silence"*, p. 133; *"Crossfire"*, p. 365; *"Reasonable Doubt"*, p. 70; *"The People Vs. Lee Harvey Oswald"* by Walt Brown, p. 623 [*for Tomlinson*: 6 H 128-134 / testimony; on video, see Part 2 of *"CBS News Inquiry: The Warren Report"*, 6/26/67, and *"Nova"*, 11/15/88; *"Triangle of Fire"* by Bob Goodman (1993), p. 111---based on what someone who had interviewed Tomlinson had told Goodman, Tomlinson allegedly described the head wound in this fashion: "the whole right, top half of his head was gone."-this statement is also quoted in *"JFK Absolute Proof"* by Robert Groden (2013), page 154; Tomlinson: unanswered letter from Vince Palamara 1998]; *"Murder in Dealey Plaza"* by James Fetzer (2000), pages 88, 93);

2)24H412-Although two FBI agents(Todd and Frazier) initialed the bullet they received from the Secret Service, Johnsen and Rowley did NOT, breaking the legal chain of custody;

3)CD7-Although the bullet was "officially" found on a stretcher in a corridor of Parkland Hospital, the FBI(Sibert and O'Neil) reported that it was found in the emergency room!;

4a)Sibert and O'Neil interview of SAIC Jerry Behn, 11/27/63-the same FBI agents bypassed Johnsen and spoke instead to Behn(not even IN Dallas) about "the location of a bullet which had been found on a stretcher at Parkland";

4b) RIF#180-10104-10481:HSCA interview of SAIC Behn- Incredibly, Behn "stated that he was in the chain of custody of CE 399... Behn received the bullet from Johnsen, then turned it over to the FBI" [WHAT ABOUT ROWLEY?];

5)Price Exhibits, Warren Commission Volume XXI-O.P. Wright, the man who allegedly gave the bullet to Johnsen at Parkland, does not even MENTION this very important find at all in his report(?!);

6)Darrel Tomlinson, O.P. Wright, Nathan Pool-all described a DIFFERENT bullet than CE399(pointed, hunting-type)["Six Seconds in Dallas"; "High Treason", p. 102; HSCA document-interview with Nathan Pool, 1/10/77; etc.].According to research done by Josiah Thompson, the bullet was found on a stretcher used by a young boy named Ronny Fuller![see also 21 H 156];

7)LBJ Library document-Memorandum to File-According to Chief James J. Rowley, CE399 "was found amongst the clothes on one of the stretchers". If that wasn't enough, Governor Connally stated in his autobiography called "In History's Shadow", "But the most curious discovery of all took place when they rolled me off the stretcher, and onto the examining table. A metal object fell onto the floor, with a click no louder than a wedding band. The nurse picked it up and slipped it into her pocket. It was the BULLET FROM MY BODY, the one that passed through my back, chest, and wrist, and worked itself loose from my thigh"(emphasis added-p. 18;"The Investigator" Feb-May 1994). Corroborating Connally's memory, from the 11/21/93 Dallas Morning News interview with Henry Wade:" I also went out to see Connally, but he was in the operating room (note the time frame).Some nurse had a bullet in her hand, and said this was on the gurney that Connally was on...I told her to give it to the police, which she said she would. I assume that's the pristine bullet"("The Investigator" Feb-May 1994). [Both John and Nellie Connally did not believe that the same bullet which hit JFK hit the Governor. Also, they never accounted for a missed shot in their three-shot scenario. Finally, they saw JFK's brain matter allover the car and on both of themselves. See 4 H 136,147-149, and 20 H 355, as well as the many sources cited on pages 85-87 of "Who's Who in the JFK Assassination"]. Finally, Gary Shaw (in the 11/22/93 "Dateline: Dallas" issue) came across this passage from the Warren Commission testimony of Parkland nurse Jeanette Standridge:

> Specter: "Did you notice any object in Governor Connally's clothing?"
> Standridge: "Not unusual"
> Specter:" Did you notice a bullet, specifically?"
> Standridge: "No"
> Specter:" Did you hear the sound of anything fall?"
> Standridge: "I didn't"

Is THIS "CE399"? What's going on here?

8)Bill Greer-Although it is an "official" fact that Agent Richard Johnsen gained possession of CE399(a.k.a. "the magic bullet", linked to Oswald's gun) via O.P. Wright (who obtained it thru Darrel Tomlinson AND Nathan Pool, who obtained it in the PRESENCE of Secret Service agent[s]) at Parkland Hospital, what has never been widely reported is the fact that Agent Greer maintained VERY close proximity to Johnsen and the bullet in question(18H799-800):

a)BOTH agents guarded the emergency room(Trauma Room 1)-Greer inside, Johnsen outside(2H126; 18H798);

b)IF the FBI's report is accurate(see # 3[CD7] above), Greer was the ONLY agent stationed inside the emergency room with JFK;

c)Johnsen rode with Greer in a car on the way to Air Force One(along with fellow agents David B. Grant, Samuel E. Silliman, Ernest E. Olsson, Jr., and Paul Landis)-and we're supposed to believe that ALL these agents remained silent about the bullet!(18H799; 18H723);

d)Greer rode with Johnsen near the casket in the REAR of Air Force One(-from the point of time starting with the swearing in of LBJ, when the MAJORITY of agents/people were up front[18H799; 2H126))...

When we consider that both Greer AND Kellerman remained silent about this bullet until it was announced by Chief Rowley that night during the autopsy(via a phone call TO Kellerman!), we have to wonder about the implications of this "silence"-in a recently uncovered HSCA document, Roy Kellerman stated that SA Johnsen told him about the bullet while they were still at PARK-LAND(HSCA document, interviews with Kellerman, outside contact report, 8/24-8/25/77)!!!! This early knowledge is troubling because of the following:

Once the autopsy at Bethesda Naval Hospital was underway, Greer "said that a bullet had been found on a stretcher-or rather as it fell from a stretcher- in Parkland Hospital...could this be the bullet that went INTO THE NECK and, in the jostling of the President on the stretcher, FELL OUT?" As author Jim Bishop reported(thru his interview with Greer[and Kellerman])," GREER"s THESIS had a supporter. Roy Kellerman ... said he remembered a Parkland doctor astride the chest of the dead President, applying artificial respiration. Kellerman... thought the bullet in the BACK...might have been squeezed out by manual pressure..."("The Day Kennedy was Shot", page 498,530; see also Tomlinson-2H412; Greer-2H127; Kellerman-2H93)!

Why would they even need Rowley's call to "alert" them to the bullet found at Parkland and given to the FBI(two agents-Sibert and O'Neil-were in attendance with Greer and Kellerman at the autopsy)?Why would Rowley "order" Kellerman to tell the autopsy doctors about something he already knew about? It gets better(or worse, depending on which way you see it)...

9)During an interview conducted on 9/29/92, the author learned that Agent Richard Johnsen DID NOT REMEMBER having possession of CE399!("The Investigator" Dec '93/Jan '94-article by author) Furthermore, Johnsen mentions in his first report that the bullet, quote, "*may*" have originated from Governor Connally's stretcher -obviously, one of the components of the "single bullet theory" is having the bullet on Connally's stretcher; if the bullet was found on JFK's stretcher(or **Ronny Fuller's**, or elsewhere), the theory is in big trouble. Interestingly, Johnsen retired in 1979, having never been questioned by the FBI, the Warren Commission, or the HSCA, and when I tried, I received very cantankerous responses(it was the day after contacting Johnsen that I received the infamous call from the Executive Secretary of the Former Agents of the Secret Service, "Percy" Hamilton Brown, telling me very angrily to "cease and desist from contacting any more of my associates...I gave you no authority to do so". As former agent Bob Lilly told me, "Who died and made him boss?!" Sam Kinney told me, "Hey, it's a free country!").As for Johnsen's 'second' report, a sort of mini-report enclosed with his first report having to do with the acquisition of CE399, it is UNSIGNED. (18H799-800;this report actually exists separately, as new documents uncovered from the LBJ Library reveal, although the same report as reproduced in the Warren Commission Volumes gives the impression it is part of the same[first] report, due to its juxtaposition on TOP of the first report).There may be more to Johnsen's present "amnesia" over this evidence than meets the eye...

10)CBS' Eddie Barker[whose son is a Secret Service agent!]interview of O.P. Wright

("*Postmortem*", p. 46)-"...I got hold of a Secret Service man and THEY [sic?] didn't seem to be interested in coming and looking at the bullet in the position it was in then. So I went back to the area where Mr. Tomlinson was and picked up the bullet and put it in my pocket, and I carried it some 30 or 40 minutes. And I gave it to a Secret Service man that was guarding the main door into the emergency room..."Who was the first agent Wright spoke to? And was his use of the word "they" a mistake? NO...

HSCA attorney Belford V. Lawson*, in charge of the Secret Service area of the "investigation", is the author of a recently uncovered memo in regard to an interview with **Nathan Pool** conducted on 1/10/77 and headlined "POOL's CO-DISCOVERY OF THE 'TOMLINSON' BULLET". In the memo, Pool mentions the fact that TWO Secret Service agents were by the elevator, one of which " remained there throughout most or all of Pool's stay". Before we can catch our breath, a THIRD Secret Service agent enters the picture; although all these men were in the immediate vicinity of the discovery of the bullet, one particular agent "was within 10 feet when Pool recognized the bullet". According to Pool, the bullet was pointed, and he added that it "didn't look like it had hit anything and didn't look like it had been in anything".

Lawson felt that further development of Pool's testimony may reveal the following:

QUOTE:" A SECRET SERVICE AGENT WAS FOR A SIGNIFICANT PERIOD OF TIME CLOSE ENOUGH TO THE ELEVATOR TO PLANT A BULLET; MAY LEAD TO AN IDENTIFICATION OF THAT AGENT...";

[re: Nathan Burgess Pool-RIF#180-10097-10261/ 7/12/78 (audio-taped) testimony before the HSCA---"...we [Pool and Tomlinson] were just standing there talking and one of us leaned up against the thing and kind of pushed it up against the wall, you know, and this bullet fell out...when it hit the wall the projectile fell of there, or the bullet..."; Question: "And was the Secret Service agent present at all times?" "He was right there by the door...Between those swinging doors...right in that area."; re: the bullet: "It looked like any G.I. issue bullet to me. It was a fairly long projectile...in pretty good condition. It wasn't beat up or anything...Didn't look like it had hit bone or anything like that...It was jacketed."; Question: "After the bullet was found and Tomlinson obtained possession of it, what did he do with it that you observed? What did you observe?" "He took it over and gave it to the guy over by the door...[the Secret Service agent] took it through the door and gave it to someone else, I assume. I don't know...I don't think there was ever a time that there wasn't a Secret Service man by that door."; re: JFK: "But that's the first time I had any idea he was dead was when they rolled him out of there because they had him covered with a-" "With a sheet?" "*No; with a purple cover.*" [emphasis added]; Question: "Did the Secret Service agents stay there after Kennedy left?" "Yes." "Was the Secret Service agent there when you left?" "I'm not sure the same one stayed there, though, but there was a Secret

Service agent there.";

[Pool: unanswered letter from Vince Palamara 1998]

ALSO: the HSCA reinterviewed Greer via an outside contact report on 12/4/78 re: "constant vigilance" over the body by the Secret Service (HSCA Record Number 1211021 [see "Best Evidence", p. 593 and "JFK: An Unsolved Murder", KRON, 11/18/88]): Greer said he was "always with the body" and that there were "no alterations at Parkland or in transit";

End of interlude

* * *

n. researcher Robert Milner, a former police officer, started a "very good" friendship with Greer in 1978; it lasted until Greer's death in 1985. Recently, Greer's second wife Mary gave Robert Bill's handwritten manuscript, presumably at least one of three Greer himself said were "salted away in the attic" during his 1978 HSCA interview. Milner will not presently reveal the specific contents of the 14-page manuscript except to say that there are no major revelations (a letter from Palamara sent to Mary Greer in March 1998, independent of Milner's statements [and also regarding these three books], went unanswered).[Milner: e-mails to Palamara, 1998];

o. "The Asheville (NC) Citizen-Times", 11/6/83 interview of Greer (see "High Treason 2", p. 572 [Palamara provided this to the author])- "I stayed with (JFK) through the examination and then through the autopsy, and was with him when they put his body in the coffin and took him to Air Force One.";

p. 2/28/85 "Washington Post"---obituary [see photos of Greer in "Six Seconds in Dallas" by Josiah Thompson (pictured with Kellerman and Hill) and the 3/17/92 tabloid "Globe" (the aforementioned Thompson picture is included but is cropped to eliminate Hill)];

q. 5/90 NBC program "Inside Report" with Fred Newcomb and Perry Adams--- focus on Greer, albeit in the "role" of alleged assassin (!);

r. 9/17/91, 10/7/91, and 9/23/92 interviews of Richard Greer, Bill's only son/ child, conducted by Vince Palamara---several interesting comments, including the absolute conviction that Bill Greer drove JFK's body out of Parkland, despite the documentation that Andy Berger was the driver of the hearse (of the casket, at least!);

s. "Murder In Dealey Plaza" by James Fetzer (2000), pages x, 26, 33, 38-39, 42, 46, 63, 105, 106, 122, 126, 128, 138, 155, 159, 160, 162, 166, 172-173, 199, 245, 352, 354

t. "JFK Absolute Proof" by Robert Groden (2013): see page 154- Greer is pictured with a nice summary of his statements

177) Secret Service Roy H. Kellerman (rode in the front seat w/ Greer) [deceased 3/84]:

a. FBI report (Sibert & O'Neill) 11/22/63 (RIF#124-10012-10239): interview with Kellerman (and Greer)---"He stated that the advanced security arrangements made for this specific trip were the most stringent and thorough ever employed by the Secret Service for the visit of a President to an American city [?!---he later denied this to Chief Rowley: 18 H 707-708]...He advised he heard a shot and immediately turned around, looking past Governor Connally...to the President. He observed the President slump forward and heard him say, "Get me to a hospital." [5 days later, later changed to "My God, I've been hit"! Kellerman would go on to dispute the actual statement he made: see 2 H 92-93. Either way, impossible]";

b. FBI Report (Sibert & O'Neill) 11/27/63 (RIF#180-10004-10466): interview with Kellerman (and Greer)---"Upon hearing a noise like a firecracker, he distinctly and positively heard the President say "My God, I've been hit."[?!---see also 2 H 104] Kellerman advised he immediately turned his head to the left rear and almost instantaneously heard two additional shots. Upon turning his head to the left, he observed President Kennedy with his left hand in back of him appearing to be reaching to a point on his right shoulder [?!]...The Presidential vehicle arrived at the Parkland Hospital in a matter of minutes...Kellerman advised he did not notice the extent of the injury to the President although HE NOTICED A WOUND IN THE BACK OF HIS HEAD [emphasis added]. The President's eyes were shut [contradicted by Powers].";

c. 18 H 724-727: Kellerman's report dated 11/29/63---"Immediately, I heard what I firmly believe was the President's voice, "My God, I'm hit!"...I accompanied the President to the emergency room. His eyes were closed BUT I COULD SEE NO VISIBLE DAMAGE TO HIS FACE [emphasis added]... [at Bethesda]I remained in the morgue and viewed the autopsy examinations...SA O'Leary was also in the morgue briefly...after the completion of the autopsy and before the embalming I summoned SA [Clint] Hill down to the morgue to view the body and to witness the damage of the gunshot wounds...Prior to our departure from the Naval Hospital I received all film, x-rays, that were used during this autopsy, and upon arrival at the White House I turned them over to SAIC Bouck.";

d. 18 H 728-729: Kellerman's report dated 11/30/63---"SA's Greer and O'Leary and myself accompanied the body to the morgue. SA O'Leary remained in the morgue only briefly.";

e. 2 H 73-74, 78-82, 85, 90-91, 93/testimony (3/9/64) [2 H 61-112]---the first shot was "...a report like a firecracker, pop. And I turned my head to the right because whatever this noise was I was SURE that it came from the right and PERHAPS into the rear, and as I turned my head to the right to view whatever it was or see whatever it was, I heard a voice from the back seat and I firmly believe it was the President's, "My God, I am hit," and I turned around and he has got his hands up her like this [indicating]...There was enough for me to verify that the man was hit...a flurry of shells come into the car (emphasis added)."; "...there have got to be more than three shots, gentlemen."; "I did not see any wounds in that man's face."; "He had a large wound this size" Specter: "Indicating a circle with your finger of the diameter of 5 inches; would that be approximately correct?" "Yes, circular; yes, on this part of the head." Specter: "Indicating the rear portion of the head." "Yes." Specter: "More to the right side of the head?" "Right. This was removed." ; "...I saw nothing in his face to indicate an injury, whether the shot had come through or not. He was clear."; "When this car was checked over that night for its return to Washington, I was informed the following day of the pieces of these missiles that were found in the front seat, and I believe aside from the skull, that was in the rear seat, I couldn't conceive even from elevation how this shot hit President Kennedy like it did. I wanted to view this vehicle, whether this was a slant blow off the car, whether it hit the car first and then hit him, or what other marks are on this vehicle, and that is what prompted me to go around and check it over myself."; (2 H 90) re: ASAIC Boring and the bullet fragments found in the limo; (2 H 91) "There was in the early---this was on the day [11/22/63] in Parkland Memorial Hospital, and this information comes from Dr. George Burkley...I asked him the condition of Governor Connally, and have they removed the bullet from him ... Dr. Burkley said that to his knowledge he still has the bullet in him...This was after we got into the hospital after the shooting, sir, between then and 2 o'clock." [Dr. Robert R. Shaw Press Conference (Connally's surgeon), 7:00 CST 11/22/63 on WFAA/ ABC (see also "*Treachery In Dallas*" by Walt Brown, p. 158: video snippet provided to author]:

"The bullet is in the leg...it hasn't been removed...it will be removed before he goes to the recovery room"(?!)- what about CE399(the stretcher bullet) that entered the record around FIVE hours earlier?]; "Gentlemen, I think if you would view the films [of the assassination] yourself you may come up with a little different answer."; "A Colonel Finck---during the examination of the President, from the hole that was in the shoulder, and with a probe, and we were standing right alongside of him, he is probing inside the shoulder with his instrument and I said, "Colonel, where did it go?" He said, "There are no lanes for an outlet of this entry in this man's shoulder"..."I said, "Colonel, would it have been possible that while he was on the stretcher in Dallas that it works itself out?" And he said, "Yes."";

f. 3/12/64 memo, Specter to Rankin re: interview of FBI agents' Sibert & O'Neill (regarding Greer and Kellerman) [see "*Post Mortem*", pp. 537-538]---O'Neill is certain that Kellerman DID state that he heard JFK say "Get me to a hospital";

g. 18 H 678: 4/29/64 report re: the drinking incident;

h. other WC references: WR 2-4, 29, 45-46, 49-50, 52-53, 57, 446, 449, 452; 2 H 45, 115, 117, 119, 121, 127, 131-133, 135, 137, 141-143, 146, 153; 4 H 130-131, 133-134, 320-321, 325, 331, 342, 346-347, 349, 351; 5 H 67, 180-181; 7 H 473; 17 H 607, 614, 615, 618, 630, 631, 632; 18 H 707-708, 722, 723, 733, 735-736, 738, 739, 740, 742-745, 746, 749, 756-757, 764, 765, 769-770, 774, 779, 795-796, 798, 810-815;

i. 11/17/64 and 5/12/65 interviews with William Manchester ("*The Death of a President*", many, included p. 160n: "Greer then looked in the back of the car. Maybe he didn't believe me." (!);

j. interviewed (?) for Jim Bishop's "*The Day Kennedy was Shot*";

k. Mentioned twice during the testimony of Dr. Pierre Finck during Garrison trial (see "*Destiny Betrayed: JFK, Cuba, and the Garrison Case*" by Jim DiEugenio, pages 295 and 300);

l. 2 telephonic interviews conducted by Fred Newcomb and Perry Adams for "*Murder from Within*" (1974 [letter from Fred Newcomb to Palamara 1/21/92]);

m. 1974 interview with Walt Brown ("*Treachery In Dallas*", p. 48;

n. 1976 interview for CFTR radio (Canada) program entitled "*Thou Shalt Not Kill*" (Newcomb and Adams were principally involved in this production)---laughs, denying that they (Greer and himself) did any of the shooting; says that they will be discussing the assassination 100 years from now;

o. 8/24 and 8/25/77 interviews with the HSCA's Jim Kelly and Andy Purdy [see also "*Killing Kennedy*" by H.E.L., p. 347]--- bullet fragment- large piece behind eye; at Parkland- face unmarked;

    FBI agent[sic] Johnsen;

    Johnsen told Kellerman at PARKLAND about bullet!- told Finck about this at autopsy (early knowledge; what about Greer, etc.?);

    While at Bethesda- received a call from BORING about TWO pieces of skull found in the car, but only remembers ONE skull fragment being examined at Bethesda!;

    "One large hole in the head and no small holes in the head"- contradicted by his OWN drawing showing a large and a small hole*** on the BACK of the head!; did NOT count film holders or x-rays and said FBI agents DIDN'T handle these items- next day: contradicts himself-" everyone counted them... I think I even counted them... I would think so.";

    "Wouldn't comment on the amended version of the receipt"(!);

    [***None of the Parkland Hospital doctors *questioned by the Warren Commission*--nor any of the nurses--- saw the small "entry" hole allegedly on the rear of the skull: 3 H 361 (Carrico); 3 H 372 and 6 H 16 (Perry); 6 H 25 (Clark); 6 H 35 (McClelland); 6 H 71 (Peters); 6 H 136 (Bowron); 6 H 141 (Henchcliffe)];

p. 12/1/78 reinterview by the HSCA's Mark Flanagan via an Outside contact report re: "constant vigilance" over the body by the Secret Service (RIF#180-10104-10248 [see "*Best Evidence*", p. 593 and "*JFK: An Unsolved Murder*", KRON, 11/18/88])---'said that no one had the chance to alter or did alter the body in transit from Dallas.";

q. 1970's contact with one of Kellerman's daughters[1 of 2] by Harold Weisberg (letter to author from 3/92---"she hopes the day would come when these men (Kellerman and Greer) could say in public what they told their families.";

r. 3/2/92 and 9/27/92 interviews with Roy's widow June Kellerman (see also the Dec. 1994 issue of "Vanity Fair" magazine-article by Anthony and Robbyn Summers, p. 88: info. provided to authors)---Roy accepted that there was a conspiracy;

s. 12/2/97 letter to Vince Palamara from June Kellerman ("KAC", Spring 1998 issue, p. 18)---"Roy did not say that JFK was difficult to protect.";

t.   *"Murder In Dealey Plaza"* by James Fetzer (2000), pages x, 26, 38-40, 59, 62-63, 67, 70, 83, 96, 123, 128, 136-138, 159, 160, 162-163, 169, 172-173, 199, 204, 244-245, 255, 275, 417

u.   *"JFK Absolute Proof"* by Robert Groden (2013): see page 154- Kellerman is pictured with a nice summary of his statements

178) Secret Service Agent Clinton J. Hill:

a.   18 H 740-745: 11/30/63 report of activities on 11/22/63---"...I heard a noise similar to a firecracker. The sound came from my right rear...I heard a second firecracker type noise but it had a different sound---like the sound of shooting a revolver into something hard. I saw the President slump more toward his left. I jumped onto the left rear step of the Presidential automobile. Mrs. Kennedy shouted, "They've shot his head off;" then turned and raised out of her seat as if she were reaching to her right rear toward the back of the car for something that had blown out... As I lay over the top of the back seat I noticed a portion of the President's head on the right rear side was missing and he was bleeding profusely. Part of his brain was gone. I saw a part of his skull with hair on it lying in the seat."; "At approximately 2:45 a.m., November 23, I was requested by ASAIC Kellerman to come to the morgue to once again view the body. When I arrived the autopsy had been completed and ASAIC Kellerman, SA Greer, General McHugh and I viewed the wounds. I observed a wound about six inches down from the neckline on the back just to the right of the spinal column. I observed another wound on the right rear portion of the skull.";

b.   2 H 138-144 /testimony (3/9/64)---"...the second noise that I heard had removed a portion of the President's head, and he slumped noticeably to his left. Mrs. Kennedy had jumped up from the seat and was, it appeared to me, reaching for something coming off the right rear bumper of the car, the right rear tail, when she noticed that I trying to climb on the car..." Specter: "Was there anything back there that you observed, that she might have been reaching for?" "I thought I saw something come off the back, too, but I cannot say that there was. I do know that the next day we found the portion [singular] of the President's head." Specter: "Where did you find that portion of the President's head?" "It was found in the street. It was turned in, I believe, by a medical student or somebody in Dallas [THE HARPER FRAGMENT!]."; "The right rear portion of his head was missing. It was lying in the rear seat of the car [this has to be separate from the aforementioned Harper fragment]. His brain was exposed. There was blood and bits of brain all over the entire rear portion of the car...one large gaping wound in the right rear portion of the head."; "...I remained with Mrs. Kennedy except for one time when I was requested to come to the morgue to view the President's body." Boggs: "...had you seen the whole body, or just the BACK of the president's head?" (emphasis added) "I had seen the whole body..."; :"I saw an opening in the back, about 6 inches below the neckline to the right-hand side of the spinal column."; re: the origins of the second shot: "It was right, but I cannot say for sure that it was rear...it had a different sound, first of all, than the first sound that I heard. The second one had almost a double sound---as though you were standing against something metal and firing into it, and you hear both the sound of a gun going off and the sound of the cartridge hitting the metal place...";

c. 18 H 685: undated report re: the drinking incident---a participant;

d. 18 H 809: undated report re: agents-on-the-limo---

"I...never personally was requested by President John F. Kennedy not to ride on the rear of the Presidential automobile. I did receive information passed verbally from the administrative offices of the White House Detail of the Secret Service to Agents assigned to that Detail that President Kennedy had made such requests. I do not know from whom I received this information...No written instructions regarding this were ever distributed...(I) received this information after the Presidents return to Washington, D. C. This would have been between November 19,1963 and November 21, 1963. I do not know specifically who advised me of this request by the President (emphasis added)."

William Manchester, in his book "The Death of a President", quotes Mr. Boring as hearing JFK tell him on 11/18/63 to "keep those Ivy League Charlatans off the back of the car" (Page 37). However, Mr. Boring was not interviewed for the book, and Mr. Boring told the author he disputes the Manchester book (interviews of 9/22/93 , 3/4/94, and letter of 11/22/97). We may never know Mr. Manchester's source for this curious statement - he told the author on 8/23/93 that "all that material is under seal and won't be released in my lifetime" - he denied the author access to his notes.

Boring told the author, in reference to JFK's alleged "desires" mentioned by Mr. Bishop, Manchester and himself in his own report: "He actually - No, I told them...He didn't tell them anything...He just - I looked at the back and I seen these fellows were hanging on the limousine - I told them to return to the car...(JFK) was a very easy-going guy...he didn't interfere with our actions at all" (emphasis added)! The author reiterated the point - Mr. Boring was still adamant that JFK never issued any orders to the agents; he even refuted Mr. Manchester's book.;

e. other WC references: WR 3-4, 48, 50-51, 53, 57, 112, 453; 2 H 62, 68, 74, 76, 79-80, 82, 97, 99, 104, 127; 4 H 349, 353; 5 H 180, 452-453, 470; 7 H 449-450, 494; 15 H 699-700; 17 H 595, 597, 607, 614, 615, 630, 632; 18 H 679, 722, 724-727, 728-729, 731, 732, 733-734, 738, 739, 746, 752-753, 755-757, 758-759, 763, 765, 768, 778, 783, 791, 796, 810-812, 814-815; 21 H 161, 242;

f. 12/3/63 newsreel re: Hill's Treasury Dept. Award ceremony (depicted in both "Inside The Secret Service" [1995, Discovery] and "The Secret Service" [1995, History Channel];

g. Original copy of award announcement sent to Richard Trask by Clinton J. Hill, 1964 ("Pictures of the Pain", pages 72 and 149);

h. 11/18/64 and 5/20/65 interviews with William Manchester ("The Death of a President", many);

i. 12/8/75 interview with Mike Wallace on "60 Minutes" (excerpts rebroadcast in Sept. 1990 and twice in Nov. 1993)---Jackie reached for a piece of the President's head that had fallen into the street; much guilt over the assassination; took early retirement and sought psychological help [the entire program presently is only available in audio format];

j.   HSCA?---they had his address and number (redacted in released list);

k.   "60 minutes" 25 year anniversary special 11/93---Hill, then (12/8/75) and now (11/93): in 1990, he and his wife made a pilgrimage back to Dallas. He believed he had done the best that he could---he found "emotional relief" [what they don't tell you is that there was a secret service reunion in Texas in 1990 and it was the former agents that got him straightened out, as both Sam Kinney and June Kellerman told me];

l.   "The Secret Service" 1995 History Channel and

m.   "Inside The Secret Service" 1995 Discovery Channel—both are new interviews and very interesting; recounts the skull particle going over the trunk of the limo, among other things;

n.   "Murder In Dealey Plaza" by James Fetzer (2000), pages 21, 26, 29, 37, 39, 44, 48, 52, 59, 61-62, 97, 120, 122, 155, 160, 167-169, 173, 198-199, 353

o.   "J. Edgar Hoover: The Father of the Cold War" by R. Andrew Kiel (2000), page 306

p.   "Inside the U.S. Secret Service" (2004) DVD

q.   Letter/ 'interview' with Vince Palamara 2005

r.   Books co-authored by Lisa Cubin: "The Kennedy Detail" (2010),

s.   "Mrs. Kennedy and Me" (2012), and,

t.   "Five Days in November" (2013) (and numerous media appearances 2010-2013): many references to the right rear of JFK's head as missing;

u.   "JFK Absolute Proof" by Robert Groden (2013): see page 150- Hill is pictured with a nice summary of his statements (see also page 156)

179) Secret Service agent John J. "Muggy" O'Leary (remained at Love Field during the assassination) [deceased 1987]:

a.   ("A Hero For Our Time" by Ralph Martin, pages 4 and 8---O'Leary was Senator Kennedy's chauffeur and a former Senate policeman before joining the Secret Service);

b.   FBI (Sibert & O'Neill) report 11/26/63 [see "Post Mortem", pp. 532-536]---listed as present at autopsy;

c.   25 H 788: report dated 11/30/63---"At the hospital I was present at the autopsy and the official picture taking of the President's body. I eventually departed the hospital about midnight and returned to the White House." Unfortunately, O'Leary was never called to testify and give details about the President's wounds;

d. other WC references: 2 H 99 (Kellerman)---"In the morgue, I should say that Special Agent Greer and myself remained all night, Mr. O'Leary only briefly."; 17 H 614; 18 H 727 (Kellerman's report dated 11/29/63)---"SA O'Leary was also in the morgue briefly."; 18 H 728-729 (Kellerman's report dated 11/30/63)--- "...I was accompanying the body of the late President Kennedy to the US Naval Hospital, Bethesda, Maryland, and would have with me Special Agents Hill, Landis, Greer, and O'Leary... SA's Hill and O'Leary rode in an accompanying vehicle... SA's Greer and O'Leary and myself accompanied the body to the morgue. SA O'Leary remained in the morgue only briefly."; 18 H 815; 22 H 97;

e. 11/10/64 interview with William Manchester ("*The Death of a President*", numerous, included p. 388, 391, 431, 435, 453, 515);

f. appears in a captioned photo (along with Hill, Landis, Boring, and others) in Mary Gallagher's 1969 book "*My Life With Jacqueline Kennedy*";

g. g) "*Murder in Dealey Plaza*" by James Fetzer (2000), page 20

180) Secret Service agent Paul E. Landis, Jr. (rode in follow-up car):

a. 18 H 758-759: report dated 11/27/63---"My reaction at this time was that the shot came from somewhere towards the front...";

b. 18 H 751-757: detailed report dated 11/30/63---"I still was not certain from which direction the second shot came, but my reaction at this time was that the shot came from somewhere towards the front, right-hand side of the road."; "... we arrived at Parkland Hospital. I immediately ran to the left rear side of the President's car, reached over and tried to help Mrs. Kennedy up by taking hold of her shoulders. She did not want to let go of President Kennedy whose head she held in her lap and she was bending over him... [I] followed Mrs. Kennedy into the hospital... I remained outside by the [emergency room] door... I rode in the follow-up car behind the ambulance which departed the hospital at 2:04 p.m.... I witnessed the swearing in of President Johnson... I helped carry the late President Kennedy's coffin from Air Force #1... ASAIC Kellerman, Admiral Burkley, and I rode in the front seat of the ambulance... I only left the 17th floor [of Bethesda Naval Hospital] twice. Once, to find ASAIC Kellerman in the hospital morgue and give him a phone message from Chief Rowley [did he see anything?]. The other time was to find a White House driver [Greer and O'Leary were drivers].";

c. 18 H 687: report re: the drinking incident---he was a participant and he did not depart the "Cellar" until 5:00 a.m.!;

d. other WC references: 2 H 68, 99, 134, 136; 5 H 452-453; 17 H 595, 597, 607, 613, 615; 18 H 679, 722, 724, 727, 728-729, 734, 738, 739, 741, 744, 746, 810, 811, 813, 814, 815;

e. HSCA?---the HSCA had his then-home address and phone number;

f. *"Columbus (Ohio) Dispatch"*, 11/20/88---"During this interview---only his second interview in 25 years---he says, "I've never gone back and read anything on
(the assassination) ... I'm about ready to ... Up until now, I didn't want to rehash
it. It was a very painful time for me." Landis remained with Mrs. Kennedy for six
months after Dallas ...";

g. [unanswered letter from Vince Palamara 1997];

h. *"Murder in Dealey Plaza"* by James Fetzer (2000), pages 26, 167, 168, 343

i. Interviewed for *"The Kennedy Detail"* book and documentary (2010)

181) JFK's Air Force Aid, Major General Godfrey "God" T. McHugh [deceased] (rode in the VIP car w/Clifton):

a. WC references: 2 H 98-99; 7 H 452-453, 469, 472; 18 H 692: confirmation that
McHugh came from Fort Worth, Texas [see reference "k)" below] and 744;

b. "After Action Report/ Summary," Gen. Wehle's Office, Military District of
Washington (MDW), 11/22/63: *attached* Memorandum for the Record dated
11/27/63 [see also Manchester, p. 670; *these documents were later released by the
Gerald Ford Library*]---Lt. Bird: "Immediately after the aircraft landed [at AAFB]
and the truck was moved up to the aircraft, I reported to Brigadier General
McHugh, President Kennedy's Air Force Aide. He then ordered me to have my
men clear the area and also informed me that the Secret Service would remove
the casket from the aircraft. I then instructed my men to descend from the truck
by a ladder on the side. Seeing that the casket was being poorly handled, I had
two (2) men remain in place on the truck. We assisted General McHugh and the
agents until they had the casket out of the aircraft.";

c. 5/6/64 interview with William Manchester (*"The Death of a President"*, many)
[see also p. 672];

d. 11/19/67 and 4/30/78 interviews with David Lifton (*"Best Evidence"*, pp. 399-
401, 413-414, 420-421, 430-432)---"McHugh believed the Warren Report was
correct ..."; "... McHugh volunteered that he had assisted in the photographing
of Kennedy's body... ."I was holding his body several times when they were turning it over and photographing it."; Lifton: "And you saw the wounds in the head
then too?" "Oh, yes; but they started fixing it up very well. You see, again, people keep saying that his face was demolished and all; he was in absolute perfect
shape, except the back of the head, top back of the head, had an explosive bullet
in it and was badly damaged ... and that had blown apart part of his forehead,
which was recuperated and put intact, back in place ... so his face was exactly as
if he had been alive. There was nothing wrong with his face."; "The back of the
head was all smashed in ... His face was not hurt." Lifton: "Where did they get
the bone to put the bone back?" "It was brought back. They found it in the car.";
"Ninety-nine percent the back, the top back of the head ... that's the portion that
had been badly damaged by the bullet ... The portion that is in the back of the
head, when you're lying down in the bathtub, you hit the back of the head.";

e. from CFTR radio interview 1976:

f.   General Godfrey McHugh: on 11/22/63, was asked to sit in a car farther back in the motorcade, rather than "normally, what I would do between the driver and Secret Service agent in charge of trip"- he admitted this was "unusual"; "back of his head blown off"; back wound was LOWER than neck wound.;

g.   5/11/78 interview with the HSCA's Mark Flanagan (RIF#180-10078-10465 [see also 7 HSCA 14])---" Brig. Gen. Godfrey McHugh, then an Air Force military aide to the President, informed the committee that Attorney General Robert F. Kennedy and Kenneth O'Donnell, a presidential aide, frequently telephoned him during the autopsy from the 17th floor suite. (102) McHugh said that on occasions, Kennedy and O'Donnell asked only to speak with him. (103) They inquired about the results, why the autopsy was consuming so much time, and the need for speed and efficiency, while still performing the required examinations. (104) McHugh said he forwarded this information to the pathologists, never stating or implying that the doctors should limit the autopsy in any manner, but merely reminding them to work as efficiently and quickly as possible:(105)"; "Ordinarily McHugh rode in the Presidential limousine in the front seat. This was the first time he was instructed not to ride in the car so that all attention would be focused on the President to accentuate full exposure.";

h.   JFK Library Oral History, 1981 (part of the "White House Staff Reflections on the New Frontier" section);

i.   2/16/81 letter to the editor, "Time" magazine---McHugh stayed with the casket after it was loaded onto Air Force One;

j.   6/21/81 "Boston Globe"---Re: Lifton's book: "absolutely absurd. It's full of lies and false implications.";

k.   interviewed for Ralph Martin's "A Hero For Our Time" (1983): see esp. pp. 519-520 re: "unbelievably heavy" casket he helped lift into Air Force One and JFK's brains sticking to Jackie's hat;

l.   "High Treason 2", pp. 567-569---interesting info. re: McHugh;

m.   "Who's Who in the JFK Assassination" by Michael Benson (1993), p. 268;

n.   Ralph Martin's Seeds of Destruction: Joe Kennedy and His Sons (1995), p. 453 [see also the Spring 1998 issue of "Kennedy Assassination Chronicles"-article by author]: In regard to the preparations for the 11/22/63 Dallas trip, General Godfrey McHugh is quoted as saying: "They'd asked me, for the first time, to please not ride in the President's car, because they want to give him full exposure. These are the exact words they used. Ken O'Donnell and the Secret Service said, 'the politicians here feel it's most important for the President to be given full exposure, to be seen coming and going...[McHugh said he normally rode in the car in which JFK was a passenger] "in the front, next to the driver, and [I] would take notes." ;

o.   "Murder In Dealey Plaza" by James Fetzer (2000), pages 97, 98, 99, 154, 161, 199

p.   "JFK Absolute Proof" by Robert Groden (2013): see page 156- McHugh is pictured with a nice summary of his statements

182) Major General Chester V. "Ted" Clifton, Military Aide to the President [deceased] (rode in the V.I.P. car in the motorcade w/ McHugh):

a. WC references: 5 H 564; 7 H 471;

b. "After Action Report/ Summary," Gen. Wehle's Office, Military District of Washington (MDW), 11/22/63 [see also *"The Death of a President"* by William Manchester, p. 670; *these documents were later released by the Gerald Ford Library*]; "At 1730 hours, Major Rutherford notified Admiral Galloway's office, advising them to provide a security cordon around the heliport at the Bethesda Naval Center, expecting arrival of the remains at approximately 1830 hours, and to turn the lights on just prior to the arrival of the remains. At 1740 hours, Colonel McGovern called and talked with Major Rutherford and stated that General Clifton radioed by phone General Mock at 1730 hours that Pres. Kennedy will be taken directly to Bethesday [sic] Naval Hospital. (2) General Clifton has indicated that as of 1730 today no definitive plans have been made for the funeral."; "...General Clifton realized that the change at the airport fowled up plans a bit, but they were not blaming MDW at all.";

c. appears on NBC film/ video shown entering Parkland Hospital;

d. appears in Cecil Stoughton's photos entering/ on board Air Force One;

e. appears on Air Force One radio transmissions [audio tapes/ transcripts; see also *"Best Evidence"*, pages 681, 686-688](code name "Watchman")---"We do not want a helicopter to go to Bethesda Medical Center. We do want an ambulance and a ground return from Andrews to Walter Reed, and we want the regular post-mortem that has to be done by law under guard performed at Walter Reed. Is that clear?";

f. 4/21/64, 8/21/64, 1/22/65, and 5/28/65 interviews with William Manchester (*"The Death of a President"*, many);

g. Co-authored the 1973 book entitled *"The Memories: JFK, 1961-1963"* w/ Cecil Stoughton and Hugh Sidey (all of whom were in the Dallas motorcade);

h. 7/15/80 interview with David Lifton (*"Best Evidence"*, pp. 688-689)---"To this day I don't know where the authority for the change came [from], because when I was on the phone telling them [we] were going to Walter Reed, that was what I had been told by Johnson or one of his staff."; "There was no decoy [ambulance]";

i. *"Air Force One: The Planes and the Presidents"* video (1981/ 1989);

j. *"America Remembers John F. Kennedy"* 1983;

k. Interviewed for Ralph Martin's *"A Hero For Our Time"* (1983);

l. *"Murder in Dealey Plaza"* by James Fetzer (2000), pages 100, 102, 154, 161

III

BETHESDA NAVAL HOSPITAL

183) Autopsy photographer John Thomas Stringer, Jr.:

a. FBI (Sibert & O'Neill) report 11/26/63 [see "*Post Mortem*", pp. 532-536]: listed as present during autopsy;

b. 11/1/66 inspection of autopsy x-rays and photographs [see "*Post Mortem*", pp. 565-573]---signed by Stringer 11/10/66 (see p. 518, Lifton, below);

c. 8/25/72 and 8/26/72 interviews with David Lifton ("*Best Evidence*", pp. 515-516, 517-518): Lifton: "When you lifted him out, was the main damage to the skull on the top or in the back?" "In the back ... In the occipital, in the neck there, up above the neck ... in the back part ... some of it was blown off---yes, I mean, toward, out of the top in the back, yes." Lifton: "Top in the back. But the top in the front was pretty intact?" "Yes, sure ... Right.";

d. HSCA RIF# 180-10093-10429 (8/12/77 interview with Andy Purdy+8/15/77 viewing of the autopsy photographs at the National Archives) [see also 7 HSCA , "*Bloody Treason*" by Noel Twyman, p. 216 and "*Killing Kennedy*" by H.E.L., pp. 31-35, 42, 44-45, 46-47, 201-202, 240, 242, 243, 267, 271, 336, 337]---"Stringer said it was his recollection that all the photographs he had taken were not present in 1966 ... he thought he had taken some interior photographs of the President's chest ("I believe so") ... Regarding photograph #42, he said the little piece of matter on the lower rear of the head was"... a piece of bone or something."... the photographs of the open head were taken while the head was held up."... Stringer remembers taking 'at least two exposures of the body cavity'"... He also remembers Dr. Burkley discussing the fact that the doctors should not conduct a full autopsy...";

e. 4/29/90, 5/11/90, and 1/20/92 interviews with Livingstone for "*High Treason 2*" (see Chapter 13, pp. 279-281)---[first interview] "... he described a large hole in the very back of the head ... he did not recall any wounds to the face."; "Yes, there was a large hole in the back of the head ... [scalp] was macerated ... the top of the head looked all right ... the top of the head was NOT gone ... it was the back of the head that was gone ... There's no way that the face was gone, because you knew who it was. Looking at him from the front, you'd never know anything was wrong."; [second interview] greatly contradicted himself;

f. "*Vero Beach Press-Journal*", 11/14/93: article by Craig Colgan---As Gary Aguilar has reported, "Craig Colgan reported Stringer's surprise when he heard, and positively identified, his own tape-recorded voice making the above statements to Lifton in 1972. He insisted in the interview with Colgan that he did not recall his ever claiming that the wound was in the rear. [?] The wound he recalled was to the right side of the head [this is the identical about-face Stringer did with Livingstone after the first interview!]. ABC's "*Prime Time Live*" associate producer, Jacqueline Hall-Kallas, sent a film crew to interview Stringer for a 1988 San Francisco KRON-TV interview ["*JFK: An Unsolved Murder*", 11/18/88, with Sylvia Chase, later of "20/20" fame] after Stringer, in a pre-filming interview told Hall-Kallas that the wound was as he described it to Lifton. Colgan reported, "When the camera crew arrived, Stringer's story had changed [another about-face]", said Stanhope Gould, a producer who also is currently at ABC and who conducted the 1988 on-camera interview with Stringer..."we wouldn't have sent a camera crew all the way across the country on our budget if we thought he would reverse himself", Gould said..."(In the telephone pre-interview) he corroborated what he told David Lifton, that the wounds were not as the official version said they were," Hall-Kallas said.";

g. ARRB interview conducted by Douglas Horne, 4/8/96 [see also "*High Treason III*" (1998), pp. 411-412]: JFK's head upon unwrapping the sheets: "It was covered with matted blood. There was a fist-sized hole in the right side of his head above his ear."; "The probe was inserted in the throat wound in the front of the neck."; "The brain was sectioned, like a piece of meat, and the sections showed all of the damage. Each section was laid out on a light box, which provided a white background in the photos, with an autopsy tag or card next to it with the autopsy number on it.";

h. ARRB deposition, 7/16/96 [see also "*High Treason III*" (1998), pp. 408-412]: Question: "Are you able to identify the hole that the doctors identified on the night of the autopsy as being the entrance wound in the skull?" "I think this was a piece of bone, but it was down near there---right about there." "You're referring to what appears to be a piece of matter or something." "Yes." "That is near the hairline?" "Mm-hmm. But it was near there." "And you're certain that that's where the doctors identified the entrance wound as being; is that correct?" "Yeah, yeah, I would think so. That's what I remember." "Do you know what that red spot is that appears to be, in layman's terms, near the cowlick?" "It looks like blood. I would say it was. There was blood all over the place. But I don't think it was anything out of the ordinary. I don't think there was a hole there for the bullet wound. You would have seen the hole." "Well, can you see the hole in any of the photographs that you're looking at?" "I haven't so far, no. But it was down, right about in here." Ordered to not talk to anyone about the autopsy by Captain John Stover; disagreed with Stover's statement that there were only 16 photos taken. Still, Stover ordered him to sign the memorandum from Stover to Kellerman verifying how many photos had been taken. The number of film holders was changed from 11 to 8.; (from 7/31/98 ARRB staff report) "The autopsy photographer, Mr. John Stringer, in painstaking and detailed testimony, explained the photographic procedures he followed at the autopsy and he raised some questions about whether the supplemental brain photographs that he took are those that are now in the National Archives. ";

i.   "*The Washington Post*", 8/2/98: article by George Lardner, Jr.: "John T. Stringer, who said he was the only one to take photos during the autopsy itself, said some of those were missing as well. He said that pictures he took of Kennedy's brain at a supplementary autopsy" were different from the official set that was shown to him. Stringer said he "gave everything" he photographed during the brain examination to Humes who then gave the film to Kennedy's personal physician, the late Adm. George Burkley. According to Humes, Burkley left the hospital with Kennedy's brain, saying that he was going to "deliver it to [Attorney General] Robert Kennedy," presumably for burial.";

j.   "*The Fort Worth Star-Telegram*", 8/2/98: article by Mike Feinsilber, AP---"And in other testimony to the board, photographer John T. Stringer questioned whether the pictures he took at a "supplemental autopsy" of Kennedy's brain are the ones preserved at the National Archives.";

k.   9/2/98 letter to Vince Palamara---"I did observe JFK's wounds and photographed them during the postmortem. As to the actual location and size, I refer you to an article published in the American Medical Association Journal 27 May 1992 entitled "At Large with Dennis Breo: JFK's death-the plain truth from the MD's that did the autopsy. *I agree with the article 100 percent.*" [!]; "William Bruce Pitzer was an ex Chief Hospital Corpsman and had been promoted to Lieutenant Commander in the Medical Service Corps and was assigned to the Television Division of the US Naval Medical School as an administrative assistant. *I knew Bill for many years, he was not a photographer and he was not in the morgue filming during the JFK postmortem examination.*"[emphasis added; in regard to Pitzer, Stringer told Allan Eaglesham the same thing earlier this year];

l.   "*Murder In Dealey Plaza*" by James Fetzer (2000), pages 9, 113, 189, 199, 201-205, 210, 212, 225, 228, 243, 245-246, 286, 301, 303, 305-307, 358, 400, 438, 447

m.   "*JFK Absolute Proof*" by Robert Groden (2013), page 156: Stringer is pictured with a nice summary of his statements

184)-185) FBI Agents James W. Sibert (deceased 4/6/2012) and Francis X. O'Neill, Jr. (deceased 2/3/2009):

a.   FBI (Sibert & O'Neill) report 11/26/63 [see "*Post Mortem*", pp. 532-536]: "... it was also apparent that a tracheotomy had been performed, as well as surgery of the head area, namely, in the top of the skull... During the latter stages of this autopsy, Dr. Humes located an opening which appeared to be a bullet hole which was below the shoulders and two inches to the right of the middle line of the spinal column. This opening was probed by Dr. Humes with the finger, at which time it was determined that the trajectory of the missile entering at this point had entered at a downward position of 45 to 60 degrees. Further probing determined that the distance travelled by this missile was a short distance inasmuch as the end of the opening could be felt with the finger… Also during the latter stages of the autopsy, a piece of the skull measuring 10 x 6.5 centimeters was brought to Dr. Humes who was instructed that this had been removed from the President's skull. Immediately this section of skull was X-Rayed, at which time it was determined by Dr. Humes that one corner of this section revealed minute metal particles and inspection of this same area disclosed a chipping of the top portion of this piece, both of which indicated that this had been the point of exit of the bullet entering the skull region… Dr. Humes stated that the pattern was clear that the one bullet had entered the President's back and had worked its way out of the body during external cardiac massage and that a second high velocity bullet had entered the rear of the skull and had fragmentized prior to exit through the top of the skull. " [see Humes/ Boswell/ Finck, below];;

b.   FBI (Sibert & O'Neill) interview of Greer and Kellerman, 11/22/63 (RIF#124-10012-10239);

c.   FBI (Sibert & O'Neill) interview of Greer, Kellerman, and SAIC Gerald Behn 11/27/63 (RIF#180-10004-10466) [for Behn interview, see "Post Mortem", p. 548];

d.   3/12/64 memo, Specter to Rankin re: interview of FBI agents' Sibert & O'Neill (regarding Greer and Kellerman) [see "Post Mortem", pp. 537-538];

e.   WC references (Sibert& O'Neill): WR 541; 2 H 92-95, 99, 131; 5 H 73; 18 H 727, 729;

f.   Sibert: TWO-HSCA rec. #002191, RIF# 180-10105-10164: interview with James Kelly and Andy Purdy, 8/25/77 [see "Killing Kennedy", pp. 343-344, and "Bloody Treason", page 100, for drawings]—"Regarding the head wound, Sibert said it was in the "…Upper back of the head."; "The head wound was in the upper back of the head…a large head wound in the upper back of the head with a section of the scull [sic] bone missing…"; his drawings depict a large wound squarely on the back of the head, as well as a small wound well down on the back, very much like the one in the autopsy face sheet; Humes and Finck agreed, after probing, that there was no exit wound of the bullet in the back: "concluded it only went so far and they couldn't find it."; "Sibert recalls that much of the piece of the missing bone section came in somewhat later"; 'Sibert said he was present when the bone piece was brought in which had been found in the limousine."; "Sibert said the doctors were discussing the amount of fragmentation of the bullet and the fact that they couldn't find a large piece. They were wondering if it was a kind of bullet, which "fragmentizes" completely."; "remember[ed] Greer say "… if I'de [sic] just been driving a little faster." He said he was driving so slow because the President insisted on it." [!]; ALSO-7 HSCA 19/ Affidavit dated 10/24/78: "As for the anterior neck wound which was described as a tracheotomy incision, I don't recall the neck wound being opened up for examination and nothing was mentioned about it being a possible bullet exit wound."; "Consideration was also given to a type of bullet which fragments completely."; "in the upper back"; Sibert "acknowledged that the statement that head surgery was performed was determined 'not to be correct following detailed inspection'";

g. Sibert:11/2/80 interview with David Lifton (*"Best Evidence"*, pp. 244-246)---would not cooperate;

h. O'Neill: TWO-RIF#180-10090-10044, HSCA rec. #006185: interview with Andy Purdy and Mark Flanagan, 1/10/78 [see *"Killing Kennedy"*, pp. 348-349 for drawings]---while stating that the autopsy doctors believed that "the bullet that entered the head struck the center, low portion of the head and exited from the top, right side, towards the front", his drawings depict an "entry" at the low rear central portion of Kennedy's skull, as well as an "exit" on the right rear quadrant of the head no more anterior than the posterior portion of the ear!; said that Admiral Galloway ordered a complete autopsy; "He does remember the doctors measuring the piece of skull that was found in the limousine and brought to Bethesda during the autopsy. O'Neill stated that in his opinion JFK could have had an open casket."; "O'Neill ended the interview by stating that he is "positive" that the bullet that entered the back came out of the back."; ALSO-Affidavit dated 11/8/78: "I do not see how the bullet that entered below the shoulder in the back could have come out the front of the throat…It was and is my opinion that the bullet entered the back came out the back. There was also no real sense either way that the wounds were caused by the same kind of bullet." Discussed the possibility of a "plastic" or "ice" bullet---one that dissolves after contact.; Admiral Galloway ordered the full autopsy "after checking with the FBI and Secret Service agents in attendance." ;

i. O'Neill: *"The Hartford (CT) Courant"*, 1/1/79: article BY Francis X. O'Neill entitled *"Kennedy Assassination Conclusions Absurd"*---a scathing, angry indictment of the HSCA's conclusions and the notion of conspiracy (in spite of his drawings!). For example, "There was no wound on his body that could conceivably under any condition come from any source other than above and in back of the president" (in spite of his drawings!);

j. O'Neill: 5/5/91, 5/20/91 and 11/20/91 interviews with Livingstone for *"Killing the Truth"*---"It was the whole massive right side of his head. Tremendous.";

k. O'Neill: 1992 video *"Research Vs. Witness: Questioning The Facts"*: interview conducted by George Michael Evica---"There was a massive wound in the right rear of the head [demonstrates this on his head at least four times] …a massive defect in the head…pretty large hole in the back of his head-bigger than an orange. [There was only a] portion of the brain in the cranium…not a total brain. It was a pretty mish-mash of total pulp. I saw them take out what remained in the area there…no cutting [needed]." There was a "beveling in, beveling out", including on a skull fragment delivered to the autopsy room which came "from Dallas". O'Neill added that, after the morticians worked on JFK, "He looked excellent. He looked like he was sleeping. The casket could have been opened...they fixed up the back [of the head] here."; Regarding the "surgery to the head area" statement, O'Neill said: "I don't know what that means. You'll have to ask Dr. Humes. He's the one who said it." In regard to the back wound ("upper back, right…right below the shoulder"), O'Neill said there was "absolutely no point of exit" and that the autopsy doctors were "totally befuddled" by this, until they came up with the idea that the bullet worked its way out via cardiac massage: "they stated, with no equivocation, this is what had happened."; denied that there was a body bag, a shipping casket, and did not know about any decoy ambulances; rode in the second car behind the grey Navy ambulance to Bethesda Naval Hospital with Pamela Turnure, George Thomas, and James Sibert. O'Neill was emphatic that the ambulance "never left my sight"; agreed with Evica that the autopsy should have been done in Texas; does not believe the single bullet theory; This video must be seen in its entirety as there are many interesting comments regarding the autopsy; highly recommended; ALSO: said that Admiral Galloway "ordered a complete and full autopsy", rectifying the situation posed by Admiral Burkley, who made the claim that Jackie said that she only gave permission for a partial autopsy;

l. 11/5/92 interview with Gerald Posner for "*Case Closed*";

m. O'Neill: "*JFK: The Case for Conspiracy*" video 1993 (see captioned photo on p.88 of Groden's "TKOAP")---"... a massive wound in the right rear... it was not in the front, it was not in the eyes";

n. Sibert or O'Neill: portrayed by actor Christopher Kosiciuka in the 1991 Oliver Stone movie "*JFK*" (See "*JFK: The Book of the Film*", page 584 [not to be confused with actor Wayne *Tippit* who portrayed "FBI Agent-*Frank*"!]);

o. Sibert & O'Neill: ARRB depositions [see also "*High Treason III*" (1998), pp. 404-407]---

Sibert, 9/11/97: Regarding the official Archives photos of the rear of the head: "Well, I don't have a recollection of it being that intact... I don't remember seeing anything that was like this photo... that wound was back here. The hair looks like it has been straightened out and cleaned up more than what it was when we left the autopsy... No. I don't recall anything like this at all during the autopsy. There was much---Well, the wound was more pronounced. And it looks like it could have been reconstructed or something, as compared to what my recollection was and those other photographs."; Claims that the Warren Commission's Arlen Specter deliberately lied about what he had said, thus falsifying the record: "That is absolutely false. There would be no way in the world I'd make a statement that I made no notes during the autopsy... [O'Neill] made many notes."; said that a "big piece of bone came in from Dallas---which was found in the limousine out in Dallas, a piece of the skull... there definitely was a large cavity... much skull missing."; re: the "surgery of the head area" statement, Sibert said that he merely wrote down the language that he heard Dr. Humes use.; re: the back wound: "it was below the scapula or the shoulders. And down far below the base of the neck... Now Humes, as I recall, didn't give any measurement on that. He did on this piece of skull that was brought in and the fragments. It was below the shoulders and to the right of the midline of the body." Sibert was asked what he thought of Gerald Ford's admission that he changed the language of the Warren Report to move the bullet wound in JFK's back much higher so that a bullet could exit the neck and strike Connally [7/3/97 news reports]: "Well, I felt like, 'Thank goodness, that is the answer.' Because I couldn't account for how that wound in the back had been moved up gradually---up to the base of the neck from down below the scapula... I have always had trouble assimilating the single-bullet theory. Seeing where that back wound was, an eyewitness there----12 inches from it, seeing them probe that. And from what I understand, the bullet holes both in the shirt and coat match the bullet wound in the back and with the first location that Humes gave us. And, of course, they tried to say that if he raised his arm up---But if you raise your arm up, you're not going to raise your shirt. It's pinned in there with your belt. Plus the fact that the President wore a back brace, I understand, that was pretty tight, too, which would help to hold down the shirt. And so, I've always had trouble with the single bullet or 'magic' bullet theory."; "There were many contradictions, as I said, what it boils down to, you had two autopsy reports. The one that's in the Archives pertaining to what occurred on the night of the 22nd of November with O'Neill and I reporting what happened there. And then you had the other one, the official autopsy report. And you had what O'Neill and I said repeated in those summary reports that were sent to Dallas, you know, out of Baltimore, by the Liaison Agent assigned to the case there. But then the findings and conclusions contained in the official autopsy report were completely different...";

O'Neill, 9/12/97: Regarding the official Archives photos of the rear of the head: "This looks like it's been doctored in some way. Let me rephrase that, when I say 'doctored.' Like the stuff has been pushed back in, and it looks like more towards the end than at the beginning. All you have to do was put the flap back over here, and the rest of the stuff is all covered on up...Quite frankly, I thought that there was a larger opening...in the back of the head...I specifically do not recall those--I mean, being that clean or that fixed up."; "a massive wound in the upper right. Back here." Question: "Just so I can say that. When you were pointing to the area above and behind your right ear---" "Yes." "Is that correct?" "That is correct, yeah."; With regard to the brain photographs, O'Neill said: "It appears to be too much...Well, from this particular photograph here, it would seem that the only section of the brain which is missing is this small section over here. To me, that's not consistent with the way I recall seeing it. I do recall a large amount of what was identified to me as brain matter being on the back of Kellerman's jacket and Greer's jacket. And, to me, that was a larger portion than that section there. This looks almost like a complete brain...In all honesty, I can't say that it looks like the brain that I saw, quite frankly. As I described before, I did not recall it being that large...I don't recall it being that large." O'Neill said that the brain WAS weighed and measured and put into a jar, but HALF of it was gone!; regarding the back wound, the autopsy doctors used "the surgical probe and with their fingers, there was absolutely no point of exit; and they couldn't go any further. And that presented a problem---one heck of a problem."; O'Neill intentionally destroyed his contemporaneous notes so that they could not be subpoenaed, claiming that this was standard FBI procedure!; O'Neill agreed with Sibert that Specter intentionally misquoted him, thus falsifying the record.; O'Neill did not recall either the metal stirrup or the towel beneath the head in some of the autopsy photos;

p.   James W. Sibert: 9/1/98 letter to Vince Palamara---"...In answering your two questions, *the head wound, which was called the fatal wound by the pathologists, was located in the right rear portion of the head. A piece of the skull was missing which was found in the limousine and brought to the autopsy room during the latter stages of the autopsy.* I have no knowledge as to whether or not Chief William Bruce Pitzer was filming that night..."[emphasis added];

q.   [O'Neill: unanswered letter from Vince Palamara 1998];

r.   *"Murder In Dealey Plaza"* by James Fetzer (2000), pages 110, 115, 174, 199, 200, 201, 208, 211, 212, 240, 244, 245, 247, 252, 255, 264-267, 278, 306, 444, 450

s.   *"In the Eye of History"* by William Law (2004)

t.   *"JFK Absolute Proof"* by Robert Groden (2013), page 155: Sibert and O'Neill are pictured with nice summaries of their statements;

u.   O'Neill's son published his father's autobiography entitled *"A Fox Among Wolves"* (2008): confirms that the statement about surgery to JFK's head came from the autopsy doctors themselves; speculates that some surgical procedure had been performed before the autopsy such as cutting of hair or removal of some tissue to view the head wound (!!!); states several times that the head wound was massive and was located in the right rear of JFK's skull; "parts of the brain were still there, but not much"; there was a small hole in the upper right rear of the back and there was no exit for this wound; states that Humes said that external cardiac massage must have worked the back bullet out of the wound in Dallas and that this solved the dilemma of the bullet found at Parkland; states that Arlen Specter's single bullet theory was "just a theory";

[12/18/63 *"Washington Post"*-article by Nate Haseltine entitled *"Kennedy Autopsy Report"*:
"President Kennedy was shot twice, both times from the rear, and would readily have survived the first bullet which was found *deep in his shoulder.* The second bullet to hit the President, however, *tore off the right rear portion of his head* so destructively as to be "completely incompatible with life." A fragment was deflected and passed out the front of the throat, creating an erroneous belief he may have been shot from two angles. These are the findings of the as yet unofficial report of the pathologist who performed the autopsy... The disclosure that a bullet hit the President in the *back shoulder, 5 to 7 inches below the collar line*..."(emphasis added);

1/26/64 *"New York Times"*:
"The third bullet, according to an autopsy in Bethesda Naval Hospital in Maryland, *ripped away a portion of the back of the President's head on the right side.* Fragments from the bullets cut a wound in the President's throat and damaged the windshield of the Presidential limousine." (emphasis added);]

186) Mortician Thomas Evan Robinson:

a.   HSCA taped interview conducted by Andy Purdy and Jim Conzelman 1/12/77 [RIF#189-10089-10178; drawing: 180-10089-10179---see also *"Killing Kennedy"* by H.E.L., p. 345 , *"Bloody Treason"* by Noel Twyman, p. 240, and *"Cover-Up"* by Stewart Galanor, p. 34]---Purdy: "Approximately where was this wound located?" "Directly behind the back of his head." Purdy: "Approximately between the ears or higher up?" "No, I would say pretty much between them.": Robinson's drawing depicts a defect directly in the central, lower rear portion of the skull. Purdy: "Could you tell how large the opening had been caused by the bullets?" "A good bit of the bone had been blown away. There was nothing there to piece together, so I would say probably about [the size of] a small orange." Purdy: "Could you give us an estimate of inches and the nature of the shape?" "Three." Purdy: "And the shape?" "Circular." Purdy: "Was it fairly smooth or fairly ragged?" "Ragged."; "I remember the bones of the skull and face badly shattered." Purdy: "Where on the face were they shattered, which of the bones?" "You cannot see that from the outside. This is looking through the opening that the physicians had made at the back of the skull."; "I can remember the probe. The probe of all this whole area. It was about an eighteen-inch piece of metal that we used." Purdy; "Do you feel they probed the head or they probed the neck?" "It was at the base of the head where most of the damage was done, the things that we had to worry about."; "Somehow I feel like there was something found in the thorax...I think that they found a piece of metal, a piece of bullet."; did not see any small wound of entry in the back of the head; described a "nasty looking" tracheotomy; *He also said there was a little wound, described as a hole of about a quarter-inch in diameter, on the right side of the forehead up near the hairline. Robinson said that he "...probably put a little wax in it."*; Purdy: "Were you the one that was responsible for closing these wounds in the head?" "Well, we all worked on it. Once the body was embalmed arterially and they brought a piece of heavy duty rubber, again to fill this area (area in the back of the head) ..." Purdy: "O.K., you had to close the wound in the back of the head using rubber... *Were there any other wounds on the head other than the little one in the right temple area, and the big one in the back?" "That's all."* [!]; *"Putting the head into the pillow of the casket would have hidden everything.";* Purdy: "You said later, when you read some things about the assassination or the autopsy, you heard or read somethings [sic] which struck you as incorrect. What would those things be?" "The time the people moved (autopsy). The body was taken...and the body never came...lots of little things like that.";

b. 8/8/91, 8/17/91, and 10/6/91 interviews with Livingstone for "*High Treason 2*" (pages 290, 580-581): "A lot of the scalp in the back was gone. We used a piece of rubber there, in the back...No one could see the hole on the pillow... no hairpiece was used. We didn't have to, because the part of the back of the head where the scalp was missing was placed on the pillow, and no one could see it. There was a hole in the pillow to take care of leakage, and that covered the missing area...The face was perfect and undamaged except for a small laceration about a half inch into the forehead, which I covered up... [the frontal bone] was perfectly intact...The face was perfect...There was one very small hole in the temple area, in the hairline. I used wax in it, and that is all that I had to do. I just put a little wax in it...I think it was on the right side...There was not enough scalp to pull together over that large wound in the back. The big hole was only in the back. We filled the skull with plaster and put back the bones, but we did not

117

have all of the bones and could not completely cover over the hole in the back. I do not remember any bone being missing on the top of the head.";

c. 11/26/63 FBI (Sibert & O'Neill) report [see "*Post Mortem*", pp. 533-536]---listed as present during autopsy;

d. "*The Day Kennedy Was Shot*" by Jim Bishop, pages 606 and 643---"Hagan just wanted the strangers to know that Gawler's was prepared. He had an embalming team waiting in an office to the left; John Van Haesen, Edwin B. Stroble, and Thomas Robinson...They would not begin their labors until the autopsy team signified that its work had been completed." [Evidently, Bishop interviewed these men: "The men of Gawler's Sons were discreet and ethical." (page 684)];

e. 6/21/96 ARRB interview [see also "*High Treason III*" (1998), pp. 436-437]: described a hole in the back of JFK's head where there was no scalp: "...centrally located right between the ears" and a "...blow-out" which consisted of a flap of skin in the right temple, which he believed to be an exit wound, based on what the pathologists said that night. There was a hole in JFK's right forehead that he filled with wax. There were also 3 small holes in his cheek which he also plugged in order to prevent any leakage of the embalming fluid.; his "...most vivid recollection of the probe is seeing it inserted near the base of the brain in the back of the head (after removal of the brain), and seeing the tip of the probe come out of the tracheotomy incision in the anterior neck. He was adamant about this recollection. He also recalls seeing the wound high in the back probed unsuccessfully, meaning that the probe did not exit anywhere."; "[the large rear head wound] just doesn't show up in this photo... [re: top of head/ superior view photo] "Robinson frowned, and said with apparent disagreement, 'This makes it look like the wound was in the top of the head.' He explained that the damage in this photograph was 'what the doctors did,' and explained that they cut the scalp open and reflected it back in order to remove bullet fragments (the fragments he had observed in a glass vial). ARRB staff members asked Robinson whether there was damage to the top of the head when he arrived at the morgue and before the brain was removed; he replied by saying that this area was 'all broken,' but that it was not open like the wound in the back of the head. Robinson said that he saw the brain removed from President Kennedy's body, and that a large percentage of it was gone 'in the back,' from the 'medulla,' and that the portion of the brain that was missing was about the size of a closed fist. He described the condition of the brain in this area as the consistency of 'soup.' He said that the brain was 'not cut up' at the autopsy.";

f. "*Murder In Dealey Plaza*" by James Fetzer (2000), pages 117, 199, 250, 259, 306;

g. "*JFK Absolute Proof*" by Robert Groden (2013), page 156: nice summary of his statements

187) Pathologist Dr. Robert Frederick Karnei, Jr.:

a. 8/23/77 interview with the HSCA (conducted by Andy Purdy and Jim Conzelman)--- Karnei assisted with the autopsy and normally would have performed the autopsy; said that there was "extensive damage" to the brain; he recalled the autopsy doctors putting the probe in and taking pictures. He said they felt the hole that was in the back was a wound of entrance and the doctors were "trying to figure out where the bullet came out."; Dr. Finck was "working with a probe and arranging photographs.";

b. 8/26/91 and 8/27/91 interview with Livingstone for *"High Treason 2"* (see Chapter 7): Livingstone: "The large defect was in the very back of the head?" "Right, yeah...Most of the brain that was missing was in the back part of the head...Most of the bone that was missing was destroyed in the back of the head."[p. 182] ;

c. *JAMA*, 10/7/92: Dr. George Lundberg's editorial---"The claim in a recent book [*"High Treason 2"*] that at autopsy the pathologists could not find the adrenals grossly, despite careful serial sections of the perirenal fat, has been independently corroborated on the record, by Robert F. Karnei, M.D., of Maryland...";

d. *"The New York Times"*, 10/6/92: article by Lawrence Altman, M.D.: "Dr. [George] Lundberg said Dr. [J. Thornton] Boswell agreed to discuss Kennedy's adrenal glands [on 8/31/92: see *JAMA* article above] after he was told that Dr. Karnei had disclosed they were missing and after Dr. James J. Humes, the other principal, released Dr. Boswell from the vow of silence.";

e. 5/21/96 ARRB interview [see also *"High Treason III"* (1998), pp. 434-435]: he did remember seeing one wound in the right side of the head approximately above the right ear, and another wound in the posterior skull, up high in the back of the head, either in the center, or just left of center (which he associated in his mind with a right-front to left rear trajectory, or vice-versa). He also said that the upper posterior skull sagged a bit; i.e., was a bit concave in shape.; "...remembered repeated instances, during the numerous attempts to probe the back wound, when photographs were taken of a probe in the President's body (at approximately 9:00 P.M.), and seemed more certain of this recollection than of any other during his ARRB interview. He remembers that John Stringer was photographing the autopsy... He said that there was a second person taking photographs [Pitzer? Knudsen?], whom he initially described to ARRB staff as a FBI or S.S. agent..." due to the man's civilian attire and the assumption that all civilians in the autopsy room were federal agents.;

f. [unanswered letter form Vince Palamara 1998]

g. *"Murder In Dealey Plaza"* by James Fetzer (2000), pages 113, 199-200, 208, 225, 228, 243, 245-246, 278, 284, 301;

h. *"JFK Absolute Proof"* by Robert Groden (2013), page 156: nice summary of his statements

188) Joseph E. Hagan, Chief Asst. to Joseph H. Gawler, undertaker[Hagen]:

a. 5/18/64 interview with William Manchester ("*The Death of a President*", pp. 432-433);

b. FBI (Sibert & O'Neill) report 11/26/63 [see *"Post Mortem"*, pp. 532-536]---listed as present during autopsy;

c. *"The Day Kennedy Was Shot"* by Jim Bishop, pages 606 and 643---"Hagan just wanted the strangers to know that Gawler's was prepared. He had an embalming team waiting in an office to the left; John Van Haesen, Edwin B. Stroble, and Thomas Robinson ... They would not begin their labors until the autopsy team signified that its work had been completed." [Evidently, Bishop interviewed these men: "The men of Gawler's Sons were discreet and ethical." (page 684)];

d. 8/15/91 and 8/28/91 interviews with Livingstone for *"High Treason 2"* (see pages 137, 196, and 581; see also *"Killing the Truth"*, pages 653, 680, 681, and 728): "I couldn't remember any bone missing in the face or from the frontal bone. That was pretty well intact to the best of my memory."; there were a lot of pictures taken from the gallery; "There was extensive damage to the President's head, most of it back up in here (indicating with his hand the rearward right side and the back) ... We had to replace just all of that area with plaster of paris due to the extent of the wounds that were there ... If it hadn't of been that big, we wouldn't have had to use plaster of paris, see ... Quite a bit of bone was lacking ... we had no problems in here (indicating the area of the coronal suture) ... Back up in here (again gestures back of head), his head would have been down in the pillow and, if I remember correctly, we had taken a little out of the pillow where his head would fit down in the pillow."; The face was undamaged except for a small laceration extending about a half inch into the forehead towards the right eyebrow, which can be seen in the right profile photograph;

e. 3/31/93 interview for *"Killing the Truth"*, p. 740---It was Hagen who wrote the document from Gawler's, which read "Body removed from metal shipping casket at USNH at Bethesda". However, Hagen said that "The only reason we used that phrase was to identify the casket as a casket and as metal. ;

f. [unanswered letter from Vince Palamara 1998]

g. *"JFK Absolute Proof"* by Robert Groden (2013), page 156: nice summary of his statements

189) Paul Kelly O'Connor, Bethesda laboratory technologist (deceased August 2006):

a. FBI (Sibert & O'Neill) report 11/26/63 [see *"Post Mortem"*, pp. 532-536]---listed as present during autopsy;

b. 7 HSCA 15 and

c. HSCA outside contact report, 6/28/78---the body was *wrapped* in a rubber "body bag", as quoted in vol. 7. However, the outside contact report states that O'Connor said "the body was *in* a rubber 'body' bag." [emphasis added]; said that no missiles were discovered at any time during the autopsy;

d. 8/25/79 interview with David Lifton (*"Best Evidence"*, photo 37+pp. 598-606)---re: "the shipping casket" and JFK being "in a body bag"; (p. 601) "... he didn't have any brains left ... The wound in his head was terrific ... eight by four inches ... The wound was in the occipital-parietal area ... clear up around the frontal area of the brain...the cranium was empty..."; (p. 604) the wound in the throat was "a great big hole in his larynx...the esophagus was laid open";

e. *"Best Evidence: The Research Video"* ([Oct.] 1980/ 1990):1980 filmed interview [clips repeated in *"The Fifth Estate-Who Killed JFK?"* 1983 CBC, "Nova" special, 11/15/88, *"Dispatches: The Day The Dream Died"*, 11/16/88 London, and *"A Current Affair"*, 9/3/90 and 9/4/90]---re: body bag, shipping casket, no brain left in skull;

f. *"On Trial: Lee Harvey Oswald"* 1986 Showtime---more of the same: "we were interfered with constantly... Admiral Burkley interfered constantly"; "body bag... body bag unzipped"; "brains literally blown out of his head; he had none...There was no brain-[just] pieces of brain matter... half a handful...The brain was gone, for all practical purposes, it was gone."; "had a monstrous hole in his head.";

g. *"The Men Who Killed Kennedy"* 1988---"The whole side of his head was gone. I don't know where those things [the autopsy photos] came from but they are wrong. Totally wrong.";

h. *"JFK: An Unsolved Murder"*, KRON, 11/18/88 [clips repeated in *"JFK: The Case for Conspiracy"* video 1993]: "My job was to remove the brain. There was no brain to remove. The brain wasn't there."; Regarding the autopsy photos, O'Connor said: "No, that doesn't look like what I saw. I saw a lot worse wound extended way back here [demonstrated top and rear of head as missing]...an open area all the way across into the rear of the brain."; talks about the order not to talk about what he saw;

i. 4/19/90, 4/20/90, 5/9/90, 5/18/90, 6/3/90, 6/11/90, 6/30/90, 10/8/90, 4/6/91 [unreleased video: see photo section in *"High Treason 2"*, as well as his two drawings and comments on the autopsy photos], 5/18/91, 5/26/91, 6/8/91, 6/9/91, 6/10/91, 6/11/91, 9/23/91, and 4/19/93* interviews with Harry Livingstone for *"High Treason 2"*, mainly Chapter 12 (*see also *"Killing The Truth"* by H.E.L., pp. 702-704)---"There was a big hunk of his scalp and hair blown out of the back of his head...The rear of the head, this is a composite forged photograph masking a large defect in the very back of the head...the throat wound is airbrushed in...The whole side of the head is airbrushed in.[!]"; "We opened it up, unzipped the body bag."; shipping casket;

j. 2 episodes of *"Hard Copy"*: 5/9/90 and 5/14/90 with Lifton (and Aubrey Rike)---on the second program, O'Connor said that "the whole right side of the President's head was blown off";

k. A.S.K. 11/91---Said that there was very little facial damage. However, he also said that he saw no hole in the back of the head [?!];

l. Credited for autopsy photos in *"JFK: Conspiracy of Silence"* by Dr. Crenshaw;

m. A.S.K. 11/92---repeated the shipping casket story;

n. AP article 6/1/92 (see *"Killing The Truth"*, pages 168 [re: Livingstone's conference], 678 and 721, and *"Killing Kennedy"*, page 222): "The bullet from the (back) wound fell out when the body was lifted from the coffin to the examining table."; "The doctors probed the hole in Kennedy's back to a depth of about 2 inches, but found no exit wound.";

o. 10/25/92 interview with Roger Feinman (see *"Between The Signal and the Noise"* by Feinman, 1993)---"My overall impression of O'Connor was that he is sincere and truthful to the best of his ability; that he remembers vignettes or anecdotes about the autopsy, some of which he has obviously discussed with other participants; but that he has great difficulty placing the events of that night into temporal or sequential order and context."; O'Connor: "...there was no surgery of any kind. And I know what surgery looks like."; "There was no brain, just brain tissue."; did not remember any sutures to the throat wound when the body arrived;

p. Groden's "TKOAP", p. 87 [his one drawing, which also appears in the 12/31/91 *"Globe"* and *"High Treason 2"* (see above)] and p. 88 [evidently from outtakes from his video]: "[There was] an open area all the way across into the rear of the brain."

q. *"Who's Who in the JFK Assassination"* by Michael Benson (1993), pp. 319-320--- good summary/ sources on O'Connor;

r. Acknowledgments, *"The Search For Lee Harvey Oswald"* (1995);

s. *"Bloody Treason"* by Noel Twyman, 1997: July 1992 interview (pp. 177-184; 204-206)—shipping casket; body bag; (p. 180) "...a huge gaping hole in the side of the president's head...The right side of the head. It went from above the hairline on the right side through the parietal and the occipital area and down around to the right temporal area of the skull...I t was a very irregular jagged wound."; ALSO: p. 214---10/22/92 drawing of the Bethesda morgue and autopsy room;

t. 1997 interviews with researcher Bill Law---re: the back wound: "There was only one...the bullet hit him in the back of the shoulder, coursed downward and went down into the plural cavity. It bruised the plural cavity, which, in turn, bruised the lung but didn't penetrate the plural cavity."; "I think he was hit four times. The first time was in the throat from the front...On the question of the head wound ... the bullets [plural] that hit him in the head blew the whole right side of his head off and most of his brains out."; "...when you look at the wound in the neck [in the photos], it looks like it has been painted on. It doesn't conform with the anatomy of the throat."; "It (the head wound) traversed from just above the hair line all the way to the back of the head. Just blown away. Part of the top of his head was gone."; "...all these [autopsy] pictures have been doctored.";

u. 10/6/98 letter to Vince Palamara---"The head wound was *approximately 20 cm. By 8-10 cm.* The wound included the complete right side of the head. Occipital, Parietal, Temporal and part of the frontal area. Approximately 80 % of the brain was missing." [emphasis added]; "P.S. There is a new book out that I worked on "Bloody Treason" by Noel Twyman. If you don't have it-get it. It's the best book ever written on the Kennedy assassination." [see reference "s)" above];

v. 11/98 appearance at JFK Lancer conference, Dallas, TX;

w. *"Murder in Dealey Plaza"* by James Fetzer (2000), pages 106, 112, 174, 199, 296, 301

x. *"In The Eye of History"* by William Law (2004)

y. *"JFK Absolute Proof"* by Robert Groden (2013), page 155: O'Connor is pictured with a nice summary of his statements

190) James Curtis Jenkins, Bethesda laboratory technologist:

a. FBI (Sibert & O'Neill) report 11/26/63 [see *"Post Mortem"*, pp. 532-536]: listed as present during autopsy;

b. TWO: 8/24/77 HSCA interview with Jim Kelly and Andy Purdy [for his drawing, see p. 346 of *"Killing Kennedy"* by H.E.L.]---Jenkins stated that when the body was unwrapped he saw a head wound in the "middle temporal region back to the occipital." His drawing clearly conflicts with official history. ; the back wound was "just below the collar to the right of the midline" and it was "very shallow... it didn't enter the peritoneal (chest) cavity."; he didn't believe that the doctor found that the probe "penetrated into the chest" and the doctors "couldn't prove the bullet came into the cavity."; Jenkins said "... with the Warren Commission findings, you can understand why I'm skeptical." He was "surprised at the conclusions the doctors reached" with regard to the head wound. Jenkins does not recall a small hole in the head as depicted on the autopsy descriptive sheet---he said that the big hole in the head would have covered the area where the little hole was drawn on this sheet. Jenkins said that the wound to the head entered the top rear quadrant from the front side.; Jenkins recalled that the doctors extensively attempted to probe the back wound. He said the probe they used was a metal one, approximately eight inches long. He said that "...most of the probe went in...between the skin..." and not into the chest cavity. He said Humes could probe the bottom of the wound with his little finger and said that the metal probe went in 2 - 4 inches. He said it was quite a "...fact of controversy..." that the doctors "...couldn't prove the bullet came into the cavity." Jenkins said he "...possibly drew the back scar..." but "...doesn't think so..." He said he is "positive" he didn't draw the head wound.";

ALSO: 6/27/78 Outside contact report by the HSCA's Mark Flanagan (RIF#180-10096-10391 [see 7 HSCA 9])--- "James Jenkins, a student laboratory technician, whose normal duties included admitting a body to the morgue and conducting an initial examination, likewise stated that the body of the President was unclothed and that it may have been wrapped in a sheet."

c. 9/23/79 interview with David Lifton (*"Best Evidence,"* photo 38+pp. 608-614, 615-619, 696)--- [p. 609]Lifton: "What was central to Jenkins's whole experience that night was his conviction, from looking at the President's head, that the fatal shot struck from the front."; [p. 616]Jenkins: "I would say the parietal and occipital section on the right side of the head---it was a large gaping area, even though, I think, as we put it back together, most of the skull, the bone itself was there. It had just been crushed, and kind of blown apart, toward the rear... I'm laying my hand on the back area of my skull. And my hand is probably five to six inches from the span of my little finger to the tip of my thumb. So if I spread my fingers and put my hand back there, that probably would be the area that was missing." Regarding the official photos depicting an essentially intact rear skull with a small bullet entry hole, Jenkins said: "That's not possible. That is totally ---you know, there's no possible way. Okay? It's not possible."; "Medical technician James Jenkins was certain the Warren Commission was wrong about the direction of the bullet that struck the head, because the large hole was at the back of the head.";

d. 9/8/90, 10/8/90, 3/25/91, 4/6/91, 4/28/91, 4/30/91, 5/5/91, 5/14/91, 5/19/91, 5/24/91, 5/25/91, 5/29/91, 6/6/91, 6/16/91, 7/14/91, and 10/19/91 interviews with Harry Livingstone for "*High Treason 2*" (see esp. Chapter 11) and "*Killing The Truth*", pp. 690-692, 709*--"I looked at the back of the head, but all I saw was the massive gaping wound…There was a hole in all of it [the scalp and the bone]. There was a hole in the occipital-parietal area… Everything from just above the right ear back was fragmented…there was [an absence of scalp and bone] along the midline just above the occipital area…I might have gone along with [a gunshot wound to the]right temple."; *"And the opening and the way the bone was damaged behind the head would have definitely been a type of exit wound.";

e. Videotaped interview with researcher Bill Law, 1998, as reflected in this 10/5/98 *LancerLINE* news story----"In an exclusive-to-LINE videotaped interview, former Navy laboratory technician James Curtis Jenkins stated that he, along with physicians and others present at the post mortem examination of the body of John Fitzgerald

Kennedy conducted at Bethesda Naval Hospital, discovered a large exit wound at the rear of the president's skull. Jenkins went on to describe [this] defect on the right rear of the head as a "blow out," or exit wound. This was a clear indication to all present of a shot that entered at the front of the head -- which is to say, a shot fired by an assassin from a position in front of the limousine, and not from the Texas School Book Depository. Also noted at the time was a possible wound of entry on the right front of the president's head. Further, Jenkins' observed a wound of entry on Kennedy's back that was located so low as to render inoperative the so-called Single Bullet Theory, without which the Warren Commission and House Select Committee on Assassinations' shared conclusion that Lee Harvey Oswald alone fired shots that hit the president cannot be supported. These and additional recollections by Jenkins, offered in response to questions posed by William Matson Law of the JFK Lancer Oral History Project, stand as evidence for conspiracy in the death of the president. Jenkins' recollection of the nature of the president's head wounds is clear. He said that there was "speculation" among the doctors conducting the autopsy that a gray substance over Kennedy's right ear was a bullet fragment. "My assumption is that this was an entry wound." When asked to examine and comment on the official autopsy photograph depicting the rear of Kennedy's head, Jenkins said that the area shown to be covered with hair (behind and slightly above the right ear) "actually was a hole." Jenkins further noted that, "I was told there was a wound in the nuchal line (near the base of the skull). I never saw it, but I could have missed it." Jenkins recalled that, "We didn't have to do a skull cap (removal) because the wound was large enough for the brain to come out." There has been informed speculation regarding the probability that never-acknowledged surgical examination of the president's body was conducted prior to the official autopsy at Bethesda Naval Hospital. Jenkins noted that, "Dr. (James) Humes, who removed the brain, made an exclamatory statement. 'The damn thing fell out in my hand.'" Jenkins said that, "The brain stem had already been severed ...Some of the areas fragmented along the sagital suture (drew) comment (to the effect) that they looked like they had been surgically extended ... some of the fragmented areas looked like they had been cut by a scalpel to expand them. "To me," said Jenkins, "this indicated that the brain had been surgically removed and then replaced." (emphasis added) Jenkins said that he personally observed the president's back wound. When asked to pinpoint its location, he responded, "Probably at T4." Jenkins further stated that the president's body cavity was opened during the official autopsy, and that, when the rear back wound was probed, it became evident that the object that had caused the wound had not transited the body. "(Autopsy pathologists) Doctors Humes and (Pierre) Finck tried to probe the (back) wound," said Jenkins. "Humes used his little finger (and a probe). I could see the finger and the probe behind the pleura in the back, they never broke the pleural cavity. The wound actually went down and stopped ... they were a little upset about it." The pleura are a lining of tissue that would have been torn by a transiting bullet such as that imagined in the SBT. "One of the things unusual to me was very little blood in the chest cavity," Jenkins observed. "I would (have to) think that there were no penetrating wounds in the chest cavity. We found none."(emphasis added) "I came out of the autopsy sure that (a) bullet had entered from the right side of the head and exited in this area (indicating the right rear of the head, behind and slightly above the ear)," said Jenkins.(emphasis added)

On November 22, 1963, James Jenkins was an E-4 in the United States Navy, attending lab technician school at Bethesda Hospital. On that fateful afternoon he had been assigned duty as a lab tech. His responsibilities included insuring that the hospital's morgue was fully equipped for autopsies. Further, during any post mortems, he would note physicians' observations regarding organ weights and other pertinent facts. Jenkins stated that he was present for the entire Kennedy autopsy (indeed, he remained on duty from 3 PM on the 22nd to 9 AM on the 23rd), with the exception of a brief period in which he obeyed an "order" to get a sandwich. He said that, given the circumstances, his appetite was less than robust, and that he quickly returned to his station. Questions have arisen regarding the identity of the individual in charge of the president's autopsy. Under oath, the physicians involved have testified that Dr. Humes was in command. Jenkins, however, remembers it differently. He said that his clear recollection is that Dr. Burkley was giving orders that were, in Jenkins' opinion, originating elsewhere, perhaps with Admiral Calvin Galloway, Humes' commanding officer at Bethesda. "The autopsy at the table was being directed from the end of the (observation) gallery ... There were more than thirty officers there, flag rank and above ... I was told that one of them was Burkley." Jenkins continued, "Dr. Humes was technically in charge of the autopsy ... (but) he was being directed by Burkley ... All of the doctors at the table were frustrated by this ... these people (in the gallery) were directing the doctors toward a conclusion (of one gunman firing from the rear) ... and (the doctors) were not finding evidence for it ... (the doctors) were under a tremendous amount of pressure." Based on his own observations and those of the pathologists as verbalized during the post mortem on the president, Jenkins said, "I came out of that autopsy expecting them to say that there were two shooters, one in the right front, one behind." (emphasis added) Was Jenkins surprised by the official autopsy results? "... what we saw that night was nothing relating to the (final and official), pathology report. There was no relation to it." (emphasis added) Which is to say, the official record of the autopsy of President Kennedy bears no relation to the facts as observed by Jenkins.

f.   [unanswered letter from Vince Palamara 1998]

g.   *"Murder in Dealey Plaza"* by James Fetzer (2000), pages 199, 301, 305

h.   *"In The Eye of History"* by William Law (2004)

i.   *"JFK Absolute Proof"* by Robert Groden (2013), page 155: Jenkins is pictured with a nice summary of his statements

191) Edward F. Reed, Jr., Bethesda X-ray technician:

a.   FBI (Sibert & O'Neill) report 11/26/63 [see *"Post Mortem"*, pp. 532-536]---listed as present during autopsy;

b.   Interview with the HSCA (RIF#180-10105-10399 [see also *"Cover-Up"* by Stewart Galanor, p. 33]): the head wound "was very large and located in the right hemisphere in the occipital region."

c.   11/25/79 interview with David Lifton (*"Best Evidence"*, photo 40+p. 619 and 696)---Believed JFK had been shot from the front because the skull wound he saw was "more posterior than anterior." ; did not see a small entry wound on the rear of the head; "It wasn't like a tracheotomy, a normal tracheotomy. It was a lot larger."; felt that the head shot came from the front;

d.   *"RT Image"*, 11/21/88 interview (see also *"High Treason 2"*, p. 152, and *"Killing The Truth"*, pp. 692-693 and 706)---saw damage to the frontal bone [?]; "... he had a large, gaping wound about the size of my fist in his right carotidal, temple, and frontal areas." [?!]. Strangely, he contradicts what he first told Lifton nearly a decade beforehand, the first account of the wounds on record by Reed.;

e.   ARRB deposition---"But which side of the skull did we X-ray? We X-rayed the left side of this patient. The left side.";

f.   f) *"Murder in Dealey Plaza"* by James Fetzer (2000), pages 112, 199

[8/15/64 "Newsweek":
"The whereabouts of these (autopsy) photographs and X-rays remains one of Washington's most puzzling mysteries. A diligent two-month inquiry... has failed to turn up a single government official who can, or will, give a simple answer to the question: 'Where are the Kennedy autopsy photos?'"]

192) Jerrol F. Custer, Bethesda X-ray technician (deceased 7/28/2000):

a. FBI (Sibert & O'Neill) report 11/26/63 [see "*Post Mortem*", pp. 532-536]---listed as present during autopsy ["Jerrol F. Crester" (sic)];

b. 9/7/77 interview with the HSCA's Mark Flanagan (RIF#180-10103-10116, Agency File Number 002339)--- "Mr. Jerrol F. Custer is included on a list of persons present during the autopsy of President John F. Kennedy. I spoke with him on the evening of September 7, 1977 in reference to his role during this event. Mr. Custer stated that in November of 1963, he served as a hospital corpsman in X-ray Technology at the Bethesda Naval Hospital. He confirmed that he witnessed the autopsy of JFK and was specifically involved in searching for fragments through the process of taking X-rays. Mr. Custer stated that numerous "total" body X-rays were taken, that numerous high-ranking people were present, and that these high-ranking officials took notes. Mr. Custer will not discuss any additional details, however, until the agreement he signed pledging silence is rescinded. Mr. Custer currently works at Monitor Hospital in the Saltsberg area. I informed Mr. Custer that the Committee would most probably contact him at a later date.";

c. 6/19/78 Outside contact report by the HSCA's Mark Flanagan (Agency File Number 013610)---" Custer was present at the autopsy of President Kennedy - I called him to ask him some questions in that regard. Custer said he was an X-ray technologist, rank HM3, and happened to be on duty in the X-ray department on the evening of Nov. 22, 1963. He was called into the autopsy room while the autopsy was in progress to assist in taking X-rays. He recalled that he used a portable machine. Custer said that he could not remember any additional details. I asked him about the persons present, the orders that were given, the types of X-rays, the photographs, the wounds, etc., Custer could not recall anything."[!];

d. 9/30/79 and 10/7/79 interviews with David Lifton ("*Best Evidence*", pp. 619-621+696): "Custer told me the President's head wound was enormous---"I could have put both of my hands in the wound. Okay?"---and that he believed he had been shot from the front."; "...when a bullet goes into the body, it goes in small and comes out big. Okay? Well, that is exactly how the skull looked. Okay?...from the front, to the back."; did not see an entry wound at the rear of JFK's head; Custer said that he exposed, and returned to the morgue, X-rays showing that the rear of the President's head was blown off.; "Custer felt the head shot came from the front.";

e. "*Best Evidence: The Research Video*" ([Oct.] 1980/1990) [clips repeated in "*The Fifth Estate: Who Killed JFK?*" 1983 CBC, "*Dispatches: The Day The Dream Died*", 11/16/88 London and "*A Current Affair*", 9/3/90 and 9/4/90]---1980 filmed interview with Custer at his home in Pittsburgh, PA; along the lines of his comments in Lifton's book;

f. "*JFK: An Unsolved Murder*", KRON, 11/18/88 [clips repeated in "*JFK: The Case for Conspiracy*" 1993 video]: When asked if the official X-ray is the one he took, Custer said "No. This area here was GONE [demonstrates the back of the head]. There was no scalp there... from the top of the head to the base of the skull. That part was gone.";

g. 12/2/88 interview with Warren Patton for the "*Jenkintown (PA) Times-Chronicle*"[see "Killing The Truth", p. 669];

h. Interview with "the authors" of "*High Treason*", p. 458---"There was a large hole in the back of the head, and there was a big hole in the scalp there ... There was a king-size hole in the back of the head, and that area was torn."; Regarding the official X-rays, Custer said "... in the lateral skull films it looks like part of the front of his face is gone. But if you look at the autopsy photographs, there's nothing gone there. His eye should have been completely gone on that film, which it never should.";

i. 1/4/88 [89?---see above], 9/29/90, 10/8/90, 10/29/90, 12/29/90, 3/20/91, 3/25/91, 3/26/91, 4/4/91, 4/28/91, 9/9/91, 9/23/91, 9/27/91, 10/23/91, 11/11/91, and **11/22/91** [unreleased video done by Vince Palamara] interviews for "*High Treason 2*" (see esp. Chapter 10)---"The scalp was so loose from the base of the skull in the occipital region to the front, it drooped."; "Skull fragments and bullet fragments. And they had me X-ray them next to the skull... Here's what he [Ebersole] told me: 'The only reason why I'm doing this is because they want to make a bust of Kennedy'"; "There was a flap of scalp in the back of the head, but it was badly shredded. As I have said, it would not make a picture like the one we now have, which shows the scalp intact."; Custer said that a missile fell from the posterior area of the President when they moved him early after the body arrived and had the appearance of a whole bullet and not a fragment, and was mutilated as though it had struck bone.; "There definitely was no brain.";

j. Reuters and AP, 5/29/92 (dispatch by Jean King of Reuters) and 5/30/92 [+5/19/92-?] (by Richard Pyle of AP) re: Livingstone's New York press conference on 5/29/92---the X-rays the government claims are of Kennedy are not, and that these were not what they took. He said they are fake. "These are fake X-rays. They show no part of the back or side of the head missing."; "There was no damage to his face and no part of his skull was missing on the forward part of his head.";[see also James P. Duffy and Vincent L. Ricci's "*A Complete Book of Facts*", 1992, pp. 142-143 and chapter 4 of "*Killing The Truth*"];

k. AP article 6/1/92---"... photos show the entire face intact and unmarked. 'That's how I remember it', Custer said.";

l. 8/31/92, "*Advance, For Radiologic Science Professionals*" by Scott Hatfield: "*RT disputes X-ray photos in JFK case.*"---"The right side of the skull on the X-rays... does not match the right side of the skull in the [autopsy] pictures. Not only that, but I remember the skull not being damaged in that area. It was all further back ... The X-rays are not the ones I took."; Custer reported having taken at least five skull radiographs, including one oblique/ tangential view of the large posterior defect.; "A bullet fell out of the upper torso of the back."; [see also "*High Treason 2*", p. 209, "*Killing The Truth*", p. 677 ,692, 696, and "*Assassination Science*", p. 111];

m. "*Killing The Truth*", pp. 309-311: Custer's letter of May, 1993---"As I have stated before, the (government's alleged) anterior/ posterior and the lateral views of the skull that were taken of JFK didn't match the X-rays that I took and which were taken that night in the morgue…The President's face didn't' show the massive damage that is quite evident in the alleged anterior/ posterior view of the skull and also on the lateral view.";

n.   11/18/93 wire story by (AP and) Reuters re: Livingstone 11/18/93 press conference including Custer [see "*Killing Kennedy*" by H.E.L., pp. 395-396 and "*Assassination Science*", p. 136]---the official x-rays are not the ones he took that night. Custer was instructed by his superior, Dr. James Ebersole, to tape bullet fragments to pieces of bones and to take X-rays of these. Custer believes the X-rays were used to help make the composites or double-exposures.;

o.   Interviews/ work with Tom Wilson, 1991 to 2000---one to two books in the making; never released (both gentlemen died in 2000)!

p.   11/17/93 Pittsburgh, PA "City Paper" article/ interview by John Hayes (Including Dr. Cyril Wecht, Tom Wilson, and Vince Palamara!)---"…I've never seen X-rays that looked like the ones they say I took. They were faked.";

q.   Spring 1995 Interview with Walt Brown: Oct. 1995 "*JFK/ Deep Politics Quarterly*: "…he told me that the proposed theory, of the photo showing both the entrance and the exit in the back of the head, was exactly the way he saw it, but had hesitated to speak out from past fears."; "he indicated that the x-rays were far more accurate than the "stare of death" photo. He also, almost casually, added that when the film was placed under the skull for the A-P x-ray, a bullet fragment fell out of JFK's neck or lower head."; Custer also provided a nice plug on the dust jacket of Walt Brown's 1995 work "*Treachery in Dallas*";

r.   Interview with Dr. David Mantik (see "*Assassination Science*", p. 157 and "*Bloody Treason*", p.231)---"Custer told Mantik that the day after the autopsy, a skull was brought to him, strangely, and he was asked to x-ray it while placing a bullet on the skull.";

s.   10/28/97 ARRB deposition [see "*High Treason III*" (1998), pp.443-446]: Question: "Are you certain that you took X-rays that included C3/C4?" "Yes, sir. Absolutely…Just one [X-ray]. And that was all that was necessary, because it showed---right there…A fragmentation of a shell in and around that…that area…There were bullet fragmentations around that area---that opening [around C3/C4]…very prevalent." Question: "Did anyone make any observations about metal fragments in the C3/C4 area?" "I did. And I was told to mind my own business. That's where I was shut down again…the two tangential views, and the AP cervical spine…In my opinion…the reason why they are not here is because they showed massive amounts of bullet fragments…I did hear…The next day…That certain pertinent things were taken care of…I heard it between two officers…One was Ebersole. And one was another radiologist [Capt. Loy T. Brown].", re: the AP view of the skull: "…it's funny how the burn mark gets in the right place. And that's pretty close to what I---my opinion---I believe was an entry wound…why couldn't he [Ebersole] see displacement of the anterior portion of the skull, and realize that it had to be coming from the… posterior portion of the skull, and realize there had to be force coming from the anterior portion of skull? He knew that. Now, he's an educated man. He has to know that."; Question: "Earlier in your deposition, you referred to some heat damage on one of the X-rays. Do you see any heat damage on this X-ray?" "It's right here. You can see it. This is where Dr. Ebersole got it too close to the heat lamp. I stated to him twice, 'Please do not put it too close.' You can see where it started to…Curdle, literally. And here, it started to burn. And isn't it funny how where it starts to burn is the area that I suggested was an entry wound [indeed, as the ARRB's Jeremy Gunn points out, the accompanying description of X-ray #1 was identified by the doctors during the 1966 inventory as being an "anterior/ posterior view of the skull, slightly heat damaged."] …I was there, I saw him do it."; Remember, also, I had stated how a portion of the skull had lifted up and pushed backwards? …Showing that there had to be a force impact this way…From the right side, you notice…the fragmentation, how it starts to get larger and larger and larger. You have equal and opposite force. Everything being pushed forward. The brain has been pushed back, and it pops the skull out." Question: "So, it's your opinion that the trauma to the head began at the front and moved towards the back of the head?" "Yes, sir. Absolutely…The larger wound would have to be further back. This one isn't as bad, toward the temporal region. It was open. But the more you went further back, the more destruction you had…Most of the destruction was towards the occipital area. This area wasn't as bad. You still had the orbital ridge. The frontal forehead was still here. But the further back you got, the worse the destruction became. And the more gaping the hole became."; repeats the episode he told Livingstone ["High Treason 2", p. 213] and myself [below] about how DR. Ebersole asked him to tape bullet fragments to pieces of bone on 11/23/63 and X-ray them, allegedly for a bust of Kennedy [deposition, p. 38, 144-145];

t.   Interviews with Bill Law, 1997, included.

3/15-3/16/98 videotaped interviews with Bill Law and Vince Palamara for JFK Lancer [see also the May 1998 "Fourth Decade" re: Pitzer and Dennis David and "In The Eye Of History" by William Law (2004)

---the longest and most detailed interview to date---covers all the comments made previously, but in more detail (and on video), along with new revelations/ unasked questions; the X-rays do not match the photos, nor what he saw(the video including the x-rays, photos, plus a blow-up of photo 40 from Lifton's "Best Evidence"); believes JFK was shot from the front and that there was a conspiracy; very suspicious of Dr. John H. Ebersole (repeats the bust-of-Kennedy episode); Custer stated that the Officer of the Day said that JFK's body was "coming in from Walter Reed…actually, he was brought in by helicopter"; saw "two different caskets": a "regular shipping casket" and the "ceremonial casket… for later on" (also depicted in a diagram he made); "the bullet came from the front"----Custer believes that an exploding bullet, not a steel-jacketed bullet, hit the head, and that there were so many fragments because a fragmented/ exploding bullet was used.; On the one hand, Custer stated that "you could drape it [scalp] over the defect", "it is possible" that this is what is depicted in the autopsy photos, and that "if you look at the [AP] x-rays, you can see bone missing in the back", he has apparently modified his position somewhat: he now states that these are indeed the x-rays he took AND that "the back of the head wasn't blown out". He pointed to the TOP REAR of the head as the location of where he saw the "massive wound" ("as if an Indian came in and scalped him"). However, he pointed to his right temple as the location of the entry wound from the front, even demonstrating where the hole appears to be in one of the autopsy photos (the empty cranium photo). In addition, he did not see the flap of skull that is depicted in the autopsy photos that night [The Back of the Head (F3) photo in "High Treason 2"] and was emphatic that there was no frontal blow out of the face. Finally, he does not believe that either alleged entry wound pointed out in the back-of-the-head autopsy photo was an entrance wound.; confirms the traditional back wound position in the autopsy photos; "there was a bruising on the pleural-thoracic area…slight discoloration"; there were "no suture marks" on the throat wound: "a big, gaping hole"; "saw fragments of the brain [in the skull]..half a handful"; "when we lifted him up to take skull films, that's when a fragment fell out of the body…the back"; Pre-autopsy manipulations? "A good possibility"; who was in control of the autopsy? "JFK's personal physician---he would make comments on everything…controlling everything every step of the way."; "one reason Pitzer was killed: he was taking movies of the body in the gallery";

u. From Chapter 7 of the *ARRB's Final Report*---"a 20-minute audiotape of a discussion between Mr. [Tom] Wilson and former Navy x-ray technician Jerrol Custer, dated 3/28/98";

v. *"Murder in Dealey Plaza"* by James Fetzer (2000), pages 107, 112, 115, 174, 199, 435, 439

w. *"In The Eye of History"* by William Law (2004);

x. *"JFK Absolute Proof"* by Robert Groden (2013), page 155: Custer is pictured with a nice summary of his statements

193) Jan Gail "Nick" Rudnicki, Dr. Boswell's lab assistant:

a. 5/8/78 interview with the HSCA's Mark Flanagan [RIF#180-10105-10397]---"the back-right quadrant of the head was missing."; saw the bullet wound "in the shoulder blade region of the back"; said that there was a discussion by the autopsy doctors about "the possibility that two bullets struck the head in the same general area, causing a massive defect.";

b. FBI (Sibert & O'Neill) report 11/26/63 [see *"Post Mortem"*, pp. 532-536]---listed as present during autopsy;

c. 10/14/90 interview with Livingstone (see *"High Treason 2"*, esp. Chapter 9; see also *"Killing The Truth"*, pp.689-690): "I remember the wounds to the throat, the wound to the rear right quadrant of the head...It was a big hole."; "…from the ear back, the scalp was either gone or definitely destroyed in that area…it would look more like it was an exit than an entrance." When asked if there was any scalp left in the right rear area of the head behind the ear, Rudnicki said, 'That was gone."; the face appeared "Normal. It looked perfectly normal, if you didn't look at the back of the head."; Rudnicki did not recall an entry wound in the back of the head; also saw "an entry wound several inches down on the back.";

d. 10/98 letter to Vince Palamara---Palamara: "Exactly where on JFK's head was the wound located?" "Right rear quadrant"; Palamara: "Do you remember if Chief Pitzer was present that night?" "No";

e. *"Murder in Dealey Plaza"* by James Fetzer (2000), pages 112, 198, 199

f. *"JFK Absolute Proof"* by Robert Groden (2013), page 156: nice summary of his statements

194) James E. Metzler, Bethesda Hospital corpsman:

a. FBI (Sibert & O'Neill) report 11/26/63 [see *"Post Mortem"*, pp. 532-536]---listed as present during autopsy;

b. Interview with the HSCA (RIF#180-10105-10401 [see also *"Cover-Up"* by Stewart Galanor, p. 33]): Helped carry JFK's body from the coffin to the autopsy table; recalled the head wound in the "right side of the head behind the right ear extending down to the center of the back of the skull."

c. 11/25/79 interview with David Lifton (*"Best Evidence"*, pp. 631-634)---"It was also his impression, from the way the wound was located toward the back of the head, that President Kennedy must have been shot in the head from the front.";

d. 5/5/91, 5/27/91, 6/1/91, 6/6/91, 6/18/91, and 9/28/91 interviews with Harry Livingstone (see *"High Treason 2"*, 89-90, 104, 128, 133, 140, 222, 229, 232, 255, 271, 274, 317, 331-332; see also *"Killing The Truth"*, pages 668, 669, 671, 673, 674, 676, 691, 703, 707*, 719, 731-732, 733, 737-738, 739)---Metzler described a large flap of scalp on the back of the head which covered up much of the huge defect.; "Metzler said there was a real jagged cut all along the hairline, just like a can opener opened it"; JFK was in the Dallas casket and "There was no body bag, I can tell you that."; *The wound was above or behind the ear, but not to the top of the head, and there was no flap as we see it now in the pictures on the right side in front of the ear. Metzler denied that it could be there.;

e. *"Murder in Dealey Plaza"* by James Fetzer (2000), pages 112, 119

f. *"JFK Absolute Proof"* by Robert Groden (2013), page 156: nice summary of his statements

195) David P. Osborne, MD: a military physician present at the autopsy at Bethesda (deceased):

a. FBI (Sibert & O'Neill) report 11/26/63 [see *"Post Mortem"*, pp. 532-536]---listed as present during autopsy;

b. 6/20/78 Outside contact report with the HSCA's Mark Flanagan (RIF#180-10102-10415 [see also 7 HSCA 15-16]) ---"thought he recalled seeing an intact slug roll out from the clothing of President Kennedy and onto the autopsy table"; "...once the doctors examined the wound closely they could determine that the bullet which entered the back passed through the throat. In regard to the head wound Osborne said that there was no question that the bullet entered the back of the head and blew off the top of the head.";

c. 11/4/79 interview with David Lifton (*"Best Evidence"*, Chapter 29: pp. 645-647, in particular): a "reasonably clean," "unmarred" bullet fell from the clothing that was around JFK's body. "The bullet was not deformed in any way...I had that bullet in my hand, and looked at it...I know the Secret Service had it...the Secret Service took it..";

d. 4/5/90 letter to Joanne Braun (see *"The Third Decade"*, 3/91 issue)---"a second (bullet) hit in the occipital region of the posterior skull which blew off the posterior top of his skull and impacted and disintegrated against the interior surface of the frontal bone just above the level of the eyes. I know this for a fact because I was the one who worked on the head, removing his brain and closed the skull so that he could have an open casket if so desired.";

e. *"Murder in Dealey Plaza"* by James Fetzer (2000), page 199

196) Dr. John H. "Jack" Ebersole, Assistant Chief of radiology (deceased 9/23/1993):

a. a) FBI (Sibert & O'Neill) report 11/26/63 [see *"Post Mortem"*, pp. 532-536]---listed as present during autopsy ["James H. Ebersole" (sic)];

b. b) one of the four Bethesda participants involved in the "Report of Inspection" of the X-rays and photographs [see *"Post Mortem"*, pp. 565-573]---signed by Ebersole 11/10/66 ;

c. c) 8/27/72 interview with David Lifton (*"Best Evidence"*, pp. 518-519)---"...I don't remember seeing any metallic fragments in the lung.... To the best of my knowledge, we actually started the autopsy formally about ten-thirty at night.";

[d) - g): "*The Ides of March ('78)?*"]

d. 3/9/78 interview with Gil Delaney of the "*Lancaster (PA) Intelligencer-Journal*"[see also "*Best Evidence*", p. 543, as part of Chapter 23 entitled "*Allegations of Dr. John Ebersole*"]---"When the body was removed from the casket, there was a very obvious horrible gaping wound to the back of the head...The front of the body, except for a very slight bruise above the right eye on the forehead, was absolutely intact. It was the back of the head that was blown off...Later on in the evening, between midnight and one A.M., a large portion of the skull was sent up from Dallas...that represented the back portion of the skull."; Ebersole came in after midnight to take more X-rays; all X-rays were taken in the morgue; "...There was, however, at the base of the throat a very neatly sutured, neatly sewn, opening that we interpreted initially as a surgical wound.";

e. 3/10/78 interview with Jack Severson of the "*Philadelphia Inquirer*"[see also

"*Best Evidence*", p. 541]---the neck wound had arrived from Dallas neatly sutured; "We found no bullet in the body."; the body came in at 8 P.M.;

f. 3/11/78 interview with the HSCA [see also 7 HSCA, as well as pp. 352-353 of "*Killing Kennedy*" by H.E.L. re: a "bust" of Kennedy]: "the back of the head was missing." Dr. Ebersole was asked, "Do you recall seeing those three fragments and X-raying the bones?" "Yes. This was maybe midnight to one o'clock when these fragments arrived from Dallas... [this obviously excludes the Harper fragment]Perhaps about twelve-thirty a large fragment of the occipital bone was received from Dallas and at Dr. Finck's request I X-rayed these. "However, Dr. Ebersole was shown the official photo of the intact back of the head---he was then asked: "Do you remember or have any independent recollection of that condition of the President when you were in the autopsy room?" "You know, my recollection is more of a gaping occipital wound than this but I can certainly not state that this is the way it looked... But had you asked me without seeing these or seeing the picture, you know, I would have put the gaping wound here rather than more forward." They ask him: "When you compare those two photographs, what inference do you draw now about the nature of the gaping wound to the President's head in terms of where it was located? Earlier, you said it was in the back of the head. Looking at these two views, how would you characterize the location of that gaping wound?" "More lateral. Much more lateral and superior than I remembered... I would have been more familiar with this aspect in positioning the head for the X-rays. I mean, this requires a forward effort to show this portion of the head on the part of the prosecutor, right?" Ebersole is then asked: "Is there a point in that photograph on the head which you take to be a bullet wound?" "[photo number]42? No, I would not want to make a statement on that basis." [!]; Dr. Ebersole was asked, "Do you remember some tentative discussion as to whether the bullet entered [the back]and then dropped out?" "Yes, a great deal of discussion of that type." "Is it your impression at that time during when the X-rays were taken and after the X-rays were taken that this was considered as a possibility?" "Yes.";

g. 3/28/78 interview with Arthur A. Smith [complete, 25-page transcript of audio tapes provided to the author with the attached drawings included; see also "*The Continuing Inquiry*", 7/78 issue; referred to in "*Best Evidence*", pp. 544-547; "*High Treason*", pp. 76-77; "*High Treason 2*", pages 152-153, 157, 215-216; "*Killing The Truth*", Appendix J: numerous; "*Killing Kennedy*", pages 112 and 215; see also Art Smith's presentation video from COPA 10/96]---"In the front there was a slight bruise above the right eye; there was a transverse wound across the lower neck in the front... slightly below [the Adam's apple]. This was, appeared to be a transverse surgically sutured, transverse surgical wound... the remainder of the body was normal from the front... in the article [referring to his statement in one of the two article above], I said the back of the head, it was more the right side of the head... Right side. A large wound deep back on the right side... Large gaping wound. I said it was blown off---wasn't correct. Traumatic, it was large, large gaping wound... Roughly irregular, very irregular circle of about so [two inches by three inches]... At least. Rough, irregular."; "...there is a very definite wound of entrance, the lower neck or back, depending on how you want to describe it, to the right of the midline."; "...twelve thirty, one o'clock in the morning when, from Dallas, three pieces of skull bone arrived, and Dr. Finck suggested I X-ray those and I did, and they were included in the archive pictures."; "...we were in communication with Dallas...We were told a bullet had been found in a blanket and now that was being sent up. That, was, as I remember, was sent up approximately the same time as the three pieces of skull bone were being x-rayed...I have no knowledge of any missile that Dr. Humes had, except possibly the one that was sent up from Dallas."; "...the biggest defect is on the right, the right side of the skull. The right parietal."; Re: the three bone fragments: "The largest might have been---two by three inches...The other two were smaller. Significantly smaller."; Smith: "Speaking about a wound of entrance; did you notice one, in the back of the head, or in the side of the head, or in the top of the head?" "No, just a gaping wound..."; Smith: "I take it you were misquoted in the papers?" "Yeah...I said the back of the head [was] blown out." Smith: "Yes. That was a misquote?" "Yes. Misquoted. I, really, ah, I may have said that---what I meant was the side." [!]; "There were two lines that I personally drew on there [the x-rays]." Smith: "For a sculptor." "For a sculptor." Smith: "You know his name? " "No. (emphatically said). About, uh, I'd have to place it roughly within a month of the autopsy, I was called by Dr. Captain James young, who was on the White House medical staff, and asked if I could, from the skull x-rays, furnish, uh, life measurements. I said, yes, I thought I could. And so I went down to the White House annex and saw the skull films. And drew a line from the, from what we call the nasean [phonetic] base of the nose, to the occipital area, on the lateral skull film, in pencil; and took careful measurements of that. Then I drew a fixed angle from it to the high point of the skull, to give me that. I also took measurements on the anterior [means AP]. I didn't draw any lines on the anterior, across the eyes, and so on. And, uh, provided Dr. Young with those measurements; for whatever reason, I don't know. I was told they were for a sculptor.";"...a wound of exit at the throat, which had been sutured...the sutured wound we saw...did seem to be neatly sutured...sewed it up. It was neat, it was surgical. Certainly in my eyes, it was.";

h.   11/2/92 and 12/2/92 interviews with Dr. David Mantik (see *"Killing The Truth"*, pages 721 and 724; *"Killing Kennedy"*, pages 210 and 390 [Mantik's letter to *JAMA*]; *"Assassination Science"*, pages 98, 104, 110, 111, 122, 136, 137, 139, and 155; *"Between The Signal and the Noise"* by Roger Bruce Feinman, p. 49)-- Ebersole stated that the back wound was not at the base of the neck; "quite surprised at the trach. He'd never want one like that!"; "[Ebersole] advised me unequivocally (on tape) that the back wound was at the level of T4."; retracted the "suture statement";

i.   interview with Brad Parker [as revealed in an unanswered letter Parker sent to James J. Humes provided to the author]---"Dr. John Ebersole gave me information which conflicted with the "official" version of events. Dr. Ebersole suggested that these discrepancies could be cleared up by consulting "the pathologists" in charge of the "autopsy." Unfortunately, this was not allowed to happen.";

j.   ARRB interview of Mrs. Marion Ebersole [deceased 9/24/2004] (Chapter 7 of

135

the *Final Report of the Assassination Records Review Board*)--- "The Review Board staff contacted the widow of Dr. John J. Ebersole, the Navy radiologist who was on duty the night of President Kennedy's autopsy at Bethesda National Naval Medical Center. Although he was not yet board-certified, he served as the consulting radiologist during the procedure. Ebersole said she did not have any of her husband's personal papers or any assassination records.";

k. *"Murder in Dealey Plaza"* by James Fetzer (2000), pages x, 112, 115, 199, 202, 225, 230, 238, 247, 253, 256-257, 267-268, 273, 285, 301, 358, 377, 433-437

l. *"JFK Absolute Proof"* by Robert Groden (2013), page 156: Ebersole is pictured with a nice summary of his statements

197) Richard A. Lipsey, aide to General Wehle:

a. TWO: 1/18/78 (audio-taped) interview with the HSCA's Andy Purdy and Mark Flanagan (RIF#180-10105-10405[see footnote on p. 619 of *"Best Evidence"*: "Lipsey insisted that Purdy tape record his interview, and Lipsey also made his own tape of the interview for his records." See also pp. 186-187 of *"Bloody Treason"* by Noel Twyman])---"Lipsey says he feels he knows "for a fact" that someone shot JFK three times and that these bullets came from behind."; said that the autopsists "were 'absolutely, unequivocally' convinced that he (JFK) had been shot three times...there were three separate wounds and three separate bullets."; "identified the entrance in the lower head as being just inside the hairline", but also made the claim that there was "no real entrance in the rear of the head...one bullet blasted away an entire portion (entrance and exit)... one bullet entered the back of the head and exited resulting in part of the face and head being blown away." [?!]; Lipsey's drawing is interesting: the diagram he drew depicts an area of the right lateral skull missing, both anterior and posterior to the ear, where he had written "same area blown away as wound." Lipsey also drew a small hole, presumably of entrance, low on the rear of the skull, which he writes was the "entrance---of bullet #2"; this wound correlated, in Lipsey's view, with the frontal neck wound: "Exit point of wound #2." Finally, he drew a wound high up in the back (at the base of the neck, actually), labeled #3, but the bullet could not be found in the body.; "Lipsey says that he recalls the doctors discussing the third bullet which he believes entered low in the neck and was deflected down into the chest cavity."; "Lipsey said the doctors followed the path of the bullet for a short distance until they lost the track at which point they removed the organs in an attempt to locate it."; "Lipsey mentioned that he and Wehle then flew by helicopter to Bethesda and took JFK into the back of Bethesda. A decoy hearst [sic] had been driven to the front."; ALSO: 7 HSCA 20, ref. No. 95: "He [Lipsey] also concluded that the entrance in the rear of the head corresponded to an exit in the neck. This conclusion could not have originated with the doctors because during the autopsy they believed the neck defect only represented a tracheostomy incision [officially speaking]. Lipsey did properly relate the preliminary conclusion of the doctors during the autopsy that the entrance wound in the upper back had no exit. The doctors later determined that this missile had exited through the throat. Thus, although Lipsey's recollection of the number of defects to the body and the corresponding locations are correct, his conclusions are wrong and are not supported by any other evidence."[Lipsey determined that there were THREE entries in the rear! See p. 100 of "*Assassination Science*" for a good discussion about this matter];

b.   8/30/79 interview with David Lifton ("*Best Evidence*", pp. 418-419, 629-630)---Lipsey said he was "absolutely" sure that a second, or "decoy", ambulance was used when the President's body was taken from Andrews Air Force Base to Bethesda Naval Hospital for the autopsy. Lipsey claimed that the ambulance in which Jackie and RFK rode contained an empty coffin and that JFK's body was in another ambulance that rode further back in the motorcade.; nothing about the nature of the wounds discussed;

c.   8/27/98 letter to Vince Palamara---"Because of the location (entrance) of the head wound, just above the earline [sic? Hairline?] and center right, in the back of the head, it was impossible for me to see the size of the entrance wound. The explosion did remove quite a bit of his scalp from the right ear forward in the hair line to the far right side of his forehead. I'm sorry I cannot offer you more information."[?];

d.   "*Murder in Dealey Plaza*" by James Fetzer (2000), page 199

e.   Lipsey's audio recorded statement: http://www.youtube.com/watch?v=G9UZ-z07eNMc

198) Maj. Gen. Philip C. Wehle, Commanding Officer of the Military District of Washington, D.C. (deceased 9/20/78):

a.   FBI (Sibert & O'Neill) Report 11/26/63 [see "*Post Mortem*", pp. 532-536]: listed as present during autopsy;

b.   "After Action Report/ Summary," Gen. Wehle's Office, Military District of Washington (MDW), 11/22/63 [see also "*The Death of a President*" by William Manchester, p. 670; *these documents were later released by the Gerald Ford Library*]: "At 1600 hours Paul Miller called General Wehle and informed him of the following information: a. Pres. would arrive Andrews at 1800 hours. B. He will be choppered from there to the Navy Medical Center for autopsy."; "White House requests that General Wehle be responsible for contacting Admiral Galloway (of Bethesda)…re: request to lay security cordon around the heliport. "; "…General Clifton realized that the change at the airport fowled up plans a bit, but they were not blaming MDW at all."; "Remains will be air lifted to Navy Medical Center in Bethesda.";

c.   4/29/64 interview with William Manchester ("*The Death of a President*", numerous);

d.   4/9/67 interview with David Lifton ("*Best Evidence*", pp. 396-397)---denied that he had been present in the autopsy room when the Dallas coffin arrived, as reported by Manchester (above): "I went into the autopsy room after that [the original casket opening] was done…I was just outside the door." Wehle did go inside later on; Wehle confirmed that two Navy ambulances were used when JFK's body was brought to Bethesda and that the team was sent in pursuit of the wrong ambulance.;

e. 8/19/77 interview with the HSCA's Andy Purdy [HSCA record # 10010042, agency file # 002086, p. 2]---Purdy reported that Maj. Gen. Wehle had been an observer during the latter stages of the autopsy. "(Wehle) noticed a slight bruise over the right temple of the President but did not see any significant damage to any other part of the head. He noted that the wound was in the back of the head so he would not see it because the President was lying face up; he also said he did not see any damage to the top of the head, but said the President had a lot of hair which could have hidden that... there could have been an open casket"; "He had no discussions with Adm. Burkley or Robert McNamara concerning orders given regarding the nature of the autopsy.";

f. 2/15/78 Outside contact report by the HSCA's Mark Flanagan (RIF#180-10080-10346)---"inquire[d] if he was still the CO of the military District of Wash. at the time of JFK's reinternment in March, 1967-he was NOT-retired in 1965";

g. [unanswered letter to Wehle's family from Vince Palamara 1998]

h. "*Murder in Dealey Plaza*" by James Fetzer (2000), pages 179, 198

199) Captain John H. "Smokey" Stover, Jr., Commanding Officer of the National Naval Medical School:

a. FBI (Sibert & O'Neill) report 11/26/63 [see "*Post Mortem*", pp. 532-536]---listed as present during autopsy ["Capt. James H. Stoner, Jr." (sic)];

b. 11/22/63 receipt, Stover to Kellerman, re: autopsy film [see "*Post Mortem*", p. 546; see also "*Best Evidence*", pp. 521-522 and photo 29];

c. 11/22/63 receipt, Francis X. O'Neill and James W. Sibert to Stover, re: "a missile" [see "*Post Mortem*", p. 266];

d. 11/24/63 Certificate, Humes to Stover re: autopsy working papers [see "*Post Mortem*", p. 525];

e. 11/26/63 memorandum from Stover (to: apparently everyone at Bethesda) [see "*Post Mortem*", p. 303]: "1. You are reminded that you are under verbal orders of the Surgeon General, United States Navy, to discuss with no one events connected with your official duties on the evening of 22 November-23 November 1963. 2. This letter constitutes official notification and reiteration of these verbal orders. You are warned that infraction of these orders makes you liable to Court Martial proceedings under appropriate articles of the Uniform Code of Military Justice."[-See also p. 185 of "*Bloody Treason*"---Paul O'Connor specifically recalls this threat];

f. 12/6/63 memo, Stover to Burkley, re: final supplementary report [see "*Post Mortem*", p. 528];

g. WC references: WR 546/ 16 H 989 (CE391) [see reference "f)" above]; 2 H 349 (Humes);17 H 47 [see reference "d)" above];

h. 9/11/64 memorandum by Pierre A. Finck [see "*Bloody Treason*" by Noel Twyman, p. 201]---"I am called by Capt. Stover, CO of Naval Med School. He tells me that Admiral Burkley, White House physician called him. The Warren Commission Report will be released to the Press shortly. However, the prosecutors involved in Kennedy's autopsy are still required not to release information to the press. Inquiries should be referred to the White House Press Office, Brig Gen Blumberg, AFIP Director, calls me within two hours, notifying me of the same White House orders.";

i. 10/29/66: identified Lt. Cmdr. William Bruce Pitzer's body and went to the Pitzer residence with Lt. Cmdr. C.A. Holston to tell Mrs. Joyce B. Pitzer the news of her husband's "suicide"[2/13/67 Board of Investigation report: see the Jan. 1998 "*JFK/ Deep Politics Quarterly*": article by Eaglesham and Palmer, as well as the Jan. 1998 "*Fourth Decade*": article by Marvin and Rose];

j. 5/11/78 interview with the HSCA's Mark Flanagan (RIF#180-10102-10407 [see also 7 HSCA 25])---"Stover observed...a wound on the top of the head, second, a wound in the upper back"; JFK's brain was placed in a stainless-steel bucket, 7-by-8 inches, which Stover placed in the closet of Admiral Calvin B. Galloway.; could not recall ever seeing an intact missile in the autopsy room that night;

k. 1/20/78 Outside contact report with the HSCA's Mark Flanagan (RIF#180-10101-10256)---"(1) does not recall how and when physical material went to White House; Admiral Burkley had control over the materials, "all material to be in his custody" (Burkley's) (2) not aware of any order of limitation of any kind (3) cannot recall the order that Admiral Galloway gave to perform a complete autopsy";

l. 4/13/80 interview with David Lifton ("*Best Evidence*", pages 630 and 651)---"I think there was a body bag...I remember seeing a body bag...I think I remember seeing a body bag peeled off."; "It seems to me that the [bullet] they found in Dallas they brought up...I think it was in a brown paper envelope...one of those slim ones with the opening across the narrow end."; Regarding his receipt for "a missile" [see reference "c)" above], Stover said: "I'm not sure that that's [the] complete round you're talking about---it's the thing I may or may not have signed the receipt for...I signed a receipt for some fragments.";

m. "*Murder in Dealey Plaza*" by James Fetzer (2000), pages 199, 205, 286

200) Chester Herschel Boyers, Jr., Chief Petty Officer in charge of Pathology Department:

a. FBI (Sibert & O'Neill) report 11/26/63 [see "*Post Mortem*", pp. 532-536]: listed as present during autopsy;

b. CD7, 283: receipt for autopsy films [see "*Post Mortem*", p. 270---"The original receipts were typed by Chester H. Bowers [sic] of the Navy "who visited the autopsy room during the final stages of such to type receipts given by FBI and Secret Service for items obtained.""];

c. 4/25/78 interview with the HSCA's Mark Flanagan (Agency File Number 013614; RIF# 180-10105-10398, Agency File Number 014462) [see also "*Bloody Treason*", p. 193]: "In regard to the wounds Boyers recalls an entrance wound in the rear of the head to the right of the external occipital protuberance which exited along the top, right side of the head towards the rear and just above the right eyebrow. He also saw an entrance wound in the right shoulder blade, specifically just under the scapula and next to it. Boyers also noted a tracheotomy incision in the neck." Boyers stated that the path of the bullet that entered JFK's upper back seemed to indicate that the bullet exited through the tracheotomy.; "...only fragments were recovered. Boyers never saw a fully intact missile."; "Concerning the wounds of President Kennedy, Mr. Boyers stated that there was a large wound to the right side and towards the rear of the head ... He estimated the massive wound in the head measured 3 inches by 3 inches.";

d. 12/4/78 affidavit to the HSCA (RIF#1012010362 [see 7 HSCA 12 and 25])---- "..Chester H. Boyers, the corpsman who typed the receipt,(70) submitted an affidavit to the committee which stated that the receipt was for two fragments that Dr. Humes removed from the skull, despite the receipt's caption of "a missile." (71) Boyers emphasized that he gave Sibert and O'Neill only missile fragments."; "Chester Boyers, one of the Navy personnel involved in the microscopic examination, informed the committee in an affidavit that he recalled preparing for analysis sections of organs on November 24, 1963, and the brain on December 2, 1963. (30) Neither Captain Stover nor Chester Boyers could recall what happened to these materials after this examination other than that Dr. Humes and Dr. Boswell, two of the autopsy pathologists, maintained possession of them at Bethesda Naval Hospital.(31)"; "I recall during the autopsy there was much use of metal probes trying to locate the passage of the bullet from the right shoulder entrance. I do not believe the actual passage was proven to have exited, at the site of the tracheotomy, i.e., by probing-due probably to deflection by bone structure."; "I noted while cutting the [brain] tissue there is a definite picture of the way the missile passed. A pencil effect, i.e., push a pencil through a piece of paper and note the results.";

e. 8/25/98 letter to Vince Palamara---"For starters you might try reading the Warren Commission report, and what Dr. Humes and Dr. Boswell had to say on the matter, rather than believing what we, Tom ,Dick, or Harry has to say about it as long as a buck is to be made." [!];

f. "*Murder in Dealey Plaza*" by James Fetzer (2000), pages 199, 212, 301, 303-304

g. "*JFK Absolute Proof*" by Robert Groden (2013), page 156: nice summary of his statements

201) Floyd Albert Riebe, a medical photographer at Bethesda [Reibe] (deceased 3/23/2008):

a. FBI (Sibert & O'Neill) report 11/26/63 [see "*Post Mortem*", pp. 532-536]---listed as present during autopsy ["Lloyd E. Raihe" (sic)];

b. 11/22/63 receipt for photographic material, Stover to Kellerman [see "*Post Mortem*", p. 546; "*Best Evidence*", p. 521]---signed it (looks like "Floyd A. Rabe, HM2, USN"!);

c. 4/20/78 interview with the HSCA [see also 7 HSCA 10]---took the autopsy photos, with Stringer, under the direction of Humes;

d. 11/26/79 interview with David Lifton ("*Best Evidence*", pp. 637-639 [misspelled "Reibe"])---"I think he was in a body bag...Yes, a rubberized bag..."; "Reibe (sic) also said he thought he took about six pictures---"I think it was three film packs"---of internal portions of the body. Again, there are no such pictures in the official collection.";

e. "*JFK: An Unsolved Murder*", KRON, 11/18/88 (repeated in "*JFK: The Case for Conspiracy*" video 1993 [see still photo on p. 88 of Groden's "TKOAP"]): "a big gaping hole in the back of the head. It was like somebody put a piece of dynamite in a tin can and lit it off. There was nothing there."; Strongly disagreed with the autopsy photos: "The two pictures you showed me are not what I saw that night." Interviewer: "What did it look like?" "It had a big hole in it. This whole area was gone...It's being phonied someplace. It's make-believe.";

f. 4/1/91, 4/2/91, and 4/5/91 *and 4/6/91** interviews with Harry Livingstone for "*High Treason 2*" (numerous, esp. pages *288, *291-293, *302, *303, *305-309, and *311[*Including *photo of himself with other principals re: Livingstone video of the Dallas conference referred to in Chapter 14*])--"Floyd Riebe...stated that some of the photographs---those showing the back of the head---are composites---forgeries---and not what either he or John Stringer took. He stated that the photographs of the back of the head does not show the large wound as it really was."; "Floyd Riebe was absolutely sure that a deep depression showing on the President's back a good six inches down from the shoulder was the rear entry wound. He pointed it out on the picture. It was "pickled in. There is a hole. Colonel Finck and Dr. Boswell had their fingers in. The tissues pulled in, pushed in there. I know for a fact Colonel Finck had his finger in there."; Re: the autopsy photos: "There's a *lot* wrong with quite a few of them. They are phony. Somebody's dream...I believe that the better part of the pictures we have here today are phony. They're paste-ups...Somebody's dreamin' about it...That's not what I saw...I believe it's fake. I believe it's a paste-up. A composite-type thing."; "O'Connor and Riebe said the body came in a body bag in a shipping casket, not in the ceremonial casket it left Dallas in, and that it was wrapped in sheets."; "A lot of this evidence was doctored to fit the story that the government wanted to put out. There had to be a conspiracy in order to do all the work that had to be done, to do all that was done to the photographs alone. Somebody had to know about it and not tell.";

g. 5/28/92 Livingstone Press Conference held in New York (Reuter Wire story by Jean King entitled "*JFK X-Rays Called Fake*" and an Associated Press story, both dated 5/29/92 ; KDKA/ CBS [Pittsburgh, PA] news story 5/29/92; Livingstone's Press Kit) [see "*A Complete Book of Facts*" by Duffy and Ricci, pages 142-143, and 402-403, as well as "*Killing The Truth*", pages 163 and 169]---"The photographs said to be of President Kennedy at the autopsy are phony. They are not the photographs that we took. The picture of the back of his head is not right. All that part of his head was missing as far as the right ear, and there was not enough scalp to pull over the wound as it is in the pictures."; "These films are doctored one way or another."; "See these here pictures? They're wrong. I don't know what this is, but that ain't the way it was. He didn't have a back of the head.";

h. AP article, 6/1/92--- "The pictures I've seen *resemble* the pictures that I'd taken. That's all I can say. The quality of (these) prints is very poor. I'd have been in deep trouble if I'd turned in work like this."; Riebe "used a flash in a room that was already brightly lit.";

i. Scott Hatfield, *RT*, "*RT Disputes X-ray Photos in JFK Case*," 8/31/92---"Riebe... said he too believes that the autopsy photographs, showing the back of Kennedy's head to be intact, are forgeries...'retouched to conceal a large exit wound from the bullet entering from the front.'";

j. Captioned photo on page 182 of Groden's "*The Killing of a President*" ["TKOAP"], apparently from outtakes from Groden's video "*JFK: The Case for Conspiracy*" (1993): Riebe demonstrates the right rear of the head as missing;

k. Acknowledgments, "*The Search for Lee Harvey Oswald*" by Robert Groden (1995);

l. ARRB deposition--- Riebe, who had earlier told several researchers that the autopsy photographs had been altered based upon his examination of photographs that have been circulating in the public domain, re-evaluated his earlier opinion when shown the actual photographs at the National Archives.;

m. "*Murder in Dealey Plaza*" by James Fetzer (2000), pages 112, 113, 174, 204, 205, 210, 212, 225, 228, 240, 246

n. "*JFK Absolute Proof*" by Robert Groden (2013), page 155: Riebe is pictured with a nice summary of his statements

202-203) Dennis Duane David, Chief of the Day, Bethesda Naval Hospital, and Lt. Cmdr. William Bruce Pitzer (deceased 10/29/1966):

a. 5/1/75, "*The News-Sun*", Waukegan, IL: article by Art Peterson entitled "*A JFK Death*"[see also *Best Evidence*", pp. 570-571: part of Chapter 25 entitled "*The Lake County Informant*"]---"Kennedy's body was brought in through a back door in an unmarked ambulance. An official motorcade from the airport contained only an empty casket..."; "He also questions the whereabouts of the memo he typed following the autopsy, at the direction of a Secret Service agent. The memo for the official record of the autopsy stated four large pieces of lead were removed...";-discusses the death of **Lt. Commander William Bruce Pitzer** : Pitzer was a close friend of David's who reportedly had taken the JFK autopsy photos and had been repeatedly threatened because of what he had seen. Dennis stated that Pitzer would not have committed suicide, and that Pitzer was left-handed.;

b. 7/2/79 interview with David Lifton ("*Best Evidence*", pp. 571-582 [for a very good summary of David, see "*Bloody Treason*" by Noel Twyman, pp. 174-174,

178, 179, 183-186, and 188])---The ornamental casket that arrived at Bethesda with Jackie was a decoy, and JFK's body was already in the hospital when it arrived, carried into the back entrance in a plain coffin("a gray metal casket") which had been delivered by a black Cadillac "ambulance", not a gray Navy ambulance; Re: the four large pieces of lead (see above), David said : "There was more material than would come from one bullet, but maybe not enough for two.";

c.   "Best Evidence: The Research Video" ([Oct.] 1980/ 1990; excerpts included in "The Fifth Estate: Who Killed JFK?" 1983 CBC and "A Current Affair" 9/4/90): details what he told Lifton above (for the book);

d.   "JFK: An Unsolved Murder", KRON, 11/18/88 [see also "High Treason", pp. 448-449 and "Conspiracy" by Anthony Summers, pp. 482-483, for a short summary of what was said]: similar in content to the above filmed interview, but makes an interesting companion piece (complete with a still photo of David circa 1963); "The casket was a plain, grey box, a metal box. Anybody who's ever been in Vietnam will know what I'm talking about. We shipped hundreds of bodies out of thee in the same kind of casket. It was just a plain, shipping casket.";

e.   4/22/90, 5/12/90, 4/25/91, 5/29/91, 6/4/91, 6/6/91, 6/14/91, and 12/17/91 interviews with Livingstone for "High Treason 2" (see esp. pages 270 ,556, and 557) and "Killing The Truth" (pages 76, 708, 735, 738, 741, 742, 744, 745-746)---According to Dennis David, **Pitzer** had filmed the autopsy: "My impression from **Pitzer's** film was that it [head wound] was a frontal entry/ rear exit wound." ("...**Pitzer** was in the gallery filming the entire autopsy with a movie camera, and David, a chief petty officer at the time---who had helped bring in the casket---helped **Pitzer** edit the film. David was a bridge partner and close friend of **Pitzer's** for many years and used to baby-sit for his children. They all believe he was murdered."); believes that the casket he saw brought in at the morgue dock before Mrs. Kennedy arrived was a shipping casket ("It was a typical shipping casket. Just like the ones we used to ship men back from Vietnam.") and that JFK's body had arrived, having been offloaded from a helicopter and then taken over to the back door in a hearse ("It came in a black ambulance."). He thinks that the bronze ceremonial casket was empty, and that Dr. Boswell had told him that President Kennedy was in a shipping casket.;

f.   9/91 letter to Joanne Braun---"As to my observations of Mrs. Kennedy, I watched her enter through the main doors, cross the lobby (rotunda) and enter the elevators directly beneath me. Several dignitaries, including Secretary McNamara, followed Mrs. Kennedy by a few feet. I do remember watching the elevator indicator to know that it went directly to the VIP suite on the 17th floor.";

g.   9/11/91 letter to Joanne Braun---"As to **Bill Pitzer's** involvement, I never asked him, 'Were you there?' or 'Did you do the filming?' I have always assumed he did, but cannot verify that he was in the autopsy room that evening. I do know that he had the film in his possession at one time. When he and I looked at a portion of the film, we remarked only on the extent of injury, apparent point of entry, etc. Bill also had some 35mm slides, which, again I assumed, were excerpts from the film. I would say the films which I *viewed* with Bill were prior to the commencement of the postmortem, as there was no evidence of a Y incision on the torso, nor was the scalp incised and peeled forward on the face as would be done during a postmortem.";

h. 10/31/91 letter to Joanne Braun---"the film slides I viewed with **Bill Pitzer** showed much the same as the pictures which you enclosed. First, I had seen and helped treat gunshot wounds and from training and experience had some idea of their effect on human flesh. Even high-powered rifle or pistol (375, M-1, M-16, etc.) entry holes are substantially smaller than their exit. It is inconceivable that anyone even vaguely acquainted with gunshot wounds would conclude that the massive wound in the *rear* of JFK's skull could have occurred from a rear-entry projectile, unless it was from grenade or mortar shrapnel, which tears and rends flesh and bone rather than pierces it. What appeared to be an entry was near the point of the arrow you drew on the right lateral picture. Also, the extension of the original tracheotomy incision to attempt to obliterate what appears to be an entry wound reinforces our impression of a frontal attack. The tracheotomy appeared to be approximately twice the length necessary.";

i. *"The Men Who Killed Kennedy"* Part 6 (1995): David discusses *Pitzer* and his suspicious death: there is even a picture of *Pitzer* included in the program, which was part of a newspaper obituary. David says that the film ("16 mm") he helped edit/ viewed with *Pitzer* depicts a "frontal entry wound" to JFK's head: "little hole about here in the [right] temple" [indicates] and "a huge gaping hole in the back [indicates with hand on right rear of head] ... I do know those films exist 'cause I was there. I saw the damn things!"(Also included in the program, re: *Pitzer*, is Lt. Col. Daniel Marvin [see below]).;

j. 12/16/96 audiotaped responses to written questions from Lt. Col. Daniel Marvin [see *"JFK/ Deep Politics Quarterly"* journal, Jan. 1998 issue: article by Allan Eaglesham and Robin Palmer re: **Pitzer**]: "Vivid in [David's] memory is his agreement with **Bill Pitzer** that those materials showed what appeared to be an entry wound in the right frontal area with a corresponding exit wound in the lower rear of the skull. Thereafter, on occasion, Dennis heard Bill refer to contacts he'd had with "agents" about the Kennedy autopsy materials on which he had worked. These references, made in the company of others and thus precluding further discussion with Dennis, were couched in matter-of-fact terms without hint of threat or intimidation.";

k. 2/14/97 ARRB interview---stated that *Pitzer* was filming the autopsy from the gallery;

l. 1998 interviews with Bill Law [see the May 1998 *"Fourth Decade"* journal, p. 19---Custer *corroborates* David re: *Pitzer*];

m. 11/98 appearance at JFK Lancer conference, Dallas, TX;

More on **Pitzer**:

n. Jan. 1987 *"The Third Decade"* article by Harry Livingstone, p. 8---Pitzer mentioned in passing re: what Lifton neglected to mention in any way in *"Best Evidence"* (Pitzer is not mentioned at all in that book);

o. Jan 1988 *"The Third Decade"* article by Harry Livingstone: *"Lt. Commander William Bruce Pitzer"* [referred to in Joanne Braun's article in the March 1991 issue, p. 11];

p.   *"High Treason"*, pp. 57-60, 95-96, 106, and 143 [see also *"A Complete Book of Facts"* by Duffy and Ricci, pp. 376-377, *"Forgive My Grief III"* (1969) by Penn Jones, pp. 95-96; *"Crossfire"* by Jim Marrs, p. 560; Groden's *"TKOAP"*, p. 84, *"Who's Who in the JFK Assassination"* by Michael Benson, pp. 363-364; *"Case Closed"* by Gerald Posner, p. 495; and *"JFK: The Dead Witnesses"* by Craig Roberts and John Armstrong, pp. 40-41];

q.   May 1995 *"The Fourth Decade"* article by Lt. Col. Daniel Marvin, p. 16---"In January 1995 Mrs. Joyce B. Pitzer told me unequivocally that she knew her husband "had parts of the autopsy that they wanted destroyed." She was speaking of our government wanting the autopsy photos he'd taken of JFK on 22 November 1963 destroyed. She told me her husband "refused to do this.";

r.   *"Killing Kennedy"* by H.E.L., pp. 336-337, 340---long quote from the May 1995 *"Fourth Decade"* article referenced above; "...Pitzer was found shot to death at Bethesda Naval Hospital on the day, October 29, 1966, when the autopsy photographs and X-rays were transferred from the Kennedy's control to the National Archives. Four days later, November 1, Humes, Boswell, Ebersole, and Stringer were asked to inventory the pictures.";

s.   Oct. 1995 *"JFK/ Deep Politics Quarterly"* journal: article by Walt Brown re: interview with Custer [see above]--- "...Commander Humes, in his Warren Commission testimony, could only name three individuals present at the autopsy (Ebersole the radiologist and two Bethesda commanders), and that by my count, there were over thirty people present. Mr. Custer indicated that the total, counting those who were in and out, would have been closer to fifty, and that it was "crazy" in there, with "people running everywhere." Among the people he noted as present were the Joint Chiefs of Staff, who, he claimed, were "in an uproar." He also indicated that the composition of the audience could best be judged from photos taken by an officer named William Pitzer. [It is possible that Custer was absent, developing film, when Pitzer's photos were exposed to light and ruined.] Custer indicated an awareness of Pitzer's death a couple of years after the autopsy and said he did not believe it was a suicide...";

t.   Sept. 1997 *"The Fourth Decade"* journal, p. 27---re: skepticism over Marvin's claim that he was the target of an attempted CIA recruitment,, while still in the Army's Green Berets, to murder Lt. Commander William Bruce Pitzer;

u.   Jan. 1998 *"The Fourth Decade"* journal: *"The Pitzer File"* (article by Daniel Marvin and Jerry Rose)---inc. both the Feb.13, 1967 Board Report [pp. 19-22] and an FBI report, dated 11/15/66, of a 11/2/66 interview of John G. Ball, Deputy Medical Examiner for Montgomery County Maryland [back cover];

v.   Jan. 1998 *"JFK/ Deep Politics Quarterly"* journal: *"The Untimely Death of Lt. Cmdr. William Pitzer"* (article by Allan Eaglesham and Robin Palmer)---see reference "j)" above; recommended reading re: Pitzer's alleged "suicide";

w.   April 1998 *"JFK/ Deep Politics Quarterly"* journal: *"Interpretations of New Information in the Pitzer Case"* (article by Allan Eaglesham)---good follow-up article to "u)" above;

x. *May 1998 "The Fourth Decade" journal, pages 11-12 and 18 (Daniel Marvin)---* inc. an excerpt from Penn Jones' book re: Pitzer [see reference "o)" above] and RIF#180-10106-10207 re: 10/11/77 interview of Penn Jones by the HSCA's David Martindale;

y. *[David: unanswered letter from Vince Palamara 1998]*

z. *"Murder in Dealey Plaza"* by James Fetzer (2000), pages 106-107, 112

aa. Presentation at JFK Lancer conference, 2003

ab. *"In The Eye Of History"* by William Law (2004)

ac. *"Without Smoking Gun: Was the Death of Lt. Cmdr. William Pitzer Part of the JFK Assassination Cover-up Conspiracy?"* by Kent Heiner (2004): regarding ***Pitzer***

ad. *"JFK Absolute Proof"* by Robert Groden (2013), page 301: regarding ***Pitzer*** (and Dennis David); page 155 and 178: David is pictured with a nice summary of his statements

204)-206) Arthur Donald "Red" Rebentisch, A Navy petty officer at Bethesda (deceased 11/21/2012), Richard Muma, dental technician, and Paul Neigler:

a. *"Grand Rapids (MI) Press"*: article by Jerry Morlock, carried by the two wire services [see also p. 701 of *"Best Evidence"*];

b. 1/24/81 AP story, *"Fort Worth Star Telegram"* and

c. 1/25/81 UPI story, *"Miami Herald"*--- the coffin came in through a rear freight entrance 30 to 40 minutes before the bronze coffin arrived: "It was a typical Navy gray shipping coffin. Just exactly as we expected. I helped take it out of the hearse. But then somebody else came and took it upstairs...We put it on a gurney and wheeled it in."; "It was about 4:30 when our chief petty officer came to me and about five other petty officers and told us to go to the back of the hospital. I'm talking about the loading ramps where they used to bring in supplies...He told all of us that we were going to be there and we were going to bring the President's casket into the mortuary. We were told not to leave our posts. The chief said we got all the ghouls and reporters and the TV and everrybody at the front of the hospital. He said there would be an empty casket in the ambulance. He said the President's body would really come in the back. We took the casket out...and pushed it down a long, illuminated hall. Now this is a service area, not the main part of the hospital."; "Rebentisch said he doubted most of Lifton's claims."; two other Navy men---***Richard [Robert] Muma***, a Bethesda staff dental technician, and ***Paul Neigler***---corroborated Rebentisch's story: Muma-"There were two ambulances that came in. One was lighted. It came up to the front door. The second one they kept dark and it went around to the back. That was the one that had Kennedy in it. It was common knowledge that there were two caskets.";

d. 1981 interview with David Lifton (*"Best Evidence"*, p. 701 [see also pp. 482-483 of *"Conspiracy"* by Anthony Summers, as well as pages 185 and 188 of *"Bloody*

Treason" by Noel Twyman])---"He provided corroboration for Dennis David's account by recalling that he had helped unload the first casket, an ordinary shipping casket, and that it had arrived at the back before the gray navy ambulance arrived at the front.Rebentisch said that *after* unloading the first casket, he went upstairs to the lobby area of Bethesda where he saw Mrs. Kennedy, who had just arrived in the navy ambulance, waiting for the elevator.";

e. 4/81, "*The Fifth Estate: The Missing Casket*", Canadian Broadcasting Corporation (repeated in the 1983 episode of "*The Fifth Estate*" entitled "*Who Killed JFK?*") [see p. 701 of "*Best Evidence*"]---interview inc. David Lifton; Rebentisch repeated the story he told as reported in the newspaper accounts above; "No, it [the casket he saw] definitely wasn't that coffin" [the ceremonial casket];

f. 5/17/91 and 5/27/91 interviews with Harry Livingstone (see "*High Treason 2*", pages 136 and 271 [O'Connor], and "*Killing The Truth*", pages 678, 733, 738-742, and 746 [see also "*A Complete Book of Facts*" by Duffy and Ricci, pp.396-397])---"What Rebentisch helped unload was the gray shipping casket from a black hearse a half hour before Kennedy came in with the [Air Force] major's body."; Rebentisch was detailed to wait out back for Dr. Pierre Finck: "They had already started the autopsy. Finck drove up and I asked him for his identification and he showed it to me and I led him in."; said the casket came in at least 20 minutes before the Kennedy party. Rebentisch was in charge of the color guard.; "There was no bronze ceremonial casket come in the back door when I was there...it was a grey metal aluminum-type shipping casket. That I remember."; "Rebentisch remembers the color guard captain, and said he died a week later from the strain." [He is correct: see "The Death of a President", p. 638];

g. 9/1/98 letter to Vince Palamara---"...The casket that was sent to "Bethesda" with the President's body in it was a military style shipping casket "*metal*", I helped move this casket-"*closed*" to the morgue.This was before the Navy ambulance arrived at Bethesda with Mrs. Kennedy. I did see Mrs. Kennedy in the rotunda at the hospital when she arrived, well "*after*" we received the president's body. I did not view the President's body, but my room mate was present during the autopsy and he did tell me of the details of that procedure..." [his emphasis];

207) Vice/ Rear Admiral (Dr.) Calvin B. Galloway, Commanding Officer of the entire Naval Medical Center [Gallaway; Holloway; deceased 1/28/1992]:

a. FBI (Sibert & O'Neill) report 11/26/63 [see "*Post Mortem*", pp. 532-536]---listed as present during autopsy ["Adm. C.B. Holloway" (sic)];

b. CD 371 / CE 397 [see also 2 H 373 and "*Post Mortem*", p. 526] :11/25/63 receipt, Galloway to Burkley---"1.Transmitted herewith by hand is the sole remaining copy (number eight) of the completed protocol in the case of John F. Kennedy. Attached are the work papers used by the Prosector and his assistants. 2. This command holds no additional documents in connection with this case. 3. Please acknowledge receipt.";

c. 11/26/63 PRS/ Secret Service document by Robert I. Bouck: receipt of materials from Burkley [see "*Post Mortem*", p. 527];

d. CE 391 / SS Control #1221 / Commission #498 / 16 H 989 / WR 546 [see also "*Post Mortem*", p. 528]: 12/6/63 transmittal letter/ receipt, Stover to Burkley via Galloway, re: forwarding of "*Supplementary report of Naval Medical School autopsy No. A63-272*"

e. 3/12/64 Memorandum, Specter to Rankin, Re: 3/11/64 Interview of Autopsy Surgeons [see "*Post Mortem*", pp. 539-540]---"On the afternoon of March 11, 1964, Joseph A. Ball, Esq., and I went to Bethesda Naval Hospital and interviewed Admiral C.B. Holloway [sic], Commander James J. Humes and Commander "J" Thornton Boswell. The interview took place in the office of Admiral Holloway [sic], who is the commanding officer of the National Naval Medical Center, and lasted from approximately 3:30 p.m. to 5:30 p.m. Commander Humes and Commander Boswell, along with Lt. Col. Pierre A. Finck, who is currently in Panama, conducted the autopsy and Admiral Holloway [sic] was present at all times... All three described the bullet wound on President Kennedy's BACK as being a point of entrance. Admiral Holloway [sic] then illustrated the angle of the shot by placing one finger on my BACK and the second finger on the front part of my CHEST which indicated that the bullet traveled in a consistent downward path, on the ASSUMPTION that it emerged in the opening on the President's throat which had been enlarged by the performance of the tracheotomy in Dallas. " [emphasis added];

f. WC references: 2 H 349 (Humes: recalled Galloway's presence at the autopsy); 18 H 727 (Kellerman's report dated 11/29/63---"...I remained in the morgue and viewed the autopsy examinations which were performed by Vice Admiral Gallway [sic], Commanding Officer, NNMC...Humes...Finck...and Boswell..."); 22 H 96 (Burkley's report: mentioned Galloway's presence);

g. mentioned several times by Dr. Pierre Finck during the Clay Shaw Trial, 2/24-2/25/69 [see "*Destiny Betrayed: JFK, Cuba, and the Garrison Case*" by James DiEugenio (1992), pages 294, 295, 300, 307, and 308; see also "*Post Mortem*", p. 236]---Question: "Who told you that three shots were heard? Who told you that?" "As I recall, Admiral Galloway heard from somebody who was present at the scene that three shots had been heard, but I cannot give the details of this."; "During the autopsy of President Kennedy there were [sic] Secret Service Agent Kellerman in that autopsy room. I asked him his name. Admiral Berkley [sic], the personal physician of Presdient Kennedy was present, and there was a third person whose name I don't recall who said to Admiral Galloway, who was there during the autopsy, that three shots had been fired."; "I personally talked to Admiral Galloway, who was referred to a third witness present at the scene. There may have been others leading us to the statement that to the best of our knowledge at that time there were three shots fired."; Question: "...you said in your report, "The second wound presumably of entry," and now you state in Court that you are positive it was an entry." "As I recall, it was Admiral Galloway who told us to put that word "presumably". "Admiral Galloway?" "Yes." "Told you to put that word "presumably"? "Yes, but this does not change my opinion that this is a wound of entry." "Is Admiral Galloway a Pathologist, to your knowledge?" "Admiral Galloway had some training in Pathology. He was the Commanding Officer of the Naval Hospital, as I recall, and at that time, in my mind, this was a wound of entry, it just was suggested to add "presumably" this was." "Did he suggest you add anything else to your report, Colonel?" "Not that I recall."; "From what I remember, Admiral Galloway was in uniform."; Finck admitted that Galloway personally ordered changes in the autopsy report after it was drafted!;

h. 5/17/78 interview with the HSCA (RIF#180-10079-0460 [see also 7 HSCA footnote 44])---Stated that various enlisted men took X-rays and photographs throughout the autopsy; said that no orders were being sent in from outside the autopsy room either by phone or in person. He said that Pierre Finck, the pathologist with the greatest expertise, seemed to be the person exercising authority and that occasionally some people, such as the senior staff members of the President, were entering and exiting the autopsy room.; recalled a discussion that attempted to determine where the missile that entered the back could have exited [see reference "e)" above]; Galloway could not remember what happened to the tissue specimens and JFK's brain, as well as where these materials were stored between the autopsy and the microscopic examination [see Stover];

i. 6/4/78 interview with David Lifton ("Best Evidence", p. 491[also: there are numerous references to Galloway throughout the book; in particular, see p. 521]): Did not do any cutting during the autopsy: "No, I was not suited up. No, I was just in uniform."; the FBI agents were kept out of the autopsy room for a while : "That's correct…you don't let a whole lot of unnecesary people into an autopsy."; repeatedly said that the Warren Report was correct, yet conceded that "there's certain things that do not make any sense.";

j. "The Washington Post", 11/23/63---"…the ambulance containing the coffin sat unattended for several minutes [at Bethesda]. A Navy cordon finally pushed the crowd back about 15 feet from the vehicle. Adm. Calvin B. Galloway, commandant of the medical center, pushed into the front seat and drove to the rear of the Hospital, where the body was taken inside." [Galloway denied to Lifton that he drove the ambulance, but did admit to riding inside.];

k. Two references in "The Death of a President" (pages 398 and 416 [see also "Best Evidence", pp. 395-396]): "Admiral Galloway lingered on the walk, detained by General McHugh." We're going to the morgue for the autopsy and the embalming,' Godfrey said. "Mrs. Kennedy doesn't want an undertaker." "We don't have the facilities. I highly recommend a funeral parlor." Godfrey pressed him. "Those are the family's wishes. Isn't it possible?" "it's not impossible," said the Admiral frowning. "It's difficult, though. And it might be unsatisfactory.";

l. "Murder in Dealey Plaza" by James Fetzer (2000), page 112

208) Elsie Boehm Closson, Galloway's secretary:

a. 7 HSCA 16, footnote 128---" Admiral Galloway instructed Elsie B. Closson, his secretary, to type the autopsy report and the supplemental report because he believed he needed a typist with a top secret security clearance. See outside contact report, Elsie B. Closson, May 4, 1978, House Select Committee on Assassinations (JFK Document No. 008135).";

b. "*Best Evidence*", p. 607---mentions "Galloway's secretary" [unnamed] as being among the "thirteen men" (sic) who were subject to Kenney's/ Stover's order not to talk;

209) Dr. George Bakeman, U.S. Navy:

a. FBI (Sibert & O'Neill) report 11/26/63 [see "*Post Mortem*", pp. 532-536]: listed as present during autopsy [it was thought by some that this was some sort of a typo for Dr. George Burkley, due to the misspellings of other names in this report. However, Burkley, misspelled "Berkley", is ALREADY accounted for on the page prior to Bakeman's name. In addition, there ARE several men named "George Bakeman" listed throughout the United States.];

b. 7 HSCA 8---"the committee could not locate this person";

c. "*High Treason 2*", p. 181: interview of Dr. Karnei---"I have no idea who Bakeman is. Unless he got in there early in the evening and came in with the body. But, no, I don't know anybody by that name that I allowed in the room.";

d. "*A Complete Book of Facts*" by Duffy and Ricci, p. 49---"no information exists regarding who he is";

e. "*Murder in Dealey Plaza*" by James Fetzer (2000), page 112

210) Lt. Cmdr. Gregory H. Cross, resident in surgery:

a. FBI (Sibert & O'Neill) report 11/26/63 [see "*Post Mortem*", pp. 532-536]: listed as present during autopsy;

b. "*The Day Kennedy Was Shot*" by Jim Bishop, p. 450---"In addition, Lieutenant Commander Gregg Cross and Captain David Osborne, chief of surgery, could be expected to be in and out of the autopsy room, depending upon whether Commander Humes required assistance." [this reads like Bishop just extrapolated from the Sibert & O'Neill report cited above];

c. 7 HSCA 8---listed as present during autopsy;

d. 4/24/78 Outside contact report by the HSCA's Mark Flanagan (RIF#180-10105-10396, Agency File Number 014460)---"The only wound Cross saw was situated in the posterior aspect of the head."[emphasis added];

e. *[unanswered letter from Vince Palamara 1998]*

211) Edwin B. Stroble, Gawler's Funeral Home (deceased 5/29/76, JFK's birthday [and before the HSCA]):

a. FBI (Sibert & O'Neill) report 11/26/63 [see "*Post Mortem*", pp. 532-536]: listed as present during autopsy;

b. *"The Day Kennedy Was Shot"* by Jim Bishop, pages 606 and 643---"Hagan just wanted the strangers to know that Gawler's was prepared. He had an embalming team waiting in an office to the left; John Van Haesen, Edwin B. Stroble, and Thomas Robinson...They would not begin their labors until the autopsy team signified that its work had been completed." [Evidently, Bishop interviewed these men: "The men of Gawler's Sons were discreet and ethical." (page 684)];

c. *"Killing Kennedy"* by H.E.L., p. 272---"Edwin Stroble and John Van Haeson also helped [Tom Robinson], all from Gawler's."

d. *"Effingham Daily News"*, 2/22/14: http://www.effinghamdailynews.com/local/x2039931337/Altamont-native-prepared-John-F-Kennedy-for-funeral

212) John Van Hoesen, Gawler's Funeral Home [Van Haesen; Van Haeson; Van Hausen]:

a. FBI (Sibert & O'Neill) report 11/26/63 [see *"Post Mortem"*, pp. 532-536]: listed as present during autopsy;

b. *"The Day Kennedy Was Shot"* by Jim Bishop, pages 606 and 643---"Hagan just wanted the strangers to know that Gawler's was prepared. He had an embalming team waiting in an office to the left; John Van Haesen, Edwin B. Stroble, and Thomas Robinson...They would not begin their labors until the autopsy team signified that its work had been completed." [Evidently, Bishop interviewed these men: "The men of Gawler's Sons were discreet and ethical." (page 684)];

c. 3/25/80 interview with David Lifton (*"Best Evidence"*, p. 666): "John Van Hoesen, of the Gawler firm, sat in the bleachers in the autopsy room. He told me: "When we got up there, nothing had been started; then we had to wait for the autopsy; and then, periodically, more pictures were being taken---you know, different angles and so forth; where the entry was, and so forth; this angle, and that angle...";

d. Undated interview with Harry Livingstone for *"High Treason 2"* (see pages 137 and 624): "No hairpiece was used."

e. 9/26/96 interview with the ARRB's Doug Horne---described the hole in JFK's head as being the size of an orange in "...the centerline of the back of the head, and its location was in the upper posterior of the skull...at or just below the cowlick area.";

f. *"Murder in Dealey Plaza"* by James Fetzer (2000), page 117

g. *"JFK Absolute Proof"* by Robert Groden (2013), page 156: nice summary of his statements

213)-214) Joseph H. Gawler, Director, Gawler's Funeral Home, and George Thomas, JFK's Valet:

a. 5/18/64, 6/1/64, 6/16/64, and 5/19/65 interviews with William Manchester ("*The Death of a President*", numerous-see esp. pages 432-433 and 670)---"Joe Gawler and Joe Hagan, his chief assistant, supervised the loading of the coffin in a hearse...The firm's young cosmetician accompanied *them* to Bethesda. The two caskets, Oneals' and Gawler's, lay side by side for a while in the morgue anteroom; then Oneal's was removed for storage and *the undertakers*, Irishmen, and **George Thomas** [Valet to the President; interviewed 5/7/64; see also 17 H 614] *were admitted to the main room.* The autopsy team had finished its work... The cosmetician then went to work...From the eight suits and four pairs of shoes *George Thomas had brought* Dave [Powers] chose a blue-gray suit, black shoes, and...a blue tie...Completely dresses, the body was wheeled into the anteroom, beside the waiting coffin...the body was transferred by physicians and *undertakers... Joe Gawler close[d] the coffin.*" [emphasis added; neither man is listed in Sibert & O'Neill's report, nor the HSCA's, of people present at the autopsy];

b. "*The Day Kennedy Was Shot*" by Jim Bishop, pages 607 and 684---"...Hagan or Gawler...leaving for the hospital."; "The men of Gawler's Sons were discreet and ethical."

c. WC references to Gawler's Funeral Home---18 H 727, 729, 745;

215) J.S. Layton Ledbetter, Chief of the Day, Medical Center Command (deceased 2/14/1997):

a. 9/25/79 interview with David Lifton ("*Best Evidence*", pages 419, 589, 592, 635 [see also p. 483 of "*Conspiracy*" by Anthony Summers and p. 250 of "*Who's Who in the JFK Assassination*" by Michael Benson])---"Well, I witnessed the arrival of two ambulances...They went to our morgue, one of them did. Actually, I don't know where the other one went."; "I know there was two helicopters involved. One never did land; and the other one, I think, was a decoy...";

b. */3/98 letter to Vince Palamara from Mrs. Layton Ledbetter---Her letter simply says, "Layton Ledbetter deceased 2-14-97";*

216) 1rst Lt. Samuel R. Bird, Officer in Charge, MDW casket team (deceased 10/18/1984):

a. "After Action Report/ Summary," Gen. Wehle's Office, Military District of Washington (MDW), 11/22/63: *attached* Memorandum for the Record dated 11/27/63 [see also "*The Death of a President*" by William Manchester, p. 670; *these documents were later released by the Gerald Ford Library*]---"The second casket team was at the left side of the truck and as it moved forward to secure the casket was disrupted by a host of agents moving forward pushing the team out of the way. The agents then placed the casket in an awaiting Navy ambulance.";

b. "*Dallas Morning News*", 11/26/63, p. 15;

c.   4/30/64 interview with William Manchester (*"The Death of a President"*, numerous; see esp. pages 390, 399 [re: "dead baby"], 430, 433-434, 593, 638, and 670);

d.   *Soldiers*, November 1964: *"Memories of the JFK Funeral: Epilogue-What Happened to the Pallbearers?"*-Article by Major Eugene Bickley---Bird was wounded in Vietnam and was confined to a wheelchair for the rest of his life;

e.   11/25/67 interview with David Lifton (*"Best Evidence"*, p. 407) [see also "A Complete Book of Facts" by Duffy and Ricci, pp. 72-73 ("on December 10, 1963, he had written in his official report that the coffin was taken from the ambulance to the autopsy room at 8:00 P.M. This conflicts with the O'Neill and Sibert report that the coffin was taken into the autopsy room at 7:17 P.M., and with autopsy chief Dr. James J. Humes's report that he received the body at 7:35 P.M." "), and "Who's Who in the JFK Assassination" by Michael Benson, p. 40]: due to a head injury, unable to help Lifton;

f.   7 HSCA 9: Outside contact report, Samuel Bird, Feb. 17, 1978, House Select Committee on Assassinations (RIF#180-10084-10000, JFK Document No. 005541)---"he did not recall too many details" but "he did record a tape, however, of the events surrounding the ceremonial aspects of JFK's assassination (Bird was head of the casket detail)";

g.   2/21/78 Outside contact report (RIF#180-10080-10481, Agency File Number 005524)-"No information pertaining to the autopsy on the tape" [see above];

h.   "*So Proudly He Served: The Sam Bird Story*" by Annette Bird, Tim Prouty, and Joan Polack (1993)

217) Robert William Rittmeyer, one of the senior instructors at the school of medical photography:

a.   10/17/77 document, Blakey to Admiral George E.R. Kinnear, II, re: request to waiver or alter the "gag order" (RIF#180-10096-10261)---Rittmeyer was one of the names listed;

b.   "*Best Evidence*", pages 638-639;

c.   *[unanswered letter from Vince Palamara 1998]*

218)-219) Army General [fnu] Curtis and Commander [fnu] Ewing, X-Ray Dept.:

a.   Chester Boyers said that these men were also present during the autopsy [4/25/78 HSCA interview with Boyers (RIF#180-10105-10398)];

220) B.R., Navy corpsman:

a.   Page 38 of "*Where were you when President Kennedy was shot?*" by Abigail ("Dear Abby") Van Buren (1993) [initials used for anonymity]: "I was a navy corpsman stationed at Bethesda Naval Hospital when news of President Kennedy's assassination was announced on the radio. All were in a state of disbelief. I was on the hospital grounds in front of the hospital when the body was brought there for autopsy. B.R., Hampton, VA";

221) "Bethesda Nurse", an Ensign in the Navy working in the OB-GYN:

a. March 1992 *"Network Publications"*: article entitled *"Bethesda Nurse"* by Woody Woodland---"Network Publications has spoken with a woman, now living in New Hampshire, who was working as a Navy nurse on the evening of November 22, 1963, at Bethesda Naval Hospital. She says that she saw a simple casket arrive by helicopter accompanied by men in trench coats, and she is convinced it contained the president's body. At her request, her identity is being protected..."; Nurse: "There was the discussion that, in fact, there had been---and this was the exact word used---that there were alterations. And the word alterations was [used] relative to the autopsy itself."; "It was announced that this helicopter would be landing and that [it] would be [carrying] the president's body.";

222) Dr. Russell Madison, a Lieutenant Colonel in the AFIP operating at Bethesda:

a. 5/25/93 interview with Roger Bruce Feinman (see *"Between the Signal and the Noise"*): Re: the back gate: "It was locked, because I'd usually go out that way and I couldn't get out...there was nobody around."[This confounds Dennis David's account of a first "ambulance" coming onto the hospital grounds from the back gate];

223) Captain/ Dr. Robert Owen "Jiggs" Canada, Jr., USN, Director/ Commanding Officer, Bethesda Naval Hospital (deceased 12/6/1972):

a. 11/22/63 Authorization For Post-Mortem Examination [see page 507 of *"Post Mortem"*]: Canada's name is *typed* in, not handwritten;

b. WC reference: 22 H 96 (Dr. Burkley's report: mentioned as being present at the autopsy);

c. 4/14/64 interview with William Manchester (*"The Death of a President"*, pages 381, 382, 396, 397, 398, 407, 415, 416)---"...[LBJ] had been Canada's patient after his massive heart attack on July 2, 1955..."; "Since the Secret Service had dislodged the regular driver at Andrews, Captain Canada had no idea where the ambulance would enter [Bethesda]."; "Jiggs Canada had once been George Burkley's shipmate...";

d. *"The Day Kennedy Was Shot"* by Jim Bishop, p. 649n---"In May 1968, Canada sent word to the author that he would not be permitted to see the empty autopsy room, unless he had an "okay from the White House.";

e. 10/11/68 *"New Orleans States-Item"*: article by Drew Pearson---"Author Jim Bishop, who is gathering research for a book to be called *The Day President Kennedy Was Shot*, stopped by the Bethesda Naval Hospital the other day for a look at the autopsy room. The visit unsettled junior officers who scurried around with his request. Bishop...merely wanted to glance around the room so he could write a firsthand description. The Naval aides, after taking up his request with Rear Adm. R.O. Canada...came back with a turn-down. Bishop explained patiently that he sought no confidential information, that he would ask no questions, that he merely wanted to look at the room where the late President's body was brought. 'I only want to see the autopsy room. I don't want it done to me in there,' he said. 'Our commanding officer says you can't see it,' replied a Lieutenant firmly. 'Is it under security?' asked Bishop. 'Why is the Navy keeping the room secret?' The answer was still negative. 'Is it all right,' asked the author, 'if I look at the lobby on the way out?'";

f. *"Best Evidence"* by David Lifton, pages 298, 395, 418, 476, 491[see also *"Who's Who in the JFK Assassination"* by Michael Benson, p. 71, and *"A Complete Book of Facts"* by Duffy and Ricci, p. 111]---Canada purposefully misled the press so that President Kennedy's body could be taken into Bethesda Naval Hoispital in secret. Canada played only a peripheral role at the autopsy and recalled nothing unusual about the body or the wounds.;

g. *"Murder in Dealey Plaza"* by James Fetzer (2000), page 112

224) (Rear) Admiral Edward C. Kenney, Surgeon General of the Navy [Kinney; Kenny] (deceased 2/22/1983):

a. WC reference: 22 H 96 (Burkley's report: mentioned as being present during autopsy ["Kenny"]);

b. *"Post Mortem"*, p. 235---excellent paragraph detailing Kinney's background;

c. *"Post Mortem"*, p. 303 [see also "Reasonable Doubt": by Heny Hurt, pp. 45-46]---"1.You are reminded that you are under verbal ordeers of the Surgeon General, United States Navy, to discuss with no one events connected with your official duties on the evening of 22 November-23 November 1963. 2. This letter constitutes official notification and reiteration of these verbal orders. You are warned that infraction of these orders makes you liable to Court Martial proceedings under appropriate articles of the Unifrom Code of Military Justice." [see Stover, above];

d. ["*Best Evidence*", pp. 607-608, 740] RE: the order not to talk---"A Navy memo stated that Burkley said "that he, as the White House Physician, had given the order." The Navy memo noted: "RADM [Rear Admiral] Kenney's role in the transmission of this order is still not clear.";

e. ["*Assassination Science*", p. 107] "On 10 November 1964, JAMA sent an inquiry [re: JFK's adrenals] to Admiral E.C. Kenney, which was forwarded to Admiral G.G. Burkley. After three months no response was received by JAMA from Burkley.";

f. 2/1/65 report of Dr. Pierre Finck to General Joseph Blumberg, p. 20---"After the completion of the postmortem examination, the Surgeon General of the Navy (Admiral Kinney) told us not to discuss the autopsy with anyone, even among the prosecutors or with the investigators involved...";

g. January 1967 report of the three autopsy doctors re: review of the autopsy photos and x-rays [see "Post Mortem", pp. 575-579: see esp. p. 575]---"The Surgeon General of the Navy [Kinney] advised Dr. Humes that the purpose of the autopsy was to determine the nature of the President's injuries and the cause of his death." [did Humes really need to be told this?];

h. Dr. Pierre Finck's testimony at the Clay Shaw trial, 2/24-2/25/69 [see "Destiny Betrayed: JFK, Cuba, and the Garrison Case" by James DiEugenio, pages 290, 292, 307, 308, and 351n; "High Treason", p. 93]: Mr. Oser: "Colonel, did you feel that you had to take orders from this Army General that was there directing the autopsy?" "No, because there were others, ther were Admirals." "There were Admirals?" "Oh, yes, there were admirals, and when you are a Lieutenant Colonel in the Army you just follow orders, and at the end of the autopsy we were specifically told---as I recall it, it was by Admiral Kenney, the Surgeon General of the Navy---this is subject to verification---we were specifically told not to discuss the case."; Mr. Oser: "Can you give me the name of the General that you said told Dr. Humes not to talk about the autopsy report?" "This was not a General, it was an Admiral." "All right, excuse me, the Admiral, can you give me the name of the Admiral?" "Who stated that we were not to discuss the autopsy findings?" "Yes." "This was in the autopsy room on the 22nd and 23rd of November, 1963." "What was his name?" "Well, there were several people in charge, there were several Admirals, and, as I recall, the Adjutant General of the Navy." "Do you have a name, Colonel?" "It was Admiral Kinney, K-i-n-n-e-y, as I recall."; Mr. Oser: "Were there any Admirals in uniform in the autopsy room?" "From what I remember, Admiral Galloway was in uniform, Admiral Kinney was in uniform...";

i. Dr. Robert Karnei, who was in charge of who was permitted into the autopsy room, said that Admiral Edward C. Kinney, the Surgeon General of the Navy, was present [8/29/77 interview with the HSCA];

j. 1 HSCA 324: Dr. Humes---"I was summoned from my home late in [the] afternoon of that day by the Surgeon General of the Navy [Kinney] and the Commanding Officer of the Navy Medical Center [Galloway], and the Commanding Officer of the Naval Medical School [Stover], and much to my surprise, was told that the body of the late President was being brought to our laboratories and that I was to examine the Presdient and ascertain the cause of death.";

k. Actor Merlyn Sexton portrayed Admiral Kenney in the Oliver Stone movie "JFK" (1991) [see "JFK: The Book of the Film", pages 158-159, for Finck's Clay Shaw trial reference to Kenney, as well as Sexton/ Kenney's small line in the movie];

l. "Murder in Dealey Plaza" by James Fetzer (2000), pages 105, 286

225)-230) Members of the MDW casket team (in addition to Bird): Coast Guard YO George A. Barnum, Navy SA Hubert Clark, Marine Lance Cpl. Timothy Cheek, Army Spec. 4 Douglas Mayfield, Army Sgt. James Leroy Felder, and Air Force Sgt. Richard E. Gaudreau:

a. *"Dallas Morning News"*, 11/26/63, p. 15;

b. **BARNUM:** 8/20/79 interview with David Lifton (*"Best Evidence"*, pp. 414-415 ; 398, 586, 626, 627, 671[see also *"A Complete Book of Facts"* by Duffy and Ricci, pp. 56-57, *"Who's Who in the JFK Assassination"*, p. 31, and *"Between The Signal and the Noise"* by Roger Bruce Feinman, pp. 83-84])---"[Barnum] explained that when he reported back for duty after the funeral, his superior at Coast Guard Headquarters directed him to write a report... Barnum was surprised to learn that his November 29, 1963 account, which he had saved primarily for his children's benefit, contained details of interest to me. Here is the portion of that account that deals with the events following the arrival of the casket team, by helicopter, at Bethesda: "We landed just prior to the President's procession. They stopped in front of the hospital, and were immediately swarmed over by people that had come to see the casket. We pushed and shoved our way through the crowd until we were beside the hearse. Immediately we were told to get into a pickup truck that was standing by and go to the rear of the hospital. We were following an ambulance that supposedly had the President's casket in it. Mrs. Kennedy had gotten out of the hearse and gone immediately into the hospital. As we arrived at the rear entrance to the hospital by the morgue, we were informed that the casket had not been driven there. We then jumped back into the pickup and returned to the front of the hospital... There were so many people that the instructions were still confusing, and we were told to return again to the rear. We di so and once again we were informed that the casket was not there. We returned again to the front and this time police had cleared a path through the people and the ambulance proceeded to the rear entrance of the morgue. We then proceeded to take the casket into the hospital in an orderly fashion... [Dr. Burkley said, regarding the shots that hit JFK, that] The first striking him in the lower neck and coming out near the throat. The second shot striking him above and to the rear of the right ear, this shot not coming out...";

c. **CLARK:** 12/19/67 interview with David Lifton (*"Best Evidence"*, pp. 408-413[*see photo 26 B*]; 398, 578, 586, 695, 696 [see also *"A Complete Book of Facts"* by Duffy and Ricci, pp. 125-126, *"Who's Who in the JFK Assassination"* by Michael Benson, p. 80, *"Conspiracy"* by Anthony Summers, p. 483, *"Bloody Treason"* by Noel Twyman, pages 174 and 211, and *"Between The Signal and the Noise"* by Roger Bruce Feinman, p. 59])---"I think there was a decoy [ambulance]... suposedly, to get the people away from the hospital... It was like a decoy was set up where we were supposed to go one way, and this decoy ambulance, I believe, went another way, to the front. And we went to the back; to the morgue."; "Hubert Clark believed a conspiracy murdered the President in Dallas...";

d. **CHEEK:** 11/19/67 interview with David Lifton (*"Best Evidence"*, p. 399; 398 [see also *"A Complete Book of Facts"* by Duffy and Ricci, p. 123, *"Who's Who in* *the JFK Assassination"* by Michael Benson, p. 77, and *"Between The Signal and the Noise"* by Roger Bruce Feinman, p. 59])---"There was a lot of confusion, because…it was supposed to be taken in the front; we got there, and it wasn't there…the body wasn't there…I believe we did follow the wrong one around to the back, and then we did come around again, after we found that it wasn't the right one. All I know is that we finally caught it, and that it was at the morgue door…";

e.   **MAYFIELD:** 12/16/67 interview with David Lifton (*"Best Evidence"*, p. 408; 398 [see also *"A Complete Book of Facts"* by Duffy and Ricci, p. 303, *"Who's Who in the JFK Assassination"* by Michael Benson, p. 289, and *"Between The Signal and the Noise"* by Roger Bruce Feinman, p. 59])---"…We went around to the back, and then we waited there, and the ambulance didn't come around right away; and we went back around [to the front]; and by this time, they were just leaving; so then we followed [it] around, and when it stopped in the back, we took it [the coffin] out and took it inside.";

f.   **FELDER:** 11/20/67 and 12/16/67 interviews with David Lifton (*"Best Evidence"*, pp. 402-406; 398, 407, 409, 584, 585, 586, 666, 695 [see also *"A Complete Book of Facts"* by Duffy and Ricci, p. 178, *"Who's Who in the JFK Assassination"* by Michael Benson, p. 130, *"Conspiracy"* by Anthony Summers, p. 483, *"Bloody Treason"* by Noel Twyman, pages 174 and 211, *"Murder In Dealey Plaza"* by James Fetzer (2000), page 106, and *"Between the Signal and the Noise"* by Roger Bruce Feinman, p. 59])---"There were two ambulances. One was supposed to be the decoy."; "…Felder was adamant---he said he saw the Dallas casket opened."; ALSO: Felder appears in the 1988 PBS program *"JFK: A Time Remembered"* (purely human-interest type comments); also: *"After Action Report/ Summary,"* Gen. Wehle's Office, Military District of Washington (MDW), 11/22/63: attached Memorandum for the Record dated 11/27/63 [see also *"The Death of a President"* by William Manchester, p. 670; *these documents were later released by the Gerald Ford Library*]---"…Sgt. Felder…marched the team to an area just outside the Air Force Cordon.[AAFB]";

g.   **GAUDREAU:** 8/26/79 interview with David Lifton (*"Best Evidence"*, p. 414[see photo 26C]; 398, 578 [see also *"A Complete Book of Facts"* by Duffy and Ricci, pp. 195-196, and *"Between The Signal and the Noise"* by Roger Bruce Feinman, p. 60])---"…I think there was some confusion, and we did go off with another ambulance…I can picture us being led somewhere, and finding something empty; and then being led somewhere else."; [**unanswered letter from Vince Palamara 1998**]

231) Sorrell L. Schwartz, a pharmacologist at the Naval Medical Research Institute, Bethesda:

a.   Letter to *"Time"* magazine, 2/16/81, p. 4---"[W]e did not lose track of the ambulance containing the bronze casket after it arrived at the medical center. On that night there were a large number of spectators around, and our intention was to get the ambulance to the morgue before the crowd gathered. The honor guard, along with a Navy enlisted-man driver, the other duty officer and me, rode to the morgue on the guard truck at high speed, believing that the ambulance was following. When we got there, the ambulance was not seen. Since the Secret Service driver [Greer] was unfamiliar with the grounds, we decided he was lost. Retracing our path, we found the ambulance still at the front of the hospital amid many onlookers. In our haste we had left without confirming that the ambulance was behind us. On the second try we did it right. At no time was the ambulance out of sight of at least several hundred people, from its arrival at the center until the bronze coffin was unloaded at the morgue.";

b. *"Between The Signal and the Noise"* by Roger Bruce Feinman, p. 60---repeats *"Time"* letter contents above;

232) Capt. Robert Weare, staff member, Bethesda Naval Hospital:

a. 4/14/64 and 6/1/64 interviews with William Manchester (*"The Death of a President"*, p. 669): not mentioned in the actual text of the book, despite these two sourced interviews;

233) Lt. Col. Paul C. Miller, Ceremonies Officer, Military District of Washington (MDW):

a. *"After Action Report/ Summary,"* Gen. Wehle's Office, Military District of Washington (MDW), 11/22/63---"At 1600 hours Paul Miller called General Wehle and informed him of the following information: a. Pres. would arrive Andrews at 1800 hours. b. He will be choppered from there to the Navy Medical Center for autopsy."; "General Wehle informed Miller here that he had seen on TV where they announced that the body would lie in state tomorrow, and asked whether or not the public would be allowed to view. The answer was no, and Miller took action to "kill" this erroneous information."; "Paul Miller advised that the Secretary Chief of Protocol at the White House informed him that a group of White House people might be out to Andrews for the arrival of the remains. General Wehle informed that McNamara and Taylor might also be there, according to his information."; "Paul Miller reiterated that the family desired a Guard of Honor on the remains at all time. General Wehle assured him this was taken care of."

b. 4/30/64 interview with William Manchester (*"The Death of a President"*, many; see esp. p. 382 [see also p. 673]): recommended Gawler's Funeral Home to Sargent Shriver;

c. *"Four Days In November"* (1964, David Wolper)---Depicted going over the funeral arrangements [this film/ video has some excellent footage of Lt. Bird's group and the MDW preparing for the funeral];

234) Chief [fnu] Mason, chief hospital corpsman/ head of histology lab:

a. Mentioned by Drs. Boswell and Karnei as being present during the autopsy and/ or the examination of the brain (*see 8/17/77 HSCA interview with Boswell*

159

and 8/29/77 HSCA interview with Karnei)---[Boswell:] "He indicated that Dr. Humes and he worked on this procedure [brain examination] with possibly two lab technicians, including Dr. Karnei (who served as chief assistant) and the chief hospital corpsman, who he believes was a man named Mason (status-HMC)... Although the autopsy supplemental report says that seven sections were taken of the brain, Dr. Boswell said he couldn't specifically recall whether or not this was the case. He said the lab supervisor, who he believes was Mr. Mason (who was head of the histology lab), would know this better than he."; [Karnei:] "He did recall a Chief Mason being around and "...thinks [Leland] Benson actually cut the slides...that day or the day after...Dr. Karnei said there are normally people assigned to clean the body after the autopsy and added that he "...keeps thinking Chief Mason was there."

235) Dr. [fnu] Dixon:

a. Mentioned by James Curtis Jenkins as being present during the autopsy (*see 8/29/77 HSCA interview with Jenkins)*--- [Jenkins:] "He recalled that Dr. Dixon came into the autopsy room once but doesn't believe he participated other than that."

236) Leonard D. Saslaw, Ph.D., a biochemist at the Armed Forces institute of Pathology:

a. 4/26/96 interview with the ARRB [important points as reported by "*The Washington Post*", 8/2/98]--- In an effort to compile a more complete record of the autopsy, the review board sought out additional witnesses and found, among others, Leonard D. Saslaw, a biochemist who recalled a loud lunchroom conversation between one of the autopsy physicians, Pierre A. Finck, and colleagues at the Armed Forces Institute of Pathology, days after the assassination.

Saslaw, who was sitting at the next table, said, "Dr. Finck was loudly lamenting the fact that the notes he had taken during the course of the autopsy on President Kennedy had disappeared, and that he had been forced to reconstruct his notes from memory.

"Dr. Finck complained," Saslaw told the board in an April 1996 interview, "that immediately after cleaning up following the conclusion of the autopsy, he looked for his notes and could not find them anywhere; and that even though others who had been at the autopsy had helped him search, that they could not be found."

Saslaw remembered Finck going on to say in angry tones hat he had been forced as a result to reconstruct his notes from memory after the autopsy was over. Saslaw said he was struck by the conversation because he was well aware as a scientist that "any observations which are not written down contemporaneously, but reconstructed from memory after the fact, are not likely to be as accurate or complete."

Asked about the lunchroom episode in a May 1996 deposition, Finck said he did not remember it. He was also vague about how many notes he took during the autopsy but confirmed that "after the autopsy I also wrote notes" and that he turned over whatever notes he had to the chief autopsy physician, James J. Humes.

It has long been known that Humes destroyed some original autopsy papers in a fireplace at his home on Nov. 24, 1963. He told the Warren Commission that what he burned was an original draft of his autopsy report. Under persistent questioning at a February 1996 deposition by the Review Board, Humes said he destroyed the draft and his "original notes."

Asked whether he remembered Finck taking any notes during the autopsy, Humes said: "I do not. I don't say he didn't, but I don't recall that he did."

"This is bizarre," said assassination researcher and author David Lifton, whose work led the board to Saslaw. "All these papers disappearing or destroyed.";

b. 5/15/96 affidavit to the ARRB [important points as reported by "*The Fort Worth Star-Telegram*", 8/2/98]--- In an affidavit, Leonard D. Saslaw, a biochemist who worked at the Armed Forces Institute of Pathology in Bethesda, Md., said that at lunch in the week following the assassination he overheard one of the autopsy doctors, Pierre Finck, "complain that he had been unable to locate the handwritten notes that he had taken during the autopsy."

Finck told the board he couldn't recall the lunchroom conversation.

But Saslaw stated that in the lunchroom, "Dr. Finck elaborated to his companions, with considerable irritation, that immediately after washing up following the autopsy, he looked for his notes, and could not find them anywhere.

"Dr. Finck concluded his story," Saslaw said, "by angrily stating that he had to reconstruct his notes from memory."

c. "*Murder in Dealey Plaza*" by James Fetzer (2000), pages 206, 286

237) Comdr. James Joseph ("Jim") Humes (deceased May 1999),
238) Comdr. J. Thornton ("Jay") Boswell, and
239) Lt. Col. Pierre A. Finck, AFIP: the three autopsy doctors at Bethesda on 11/22/63:

-HUMES (and Boswell):

a. WR 538-543 / 16 H 978-983 / CE 387 [see also "*Assassination Science*", pp. 430-435]: the autopsy report---"*There is a large irregular defect of the scalp and skull on the right involving chiefly the parietal bone but extending somewhat into the temporal and occipital regions. In this region there is an actual absence of scalp and bone producing a defect which measures approximately 13 cm in greatest diameter...*"

b. WR 544-545 / 16 H 987-988 / CE 391 [see also "*Post Mortem*", pp. 529-530, and "*Assassination Science*", pp. 436-437] supplementary autopsy report re: the brain---"*Following formalin fixation the brain weighs 1500 gms.*"

c. 2 H 347-376 / testimony (3/16/64, with *Boswell* and *Finck* present)---"The [first] wound in the low neck... The second wound was found in the right posterior portion of the scalp. This wound was situated approximately 2.5 centimeters to the right, and slightly above the external occipital protuberance which is a bony prominence situated in the posterior portion of everyone's skull. This wound was then 2 1/2 centimeters to the right and slightly above that point. The third obvious wound at the time of the examination was a huge defect over the right side of the skull. This defect involved both the scalp and the underlying skull, and from the brain substance was protruding. This wound measured approximately 13 centimeters in greatest diameter. It was difficult to measure accurately because radiating at various points from the large defect were multiple crisscrossing fractures of the skull which extended in several directions."; "...a large roughly 13 cm. diameter defect in the right lateral vertex of the skull...we concluded that the large defect to the upper right side of the skull, in fact, would represent a wound of exit. A careful examination of the margins of the large bone defect at that point, however, failed to disclose a portion of the skull bearing again a wound of---a point of impact on the skull of this fragment of the missile, remembering, of course, that this area was devoid of any scalp or skull at this present time. We did not have the bone...Some time later on that evening or very early the next morning while we were all still engaged in continuing our examination, I was presented with three portions of bone...the three pieces could be roughly put together to account for a portion of this defect...I would estimate that approximately one-quarter of that defect was unaccounted for by adding these three fragments together and seeing what was left...*However, the thing which we considered of importance about these three fragments of bone was that at the margins of one of them which was roughly pyramidal in shape, there was a portion of the circumference of what we interpreted as a missile wound. We thus interpreted it this because there was, the size was, sufficiently large for us, for it to have the curve of the skull still evident. At the point of this defect...at the area which we interpreted as the margin of a missile wound, there was a shelving of the margin.*" [Emphasis added: *see Humes' letter to Palamara*] "Scientifically, sir, it is impossible for it to have been fired from other than behind. Or to have exited from other than behind."; "In speaking of the wound in the neck, Doctor Perry told me that before he enlarged it to make the tracheotomy wound it was a "few millimeters in diameter.""; [CE399 involved in Connally's right wrist wound?---]"I think that that is most unlikely.... The reason I believe it most unlikely that this missile could have inflicted either of these wounds is that this missile is basically intact; its jacket appears to me to be intact, and I do not understand how it could possibly have left fragments in either of these locations." [Connally's thigh wound?---] "I think that extremely unlikely...I can't conceive of where they [bullet fragments] came from this missile."

d. 17 H 29-44 / CE 397 [see also "*Post Mortem*", pp. 508-523]: handwritten autopsy report: [neck wound] "Only a few mm in size 3-5 mm."; "At one angle of the largest of these [bone] fragments is a portion of the perimeter of a roughly circular wound PRESUMABLY of exit...The wound PRESUMABLY of exit was that described by Dr. Malcolm Perry of Dallas..." (emphasis added; this same language made it into the typed autopsy report [above]. For a good discussion of this matter, see Harold Weisberg's comments on the video "*Reasonable Doubt*", as well as in the book "*Selections From Whitewash*" (1994), pp. 277-278;

e. 17 H 45-46 / CE 397 [see also "Post Mortem", pp. 310-311, and "Best Evidence", photo #27] (Boswell's) autopsy descriptive (face) sheet and (Boswell's) diagram of the skull ---bullet wound well down on the back, not the neck; no weight given for the brain; verified by Dr. Burkley [see "Assassination Science", p. 16, "Bloody Treason", p. 109, and "Cover-Up" by Stewart Galanor, p.125];

f. 17 H 47 / CE 397 [see also "Post Mortem", p. 525]: 11/24/63 certificate to Capt. Stover;

g. 17 H 48 / CE 397 [see also "Post Mortem", p. 524]: 11/24/63 certificate re: the burning of certain preliminary draft notes;

h. other WC references: WR 86, 88-89; 2 H 93-94, 377, 379-383; 3 H 380-381; 5 H 142; 6 H 16-17, 25; 18 H 727;

i. 3/11/64 interview with the WC's Arlen Specter and Joseph A. Ball, Esq. (memo dated 3/12/64 on the matter, Specter to Rankin) [se "Post Mortem", pp. 539-540]--- "All three [Humes, Boswell, and Galloway] described the bullet wound on President Kennedy's back as being a point of entrance."; "According to Commander Humes, the autopsy surgeons hypothesized that the bullet might have been forced out of the back of the President on the application of external heart message after they were advised that a bullet had been found on a stretcher at Parkland Hospital.";

j. 11/26/63 FBI (Sibert & O'Neill) report [see "Post Mortem", pp. 533-536]---"During the latter stages of this autopsy, Dr. HUMES located an opening which appeared to be a bullet hole which was below the shoulders and two inches to the right of the middle line of the spinal column. This opening was probed by Dr. HUMES with the finger, at which time it was determined that the trajectory of the missile entering at this point had entered at a downward position of 45 to 60 degrees. Further probing determined that the distance travelled by this missile was a short distance inasmuch as the end of the opening could be felt with the finger."; "... since cardiac massage had been performed at Parkland Hospital, it was entirely possible that through such movement the bullet had worked its way back out of the point of entry and had fallen on the stretcher. Also during the latter stages of the autopsy, a piece of the skull measuring 10 x 6.5 centimeters was brought to Dr, HUMES who was instructed that this had been removed from the President's skull. Immediately this section of skull was X-rayed, at which time it was determined by Dr. HUMES that one corner of this section revealed minute metal particles and inspection of this same area disclosed a chipping of the top portion of this piece, both of which indicated that this had been the point of exit of the bullet entering the skull region. On the basis of the latter two developments, Dr. HUMES stated that the pattern was clear that the one bullet had entered the President's back and had worked its way out of the body during external cardiac massage and that a second high velocity bullet had entered the rear of the skull and had fragmentized prior to exit through the top of the skull.";

k. 4/15/64 FBI memorandum, L.J. Guthier to Mr. Callahan, regarding 4/14/64 conference "Examination Of Visual Aids By President's Commission"---"Staff members of the President's Commission and specialists of the armed services,

Drs. Humes, Heany, Fink [sic], Light and Olivia (ph.) attended a conference on 4-14-64 for the purpose of reviewing motion pictures and slides of the assassination site. Representatives of the Secret Service and the FBI were present to assist in projecting the film and the use of the scale model. Dr. Humes, U.S. Navy Commander, who performed the autopsy on the President, appeared to lead the discussion throughout the 4-hour session. *All of his associates were generally in agreement with previous findings of the Commission as to where Shots 1.2 and 3 approximately occurred. The most revealing information brought out by the doctors is as follows [here, one of the FBI agents who received this memo hand-wrote: "This is speculative" with a smiley-face!]: 1. That Shot 1 struck the President high in the right shoulder area,* penetrating the torso near the base of the neck damaging the flesh of the throat but not tearing the throat wall. This bullet, according to the doctors, continued and entered Governor Connally's right shoulder, emerging below the right nipple. The velocity of the missile, according to the doctors apparently was snagged in the coat and shirt, eventually falling out on Connally's stretcher. *2. That Shot 2 struck the wrist of the Governor, continuing on into his thigh. 3. That Shot 3 struck the right side of the President's head, carrying much bone and brain tissue away, leaving a large cavity.* There is nothing controversial about where Shot 3 occurred inasmuch as the Zapruder movie indicates with much clarity where this happened. *Heretofore it was the opinion of the Commission that Shot 1 had only hit the President, that Shot 2 had entered the Governor's right shoulder area penetrating his torso through the chest area emerging and again entering the wrist and on into his leg."* [emphasis added]: among other things, there is no accounting for the shot that missed and went on to injure witness James Tague!; From page 3 ("Addendum" re: proposed re-enactment): "It is our opinion [the FBI's] that it would be undesirable for the FBI to become involved as the speed of the car, protection measures, etc., were the basic responsibilities of Secret Service at the time. We would prefer not to become identified with the actual scene and happenings at the assassination in the minds of the public." [emphasis in original] (!);

l. 11/2/66, 11/3/66, 9/7/78, and 11/9/79 interviews with David Lifton (*"Best Evidence"*, pp. 243-244, 256-259, 474, and 647-648 [audio tape of Lifton's 11/3/66 interview played at the 4/3/93 Chicago Symposium-on video]);

m. *11/1/66 Report of Inspection (by Humes, Boswell, Ebersole and Stringer)of X-rays and photos at the National Archives (signed 11/10/66) [see "Post Mortem", pp.565-573];*

n. 1/10/67 CBS memo, Robert Richter to Les Midgley [see *"Killing Kennedy"* by H.E.L., p. 195]---"Jim Snyder of the CBS bureau in D.C. told me today he is personally acquainted with DR. Humes. They go to the same church and are personally friendly. Snyder also knows Humes's boss in Bethesda; he is a neighbor across the street from Snyder. Because of personal relationships Snyder said he would not want any of the following to be traced back to him; nor would he feel he could be a middle-man in any CBS efforts to deal with Humes. Snyder said he has spoken with Humes about the assassination. In one conversation Humes said one X-ray of the Kennedy autopsy would answer many questions that have been raised about the path of the bullet going from Kennedy's back through his throat. Humes said FBI agents were not in the autopsy room during the autopsy;

they were kept in an anteroom, and their report is simply wrong. Although initially in the autopsy procedure the back wound could only be penetrated to finger length, a probe later was made---when no FBI men were present---that traced the path of the bullet from the back going downward, then upward slightly, then downward again exiting at the throat. One X-ray photo taken, Humes said, clearly shows the above, as it was apparently taken with a metal probe that was left in the body to show the wound's path. Humes said that a wound from a high-power rifle, once it enters a body, causes muscle, etc., to separate and later contract; thus the difficulty in initially tracing the wound's path in the case of Kennedy. Also, once a bullet from a high-power rifle enters a body, its course can be completely erratic; a neck wound could result in a bullet emerging in a person's leg or anywhere else. Humes refused to discuss with Snyder the 'single-bullet' theory in which the Warren Commission contends the same bullet described above went thru both Kennedy and Connally. Humes also said he had orders from someone he refused to disclose--other than stating it was not Robert Kennedy---to not do a complete autopsy. Thus the autopsy did not go into JFK's kidney disease, etc. Humes's explanation for burning his autopsy notes was that they were essentially irrelevant details dealing with routine body measurements, and that he never thought any controversy would develop from his having done this.";

o. *1/20/67 Dept. of Justice-requested inspection (by Humes, Boswell, and Finck) of X-rays and photos (signed 1/26/67) [see "Post Mortem", pp. 575-579];*

["President Johnson's notes on conversation with acting Attorney General Ramsey Clark---January 26, 1967"(LBJ Library)-"On the other matter, I think we have the three pathologists and the photographer signed up now on the autopsy review and their conclusion is that the autopsy photos and X-rays conclusively support the autopsy report rendered by them to the Warren Commission though *we were not able to tie down the question of the missing photo entirely but we feel much better about it and we have three of the four sign to an affidavit that says these are all the photos that they took and they do not believe anybody else took any others. There is this unfortunate reference in the Warren Commission report by Dr. Humes to a picture that just does not exist as far as we know. I am checking further to see where the pictures were at all times.*"(emphasis added)]

p. 6/26/67 (part 2) and 6/28/67 (part 4) appearances on *"CBS News Inquiry: The Warren Report"* [for a transcript, see *JAMA*, 10/7/92, Vol. 268, No. 13; transcript provided to the author by Bill Drenas]---"There were two wounds of entrance, and two of exit [:] Posteriorly, one low in the right posterior scalp, and one in the base of the neck, on the right... [entrance wound in head] That was posterior, about two and a half centimeters to the right of the midline, posteriorly... and the exit wound was a large irregular wound to the front and side---right side of the President's head.";

q. 8/17/77 interview with the HSCA's Andy Purdy [RIF# 180-10093-10429; see also 7 HSCA 13]---"I [Purdy] asked him whether the [entry] wound was in the upper or lower part of the head. Dr. Humes said that it was in the 'lower head' area. I asked Dr. Humes about his knowledge of the Clark Panel Report. He said he knows some of the people who served on it and he thought they confirmed the essential findings of the autopsy doctors. I cited to him the Clark Panel's recitation of their determination that the autopsy doctors had miscalculated the location of the head wound by a vertical distance of approximately 100 milli-meters (they said the autopsy doctors place the wound that much lower than it really was). Dr. Humes stated categorically that his physical measurements are correct and emphasized that he had access to the body itself and made the mea-surements of the actual head region. In addition, he said that photographs and X-rays have inherent limitations which are not present when one is examining the subject."; "Both Dr. Humes and Dr. Burkley informed the Committee that these [skull] fragments were placed back in the skull of the President."; the bullet wound in the back was found right away during the complete examination that was made of JFK's body before the autopsy work began; specifically recalled that Kodachrome photographs were taken of the President's chest---these photos are missing from the current collection;

r. *9/16/77 interview (Humes and Boswell) with the HSCA's Forensic Pathology Panel (7 HSCA 243-265 / Addendum I [see also "Mortal Error", pp. 321-324])---[en-trance wound]*HUMES: *"Below the external occipital protuberance... That's an el-liptical wound of the scalp which we described our protocol. I'm quite confident. And it's just to the right and below by a centimeter and maybe a centimeter to the right and Maybe 2 centimeters below the midpoint of the external occipital protuberance. And when the scalp was reflected from there, there was virtually an identical wound in the occipital bone... There was what we interpreted to be an exit wound, in the location to which I point. The bone that would correspond and complete that circle or ellipse, that might have been made by that exit wound, was missing at the time we began the examination. Later on that evening, several hours into the evening, we were presented with another fragment of bone, not the one that you are examining now, and that fragment had a corresponding semicircular defect which almost completed this, what we interpreted to be an exit wound, but not quite. And we never had the privilege of examining the fragments or photographs of this fragment [THE HARP-ER FRAGMENT] that you now examined until this afternoon, and I was unaware of its existence until about 3 weeks ago.";* BOSWELL: *"It's to the right and inferior to the external occipital protuberance."[see also pages 120 and 358 of "Assassination Science"]*;

s. 9/7/78 HSCA testimony (broadcast by PBS [1 HSCA 323-332; see *"Best Evidence"*, pp. 549-553, as well as photo 36]; short, silent clip rebroadcast on KRON's program *"JFK: An Unsolved Murder"*, 11/18/88)--- Humes: "[*the small droplet in the lower portion of Fox-3/ F-48 in the HSCA Exhibits*]wound of entry and that that was the only wound of entry."; "I don't know what that is [*alleged defect in the cowlick area, more prominent in the Ida Dox drawing*]. No. 1, I can assure you that as we reflected the scalp to get to this point, there was no defect corresponding to this in the skull at any point. I don't know what that is. It could be to me clotted blood. I don't, I just don't know what it is, but it certainly was not any wound of entrance.";

"Mr. CORNWELL. Now, I would like to ask you today if you have had at least a greater opportunity to look at the photographs along the lines that I have just indicated to you and if, after doing so, you have a more well-considered or a different opinion or whether your opinion is still the same; as to where the point of entry is?

Dr. HUMES. Yes, I think that I do have a different opinion. No. 1, it was a casual kind of a discussion that we were having with the panel members, as I recall it. No. 2, and I think before we talk about these photographs further, if I might comment, these photographs were made on the evening of November 22, 1963. I first saw any of these photographs on November 1, 1966, almost 3 years after the photographs were made, which was the first opportunity that I had to see those photographs.

At that point, Drs. Boswell, Finck and I were asked to come to the National Archives to categorize these photographs, label them, identify them and we spent many hours going through that. It was not the easiest thing to accomplish, I might say, after 3 weeks short of 3 years. But we identified them and I think in light of the very extensive opportunity that various panels of very qualified forensic pathologists have had to go over them, we did a reasonably accurate job in cataloging these photographs. So, I saw them on that occasion. I saw them again on the 27th of January of 1967 when we again went to the Archives and made some summaries of our findings.

I go back further to the original autopsy report which we rendered, in the absence of any photographs, of course. We made certain physical observations and measurements of these wounds. I state now those measurements we recorded then were accurate to the best of our ability to discern what we had before our eyes.

We described the wound of entrance in the posterior scalp as being above and to the right of the external occipital protuberance, a bony knob on the back of the head, you heard Dr. Baden describe to the committee members today. *And it is obvious to me as I sit here how with this his markedly enlarged drawing or the photograph that the upper defect to which you pointed or the upper object is clearly in the location of where we said approximately where it was, above the external occipital protuberance; therefore, I believe that is the wound of entry.* It relative position to boney structure underneath it is somewhat altered by the fact that there were fractures of the skull under this and the President's head had to be held in this position thus making some distortion of anatomic views produced in this picture.

By the same token. the object in the lower portion, which I apparently and I believe now erroneously previously identified before the most recent panel, is far below the external occipital protuberance and would not fit with the original autopsy findings." [emphasis added];

"Mr. CORNWELL. I would ask you if you would mind stepping to the easel and describing for us what your view, or your opinion, would be as to the location of the entry wound on that X-ray.

Dr. HUMES. OK. I believe, particularly in this rather enhanced picture, I might say, it is a pleasure to have such because I didn't have anything of this kind formerly, that this would be the point of entrance.

Mr. CORNWELL. For the record simply, would you try to describe the point that you just indicated?

Dr. HUMES. Well, in this approximate area would be about where external occipital protuberance would be, the knob we can feel in the back of our head. This would be above it. There is a great enlargement here, so it looks considerably further away than it would be on a standard size film or on the skull and I believe this is above the external occipital protuberance.";

"Your initial autopsy report indicated that, as you have just stated, the wound was, indeed, above, I believe the report is worded in terms of "slightly above," the external occipital protuberance.

The testimony today indicates that the panel places that at approximately 10 centimeters above the external occipital protuberance. Would that discrepancy be explainable?

Dr. HUMES. Well, I have a little trouble with that; 10 centimeters is a significant--4 inches"

Mr. CORNWELL. I would like to simply ask you a few specific questions in order to determine----

Dr. HUMES. I go back to the fact there was only one, period. [emphasis added]";

t.   12/10/80 [HUMES], 2/5/88 [HUMES and BOSWELL],9/5/91[HUMES], and 10/7/91 [BOSWELL] interviews with Harry Livingstone (see "High Treason", pp. 57-59, and "High Treason 2", p. 152, see also "Killing Kennedy", pp. 239-240)---Boswell, regarding the rear head entry wound: "It didn't move!": the entry wound was low down on the head near the hairline.; Boswell said that Pitzer as not present at the autopsy; Boswell said that the spinal cord was not removed; Humes would not retreat from the low-entry position on the head;

[7 HSCA/ *"Killing the Truth"*, p. 180---

"The panel continued to be concerned about the persistent disparity between its findings and those of the autopsy pathologists and the rigid tenacity with which the prosecutors maintained that the entrance wound was at or near the external occipital protuberance."]

u.   1984 interview with Henry Hurt (*"Reasonable Doubt"*, p. 427): "[Lifton's] book is so ridiculous it's incredible." However, Humes refused to discuss the details of the issues raised in *"Best Evidence"*;

v.   Portrayed by actor Chris Robinson in the Oliver Stone Movie "*JFK*" (1991) [see "*JFK: The Book of the Film*", pages 159 and 584];

w.   *JAMA, May 27, 1992-Vol 267, No. 20: "JFK's Death---the plain truth from the MDs who did the autopsy" by Dennis L. Breo (interview with James J. Humes and "J" Thornton Boswell [inc.4 photos of Humes and Boswell from 1992, as well as a photo of all three autopsy doctors: this same photo can be found on p.74 of "TKOAP"])*

Humes:"... I am tired of being beaten upon by people who are supremely igno-rant of the scientific facts of the President's death... "If a bullet or a BB were fired through that window, it would leave a small hole where it entered and a beveled crater where it exited. That is what 'J' and I found when we examined the Presi-dent's skull. There was a small elliptical entrance wound on the outside of the back of the skull, where the bullet entered, and a beveled larger wound on the inside of the back of the skull where the bullet tore through and exploded out the right side of the head. When we recovered the missing bone fragments and reconstructed this gaping wound where the bullet exited, we found this same pattern - a small wound where the bullet struck the inside of the skull and a beveled larger wound where it exited. This is always the pattern of a through-and-through wound of the cranium - the beveling or crater effect appears on the inside of the skull at the en-trance wound and on the outside of the skull at the exit wound. The crater effect is produced when the bony tissue of the skull turns inside out where the bullet leaves."; "His identifying facial features were all intact and there he was, the Pres-ident of the United States, now dead at age 46 with a terrible wound of the head. He wasn't that much older than me, and other than the head wound, he looked perfectly normal. He was a remarkable human specimen and looked as if he could have lived forever. It was very, very distressing."; " I'd done gunshot wounds before and this one was perfectly obvious - there was a huge hole on the right side of the President's head that only could have resulted from the exit of a high-velocity missile."; Boswell adds, "Sure, there were FBI and Secret Service people observing the autopsy and talking on their radios to people outside the room, and we could hear a play-by-play of what we were doing and talking about, but nobody tried to interfere and we were able to focus on the matter at hand." He adds, "The FBI and Secret Service told us that two fragments of the President's skull had been recov-ered in Dallas and were being rushed to Bethesda and that bullet fragments had also been recovered in Dallas."; "The fatal wound was blatantly obvious," Humes recalls. "The entrance wound was elliptical, 15 millimeters long and 6 millimeters wide, and located 2.5 centimeters to the right and slightly above the external oc-cipital protuberance. The inside of the skull displayed the characteristic beveled appearance. The x-rays disclosed fine dustlike metallic fragments from back to front where the bullet traversed the head before creating an explosive exit wound on the right temporal-parietal area. These fragments were not grossly visible. Two small fragments of bullet were recovered from inside the skull - measuring 3 by 1 millimeters and 7 by 2 millimeters.

"The head was so devastated by the exploding bullet and the gaping jagged stellate wound it created - it blew out 13 centimeters of skull bone and skin - that we did not even have to use a saw to remove the skullcap. We peeled the scalp back, and the calvarium crumbled in my hands from the fracture lines, which went off in all directions. We made an incision high in the spinal cord and re-moved the brain, which was preserved in formalin. Two thirds of the right cere-brum had been blown away.

"After the brain was removed, we looked more closely at the wound, and not-ed that the inside of the rear of the skull bone was absolutely intact and beveled and that there could be no question from whence cometh that bullet - from rear to front. When we received the two missing fragments of the President's skull and were able to piece together two thirds of the deficit at the right front of the head, we saw the same pattern on the outer table of the skull - a bullet that traveled from rear to front. Every theorist who says the bullet came from the front has ignored this critical irrefutable diagnostic fact. We did everything within the means of reasonable people to record with x-rays and photos what we saw."; Boswell adds, "Having seen the clothing, I now know that I created a terrible problem with my own autopsy drawings. My drawings of the bullet holes on the night of the autopsy did not precisely match up with the actual holes in the clothing, because we were not aware that the President's suit jacket had humped up on his back while he waved at the spectators. These errors were later exploited by the conspiracy crowd to fit their premises and purposes." The clothing was kept in the National Archives, along with the rest of the autopsy materials."; What happened to the brain? Boswell says, "I believe that it was buried with the body." Humes says, "I don't know, but I do know that I personally handed it over to Admiral Burkley and that he told me that the family intended to bury it with the body. I believe Admiral Burkley.";

x. 1992 and 8/14/93 interviews with Brad Parker [summarized in Parker's letter to Humes dated 9/15/93 which went unanswered]---"I just wanted to tell you that your outburst during our telephone conversation of August 14 has shed new light on the entire assassination for me. When I spoke to you a year ago, I found you to be a cordial and seemingly honest man of integrity. Your very nature made me overlook the many documented instances of contradictory testimony which you have given...Your apparent explosive temper, your varying descriptions of the wounds (such as the entry wound in the head being moved from "2.5 cm laterally to the right and slightly *above* the external occipital protuberance" to "the right and *inferior* to the right of the external occipital protuberance"), and your refusal to answer a few simple questions are the reasons why your "autopsy" will be forever questioned.";

y. Humes only: 11/2/92 and 11/4/92 interviews with Gerald Posner ("Case Closed", pages 300 and 301n);

z. *11/17/93: Gerald Posner's testimony before the Conyers Committee---said that he interviewed Humes and Boswell[although his alleged interview with Boswell is NOT cited in "Case Closed"] and that the HSCA had them change their minds re: the placement of the rear head entrance wound: "It is in fact correctly placed 4 inches higher" and, thus, they allegedly confirmed their [second] HSCA placement of the head wound;*

[Humes/Boswell:
WC: to the right and just above the external occipital protuberance (EOP);
HSCA #1: to the right and 1-2 cm below the EOP;
HSCA #2 (public session): near the cowlick 10 cm above the EOP;
JAMA: back to the WC placement---to the right and just above the EOP;
According to Posner: back to HSCA #2 position!]

aa. *Humes and Boswell: 3/30/94 (audio-taped) interviews with Dr. Gary Aguilar [provided to the author; see also "Killing Kennedy" by H.E.L., pages 251, 300, 391 and*

398; "Assassination Science" by Prof. James Fetzer, page 122; "Breach of Faith" by Dr. William Truels, pages 70 and 73]---Boswell said that Humes' testimony to the HSCA "might be suspect" and that their autopsy report was the most valid: "have to take what has been said subsequent to the autopsy with a grain of salt."; Boswell said that the large defect was 13 cm across _after_ the bone fragment completing the entry hole was inserted at the EOP, along with two other bone fragments. It was 17 cm without it [see Boswell's diagram of the skull]. Thus, what we see in the Rydberg diagram is a depiction of the skull AFTER the bone fragment was put back in place ;Boswell denied that Posner ever spoke to him, which, strangely, IS borne out by Posner's book [both editions], but NOT by his Conyers' Committee testimony!; Both Humes and Boswell denied that they had changed their minds about the location of JFK's skull wound entrance, as alleged by Posner;

ab. Humes:2/13/96 ARRB deposition (almost 7 hours in length!)[See also "High Treason III" (1998), pp.446-455]---Humes does not deny probing [see Robert Knudsen], but says it wasn't effective.; categorically denied talking to Dr. Livingston [see below]; spent 30-45 minutes examining the cranium after the brain was removed (!); "It was handwritten notes and the first draft that was burned."; Regarding Barkley's placement of the back wound at the level of the third thoracic vertebra, Humes said "I think that's much lower than it actually was", yet says that the back wound was at the second-centimeter line as depicted in the autopsy photo of JFK's back showing the ruler and the bullet hole [p. 78 of "TKOAP"]; "This is funny---it's a strange way to depict the posterior portion of the skull, is all I can tell you. There was no significance. It was just a hole. But it was further down, you see. It wasn't way up there." Gunn: "I note _here_ is the external occipital protuberance." "Yes." Gunn: "Can you describe generally where there was any missing bone from the posterior portion, to the best of your recollection?" "There basically wasn't any [bone]. It was just a hole. Not a significant missing bone." The exit wound was mostly parietal-temporal; Now unable to identify the entrance wound in the back of the head: he could not pick EITHER alleged wound as borne out by the HSCA! He doesn't have the "foggiest idea" of what the marking is towards the BOTTOM of the photo, while he cannot see ANY wound in the upper area in the black and white copy of Fox #3 [p. 83 of "TKOAP"]---"...the photographs I think create ambiguity. For me they do, much to my displeasure and dismay. I thought they would erase ambiguity rather than create it."; With regard to the X-rays, Humes said he had previously seen fragments corresponding to a small occipital wound in the x-ray, but now doesn't see it [ARRB222]. He also said he doesn't understand the big, non-opaque area that takes up half the skull. Humes did not remember seeing this the night of the autopsy: "I don't understand this great big void there. I don't know what that's all about... there's aspects of it [the X-ray] I don't understand. I don't understand this big void up---maybe a radiologist could explain it [Dr. David Mantik has an explanation for it...]. I don't know what this big non-opaque area that takes up half of the skull here, I don't understand that...I don't remember it." ; Humes said that there was very little scalp missing and they pretty much were able to close up the skull when it had been reconstructed with a mortician's rubber dam put in the back of the head after the autopsy [see "High Treason 2", pp. 184-185].;

Humes was insistent that the entry of a bullet into the back of the head was near the hairline and to the right, and that the entry hole in the scalp exactly coincided with the hole in the skull, and that the small entry hole in the skull, assembled when a second, large bone fragment arrived from Dallas and was fit into place on the skull, showed a coning effect on the inside of the skull, which indicated a wound of entry there: "...because it was shelved on the outer table, and we almost could put it all together, that wound.";

ac. 3/11/96 from Humes to the ARRB's Jeremy Gunn [see also *"High Treason III"* (1998), pp. 448-449 and 543]---"Both during my testimony before the House Select Committee on Assassinations, and during this deposition I experienced great difficulty in interpreting the location of the wound of entrance in the posterior scalp from the photograph. This may be because of the angle from which it was taken, or the position of the head, etc. It is obvious that the location of the external ocipital protuberance cannot be ascertained from the photograph. I most firmly believe that the location of the wound was exactly where I measured it to be in relation to the external occipital protuberance and so recorded it in the autopsy report. After all that was my direct observation in the morgue and I believe it to be far more reliable than attempting to interpret what I believe to be a photograph which is subject to various interpretations.";

ad. 9/98 letter to Vince Palamara---VMP: "I understand that skull fragments were brought to the autopsy during the later stages...in fact, wasn't the entry wound in the rear of JFK's head found on just such a skull fragment?" Humes: *"No-J.J.H"* [emphasis added: see 2 H 354]

ae. *"Murder In Dealey Plaza"* by James Fetzer (2000), pages x, 7, 105, 112-115, 182-183, 192, 199, 202-203, 205-206, 212, 224-225, 228, 230, 232, 234, 241, 243, 246-248, 253, 256-257, 261, 264, 266-270, 272, 283, 285-293, 297, 300-310, 336, 358, 433-434, 436, 439, 443-452

af. *"JFK Absolute Proof"* by Robert Groden (2013), page 155: Humes is pictured with a nice summary of his statements (see also 165, 178, 186)

-BOSWELL:

a. 2 H 376-377 (testimony)---basically just agrees with Humes' testimony;

b. other WC references: WR 86, 88; 2 H 348-350, 354-355, 373, 383; 5 H 142; 6 H 25; 18 H 727;

c. 11/25/66 *"Baltimore Sun"* article by Richard H. Levine---"The pathologists had already been told of the probable extent of the injuries and what had been done by physicians in Dallas."; "'The wound in the throat was not immediately evident at the autopsy,' Dr. Boswell said, 'because of the tracheotomy performed in Dallas...We concluded that night that the bullet had, in fact, entered in the back of the neck, traversed the neck and exited anteriorly.'";

d. 11/24/66 AP article: *"JFK Autopsy Doctor Admits Sketch Error"*---Boswell claimed that his drawings were highly inaccurate (!);

e.   interview with Josiah Thompson (*"Six Seconds In Dallas"*; see also *"Crossfire"*, p. 371, and *"Who's Who in the JFK Assassination"*, pp. 46-47)---Boswell said that all three autopsy doctors probed the back wound with their fingers but could not penetrate past an inch or so. A thin metal probe was also used but no bullet track could be located.;

f.   1/26/68 letter from Boswell to Attorney General Ramsey Clark [see *"Post Mortem"*, p. 574, as well as in *JAMA*, May 27, 1992-Vol 267, No. 20: *"JFK's Death---the plain truth from the MDs who did the autopsy"* by Dennis L. Breo (interview with James J. Humes and "J" Thornton Boswell***)]---"As you are aware, the autopsy findings in the case of the late President John F. Kennedy, including x-rays and photographs, have been the subject of continuing controversy and speculation. Dr Humes and I, as the pathologists concerned, have felt for some time that an impartial board of experts, including pathologists and radiologists, should examine the available material. If such a board were to be nominated in an attempt to resolve many of the allegations concerning the autopsy report, it might wish to question the autopsy participants before more time elapses and memory fades; therefore, it would be my hope that such a board would be convened at an early date. Dr Humes and I would make ourselves available at the request of such a board. I hope that this letter will not be considered presumptuous, but this matter is of great concern to us, and I believe to the country as well."; ***"Four physicians were subsequently appointed to a blue-ribbon panel to evaluate the original autopsy. The four included:

- William H. Cames, MD, professor of pathology at the University of Utah, Salt Lake City, and a member of Utah's Medical Examiner's Commission. He was nominated by J. E. Wallace Sterling, the president of Stanford University.

- Russell S. Fisher, MD, professor of forensic pathology at the University of Maryland and chief medical examiner of the state of Maryland. He was nominated by Dr Oscar B. Hunter, Jr, president of the College of American Pathologists.

- Russell H. Morgan, MD, professor of radiology at The Johns Hopkins University School of Medicine, Baltimore, Md. He was nominated by Dr Lincoln Gordon, president of The Johns Hopkins University.

- Alan R. Moritz, MD, professor of pathology at Case Western Reserve University, Cleveland, Ohio, and former professor of forensic medicine at Harvard University, Cambridge, Mass. He was nominated by Dr John A. Hannah, president of Michigan State University.

None of the four had any previous connection with prior investigations or reports on the President's assassination. After an exhaustive study of all relevant materials, the four members of the panel signed and submitted a 16-page report to Attorney General Clark in April 1968, unanimously concluding:

"Examination of the clothing and of the photographs and x-rays taken at autopsy reveal that President Kennedy was struck by two bullets fired from above and behind him, one of which traversed the base of the neck on the right side without striking bone the other of which entered the skull from behind and exploded its right side. The photographs and x-rays discussed herein support the above-quoted portions [the conclusion] of the original Autopsy Report and the above-quoted medical conclusions of the Warren Commission Report."----except that the Clark Panel found that the rear head entrance wound was FOUR INCHES HIGHER than the autopsy doctors said it was located [see "*Post Mortem*", pp. 580-596, and "*Mortal Error*", pp. 313-320]!

g. 8/16/77 interview with the HSCA's Andy Purdy, Colleen Boland, and Jim Kelly (RIF#180-10093-10430)---"Regarding the head wound, Dr. Boswell said the wound was fairly low in the back of the head and that the bone was completely gone above the entry wound. He said that during the autopsy, a piece of skull fragment was brought in which included a portion which corresponded to the missing half of the entry wound in the head...Regarding the head wounds he said the entry hole was only approximately half in evidence, the other half being part of the skull fragment which was brought in...Regarding the autopsy face sheet, Dr. Boswell said that the entry wound to the head, if not exactly accurate, may have been '...possibly off a little to the left."; Boswell said it was "ridiculous to do the post here" (at Bethesda) but "He was told that Dr. Burkley had insisted that the President be brought there [to Bethesda Naval Hospital]...[Burkley said that the police had] captured the guy who did this, all we need is the bullet. We argued with him at that point...saying the autopsy must be complete and thorough. Dr. Burkley indicated he wanted just a limited autopsy to the thorax, and this was then extended to the head. Dr. Humes insisted there be a complete autopsy, saying, for example, the adrenals were extremely important. Dr. Burkley said it would be okay to examine the adrenals if they could reach them through the upper opening. Dr. Boswell reached down and tried to reach the adrenals but could not and Dr. Burkley agreed that they could do a full autopsy." Dr. Burkley made it clear that he wanted the information on the adrenals reported informally. Boswell also said that Robert McNamara seemed to have acted as liaison between the Kennedy family and Dr. Burkley---McNamara kept his head throughout and, although never actually in the autopsy room, was working out of the room where the Kennedy family was staying (on the 17th floor).; He said that no one gave orders not to probe the back wound [!] and that Humes probed the back wound with both a metal probe and his little finger.; He remembered seeing part of the perimeter of a bullet hole in the anterior neck; Boswell "thought a photograph was taken of the lung."; Said the radiologists agreed that there was no damage to the cervical spine, although there was a small fleck/ metal fragment in the spinal canal; "...we had gotten ourselves in dutch with the neck and throat wounds with regard to the Secret Service." [?]; Dr. Robert Karnei, a resident "who served as chief assistant" during the autopsy, was also present during the brain examination;

h. 8/11/78 interview with the HSCA---Boswell said that the X-rays and photos were of poor quality; said that he looked for the adrenals and they were atrophied; Burkley supervised the autopsy, acting as liaison for the Kennedy family; claimed that they were NOT aware the tracheostomy was performed on the throat wound before they spoke with Perry; said the trachea was not removed and that there wasn't much trauma to the neck area; said that JFK's brain was so torn up it would not show a bullet track;

i.   11/28/78 Outside contact report by the HSCA's Mark Flanagan (RIF#180-10101-10270)---"Called to ask Dr. Boswell to respond to Dr. Humes' change in opinion re: the entrance wound location in the rear of the President's head. Dr. Boswell said he still agrees with the original report and does not wish to change his opinion.";

j.   7/5/79 interview with David Lifton (*"Best Evidence"*, pages 319, 320, 688 and 689)---"Boswell told me... that he personally made the 10 by 17 cm measurements using a centimeter scale.";

k.   10/2/90 and 9/1/91 interviews with Richard Waybright and Harry Livingstone, respectively, for *"High Treason 2"* [H.E.L.'s 10/7/91 interview referenced above] (see Chapter 8, pp. 191-201 [see also *"Killing the Truth"*, page 680]): Boswell "appeared to be troubled by the X-rays and continued to look at them. He stated that they did not look right, but that he would have to see the originals before he could make a valid judgment."; "Dr. Boswell explained that it [small crescent shape at the bottom of the skull diagram sheet] was a drawing of a crescent-shaped piece of skull that was brought into the autopsy room later."; "with rigid tenacity [Boswell] maintained that the entry wound was at or near the occipital protuberance."; "Dr. Boswell indicated that the entrance wound was located at the rear of the head where a small piece of brain tissue is visible in the autopsy photographs. He stated that the 'bullet hole' that Ida Dox has highlighted in her drawings of the President's head is not the entrance wound but possibly may be blood or a mixture of blood and water."; Boswell: "...there was a pretty good amount of the skull that was---first of all there was a piece of the skull on the pavement down in Dallas..."; Re: the right frontal bone: "It was intact";

l.   8/31/92 interview with Dennis Breo, as reported in the 10/7/92 JAMA---"On August 31, 1992, Dr. Boswell confirmed, on the record, that serial sections of the perirenal fat pads demonstrated no gross evidence of adrenal cortex or medulla... diagnostic of severe Addison's disease..." [*see Karnei, above*];

m.   2/26/96 ARRB deposition (*inc. life-sized plastic model of a human skull on which Boswell marked the location of the head wound*) [see also *"High Treason III"* (1998), pp. 455-472]---Boswell reaffirmed the rear head entrance wound as being near the EOP. Question: "Did you at any point ever change your mind about the location of the entrance wound in the skull?" "No."; Question: "I'd like to draw your attention in the color photograph to the round, reddish marking just to the right of the ruler, very near the top of the ruler." "Yes." "Could that round or ovular-shaped marking be the entrance wound?" "No."; like Humes, said that there was some disruption to the cerebellum; stated that the scalp was loose and would fall down over the skull defect unless it was held up in place ("I think that I probably was pulling the scalp up."), thus their holding it up over the defect to photograph the entry hole into the scalp; says they've "always looked for" the photo of the interior of the chest, that they tried to find it on previous occasions because it was such an important photo. In all, Humes and Boswell both identify three photos that are missing: color photos showing the tunneling of the entry hole into the scalp, one depicting the interior of the skull and the entry hole, and the aforementioned photo of the interior of the chest.; Question: "Just to try a different description, because we're trying to put this into words where we're looking at photographs, would it be fair to say---again, we are imaging President Kennedy is standing erect, although he's lying down in this photograph. So with the ruler pointing up, would the portion as it would appear on this photograph to the left of his right ear all be the portion of the skull that was missing?" Boswell: "Yes." [!]; Re: the location of the entry in JFK's back---Question: "If you had to match the entrance wound that you can see on the photograph in view 4 to one of the vertebra, would you be able to give an approximate location, either C7 or C4 or T3, whatever?" Boswell: "Well, it's certainly not as low as T4. I would say at the lowest it might be T2. I would say around T2."; Two lies-Question: "Were the organs of the neck dissected?" "Yes." Question: "Did you reach the conclusion that there had been a transit wound through the neck during the course of the autopsy itself?" "Oh, yes."; Question: "Do you remember whether the fresh brain was weighed?" "I doubt that it was weighed …"; "… the morticians were able to cover this defect completely by using some sort of plastic to cover the brain cavity, because there wasn't much bone to replace the brain cavity. But they were able to use his scalp to almost completely close the wound." Question: "So it would be fair to say that although there was a very large piece of skull missing, there was very little scalp missing?" "Right."; Question: "Would it be your impression that, first, the markings that are contained in the face sheet, Exhibit 1, and in the autopsy protocol are accurate?" "Yes."; Question: "Let me draw your attention to a white semicircular marking in what appears to be in the right orbit, and I'll say that's on the left side of the X-ray we're looking at now. Do you see that white apparently radiopaque object? " "Yes." "Do you know what that object is?" "No." "Do you know whether that is an artifact that is just there as part of either the developing process or whether that is a missile fragment?" "No, I can't tell you that. I don't remember the interpretations. I see a lot of metallic-looking debris, X-ray opaque material …" "Can you relate that, again, apparently large object to any of the fragments that you removed?" "No. We did not find one that large. I'm sure of that." (emphasis added); re: the right lateral X-ray: "I don't think I can identify the entrance wound …I don't see that in this X-ray." Question: "Does that depressed fracture [in the cowlick/ Clark Panel/ HSCA location] correlate in any way to the entrance wound that you observed on the night of the autopsy?" "I think it's a long way from it. I think that's quite a ways from the entrance wound."; re: the apparent trail of dustlike fragments seen in the X-rays across the top of the skull: "I see the line here, but it doesn't connect with the wound of entry, although they say it does there [in the autopsy report]."; once again, Boswell states that the bullet hole of entry was only to be found when a bone fragment arrived from Dallas and they could see that it was beveled in one place and fit on the skull where there was a semi-circular hole with interior beveling.;

n. [no relation to the "Dr. Boswell" from Baylor Hospital who treated DPD Detective Paul L. Bentley's injured foot on 11/26/63! [See *With Malice: Lee Harvey Oswald and the Murder of Officer J.D. Tippit*" by Dale K. Myers (1998), p. 562];

o. [unanswered letter from Vince Palamara 1998]

p. *"Murder In Dealey Plaza"* by James Fetzer (2000), pages x, 112, 113, 182, 183, 186-187, 192, 199, 202-203, 205, 228, 229, 230, 237, 246-247, 250, 252, 256, 266-268, 272, 284-289, 293, 295, 300, 301-303, 305-310, 336, 358, 433, 434, 436, 439-445

q. *"JFK Absolute Proof"* by Robert Groden (2013), page 155: Boswell is pictured with a nice summary of his statements

-FINCK:

a. 2 H 377-384 / testimony---while he "agreed" with the testimony of Humes, Finck also agreed with him that all of Connally's wounds were not made by CE399: "...there are too many fragments described in that wrist."; "The bullet entered in the back of the head and went out on the right side of the skull, producing a large wound, the greatest dimension of which was approximately 13 centimeters.";

b. other WC references: WR 86, 88; 2 H 93-94, 103, 348, 350, 352, 355, 358, 360, 373, 375, 377; 5 H 142; 6 H 25; 18 H 727;

c. 2/1/65 memorandum to Brig. Gen.. J.M. Blumberg, MC, Director, Armed Forces Institute of Pathology [*see Blumberg, below*; see also 7 HSCA 101, 122, 135, 191; *"Between the Signal and the Noise"* by Roger Bruce Feinman, pp. 34-37]

"The scalp of the vertex is lacerated. There is an open comminuted fracture of the cranial vault, many portions of which are missing. .The autopsy had been in progress for thirty minutes when 1 arrived. Cdr Humes told me that he only had to prolong the lacerations of the scalp before removing the brain. No sawing of the skull was necessary. The opening of the large head wound, in the right fronto-parieto-occipital region, is 130 millimeters (mm) in diameter. I also noticed another scalp wound, possibly of entrance, in the right occipital region, lacerated and transversal, 15 x 6 mm.. Corresponding to that wound, the skull shows a portion of a crater, the beveling of which is obvious on the internal aspect of the bone; on that basis, I told the prosecutors and Admiral Galloway that this occipital wound is a wound, of ENTRANCE. No EXIT wound is identifiable at this 'time in the skull, but close to midnight, portions of the cranial vault are received from DALLAS, Texas. X ray films of these bone specimens reveal numerous metallic fragments. Two of the bone specimens, 50 mm in diameter, reveal BEVELING when viewed from the external aspect, thus indicating a wound of EXIT. Most probably, these bone specimens are part of the very large right skull wound, 130 mm in diameter and mentioned above. This right fronto-parieto-occipital wound is therefore an EXIT. There is another wound, in the region of the right trapezious muscle, at 140 mm from the right acromion and at 140 mm from the tip of the right mastoid process (I took these measurements). The wound is OVAL, 7 x 4 mm, and shows well demarcated edges. This wound cannot be probed with the soft probe available. There is subpleural hemorrhage in the right apical mesial region. The apex of the right lung is hemorrhagic, without laceration of the pleura.";

d. 6/65 article in *"Military Medicine"*;

e. 2/24/69 and 2/25/69 testimony in the Clay Shaw trial (*see Kellerman, Gallo-way, and Kenney, above*) [see *"Destiny Betrayed: JFK, Cuba, and the Garrison Case"* by James DiEugenio (1992), pp. 288-309/ Appendix A+page 197, inc. a photo of Finck from 2/24/69]---"...the wound of the head with entry in the back of the head and exit on the right side of the head...."; Mr. Oser: "Was Dr. Humes running the show?" "Well, I heard Dr. Humes stating that---he said, "Who is in charge here?" and I heard an Army General, I don't remember his name, stating, "I am." You must understand that in those circumstances, there were law enforcement officials, military people with various ranks, and you have to co-ordinate the operation according to directions."; Mr. Oser: "Colonel, did you feel that you had to take orders from this Army General that was there di-recting the autopsy?" "No, because there were others, there were Admirals." Mr. Oser: "There were Admirals?" "Oh, yes, there were Admirals, and when you are a Lieutenant Colonel in the Army you just follow orders, and at the end of the autopsy we were specifically told---as I recall, it was by Admiral Kenney, the Sur-geon General of the Navy---this is subject to verification---we were specifically told not to discuss the case...without coordination with the Attorney General [RFK]."; "I did not dissect the track in the neck...We didn't remove the organs of the neck...I was told that the family wanted an examination of the head, as I recall, the head and chest, but the prosecutors in this autopsy didn't remove the organs of the neck, to my recollection...As I recall I was told not to but I don't remember by whom."; "When there are so many fractures in so many directions producing so many lines and fragments in the bone, *a photograph will be more accurate than descriptions.* [emphasis added: see below];

f. 2/25/69 *"New York Times"*---the autopsy would not qualify as a "complete" au-topsy by the standards of the American Board of Pathology because of certain restrictions which were imposed, including not dissecting out the entire bullet track through the base of the neck on the right side.;

g. 3/11/78 interview with the HSCA [see 7 HSCA 115]---Finck *"believed strongly that the observations of the autopsy pathologists were more valid than those of in-dividuals who might subsequently examine photographs."* [emphasis added: see above]; Andy Purdy: "Was there discussion where the entry was in the head specifically when you examined the photographs?" "In January 1967, I would say there was..." Andy Purdy: "When you examined the photograph in 1967, did you consider or was it pointed out to you the red spot in the higher portion on the head that we pointed out to you?" "I don't remember. If it is not in the [Dept. of Justice]memorandum, I cannot remember...I don't know what it is. *How are these photographs identified as coming from the autopsy of President Ken-nedy?"* [emphasis added]; "Well, I would say that this was the wound of entry to the right of the external occipital protuberance. "; "It [the entry wound] was *above* the external occipital protuberance...*Slightly above it*...It was 2.5 centi-meters to the right of the midline." [emphasis added; Humes said the wound was *below* the EOP, and both Humes *and* Boswell insisted on this position to the same panel of doctors the previous year]; Question: "Did you see the wound of entry in a separate piece of bone that was handed to you or was that still hooked on the body?" "*It was definitely attached to the body, the wound of entry.*" [empha-sis added; Finck is thus refuting Boswell's claim, *as did Humes in his letter to the author*]; "the probing was unsuccessful…";

h. 3/12/78 interview with the HSCA----"I think that the doubts and the contro-versies now arise from the fact that the people used these photographs as a basis for interpretation, saying they don't fit the autopsy report. And that's what both-ers people and *that's why I came back*---to clarify that situation as well as I can after all that time. At the time of the autopsy, I palpated the scalp of President Kennedy, I examined it. Outer and inner surfaces of the scalp in the back of the head…try[ing] to summarize my opinion about this photograph, *having exam-ined the scalp myself, I don't think there is much point in arguing about the so-called wound seen high in the scalp*…for the good reason that, at that level I did not see in the scalp of President Kennedy, a perforating wound of the scalp." [emphasis added];

i. Portrayed by actor Peter Maloney in the 1991 Oliver Stone movie "*JFK*" (see "*JFK: The Book of the Film*", pp. 158-159 and 584);

j. "*Mortal Error*" by Bonar Meninger (1992): "Finck, contacted at his home in Switzerland, declined to discuss the assassination or autopsy."

k. 8/19/92 interview with Dennis L. Breo as reported in the 10/7/92 JAMA article "*JFK's death, part III---Dr. Finck speaks out: 'Two bullets from the rear.'*": [written response to Breos' question] "The FATAL WOUND-entry 25mm to the right of the external occipital protuberance and slightly above. After removal of the brain, the beveling of the internal table (of the skull) indicates this was a wound of entry."; "The generals did NOT interfere with the autopsy." [how about the Admirals?];

l. 5/24/96 ARRB deposition [aka "I don't recall"; see also "*High Treason III*" (1998), pp. 412-416]: "It was clear that there was a wound of entry in the upper back"; very from that the entry into the back of the head was 2.5 cm to the right and slightly above the external occipital protuberance, precisely where it was placed at the time of the autopsy;

m. "*Murder In Dealey Plaza*" by James Fetzer (2000), pages 112-113, 182-183, 192, 205-207, 212, 225, 228, 230, 235, 237, 243, 247, 285-297, 300, 303-309, 433-434, 445

IV

MISC.

240) John C. "Jack" Metzler, Superintendent, Arlington National Cemetery:

a.   "After Action Report/ Summary," Gen. Wehle's Office, Military District of Washington (MDW), 11/22/63---"Should call Mr. Metzler to make arrangements with the Gawler Funeral Home to have ambulance come out and pick up the President's body."; "At 1610 hours, General Wehle called Mr. Metzler, Superintendent, Arlington National Cemetery, and informed him to contact Gawler Funeral Home and make arrangements as prescribed.";

b.   4/30/64, 8/10/64, 6/21/65, and 7/7/65 interviews with William Manchester (*"The Death of a President"*, many [see also p. 673]);

c.   5/5/78 interview with the HSCA: outside contact report (7 HSCA 31);

241)-242) Capt. Walter R. Bishop, Artillery Officer, and Sgt. 1rst Class Allen J. Eldredge, Wreath Bearer (deceased 10/19/2004) (both from Lt. Bird's 3rd Infantry Division):

a.   Both interviewed by William Manchester on 4/30/64 for *"The Death of a President"* (see pages 660 and 662): neither man appears in the actual text of the book, despite these sourced interviews;

243) 1rst Lt. Donald W. Sawtelle, Honor Guard Commander, 3rd Infantry:

a.   4/30/64 interview with William Manchester (*"The Death of a President"*, pages 410, 421, 442, 462, 517 and 667);

244) Dr. Leonard Heaton, the Army's Surgeon General, Walter Reed Hospital (deceased 9/10/1983):

a.   Air Force One radio tapes/ transcripts [see also *"Best Evidence"*, pages 681, 684, 686]-Clifton to Heaton: "We do not want a helicopter for Bethesda Medical Center we do want an ambulance and a ground return from Andrews to Walter Reed, and we want the regular postmortem that has to be done by law under guard performed at Walter Reed. Is that clear? Over." Heaton: "That is clear, General Clifton.

You want an ambulance and another limousine at Andrews and you want the regular post-mortem by law done at Walter Reed." Clifton: "That is correct.";

245) Capt. [fnu] Patton, special events officer, Military District of Washington (MDW):

a. Daily Staff Journal/ Duty Officer's Log, Military District of Washington (MDW) headquarters, November 22, 1963---At 5:00 P.M., Capt. Patton informed the MDW that the "President's remains will arrive AAFB 18:05 hrs.";

b. Memorandum For The Record, 1rst Lt. Samuel R. Bird, 11/27/63---"Upon landing at Andrews Air Force Base, Maryland, at approximately 1730 hours, I reported to Captain Patton, special events officer, Military District of Washington...Captain Patton instructed me to be prepared to take three courses of action. First, that the all Army Casket Team would remove the remains from the Presidential Aircraft. Second, that a joint armed forces casket team would be formed if personnel from the other services arrived prior to the arrival of the aircraft. Third, that the Presidential Aircraft had radioed that Secret Service Agents aboard the aircraft would remove the President's casket.";

246)-251) Secret Service (PRS) Special Officer (SO)/ Photographer James K. "Jack" Fox (deceased 1987),
Lt. (jg.) Vincent Madonia, USN,
(Mrs. Kennedy's personal) White House Photographer (Chief Petty Officer) Robert L. Knudsen, USN (deceased 1/89),
Saundra Kay "Sandy" Spencer, a lab technician at the Naval Photographic Center, Joe O'Donnell, a government photographer employed by USIA in 1963, and Carol Ann Bonito:

a. CD 80, p. 3; RIF# 180-10001-10041 [see Kinney, above, as well as Bouck]---photographed the Presidential limousine in the White House garage at 4:00 P.M. on 11/23/63;

b. 4/26/65 Memorandum of Transfer (re: transfer of autopsy/ related materials) [see "Post Mortem", p. 558]---mentioned twice: "Office Memorandum from James K. Fox to SAIC Bouck Nov. 29, 1963, concerning the processing of film in the presence of **Lt. (jg) V. Madonia, USN** (orig. & 2 ccs)" and "Orig. memo from Lt. Madonia to J.K. Fox, U.S. Secret Service, White House, Special Officer, dated Nov. 29, 1963, concerning receipt of certain films and prints and the processing thereof (Orig. & 1 cc)";

c. c) 5/19/70 letter from Secret Service Assistant Director Thomas J. Kelley to Harold Weisberg [see "Post Mortem", p. 274; RIF#180-10109-10368: 2/67 SS statement signed by Kellerman, Bouck, Edith Duncan, Fox, and Kelley---see also the Summer 1998 issue of "Kennedy Assassination Chronicles" journal]---"On or about November 27, 1963, Bouck gave the photographic film to Secret Service employee, James K. Fox, who took the film to the U.S. Navy Photographic Laboratory. The black and white film was processed, black and white negatives were developed, and colored positives were made from the colored film. The processing and development was done by **Lieut. V. Madonia, U.S. Navy**, at the laboratory. Fox remained with the film at the laboratory and all the photographic film was returned to Mr. Bouck the same day. The processed film was placed in a combination lock-safe file; the combination was known only to two persons. A few days later, black and white prints were made by Mr. Fox in the Secret Service photographic laboratory. On or about December 9, 1963, Mr. Fox took the colored positives back to the U.S. Navy Photographic Laboratory and observed while enlarged color prints were made. All the color positives and prints were returned by Fox at 6 p.m., the same evening and returned to the locked safe.";

d. 8/6/77 HSCA interview of SAIC of PRS Robert I. Bouck (RIF# 180-10097-10141)---"Bouck said that James Fox was his photographer at the White House and believes that he processed the black and white prints ("...little snapshots..."). Bouck said "...I believe they had nothing to do with the big prints or the color ones." Bouck said that James Fox processed one or two or several rolls of color film at another facility.";

e. 8/7/78 interview with the HSCA's Andy Purdy (RIF# 180-10077-10107)---[Purdy's notes on call] "Who developed film? He did black and white at Secret Service lab. Color was done at Naval Processing Center---recalls **Lt. Madonnia** [sic] (he wrote memo on it.)---White House photographer [**Robert L. Knudsen**] was in drying room. He (Fox) checked and there was film on each side of color film holders. (some black+white missing) Negatives put in files 4-5 days.---Bouck then ordered him to have prints made. He + **Knudsen** did it. *Two women in drying room passed out when came [film] through* [most likely **Saundra Kay Spencer and Carol Ann Bonito**]. He did not help **Knudsen** put prints in holders. Recalls one or two sets of prints being turned over to Bouck. (It was four years after assassination that he was asked for statement.) *Burkley* told Fox to have prints made up, he went to Bouck for okay. He said fine but would need special arrangement for color. **Knudsen** not there when black and white done. No metal probes present; doctors were taking measurements, ruler and hands visible in autopsy photos." [emphasis added];

f. *"Best Evidence"* by David Lifton, page 703 [+ autopsy photos] (see also p. 427)---"In 1981, I received a letter from Maryland radio journalist Mark Crouch saying he knew someone who had a set of the autopsy photographs, the same photographs that were at the National Archives. He subsequently introduced me to James K. ("Jack") Fox, formerly a photographer with the Intelligence Division of the Secret Service. Documents from the House Assassinations Committee establish that Fox was one of a few officials who had access to the processing [*see 7 HSCA 23-24*] On three occasions, he supervised their processing. According to Fox, shortly after the assassination he was told by Secret Service Agent Roy Kellerman: "Here, make a set of these for yourself. They'll be history someday." Fox showed me the pictures he had, and later I was able to obtain a set.";

g. ***Vincent Madonia, the officer in charge of the color photo lab***: 6/21/96 and 11/27/96 interviews with the ARRB---"... he did not recall any transparencies being developed, only prints. He said there was no good system for making prints from color positive transparencies. NPC [Navy Photographic Center in Anacostia] had the capability to develop transparencies and make internegatives, but he did not remember this happening following the JFK assassination."; he knew Robert Knudsen and "..he may have been there that weekend (right after the assassination) ... take that out of your notes, I shouldn't have said that, I'm not sure." (!);

h. *"Nova"*, PBS, 11/15/88 and

i. *"JFK: An Unsolved Murder"*, KRON, 11/18/88 [later excerpted on *"JFK: The Case for Conspiracy"* video by Robert Groden w/ *narration by Mark Crouch*, 1993]: a few of the autopsy photos appear (Lifton appeared on each program, as well; the latter, as a paid consultant);

j. *"High Treason"* by Robert J. Groden and Harrison Edward Livingstone (1989/ 1990)-Fox---and Crouch---are *credited, along with David Lifton,* on p. 484 of the 1990 BERKLEY edition onward. The autopsy photos, with one exception, were merely copied from "Best Evidence";

k. *"Conspiracy"* by Anthony Summers (1989 PARAGON HOUSE EDITION): 2 of the Fox photos used (Fox and Crouch credited, along with David Lifton, on p. 639);

l. *"Best Evidence: The Research Video"* (THE 1990 RHINO RELEASE): the autopsy photos appear near the end of the program (Fox and Crouch credited), and the Fox photos appear when Lifton guests on *"Hard Copy"* in May 1990;

m. *"JFK"* movie by Oliver Stone---the autopsy photos appear here, as well (Fox and Crouch credited; both Groden *and* Lifton were technical advisors);

n. 12/31/91 *"Globe"* tabloid---autopsy photos inc. in Groden article (*later* credited to Fox and Crouch);

o. 1992 video produced by Mark Crouch and Harry Livingstone---dissects all the Fox autopsy photos in detail;

p. *"High Treason 2"* by H.E.L. (1992), pages 90, 99, 137-138, 245, 300, 314, 318, 322, 327-328, 333-334 [+ complete Fox set]---"In his interviews with James Fox, Mark Crouch reports that even some members of the Secret Service believed an agent was lost."; "Mark Crouch tells me that his friend, Secret Service man James Fox, described the burning of most of the autopsy photos and X-rays and other assassination related materials two weeks after the autopsy.";

q. "During interviews conducted on 1/28/92 and 9/23/92 respectively [with Mark Crouch], the author obtained startling new information:

While all three major television networks reported that "A Secret Service agent and a Dallas policeman were shot and killed" on 11/22/63, only to be officially "corrected" later by Secret Service officials, this author learned from Crouch that Agent Fox stated that the story was <u>true</u>! According to Crouch, Fox was working in the Executive Office Building on 11/22/63 (where the PRS worked out of) when he was asked by SAIC of PRS Robert Bouck to get ready a detail of four to six agents to assist in retrieving the body and casket of the unnamed Secret Service agent. Fox told Crouch, "we lost a man that day - our man," and qualified his remarks by stating that he was NOT referring to JFK! This was a deathbed confession of sorts - Fox died not long [1987] after telling Crouch this in the early 1980's. (Interestingly, although having heard the news reports that stated that the President's *limousine* raced to Parkland Hospital after the shooting, Mrs. Bill Greer thought for several hours that her husband had perished that day! Since she knew that Greer was the <u>driver</u> of JFK's car, this appears to be a strange admission.)("Death of a President", page 354; interview with Richard Greer 10/7/91)";

r.   The Fox set appears in the 1992 book "*JFK: Conspiracy of Silence*" by Crenshaw, but they are credited to Paul O'Connor [Tom Wilson also had a set during 1991/ 1992] (during Crenshaw's appearance on "*20/20*" in April 1992, one of the Fox photos appears);

s.   A mixture of Fox and Groden autopsy photos appear in "*The Killing of a President*" (1993) and in "*JFK Absolute Proof*" by Robert Groden (2013) [one of Groden's color photos appears in "*The Men Who Killed Kennedy*" to which he appeared as a consultant (1988/ 1991/ 1995)], and several of the Fox photos appear in Robin T. Deloria's "*Mirror of Doubt*" (1993); one Fox photo appears (w/ credit) on page 132 of Stewart Galanor's "*Cover-Up*" (1998);

t.   *"Killing The Truth" by H.E.L. (1993), pages 269-288 (most of chapter 9), 401, and 428-434 (Crouch's article)[inc. 2 of the Fox photos]---recommended reading regarding Fox, Crouch, Lifton, and Groden, as well as the chain of possession of the (Fox) autopsy photos;*

u.   "*In the Line of Fire*" movie (1993): one of the Fox photos appears and Fox---and Crouch---are credited;

v.   "*Treachery in Dallas*" by Walt Brown (1995), pp. 54-55 [+ 2 Fox photos];

w.   "*Killing Kennedy*" by H.E.L. (1995), pages 32, 33, 196, and 352;

x.   "*Bloody Treason*" by Noel Twyman (1997), pp. 223-224 [+the Fox set];

y.   July 1997 "*JFK/ Deep Politics Quarterly*" journal: article by Mark Crouch entitled "*Jim Fox and the Dead Secret Service Agent Story*";

z.   "*Pictures of the Pain*" by Richard Trask" (1994), pages 25 (*inc. PHOTO*), 28, 365, and 384 [see also "*That Day In Dallas*" by Richard Trask (1998), pages 10, 11 (*inc. PHOTO*) 14, and 15]: good information on **Robert L. Knudsen**;

aa.   7/31/98 Associated Press story by Deb Riechman---"New testimony released Friday about the autopsy on John F. Kennedy says a second set of pictures was taken of Kennedy's wounds -- pictures never made public.

The existence of additional photographs -- believed taken by White House photographer **Robert L. Knudsen** during or after the autopsy at the National Naval Medical Center in Bethesda, Md. -- raised new questions about how the autopsy was conducted, a subject of intense debate for 35 years.

But the new evidence sheds no light on the whereabouts of the second set of pictures.

Kennedy was killed Nov. 22, 1963. The following year, a commission chaired by then-Chief Justice Earl Warren concluded the killer was Lee Harvey Oswald and that he acted alone and was not part of a conspiracy. That conclusion has been challenged ever since.

"One of the many tragedies of the assassination of President Kennedy has been the incompleteness of the autopsy record and the suspicion caused by the shroud of secrecy that has surrounded the records that do exist," said the Assassination Records Review Board, which made the new testimony public.

The board, created by Congress to collect all pertinent records concerning Kennedy's murder, said the doctors who conducted the autopsy may have had the best of intentions -- protecting the privacy of the Kennedy family. But ``the legacy of such secrecy ultimately has caused distrust and suspicion," the board said.

One set of autopsy photographs, now at the National Archives, has been known to exist for years, and some of the pictures have been widely published. But the new testimony documents the existence of another set.

In 1997, the review board located **Saundra K. Spencer**, who worked at the Naval Photographic Center in 1963. She was shown the archives' autopsy photos and concluded they were not the pictures she had helped process.

Those she had worked with, she said, had ``no blood or opening cavities." They were "quite reverent in how they handled it," she said.

She theorized that a second photographer took pictures of a cleaned-up corpse and speculated that was done at the request of the Kennedy family in case autopsy pictures had to be made public. ``The only thing I can think of is that a second set of autopsy pictures was shot for public release, if necessary."

The film was brought in, she said, by an agent she believed was with the FBI. "When he gave us the material to process, he said that they had been shot at Bethesda and they were autopsy pictures."

She was told, she said: ``Process them and try not to observe too much, don't peruse."

Knudsen's widow, Gloria, told the review board that her husband told her that photographing the dead president was "the hardest thing he had ever had to do in his life."

He appeared before the House Select Committee on Assassinations, which in the late 1970s reopened the official investigation into the killings of both Kennedy and Martin Luther King Jr., and his widow said he later told her that four or five of the pictures the committee showed him did not represent what he saw or photographed that night and that one of them had been altered.

"His son Bob said that his father told him that 'hair had been drawn in' on one photo to conceal a missing portion of the top-back of President Kennedy's head," according to a review board memo about a meeting with Knudsen's family.[5/7/96]

Gerald Posner, author of ``*Case Closed*," a 1993 book that argues that the

Warren Commission's central conclusion – that Oswald alone killed Kennedy -- is correct, though the new information was important and would ` `give grist to the conspiracy theorists for the next two generations."

"There's such controversy over the wounds on President Kennedy and the discussion over what the autopsy doctors have discussed and said and what the autopsy photos show that the existence of any additional photographs could be significant," he said.

Added David Lifton, author of ` `Best Evidence," a 1981 book concerning medical evidence about the assassination, ` `It's of tremendous significance that there's another camera and its existence and its product have been concealed all these years,' Lifton said. ` `We've got a credible paper trail about another camera and film but no pictures." [emphasis added];

ab. "The Washington Post", 8/2/98: article by George Lardner, Jr. :" Other new witnesses dealt with photographs believed to have been taken at Bethesda by the late White House photographer

Robert L. Knudsen, perhaps after the autopsy had been concluded and the embalming procedure had begun.

Saundra K. Spencer, who worked for Knudsen in "the White House lab" at the Naval Photographic Center in 1963, said she helped develop color negatives from film brought to her by an agent she thought was with the FBI.

"He said that they had been shot at Bethesda and they were autopsy pictures," Spencer testified in a June 1997 deposition. The agent told "us to process them and try to not observe too much, don't peruse."

Shown official autopsy photographs of Kennedy from the National Archives, Spencer said they were not the ones she helped process and were printed on different paper. She said "there was no blood or opening cavities" and the wounds were much smaller in the pictures she worked on, unlike in usual autopsy photos. "It was quite reverent in how they handled it."

Knudsen's widow, Gloria, and two of his children said he told them he had "photographed the autopsy of President Kennedy" and that "it was the hardest thing he ever had to do in his life." He also told them that "the Secret Service took the film from him as soon as he had exposed" it." [emphasis added];

ac. **Robert L. Knudsen**: 8/11/78 [audio-taped?] interview with the HSCA's Andy Purdy (RIF# 180-10105-10333) [see also "High Treason III" (1998) pp. 428-432]:
Purdy: "Where did the probes go through the body?"
Knudsen: "From the point where the projectile entered to the point where the projectile left."
Purdy: "Where were those two points?"
Knudsen: "From the entry to the exit."
Purdy: "Where were the entry and exit points?"
Knudsen: "Being under oath, I cannot tell you I do not know, because I do know, but, at the same time, I do feel I have been sworn not to disclose this information and I would prefer very much that you get one of the sets of prints and view them.";

"There are close-up and half body photographs, including ones with metal probes through the wounds of JFK"; seven sets of prints made, given to: RFK, National Archives, Kennedy Library, Ted Kennedy, possibly Secret Service.;
Purdy: "What other things besides the body did you see, other than the rulers?"
Knudsen: "What appeared to be stainless steel probes."
Purdy: "About how long were they?"
Knudsen: "The probes?"
Purdy: "Yes."
Knudsen: "I would estimate about two feet."
Purdy: "Was there one probe that you saw through the body, or were there more than one?"
Knudsen: "More than one. Here again, we are getting into this grey area of what I was instructed not to discuss."; "I am certain…there were the probes showing the point of entry and exit…It seems to me that the entry point was a little bit lower in the back---well, the point in the back was a little bit lower than the point in the front. So the probe was going diagonally from top to bottom, front to back…Right about where the neck-tie is."
Purdy: "Approximately how much lower than that would you say the other probe, which went through the chest cavity?"
Knudsen: "I would put it six, seven inches."
Purdy: "From the side view, you saw both probes?"
Knudsen: "Right."
Purdy: "You just indicated where the probe came out, on the lower---"
Knudsen: "It seemed to me that it was right around mid chest.";
Knudsen mentions one of the women in the lab as "**Sandy Spencer**"; "*JFK Absolute Proof*" by Robert Groden (2013), page 155: Knudsen is pictured with a nice summary of his statements.

ad. **Saundra Kay Spencer**: 12/13/96 interview with the ARRB [see also "*High Treason III*" (1998), pp. 416-418]---"Views were 'body shots,' and not like the normal autopsy photographs she had experience with from her previous duty at Pensacola, in that there was no one in the background, and she does not remember any instruments in the photographs; the views were also unlike other autopsy photographs she had seen, in that the body of the President was 'very clean,' explaining that there was 'no blood and no gore' visible; she remembered no measuring devices visible either; no identification tags or cards visible in any of the photos; a wound at the base of the front of the President's neck which was circular, and about the size of the round end of a person's thumb; she remembers a wound in the back of the President's head which she described as a 'blown out chunk' about 2 to 2.5 inches wide located in about the center of the back of the President's head, about 3 or 4 inches above the hairline at the back of his head… she remembered no damage to the right side of the President's head."; ***Carol Ann Bonito***: helped Spencer develop the autopsy photos;

ae. **Saundra Kay Spencer**: 6/5/97 deposition with the ARRB (+drawing of wound in JFK's skull as depicted in photograph of the back of Kennedy's head) [see also "*High Treason III*" (1998), pp. 416-418, 421-425, 501-536]---Spencer was a lab technician at the Naval Photographic Center on the night of November 22, 1963. Someone ["Fox", apparently James K. Fox] brought in 4 x5 holders of film for her to develop and warned her not to examine them. She examined the original autopsy photos at the National Archives and found that they were printed on a different type of Kodak paper than the prints she made for "Fox". And the appearance of the President's body was markedly different from the autopsy photos.; "...the prints that we printed did not have the massive head damages that is visible here...The face in the photographs we did, did not have the stress that these photos---on the face that these photos show...The face, the eyes were closed and the face, the mouth was closed, and it was more of a rest position than these show."; "They had one [photo]showing the back of the head with the wound at the back of the head...It appeared to be a hole, inch, two inches in diameter at the back of the skull here....it was just a ragged hole."; "[the throat wound] ...it appeared just indented. It was...clean, pristine...it wasn't an immediate wound, it had some cleaning done to it or something." She described the throat wound depicted in the current autopsy photos as "a large, gaping gash type."; Q: "So, just to make sure that I am understanding correctly, previously, in your deposition, you described a wound, a small, circular wound in the back of the head, approximately two inches or so as I recall that you stated whereas, these show a much larger injury, is that correct?" Spencer: "That is correct."; "I would definitely say they [the current autopsy photos and the ones she took] were taken at different times...between those photographs and the ones that we did, there had to be some massive cosmetic things done to the President's body...I would say [the photos she took were made] probably afterwards [of the current photos available]." Q: "So you would think that the photographs that you developed were taken after reconstruction of the body?" "Yes."; "The only organ that I had seen was a brain that was laid beside the body...by the side of the body, but, it didn't appear that the skull had been cut, peeled back and the brain removed. None of that was shown. As to whose brain it was, I cannot say... it was on the mat on the table." Q: "In the photograph that you saw in November of 1963, with the brain lying next to the body [corroborating Stringer], were you able to observe whether there had been any damage to the brain?" Spencer: "No, it was not damaged as this brain, as the brain on these photographs were...the ones that we just viewed [the ones currently available]."; "Like I said, the only thing I can think of is that a second set of autopsy pictures was shot for public release if necessary."; (the following names were mentioned during Spencer's deposition: **Ashton Thomas Larr, Joseph M. Somers, Chief Strickland, and Leo Marshall**, the Chief in Charge of the NPC color lab);

af. [Spencer: unanswered letter from Vince Palamara 1998];

ag. **_Spencer:_** 1998 audio-taped interview with Bill Law for JFK Lancer's Oral History Project (see the Summer 1998 issue of *Kennedy Assassination Chronicles* journal)---parallels her ARRB deposition: "The two [wounds] that I remember were the back of his head and the one at his throat. The throat wound was small, slightly off to the right. It was just about thumbnail size...It was just a rounded wound."; Regarding the head wound: "It was about two and a quarter [inches] around. If you were wearing a ball cap, the back of the cap would be slightly off to the right…There was none of the massive head trauma that is shown in those photos [the official Archives version]…it would have to be an exit wound…his face looked normal and relaxed." The top and front of JFK's head was intact.; "There was one [photo] of the brain next to him…it's almost like they reconstructed his head for the photos so that if they had to show the public something that's what they would show." The brain she saw was not damaged: "…I doubt that it was his…"; Regarding the back wound: "…there was only one wound and that was in his shoulder."; regarding the photos SHE saw, in general: "They weren't like autopsy pictures. They did not have the incisions, you know, or the cutting of the head."; "*JFK Absolute Proof*" by Robert Groden (2013), page 156: Spencer is pictured with a nice summary of her statements.

ah. **Gloria Knudsen:** 5/7/96 conversation with the ARRB [see also "*High Treason III*" (1998), pp. 493-494]---"About 3:00 that afternoon [11/22/63], her husband got a telephone call, from the Secret Service she believes, and was ordered to go to Andrews AFB, meet the airplane, and accompany the body to Bethesda.";

ai. **Gloria Knudsen and children Bob and Terri:** 5/10/96 conversation with the ARRB's Douglas Horne [see also "*High Treason III*" (1998), pp. 494-497]---"All three family members recounted that Mr. Knudsen had told them he photographed the autopsy of President Kennedy, and was the only one to do so… He [Knudsen] witnessed and photographed probes inserted in the President's body which left no doubt of the number and direction of bullet trajectories; son Bob thought that his father had described 3 probes in the body (2 in the thorax/neck, and one in the head)…after he appeared before the HSCA in 1978, he told his family (at different times) that 4 or 5 of the pictures he was shown by the HSCA did not represent what he saw or took that night, and that one of the photographs he viewed had been altered. His son Bob said that his father told him that "hair had been drawn in" on one photo to conceal a missing portion of the top-back of President Kennedy's head…Mrs. Gloria Knudsen said that her husband Robert had told her that the whole top of the President's head was gone, and that the President's brain(s) were largely missing (blown out)."; His family said he "appeared before an official government body...sometime in 1988, about 6 months before he died...on Capital Hill...may have been a Congressional inquiry of some kind…Mr. Knudsen came away from this experience very disturbed, saying that 4 photographs were "missing" and that one was "badly altered"…the wounds he saw in the photos shown him in 1988 did not represent what he saw or took. He also told them that some of the details in the room in the background of the photos were "wrong." He had recounted that this experience was a waste of time for him because as soon as he would answer a question consistent with what he remembered, he would immediately be challenged and contradicted by people whom he felt already had their minds made up…Mr. Knudsen expressed skepticism with his daughter Terri over the years about the conclusions of the Warren Report in regard to the President's wounds and the manner in which he was shot, because of the observations he had made the night of the autopsy.";

aj. **Gloria Knudsen**: 10/8/96 conversation with the ARRB's Douglas Horne [see also "*High Treason III*" (1998), pp. 498-500]---"...she said she spoke last week with some former Navy people who in one case (along with her husband, Robert Knudsen) saw, and in another case helped Robert Knudsen print, photos of President Kennedy's autopsy...these people were of the belief that he may well have been present at the autopsy...She elaborated that one of the former Navy people she called said that he did recall one particular photo which showed the back of the President's head "blown out"...she said the person to whom she spoke last week definitely said the "back" of the head was blown out in the photograph he sighted. She told me that her husband told her on one occasion that he knew who had had custody of the autopsy photographs, and that he therefore could deduce who had been responsible for some of them disappearing, but that he was not going to stick his neck out, because he had a family to protect. She also reiterated her husband's firm belief that the photographs of the back of the head which show it to be intact were forgeries...Gloria Knudsen told me that their house was burglarized shortly after the HSCA deposed her husband, and that she had always wondered if there were any connection between the two events."; (Dr. Randy Robertson had also made contact with Mrs. Knudsen, which was the reason for this particular contact.);

ak. **Joe O'Donnell**: 1/29/97 interview with the ARRB's Jeremy Gunn and Douglas Horne [see also "*High Treason III*" (1998), pp. 418-420]--"frequently detailed to the White House"; Within the week after JFK's murder, O'Donnell said _Knudsen_ showed him an autopsy photograph revealing "a hole in the forehead above the right eye which was a round wound about 3/8" in diameter which he interpreted as a gunshot wound," and "a hole in the back of the head, about 2" above the hairline, about the size of a grapefruit; the hole clearly penetrated the skull and was very deep." A few days later, Knudsen showed him another photo which showed the back of the head *intact*: "he remembers seeing neatly combed hair which looked slightly wet, or damp in appearance." He also saw photos of JFK with probes in him.;

al. **Joe O'Donnell**: 2/28/97 interview with the AARB's Gunn, Horne, David Marwell, and Dave Montague [see also "*High Treason III*" (1998), p. 420]---"O'Donnell said he remembers a photograph of a gaping wound in the back of the head which was big enough to put a fist through, in which the image clearly showed a total absence of hair and bone, and a cavity which was the result of a lot of interior matter missing from inside the cranium. He said that another image showed a small round hole above the President's right eye, which he interpreted as an entry wound made by the same bullet which exited from the large wound in the back of the head.";

am. **Carol Ann Bonito**: junior to Saundra Kay Spencer in rank, Bonito helped her develop the autopsy photos [see Spencer's 12/13/96 ARRB interview; see also "*High Treason III*" (1998), pp. 417-418];

an. Bonito: unanswered letter from Vince Palamara 1998

ao. "*Murder In Dealey Plaza*" by James Fetzer (2000), pages 9, 188-189, 200, 201, 209, 225, 228, 241, 242, 243, 245, 246, 250, 252, 269, 273, 274, 275, 276, 277, 278, 279, 284, 291, 296, 301, 354

ap. Joe O'Donnell: "The Men Who Killed Kennedy" (2003) DVD

aq. Sandra Spencer: "In The Eye Of History" by William Law (2004)

ar. Joe O'Donnell: "*JFK Absolute Proof*" by Robert Groden (2013), page 156: O'Donnell is pictured with a nice summary of his statements.

252) Captain Michael D. Groves, MDW Honor Guard (deceased 12/3/63):

a. "*Killing the Truth*" by H.E.L., p. 742---"Rebentisch remembers the color guard captain, and said he died a week later from the strain." [*He is correct: see "The Death of a President", p. 638*];

b. "*JFK: The Dead Witnesses*" by Craig Roberts and John Armstrong (1995), p. 3---"Captain Groves, who commanded the JFK Honor Guard for Kennedy's funeral, died under mysterious circumstances seven days after the funeral. While eating dinner, he took a bite of food, paused briefly as a pained look came over his face, then passed out and fell face down into his plate. He died instantly. On December 12th, his possessions and mementos---which had been sent home to Birmingham, Michigan---were destroyed in a fire of mysterious origin. The Honor Guard, for some mysterious reason, had been practicing for a presidential funeral for three days before the assassination. Captain Groves was 27 years old at the time of this death. Cause of death: Unknown. Possibly poison.";

c. From internet SSN Death listing:
Name: MICHAEL GROVES
Born: 19 Aug 1936
Died: Dec 1963
Residence: (No Location Given)
Last Benefit: (No Location Given)
SSN: 375-36-8313
Issued: (Between 1953 and 1954)

253) USMC Sgt. R.E. Boyajian, in charge of the guards in the halls in Bethesda 11/22-11/23/63:

a. R.E. Boyajian, USMC report to his C.O. of 26 November 1963---At 0345, the casket was removed from the morgue. At 0350 Mrs. Kennedy departed with the casket for the White House;

254)-255) Janie B. Taylor, biologist at the National Institute of Health (NIH), across the street from Bethesda Naval Hospital, and [fnu] Israel, one of 2 African-American orderlies allegedly present during the autopsy:

a. 11/24/95 ARRB interview of Taylor [see also "*High Treason III*" (1998), pp. 439, 492-493]--- "A man named Clarence ***Israel*** (deceased) of Rockville, MD told Taylor that *his brother (deceased and no name given)* was one of two African-American orderlies present in the autopsy room of the Medical Center the day of the autopsy. Israel said his brother had not mentioned the story to anyone including his wife & daughter who his brother outlived. His brother wanted to insure that his story was known because he was verbally threatened by a guard at the time of the autopsy. Taylor said that African-Americans during that time period were often ignored and that non-African-American workers in many workplaces would assume that an African-American's presence did not count. She believed that activities were often done in their presence with the perception that the activities would never be reported. Israel told her the orderlies saw one doctor was in the autopsy room at the Medical Center who was waiting for some time prior to the arrival of the body and any other physicians. When the body arrived, many people were forced out of the room and the doctor performed some type of mutilation of three bullet punctures to the head area. The doctor was working at a very "hurried" pace and was done within a few minutes, at which point he left the autopsy room. " [see Dr. Michael Miller, below];

256) Captain/ Dr. Loy Thietje Brown, head of Radiology Dept.

a. 8/29/91 interview with Harry Livingstone (*"High Treason 2"*, page 214): "...he said that he had heard about the assassination in Chicago almost immediately. At once, he called his department at Bethesda and told them to get ready, and then started driving east as fast as he could. Brown denied having been present at any taping of bullet fragments to bone fragments the day after the autopsy [as alleged by Jerrol Custer: see pages 213 and 216; see also page 188]";

b. *"Killing Kennedy"* by H.E.L., pages 112 and 201---"the regular chief [of radiology], Dr. Loy Thietje Brown, was in Chicago for the RSNA meetings ... Dr. John Ebersole took his place."

257) Dr. Joseph Theodore Brierre, Navy pathologist at Bethesda:

a. 8/7/91 interview with Harry Livingstone (*"High Treason 2"*, pp. 53-54, 58; *"Killing The Truth"*, p. 730)---"diagnosed Pott's disease in the President"; "He would not have lived through a second term"; Dr. Burkley was "no doctor at all."; "The histological work was done at Bethesda, not downtown, according to Dr. Joseph Brierre."

258) Dr. Robert B. Livingston, chief of the U.S. Neurobiological Laboratory; Scientific Director of both the National Institute for Mental Health and the National Institute for Neurological Diseases and Blindness in both the Eisenhower and Kennedy administrations (deceased 4/26/2002):

a. 5/2/92 letter/ fax to Harry Livingstone (*"Killing The Truth"*, pp. 114-115; *"Killing Kennedy"*, p. 7, 193, 207, 208, 216, 276, 316, 354; *"Bloody Treason"* by Noel Twyman, pp. 201-202; for the actual letter, in the form of a letter to Lifton, see *"Assassination Science"*, pp. 168-171)---Livingston told Dr. Humes *before* the autopsy started that the Dallas doctors saw an entry bullet wound in the throat; "Also relevant, I learned from a former classmate of mine from Stanford who was then a reporter for the St. Louis Post-Dispatch, Richard Dudman, that he was one of the White House press group that accompanied the President to Dallas. Not getting much information from the Parkland Hospital, Dick went out to inspect the Lincoln limousine in which the President and Connally and their wives had been riding. He thought he saw, for certain, that there was a through-and-through hole in the upper left margin of the windshield. He described the spraying-splintering of glass at the margins as though the missile had entered from in front of the vehicle. When he reached over to pass his pencil or pen through the hole to test its patency, an FBI or Secret Service man roughly drew him away and shooed him off, instructing him that he wasn't allowed to come so close to that vehicle.."; "Incidentally, sometime later, I learned that the Secret Service had ordered from the Ford Motor Company a number of identical Lincoln limousine windshields---"for target practice.";

b. 11/18/93 New York news conference (see *"Killing Kennedy"*, p. 396, for a reprint of the Richard Pyle [of AP] wire story, as well as *"Assassination Science"*, pp. 161-166 [full-length version], and *"Bloody Treason"*, pp. 201-202)---extended version of his 5/92 letter to Lifton/ fax to Livingstone cited above;

c. 11/22/93 presentation at the ASK conference in Dallas, TX (see *"Bloody Treason"*, pp. 193, 201-202)---see reference "a)" above;

d. 1/20/94 interview with Harry Livingstone (*"Killing Kennedy"*, pp. 266-267)---"The Supplemental Autopsy Report stated that the brain weighed 1,500 grams, much too heavy and more than an average adult male brain, let alone one that had lost much of its mass. The fixative formalin solution could not add any significant amount to the brain weight.";

e. 7/7/94 letter to Noel Twyman (*"Bloody Treason"*, p. 89)---"The autopsy pathologists also did not dissect the throat wound to see where it went, despite being informed by telephone before the autopsy (as a suggestion) to do so by the chief of the U.S. Neurological Laboratory at the time, Dr. Robert Livingston.";

f. Two filmed segments in Prof. James Fetzer's 1994 video *"JFK: The Assassination, The Cover-up, and Beyond"*---Livingston reads his prepared remarks originating from his 5/92 letter/ fax: see pages 170-171 of *"Assassination Science"*;

g. Interviews with Noel Twyman (*"Bloody Treason"*, pages xi and 190; see also pages 89, 193, 201, and 202): "provided many hours of consultation and advice";

h. *"Assassination Science"* by Prof. James Fetzer (1997/1998), numerous, esp. pages 161-175 and 366[for photos of Livingston himself, see pages 166 and 194]---Livingston was one of the contributors to this book; "Robert Livingston has concluded that diagrams of the brain in the National Archives must be of some brain other than that of John F. Kennedy.";

i. *"Murder in Dealey Plaza"* by James Fetzer (2000), pages v, 8, 113, 138, 212, 259, 261, 285, 297, 300, 306, 310, 421

j. j) *"The Men Who Killed Kennedy"* (2003) DVD

259) "Dr. Michael Miller" [or Morgan]:

a. "*High Treason 2*", pages 271, 311 and 549---Paul O'Connor (5/26/91 interview with H.E.L.): "I was told by this so-called Dr. Michael Miller that 'the body was altered at Walter Reed or at Bethesda and he thinks it was Bethesda, and put back in the coffin and taken around the corner and down back of the hospital to the morgue.'"; "A "Dr. Morgan" or "Miller" in the Baltimore, D.C. area called Paul O'Connor late one night and said that someone---we'll call him X---took a ball-peen hammer to the head either at Walter Reed or Bethesda. O'Connor thinks he said it was Bethesda---"to disrupt the wound and the physical characteristics of the wound." Paul thought that X had something to do with it. X transferred out after the autopsy.";

260) Dr. Bruce Smith, deputy director of the AFIP:

a. *JAMA*, May 27, 1992-Vol 267, No. 20: "*JFK's Death---the plain truth from the MDs who did the autopsy*" by Dennis L. Breo (interview with James J. Humes and "J" Thornton Boswell): Humes: "My orders were to find the cause of death and I was told to get anyone I thought necessary to help do the autopsy, but to limit it to only the help I needed. Hell, I could have called in people from Paris and Rome if I thought it necessary, but as it turned out, I didn't. About this time, I also received a phone call from Dr. Bruce Smith, the deputy director of the Armed Forces Institute of Pathology [AFIP], offering me whatever help I might need. Bruce was a friend and I thanked him, saying I would call later if I needed help."; Boswell: "Early in the afternoon, we received a call from Dr. Bruce Smith from AFIP, saying, 'The President's body is on its way to Bethesda for an autopsy.' I argued, 'That's stupid. The autopsy should be done at AFIP [which was located five miles away at the Walter Reed Army Medical Center].' After all, the AFIP was the apex of military pathology and, perhaps, world pathology. I was told, 'That's the way it is. Admiral [George] Burkley [the President's personal physician] wants Bethesda.' Apparently, Admiral Burkley had called the AFIP from Air Force One en route from Dallas. Later, I was told that Jackie Kennedy selected Bethesda because her husband had been a Navy man."; Humes: "Dr. Bruce Smith [the deputy director of the Armed Forces Institute of Pathology] had initially thought that we might want a neuropathologist as a consultant, but once we opened the casket and saw the devastating nature of the President's head wound, we knew that there was no need for the skills of a neuropathologist. I called Dr. Smith back and told him what we had found, and he decided to make available Dr. Pierre A. Finck, who was one of the AFIP's experts in ballistics.";

261) Harold Alfred "H.A." "Skip" Rydberg, hospital corpsman/ medical illustrator:

a. WC reference: 2 H 349-350 (Humes);

b. 16 H 977 and 984: CE 385, 386, and 388---Rydberg's inaccurate drawings;

c. Rydberg's drawings: numerous appearances in the critical literature, inc. "*Cover-Up*" by Stewart Galanor, pp. 129-131 [all 3, in color], "*Assassination Science*", page 438 [all 3], "*Best Evidence*", "*Reasonable Doubt*", "*High Treason*", and "*TKOAP*";

d. "*Murder in Dealey Plaza*" by James Fetzer (2000), pages 182, 229, 231, 248

e. Presentation at JFK Lancer conference, 2003

f. "*In The Eye of History*" by William Law (2004)

g. "*JFK Absolute Proof*" by Robert Groden (2013), page 156: Rydberg is pictured with a nice summary of his statements.

262) Major General Joseph M. Blumberg, Commanding Officer of the AFIP (deceased 5/19/1984):

a. WC reference: 2 H 349 (Humes);

b. 2/1/65 memorandum, Lt. Col. Pierre A. Finck to Blumberg [*see Finck above*];

c. 7 HSCA 16, 20, 101, 122, 135, and 191---see reference "b)" above;

d. "*Best Evidence*" by David Lifton, pp. 529-530n;

e. "*Between The Signal and the Noise*" by Roger Bruce Feinman (1993), pp. 34-37;

f. "*Case Closed*" by Gerald Posner (1993), p. 300;

g. "*Killing Kennedy*" by H.E.L. (1995), pages 150, 189, 250, and 255;

h. "*Assassination Science*" by Prof. James Fetzer (1997/1998), pages 94, 99, and 300;

i. "*Murder in Dealey Plaza*" by James Fetzer (2000), pages 247, 303, 306

263) M. Wayne Balleter, chief medical photographer, Methodist Hospital:

a. 7 HSCA 122---took photographs of the Harper fragment on 11/25/63;

264) Bobby M. Nolan, Texas Highway patrolman:

a. WC reference re: "bullet fragments taken from body of Governor Connally": 24 H 260 / CE2003 [see also "*Cover-Up*" by Gary Shaw and Larry Ray Harris (1976), p. 160, and "*Bloody Treason*" by Noel Twyman, p. 113]: evidence sheet with alteration---2 6.5 spent rounds changed to 3;

b. "*Cover-Up*" by Shaw and Harris (1976), p. 159 [see also "*Bloody Treason*", p. 112]: original evidence sheet [see above];

c. 7 HSCA 156---" Bobby M. Nolan, Texas Highway patrolman, Tyler district, was interviewed relative to a bullet fragment removed from the left thigh of Governor

Connally, which was turned over to him at Parkland Hospital in Dallas for delivery to the FBI. Nolan stated his instructions were apparently not clear at the outset and that following contact with his superior officers while at the Dallas Police Department, he turned the bullet fragment over to Captain Will Fritz [Dallas Police Department.] at approximately 7:50 p.m. He stated he had no further information concerning the matter and that his only participation in this series of events was the acceptance of the fragment and delivery of same to Captain Fritz.";

265) Tom Joyce, aide and friend of the Kennedy brothers:

a. *"Killing the Truth"*, p. 652---"Tom Joyce, aide and friend to the Kennedy brothers who was familiar with the wounds, ha[s] indicated that the photograph of the head published by the House Select Committee is false."

266) Betty J. Harrison, Secretary to Dr. Earl Rose:

a. *"With Malice: Lee Harvey Oswald and the Murder of Officer J.D. Tippit"* by Dale K. Myers (1998), pages 239-240 [inc. information gleaned from a 2/28/83 interview Myers had with Harrison];

267) Dr. Paul C. Moellenhoff, surgery resident at Methodist Hospital (removed a bullet from DPD Officer J.D. Tippit's stomach for i.d. purposes):

a. WC reference : 24 H 260 / CE2003 [see also *"Cover-Up"* by Gary Shaw and Larry Ray Harris (1976), p. 160, and *"Bloody Treason"* by Noel Twyman, p. 113]: evidence sheet with alteration---2 6.5 spent rounds changed to 3;

b. *"Cover-Up"* by Shaw and Harris (1976), p. 159 [see also *"Bloody Treason"*, p. 112]: original evidence sheet [see above];

c. *"The Day Kennedy Was Shot"* by Jim Bishop, pages 319-320, 478;

d. *"With Malice: Lee Harvey Oswald and the Murder of Officer J.D. Tippit"* by Dale K. Myers (1998), pp. 115-116, 198, 239, 372-373, 391, 464, 486, 611, 630, 638, and 639 [inc. information gleaned from Myers' 3/4/83 interview of Moellenhoff];

268) Dr. Richard A. Liguori, Methodist Hospital (pronounced DPD Officer J.D. Tippit dead)[Liquori]:

a. 11/29/63 interview with the FBI (CD 5/81 [see also *"With Malice: Lee Harvey Oswald and the Murder of Officer J.D. Tippit"* by Dale K. Myers (1998), page 485]);

b. *"With Malice: Lee Harvey Oswald and the Murder of Officer J.D. Tippit"* by Dale K. Myers (1998), pp. 116, 372-373, 447, 464, and 486; Note: the two Dudley Hughes Funeral Home ambulance attendants were **Jasper "J.C. / Clayton" Butler and William "Eddie" Kinsley**---see Myers' book, pp. 101, 102, 103-105, 107, 109, 115, 124, 198, 235, 300, 368, 372, 608, 611, 639, and 652;

269) Nurse Lottie Thompson,

a. *"With Malice: Lee Harvey Oswald and the Murder of Officer J.D. Tippit"* by Dale K. Myers (1998), pages 198, 375, and 630 [inc. information gleaned from a 1981 interview David B. Perry had with Thompson];

270) Leland W. Benson, civilian Supervising Histo-Pathology Technician at Bethesda:

a. 8/16/77 interview with the HSCA (RIF#180-10093-10414)---" Benson was Supervising Histo-Pathology Technician at the time and supervised the processing of tissue from JFK's autopsy. He was not on duty after 4PM on the 22nd of November and did not return to duty at the Lab until Monday morning, November 25, 1963.The normal procedure at that time was for the Pathologist performing the autopsy to forward sections of tissue from either autopsies or surgery to the Lab. In Autopsy [sic], a routing slip was filled out with the numerical notation of how many sections of tissue were being forwarded to the lab and sent along with the sections up to Benson's Histo-Pathology Lab. In Kennedy's case, Benson recalls that a routing slip was sent on Monday morning and the sections were processed into wax blocks which were then shaved into micro sections and stained by hand. The finished slides were then given to a pathologists to read. All slides and gross tissue were returned to Dr. James Humes, the Pathologists [sic] who handled the Kennedy autopsy on November 22, 1963. Nothing was kept in the Lab and no record made of intake or processing. Humes would make whatever notes were necessary. Benson said Bethesda did an average of 300 autopsies a year. The brain tissue was processed to the best of his recollection. Brains removed at autopsies are usually fixed in formalin and then kept in a chrome "bucket" of formalin. He said that he did not see Kennedy's brain at any time and does not know where it is today. He said that is possible that the brain and tissues were sent to the Armed Forces Institute of Pathology at Walter Reed Hospital on 16th Street. Sometimes teaching slides are made and the brain is used as a teaching specimen. Benson said he was questioned in 1964 by representatives from the Warren Commission about his knowledge of the autopsy and NNMC procedures. He could not recall who questioned him.[?]";

b. Mentioned by Chester Boyers and Dr. Robert Karnei as being involved/ with the brain examination (*HSCA Affidavit of Boyers and 8/29/77 HSCA interview with Karnei*);

c. *"Murder In Dealey Plaza"* by James Fetzer (2000), pages 301, 303

271)-272) Chief [fnu] Ewald, bacteriology, and Chief [fnu] Norman:

a. Mentioned by James Curtis Jenkins in his *8/24/77 HSCA interview*---"Mr. Jenkins said he participated in two or three autopsies each time he was on duty, and he usually finished about 3-4 A.M. Jenkins said the individuals who outlined the standard operating procedure to him were "probably" Chief Ewald, (bacteriology) and/ or Chief Norman (who dealt with the "academic part").";

273) B.O. Turner, lab technician, HM1:

a. Mentioned by Chester Boyers as being a person he recalls who was "involved with the case who [was] not present in the autopsy room" (*see Boyers' HSCA affidavit*);

274) Mrs. [fnu] Gorman, Dr. Humes' secretary:

a. Mentioned by Chester Boyers as being a person he recalls who was "involved with the case who [was] not present in the autopsy room" (*see Boyers' HSCA affidavit*);

275) Dr. [fnu] Fobes, laboratory Dept.:

a. Mentioned by Chester Boyers as being a person he recalls who was "involved with the case who [was] not present in the autopsy room" (*see Boyers' HSCA affidavit*);

276) Stanley Miller, James C. Jenkins' partner:

a. Mentioned by James Curtis Jenkins during his *8/24/77 HSCA interview*---"Mr. Jenkins said that two people "pulled duty" together. He said they usually wore scrub clothes. He said his usual partner was Stanley Miller who was not present that evening for some unknown reason. He said that on that night [11/22/63] he was working with Paul O'Connor (O'Connor later married Jenkins's wife's cousin).";

277) Earl McDonald, medical photographer:

a. 5/14/96 ARRB interview [see also "*High Treason III*" (1998), pp. 437-438]---re: "general observations of discrepancies between the official collection of autopsy photos at NARA and what he would expect to see if he had shot the autopsy photos himself." McDonald said that there are no autopsy tags, no whole body photos, no photograph of the brain (at autopsy) immediately following removal from the cranium, no photograph of the inside of the skull (following the removal of the brain), no photograph of the reassembled skull, no photograph of the chest cavity, no close-up of the back wound, and no wide-angle view and/ or medium-field view of the cranium.; "...he said he would grade them [the official photos] 'quite low' because, among other reasons, the collection was not comprehensive."; "...he never saw the stirrup used (for the head of the deceased) as it is in the autopsy photographs of President Kennedy [FBI agent Sibert told the ARRB the same thing], but instead saw a wooden chock or block, and said that there was no wooden furniture where it appears in the photos, and no telephone where it appears in the photos."; "…the photographer who shot the autopsy would always develop his own film (both B&W and color) in the lab at Bethesda, that this was virtually mandatory. He could not recall one instance of autopsy or medical film being taken to the Navy Lab at Anacostia for developing; he thought that would be very strange, since he said that facility was surrounded by barbed wire, had the reputation of doing 'secret' photo-intelligence work of some kind, and everyone knew no one was supposed to talk about the kind of work that went on at Anacostia.";

b.   *"Murder In Dealey Plaza"* by James Fetzer (2000), page 246

278) Ken Vrtacnik, AFIP:

a.   11/13/96 ARRB interview [see also *"High Treason III"* (1998), pp. 438-439]---Vrtacnik "volunteered that he had seen President Kennedy's brain during the 1964-65 period, which he stated had been kept in a locked room at the AFIP (Armed Forces Institute of Pathology) National Museum of Health and Medicine… the item on display was one long section, tan in color, immersed in liquid, laying in a stainless steel tray inside a glass case. He repeatedly stated that it had wooden pegs (or arrows) through it which were routinely used in gunshot wound cases to show the trajectory of bullets… it was labeled "President Kennedy's Brain" or words to that effect… and it made a big impression on him at the time because of his interest in the assassination, and because of the tight control placed on viewing of the specimen.";

279) Dr. Richard L. Davis, a neuropathologist:

a.   February 1996 ARRB interview of J. Thornton Boswell---Boswell said he thought Davis was present at the supplemental examination of the brain.;

b.   2/27/97 ARRB interview [see also *"High Treason III"* (1998), pp. 440-441]: "I never saw President Kennedy's brain." However, Dr. Davis knew that the brain would normally be weighed twice: first, immediately after removal, which was not done on 11/22/63; and, second, at the supplemental examination (after fixation), before any procedures were performed.;

c.   *"Murder in Dealey Plaza"* by James Fetzer (2000), pages 305, 307, 441

280) Velma Reumann (Vogler):

a.   10/4/96 ARRB interview [see also *"High Treason III"* (1998), pp. 441-442]---"has a strong, independent recollection of Navy Photographic Center personnel boxing up all photographic materials (everything we---the film department---had) related to the assassination on the orders of Robert Kennedy and sending them to the Smithsonian Museum for permanent storage sometime within 6 months or so after the assassination… She said she was certain of this because she, herself, was required to call an official at the Smithsonian to discuss the imminent transfer, and recalls the individual to whom she spoke was a surprised by the selection of the Smithsonian as she was.";

b. *"Murder in Dealey Plaza"* by James Fetzer (2000), page 276

V

VARIOUS MOTORCADE OCCUPANTS

281) Lt. Col. George L. Whitmeyer, East Texas Section Commander of the Army Reserve, rode in pilot car in motorcade (deceased 1978):

a. WC references: 4 H 170 (Curry: listed as "Wiedemeyer"!); 21 H 578-579; 24 H 324 (Senkel's report); 24 H 326 (Turner's report);

b. 1970 interview with Larry Haapanen [*3/9/94 letter from Haapanen to author*]---"Lt. Col. Whitmeyer was simply "along for the ride" with DPD Deputy Chief Lumpkin, who was an Army reserve officer and invited Whitmeyer, his Army advisor, to accompany him. Whitmeyer didn't have very much to say about the events in Dealey Plaza---mostly, he explained what he was doing there.";

c. 1/31/78 HSCA interview of Secret Service agent Winston Lawson (RIF#180-10074-10396)---"Mr. Lawson acknowledged that Lt. Col. George Whitmeyer, who was part of the Dallas District U.S. Army Command, who Lawson said "taught Army Intelligence" and who rode in the pilot car, "wasn't scheduled" to be in the motorcade. [as 17 H 615, Lawson's scheduled motorcade list, bears out]. Mr. Lawson denied that the presence of Col. Whitmeyer had anything to do with Lawson's prior service in the CIC.";

d. "*Deep Politics and the Death of JFK*" by Peter Dale Scott (1993), pp. 273-274;

e. 9/28/98 letter from George Whitmeyer JR. to Vince Palamara----"My father passed away in 1978 and therefore the answers to your questions are somewhat based on personal recollection of his information given to me. In regards to your first question, my father was invited by Col. George Lumpkin (ret.) (deceased) to ride in the point [sic] car of the motorcade. He was not a scheduled participant. I think that Col. Lumpkin was with the Dallas Police Department at the time. In regards to your second question, the point car i/n which my father was riding had already passed under the underpass and was turning onto Stemmons freeway when the assassination took place. They only saw the Presidential limousine speeding by on its way to Parkland Hospital. At that time, the car my father was in returned to downtown Dallas and to the area of the Texas School

Book Depository. Therefore, he did not see or hear the actual assassination nor did he go to parkland Hospital."

f.   *"Murder in Dealey Plaza"* by James Fetzer (2000), pages 22, 30

282) Jacob L. "Jack" Puterbaugh, Democratic National Committee advance man, rode in pilot car in motorcade (deceased):

a.   WC references: (Lawson) 4 H 320, 322, 336-337, 341; (Sorrels) 7 H 335; 17 H 611, 615, 618, 619, 620, 621, 623, 625, 626, 630; 18 H 730, 761, 776; 21 H 546;

b.   9/5/70 interview with Larry Haapanen [transcript provided to the author from Haapanen]---"He said that he had no part in the actual selection for the luncheon [contrast this with 18 H 715, Rowley]...he had been told by Lawson that there would be a total of four people in the car, but that it turned out that there were five [the addition of Whitmeyer, above]...Puterbaugh said that the pilot car stopped about 50 feet from the presidential limousine at Parkland, and that he got out and tried to keep back unauthorized people...he had heard someone say at Parkland that it looked very bad for the President, and had assumed that Kennedy had been killed...Puterbaugh said he has some doubts about the validity of the Warren Commission's findings, since "the ballistics stuff doesn't add up.""";

c.   *"The Advance Man"* by Jerry Bruno and Jeff Greenfield (1971), pp. 93-94;

d.   4/14/78 interview with the HSCA (RIF#180-10080-10069)---"Puterbaugh met Forrest Sorrels, the SAIC of the Secret Service in Dallas, and drove the alternative motorcade routes with him."; "...he heard shots...They [the pilot car] pulled over and let the motorcade pass."

e.   *1/3/98 letter to Vince Palamara [see also the Spring 1998 issue of the Kennedy Assassination Chronicles journal]*

f.   *"Murder in Dealey Plaza"* by James Fetzer (2000), pages 30, 128

283) DPD Sergeant Samuel Q. Bellah, one of the three advance motorcycle officers in motorcade (deceased 9/11/2011):

a.   WC references: 7 H 581, 588; 19 H 134; 20 H 489;

b.   *"Fairfield (TX) Recorder"*, 11/17/88: based off interview with Bellah (photo included) [provided to the author by Bellah]: "On the night before his assignment, Bellah reviewed the planned route with his captain. The route was not the original that was to go straight through Dealey Plaza, but a revised route. The original plan would have skirted the Texas Book Depository building by a block, but the altered plan turned to pass directly in front of the building...Bellah, who was riding in front of the presidential limousine, received a radio message that Kennedy had been shot and was ordered immediately to the book building. "We had to find out who did the shooting," he recalls."; "The fact that Ruby was in the basement of the city jail still puzzles Bellah because security was so tight there that the motorcycle sergeant was even required to show identification before being admitted to the building a few hours earlier. Bellah reports that Ruby was well known by Dallas police officers and that he was a supporter of the department. That still did not give permission for him to be in the jail basement as Oswald was being moved. "That's always been a mystery. I still don't know how he got in," the former policeman says."

c. *"Presidential Motorcade Schematic Listing"* by Todd Wayne Vaughan (1993), p. 3;

d. *"Pictures of the Pain"* by Richard Trask (1994), pages 154, 233, 234, 519, and 616 [see also Trask's *"That Day in Dallas"* (1998), page 60]

e. 9/98 letter to Vince Palamara---did not observe JFK's wounds

284) DPD Stavis "Steve" Ellis, one of the five lead motorcycle officers in the motorcade [Starvis] (deceased 8/10/2005):

a. WC references: 7 H 581; 12 H 135; 19 H 134; 20 H 489;

b. [*See Kinney above*];

c. 4/21/71 interview with Gil Toff (for *"Murder from Within"* [see also *"Best Evidence"*, pages 370-371n]): saw a hole in the windshield

d. CFTR radio CANADA interview 1976;

e. 8/5/78 interview with the HSCA (12 HSCA 23; see also *"Crossfire"* by Jim Marrs, p. 14, *"High Treason"*, p. 22, *"Who's Who in the JFK Assassination"* by Michael Benson, p. 125, and *"A Complete Book of Facts"* by Duffy and Ricci", p. 171)---reported seeing a bullet strike the pavement "alongside the first car in the motorcade, approximately 100 to 125 feet in front of the car carrying President Kennedy. Ellis said that just as he started down the hill of Elm Street, he looked back toward President Kennedy's car and saw debris come up from the ground at a nearby curb. Ellis thought it was a fragment grenade. Ellis said also that President Kennedy turned around and looked over his shoulder [?]. The second shot then hit him, and the third shot 'blew his head up.'"

f. Interview with Todd Wayne Vaughan (see Vaughan's book, page 4);

g. *"Pictures of the Pain"* by Richard Trask (1994), pages 61, 234, 475, 616

h. *"No More Silence"* by Larry Sneed (1998), pp. 142-153+photos;

i. 9/8/98 letter to Vince Palamara---"Yes, I did see a hole in the limousine windshield at Parkland Hospital. I did not see the bone fragment. The officer on the escort with me said there was one fragment, approximately 6 or 7 inches around."

j. *"Murder in Dealey Plaza"* by James Fetzer (2000), pages 36, 147, 148, 172, 139-140

285) Secret Service Agent Winston G. "Win" Lawson, one of the two advance agents for the Dallas trip, rode in lead car in motorcade:

a. a) WC references: WR 29-32, 39, 43, 53, 57, 202, 204, 431, 445-449, 452; 4 H 317-358 (testimony); 2 H 64, 66-68, 74, 76, 78, 80, 97, 105-106, 109-111, 142;

4 H 161, 171, 173-174, 314; 5 H 462; 7 H 335-339, 344-346; 12 H 28, 93; 17 H 593-626, 628-634; 18 H 722, 725, 730, 735, 739, 741, 742, 744, 751, 761, 762, 777, 778, 785, 786, 788, 789, 790, 791, 792, 793, 795, 797, 798, 810, 811, 814; 21 H 546-548; although Lawson helped remove JFK from the limousine onto a stretcher at Parkland, he was asked nothing (on the record) about the wounds, nor did he volunteer any such information in his reports!;

b. 1/31/78 HSCA interview of Secret Service agent Winston Lawson (RIF#180-10074-10396)---"As for the President's wounds, Mr. Lawson remembers only that they were head wounds and that they were concealed from his view by the presence of blood and then by a coat placed over JFK's head [by Clint Hill]."

c. "*Mortal Error*" by Bonar Meninger (1992), p. 233;

d. 9/27/92 interview with Vince Palamara

e. "*Inside The Secret Service*" video (1995, Discovery Channel);

f. "*Murder In Dealey Plaza*" by James Fetzer (2000), pages 26, 27, 31, 34-35, 122, 160-161, 168-169

g. "*The Secret Service*" by Philip Melanson (2002/2003)

h. C-SPAN, 2003

i. "*Dallas Morning News*", 11/22/03

j. 2004 correspondence with Vince Palamara

k. Lawson stated that he "saw a huge hole in the back of the president's head," as reported in *The Virginian-Pilot* on June 17, 2010.

286) Forrest V. Sorrels, SAIC of the Dallas Secret Service office, rode in lead car in motorcade (deceased 11/6/93):

a. 7 H 332-360 and 13 H 55-83: testimony;

b. 7 H 592: affidavit;

c. Other WC references: WR 29, 31-32, 39, 43, 52, 156, 204, 206, 210, 445-446, 448-449, 452; 1 H 174, 177, 184-187, 260; 2 H 15, 68, 109, 182, 187, 199-200; 3 H 145-147, 150, 158, 160; 4 H 161, 170, 173-174, 197-199, 222, 227-228, 323-324, 326, 330-331, 336, 340, 344-346, 355-358, 470; 5 H 47, 206, 218, 245-249, 257, 461, 613; 6 H 234, 324, 408; 7 H 155, 257, 266, 297, 301, 537, 575, 580, 586, 590; 10 H 281, 309; 11 H 386; 12 H 21, 28, 84, 105, 368, 413-414, 430-433, 441-442; 13 H 4, 25-26, 34, 50-51, 103, 229; 14 H 95, 109-110; 15 H 65, 129, 465; 16 H 922-923; 17 H 595, 601, 607, 609, 615, 619, 620, 621, 622, 623, 624, 625, 628, 630, 631, 633; 18 H 722, 730, 761, 788, 789, 810; 21 H 536-547; 21 H 548 (report dated 11/28/63): "I looked towards the top of the terrace to my right as the sound of the shots seemed to come from that direction.";

d. 2/27/64 FBI interview---"Mr. Forrest V. Sorrels...advised that he was at the Parkland Memorial Hospital when President Kennedy was brought to the hospital and said *that he remained there until his body was taken to Love Field* [?!]. Mr.

Sorrels stated that there were no photographs taken of President Kennedy at the Parkland Hospital. He stated there were no photographs taken of him as he was being taken into the Parkland Hospital on a stretcher." [Emphasis added];

e. 3/15/78 interview with the HSCA (RIF#180-10074-10392)---"He believed the President was dead before he arrived at the hospital. After arriving at Parkland Hospital, he decided that he could be of more help back at the scene of the shooting."

f. 8/20/78 interview with *Dallas Morning News* reporter Earl Golz (see 8/27/78 DMN article by Golz; notes courtesy AARC): wouldn't cooperate;

g. **1/28/92 and 9/27/92 interviews with Vince Palamara ---"The Warren Report stands";**

h. *Murder in Dealey Plaza*" by James Fetzer (2000), pages 19, 20, 24, 26, 32, 34, 42, 54, 85, 160

[June Kellerman, widow of the late Roy H. Kellerman, and daughter: see Kellerman, above]

[Richard Greer, son of the late William R. Greer: see Greer, above]

[Samuel A. Kinney: see Kinney, above]

[David F. Powers: see Powers, above]

[Bobbie Jacks, widow of Hurchel D. Jacks: see Jacks, above]

287) Secret Service Agent Rufus W. Youngblood, rode in LBJ's car in motorcade (deceased 10/2/96):

a. WC references: WR 3, 46, 48, 51-52, 57-58, 453; 2 H 143-155 (testimony); 5 H 561-563, 565; 7 H 450, 474-475, 478; 17 H 595, 607, 613, 615; 18 H 681-682 (his report re: the drinking incident), 722, 724, 728, 735, 736, 737, 738, 747, 766-772 (his report), 773, 774, 775, 776, 777, 778, 779, 780, 781, 783, 801, 810, 811, 812, 813, 814;

b. 12/17/68 LBJ Library Oral History (inc. on audio tape);

c. His book "*20 Years with The Secret Service*" (1973);

d. HSCA contact/ interview (they did have his address)-?;

e. *10/22/92 and 2/8/94 interviews with Vince Palamara;*

f. "*Presidential Motorcade Schematic Listing*" by Todd Wayne Vaughan (1993), p. 12---based off a 3/5/93 interview Vaughan had with Youngblood

g. "*The Secret Service*" video (1995, History Channel);

h. 10/2/98 letter and photo from Howard Donahue ("*Mortal Error*") re: Youngblood---Donahue sent me a blow-up of a color photo of himself talking to Rufus Youngblood at a conference in Memphis, Tennessee back in 1996, as they had served in the very same Air Force unit, the 91st Bomb Group, in WWII!; Donahue: "…I am puzzled about the number of spectators who claimed to have smelled gunpowder---" Youngblood: "So did I after the last shot." [*Smell of gunpowder---see also 6 H 165+"POTP", p. 441 (Tom Dillard), 6 H 233 (DPD Earle Brown), 7 H 487+Capitol Records' "The Controversy"/ interview with Larry Schiller and Richard Lewis (Mrs. Elizabeth "Dearie" Cabell and re: Congressman Ray Roberts), 7 H 512+CD5, pp. 66-67 (Mrs. Donald Baker), 20 H 351 (Kantor re: Ralph Yarborough) + "The Death of a President", p. 156, "Murder From Within", page 65/ interview with Newcomb&Adams, "The Truth About The Assassination" by Charles Roberts, page 17, "Crossfire", p. 16 (all 4 re: Yarborough) , DPD B.J. Martin (see below), DPD Joe M. Smith (CD205, p. 310+"Texas Observer", 12/13/63+"Murder From Within", pages 65 and 92+"Conspiracy", p. 29), and Beverly Oliver ("Nightmare In Dallas", p. 122); ALSO: re:* **smoke**---- *22 H 833 (James L. Simmons), "Rush To Judgment" film 1966 (Simmons, Richard Dodd, Sam Holland, and Lee Bowers), 22 H 834 (Nolan Potter), 22 H 836+"No More Silence" by Larry Sneed, pp.79-83 (Clemon Earl Johnson), 19 H 480, 514, 530 (Holland), 6 H 243 (Holland testimony), 19 H 485 (Austin Miller), Thomas Murphy: 5/6/66 interview ("Best Evidence", pages 16 and 723, and "Cover-Up" by Stewart Galanor, page 59), Walter Winborn: 3/17/65 and 5/5/66 interviews ("Best Evidence", pages 16 and 723, "Cover-Up" by Stewart Galanor, pages 59-60), and 6 H 230 (Frank Reilly), as well as Jean Hill ("Crossfire", p. 38), Beverly Oliver ("Nightmare In Dallas", p. 122), W.W. Mabra ("Crossfire", pp. 19-20, and "No More Silence", p.519), and Ed Hoffman ("JFK Breaking The Silence", p. 18). Also, see page 204 of Groden's "TKOAP" for a still photo from the Dave Weigman film which seems to show a puff of smoke lingering out from the trees on the knoll. In addition, the Nix film, the John Martin film, and the Patsy Paschall film are all alleged to have evidence of smoke/ flashes on them.*];

i.   "Murder in Dealey Plaza" by James Fetzer (2000), pages 27, 37, 56, 60, 63, 67, 83, 160-163, 168-169

288) Secret Service Agent Jerry D. Kivett, rode in V.P. 's Secret Service follow-up car (deceased 6/26/2010):

a.   WC references: 2 H 147, 149, 152-154; 5 H 565; 7 H 474; 17 H 595, 601, 608, 615, 621; 18 H 722, 766, 767, 769, 770, 773, 774, 776-781 (his reports), 782, 783, 810, 811, 812, 813, 814;

b.   HSCA contact/ interview (they did have his address)-?;

c.   12/8/97 letter to Vince Palamara (see also the spring 1998 Kennedy Assassination Chronicles journal);

d.   "Murder in Dealey Plaza" by James Fetzer (2000), page 67

e.   2004 interview/ correspondence with Vince Palamara

[Milton T. Wright: see Wright, above]

289) Cecil W. Stoughton, White House Photographer, rode in Camera Car #2 in motorcade (deceased 11/3/2008):

a. WC references: 2 H 98; 18 H 771, 775, 781, 813;

b. His book, co-authored w/ Clifton and Sidey, entitled "*The Memories-JFK: 1961-1963*" (1973);

c. Interview with David Lifton ("*Best Evidence*", p. 677);

d. 11/22/83 appearance on "*Good Morning America*";

e. 5/6/85 (letter), 7/10/85, and 4/23/86 interviews with Richard Trask (see "*Pictures of the Pain*", pp. 22-54): "Stoughton recalls that a man was washing the [rear limousine] seat "with a cloth, and he had a bucket. There was blood all over the seat, and flower petals and stuff on the floor."

f. 11/93 Disney Channel special "*With the President*";

g. "*Biography: JFK, Jr.*" (1995) A&E Channel;

h. 1/23/97 letter to Richard Trask (see "*That Day in Dallas*", pp. 9-56);

i. 11/30/95 and 11/20/97 letters to Vince Palamara (see the spring 1998 issue of Kennedy Assassination Chronicles journal);

j. Appearance at The Sixth Floor Museum, 1998;

k. "*Murder in Dealey Plaza*" by James Fetzer (2000), page 168

290) Henry Dashiell Burroughs, AP B&W still photographer, rode in Camera Car #2 in motorcade:

a. 3/85, 8/21/85, 8/27/85, and 12/85 letters/ contacts with Richard Trask ["*Pictures of the Pain*" by Richard Trask (1994), pages 37, 49, 50, 306, 318, 393-395, 397-399, 402, 404, 406-408, 410-412, and 455]---"My recollection was hearing four shots."; "I took a picture of cleaning out the car…"

b. "*That Day in Dallas*" by Richard Trask (1998), pages 30, 51, 52, and 71

c. 10/14/98 letter to Vince Palamara---"I was a member of the White House pool aboard Air Force One when we arrived with JFK in Dallas on that fateful day. *We, the pool, were dismayed to find our pool car shoved back to about #11 position in the motorcade. We protested, but it was too late.* The President had come to Texas primarily to mend political fences. That of course was the reason he brought Mrs. Kennedy too. The cars in the motorcade behind the President's and Secret Service and wire service car were all filled with local politicians. After the President's limousine turned the corner at the book depository we could not see him, but we heard the shots *and the motorcade stopped.* Looking across the park, in the far distance, I spotted the Queen Mary (the Secret Service follow-up car). An agent was standing and displaying an automatic rifle. Very unusual; I had never seen them display weapons before. That's when we knew for sure that something very serious had occurred. Maj. Cecil Stoughten [sic], White House official photographer, convinced our driver, a local sheriff, to get out of the motorcade, and we eventually arrived at Parkland Hospital. The scene at the emergency entrance was utter chaos. The limousines that had carried the Presidential party and the Vice-Presidential party were askew. *An agent with a stainless steel hospital bucket was cleaning up the rear seat of the President's limousine. Flowers were strewn over rear seats of both limos.* A handful of people had clustered across the roadway. Many were crying. Secret Service had blocked off entrance to the Hospital, but after a short *while Malcolm Kilduff, Assistant Press Secretar[y]*, *came out and told me that things looked pretty bad. The President was in serious condition.* Short while later, Kilduff called a press conference in one of the hospital classrooms and made the official announcement that the President was dead. I was the only AP man at that briefing. I ran out looking for an AP reporter or a phone; spotted Jack Bell, AP's top political reporter, on a hospital office phone. I reported what I had. He handed me the phone and said, "Dictate it." Shortly afterward, Frank Cancellare, UPI photographer, and I, wandered out to the hospital entrance looking for some sign of the Presidential party. We saw a limousine speeding off, and through the rear window we could spot that unmistakable pillbox hat of Jacqueline Kennedy's. We grabbed a cab and headed for Air Force One at Love Field. When we arrived, Air Force One had been cordoned off by Army troops, but the ramp was still in place. Before we could worry about what to do, the plane door opened and out popped Maj. Cecil Staughten [sic]. He saw us standing by and came over. He had a roll of film in his hand, and announced that he had just photographed the swearing-in of President Johnson, and asked me if AP would process the pictures and pool them with UPI. Cancellare and I readily agreed and that's how that famous picture aboard Air Force One was transmitted to the world. Hope this is of some help. You are the first historian to ask me about that tragic day." [Emphasis added];

d. *"Murder in Dealey Plaza"* by James Fetzer (2000), page 120

291) DPD Marrion L. Baker, motorcycle officer in motorcade:

a. 3 H 241-270 / testimony---see Chaney, reference "c)", below; (3 H 244 re: change of instructions) "When we got to the airport, our sergeant instructed me that there wouldn't be anybody riding beside the President's car."

b. 7 H 592 / affidavit;

c. Other WC references: WR 5-6, 149, 151-154, 156, 252; 3 H 221-228, 236, 240, 270, 280, 291; 4 H 163, 213; 6 H 297, 329, 331; 7 H 385-386, 543; 20 H 489; 26 H 679 [see also p. 159 of Stewart Galanor's *"Cover-Up"*];

d. Early 1970's interview with Fred Newcomb and Perry Adams for *"Murder from Within"* (1974), pages 72 and 98;

e. *"On Trial: Lee Harvey Oswald"* 1986 [see *"An Annotated Film. TV, and Videography 1963-1992"* by Anthony Frewin, p. 52---was he edited out of Showtime broadcast?]

f. *"The Men Who Killed Kennedy"* 1991/1995;

g. Portrayed by actor Bill Pickle in the 1991 Oliver Stone movie *"JFK"* (see *"JFK: The Book of the Film"*, pp.168-168 [inc. comments from a March 1991 interview] and 585);

h. *"Who's Who in the JFK Assassination"* by Michael Benson (1993), pp. 23-24---lists many other sources, as well

i. *"No More Silence"* by Larry Sneed (1998), pp. 123-126+photos;

j. 10/98 letter to Vince Palamara---Palamara: "Are you aware of any orders not to have the motorcycles ride right beside JFK's limousine?" Baker: "Yes"; did not know why the press photographers were out of their usual position (in front of JFK) [see 6 H 163+ *"J. Edgar Hoover: The Father Of The Cold War"* by R. Andrew Kiel (2000), page 302];

k. *"Murder in Dealey Plaza"* by James Fetzer (2000), pages 33, 37, 40, 46, 121, 172, 341, 366

l. "J. Edgar Hoover: The Father of the Cold War" by R. Andrew Kiel (2000), page 302

292) Congressman Lindley Beckworth, rode in Congressman's Car #2 (deceased 3/9/1984):

a. WC references: 17 H 614, 616;

b. 10/5/98 letter to Vince Palamara from Beckworth's son Gary---"My father Lindley was there. He passed away in 1984 from natural causes. One item of interest is that on Air Force One from Amon Carter Intl. Field-Fort Worth to Dallas-Love Field, he gave the President a Dallas Morning News which may have been the last newspaper seen by the President. They had stayed at the Hotel Texas in Ft. Worth the night before."

293) DPD James M. Chaney, one of the Presidential motorcycle officers in the motorcade (deceased April 1976):

a. WFAA/ ABC interview with Bill Lord, 11/22/63 [audio portion rebroadcast in May 1976 on CFTR radio's special *"Thou Shalt not Kill"*; see also *"Killing Kennedy"* by H.E.L., pp. 151-152, *"That Day In Dallas"* by Richard Trask, pages 115 and 119, and *"High Treason"*, p. 232]--- Chaney explained that he was "riding on the right rear fender" of JFK's limo during the shooting, and that "the President was struck in the face" by the SECOND shot. Lord ended the interview by telling the audience that "(Chaney) was so close his uniform was splattered with blood"!

b. 11/24/63 *"Houston Chronicle"* [see also 2 H 43-45]---quoted as stating that the first shot missed entirely and that the Presidential limousine stopped momentarily after the first shot;

c. Other WC references: 3 H 266 (DPD Marion Baker: "I talked to Jim Chaney, and he made the statement that the two shots hit Kennedy first and then the other one hit the Governor...he knew they came from behind him but he didn't know where."); 4 H 161 (Curry: notified by Chaney); 6 H 294 (Hargis) ; 12 H 28 (Curry again); 19 H 134; 20 H 489; 25 H 284 (Chaney's 11/28/63 report re: Ruby);

d. *"Four Days in November"* (1964, Wolper) film/ video;

e. Early 1970's interview with Fred Newcomb and Perry Adams for *"Murder From Within"* (see pages 66 and 93)---"James M. Chaney, on the right, stated that all four [of the Presidential motorcycle officers] were hit with the "spray."; ALSO: "The bloody condition of Chaney's motorcycle and clothing were later noted by Sgt. Stavis Ellis at Parkland Hospital." (pages 66 and 93);

f. *"Crossfire"* by Jim Marrs (1989), p. 14---Chaney "told newsmen the next day that the first shot missed."

g. *"JFK: The Dead Witnesses"* by Craig Roberts and John Armstrong (1995), pp. 125-126---Chaney "stated to the local press that he witnessed separate shots hit Governor Connally and the President";

h. *"That Day in Dallas"* by Richard Trask (1998), p. 116: captioned photo of Chaney;

i. *"Murder In Dealey Plaza"* by James Fetzer (2000), pages 36, 40, 121, 147, 172, 341

294) DPD Robert Weldon "Bobby" Hargis, one of the Presidential motorcycle officers in the motorcade:

a. 11/24/63 *"New York Daily News"*, p. 100 [see also *"Murder From Within"*, pages 66 and 93, and *"Cover-Up"* by Stewart Galanor, p. 37]---"Hargis was struck so hard by a piece of skull bone that he said, "I thought at first I might have been hit." [Note: Hargis denied that he ever said this during an interview with Ian Griggs in 1995];

b. 6 H 293-296 / testimony----"...it sounded like the shots were right next to me... they probably could have been coming from the railroad overpass, because I thought since I had got splattered, with blood---I was just a little back and left of---just a little bit back and left of Mrs. Kennedy..."; "...it seemed like his head exploded, and I was splattered with blood and brain, and kind of bloody water."

c. Other WC references: 6 H 290, 292; 19 H 134; 20 H 489;

d. *"The Men Who Killed Kennedy"* 1991/1995---said that fellow DPD motorcycle officer "Buddy" Brewer pointed out to him a small piece of the President's bone and brain that was stuck to his lip

e. *"JFK: That Day in November"* NBC 11/22/88;

f. Mark Oakes Eyewitness Video 1991;

g. Mark Oakes *"Eyewitness Video III"* 1998 [from 6/26/95]---Regarding the blood/ debris from JFK's head: "It hit me, it got Billy Joe Martin; it showered everything in the car behind it [indicating]" (this corroborates Sam Kinney's statements to Palamara); "I had a piece of skull on my lip...piece of his brain, piece of his bone...my motorcycle had stuff all over it" including his helmet.; "one [shot] hit his head...busted his head wide open." Hargis pointed to his right temple twice; Regarding Greer: "That guy slowed down, maybe his orders was to slow

212

down…slowed down almost to a stop." Believes Greer gave Oswald the chance to kill JFK.

h. *"Murder in Dealey Plaza"* by James Fetzer (2000), pages 40, 121, 341, 343

295) DPD William Joseph (Billy Joe) "B.J." Martin, one of the Presidential motorcycle officers in the motorcade (deceased 1989):

a. 6 H 289-293 / testimony---"There was blood and other matter on my windshield and also on my motor."

b. other WC references: 3 H 265-266; 19 H 134; 20 H 489;

c. Early 1970's interview with Fred Newcomb and Perry Adams for *"Murder From Within"* (pages 33, 42, 58, 64-65, 71, 76, 89, 92, 96, 101 [see also "Killing Kennedy" by H.E.L., p. 152])---"It is likely that he [referring to Gov. Connally] smelled gunpowder too [as Martin did].".; saw the limousine stop "…just for a moment.".; Martin "said that at morning muster the four [Presidential motorcycle officers] were ordered that under no circumstances were they to leave their positions "regardless of what happened."" [**See also** *3 H 244+"No More Silence" by Larry Sneed, p. 123 (Baker), 4 H 171 (Curry), 6 H 293 (Martin), and 20 H 489: DPD Capt. Perdue Lawrence's 11/21/63 personnel assignments (same as the HSCA's JFK Exhibit F-679); Curry's interview with Newcomb and Adams (below); Baker's letter to Palamara, above; "No More Silence" by Larry Sneed (1998), p. 162/ DPD H.B. McLain*];

d. *"American Illustrated History"*, Nov. 1988, p. 17: interview with Edward Oxford;

e. "J.B. Marshall" in Jean Hill's 1992 book (with Bill Sloan) entitled *"JFK: The Last Dissenting Witness"* [Martin was Hill's alleged paramour];

f. *"Murder in Dealey Plaza"* by James Fetzer (2000), pages 40, 121, 155, 172, 341

[John and Nellie Connally, Jackie Kennedy, Clint Hill, Paul Landis, George Hickey, Godfrey McHugh, Ted Clifton, Admiral George Burkley, Seth Kantor, Joe H. Rich, Merriman Smith, Evelyn Lincoln, and Larry O'Brien: see above]

296) DPD Douglas L. Jackson, one of the Presidential motorcycle officers in the motorcade (deceased):

a. WC references: 19 H 134; 20 H 489;

b. Early 1970's interview with Fred Newcomb and Perry Adams for *"Murder from Within"* (pages 60, 66, 71, 89, 90, 93, and 96 [see also "Killing Kennedy" by H.E.L., pages 144 and 152): "Mr. Connally was looking back toward me. And about that time then the second shot went off. That's the point when I knew that somebody was shooting at them because that was the time he [Connally] got hit---because he jerked. I was looking directly at him…he was looking…kind of back toward me and…just kind of flinched."; Jackson "stated that he was not hit [with blood/ debris]. This is possible because Jackson had begun to lag behind

the limousine and was about ten feet away from it at the time of the fatal shot.";
"...that car [JFK's limo] just all but stopped...just a moment."

c. DPD James C. Bowles' manuscript "*The Kennedy Assassination Tapes*"---includes
a personal diary entry made on 11/22/63 by Jackson

d. "*Murder in Dealey Plaza*" by James Fetzer (2000), pages 121, 172, 341

297) DPD Chief Jesse E. Curry, driver of the lead car in the motorcade (deceased June 1980):

a. 11/20/63 televised warning to Dallas citizens (see "*Four Days In November*",
1964);

b. 11/22-11/24/63 televised statements, ABC, CBS, NBC (see also "*Rush to Judgment*")

c. 4 H 150-202 [not consulted about motorcade route: 4 H 169; see also CD 5, p.
4: learned of the route 11/21/63 via Lawson and Sorrells]; 12 H 25-42; 15 H
124-133 / testimony;

d. 15 H 640 / affidavit;

e. Other WC references: too numerous to list (see "*Referenced Index Guide to the
Warren Commission*" by Walt Brown, 1995, pp. 46-47 and 294;

f. 8/69 LBJ Library Oral History (audiotape)---there was no radio contact between the lead car and the limousine and Lawson's portable radio was not working too well at the time

g. His book "*JFK Assassination File*" (1969), pages 32, 34---"No hospital attendants
were at the emergency entrance...The back seat was a gory sight---blood was
everywhere...Even amid the confusion the Chief Executive looked dead. Visible respiration was gone; his eyes were dilated and fixed...Agent Hill finally
convinced her [Jackie] to let go of the President. Apparently she didn't want
anyone to see that the BACK of the President's head was partially blown off."
[Emphasis added]; "As Dr. Perry took charge he sized up the situation. A small
neat wound was in the throat. The back of the head was massively damaged and
blood from this wound covered the floor and the aluminum hospital cart. Dr.
Perry examined the throat wound and assessed it as the entrance wound...at the
time Dr. Perry insisted that the President was shot from the front----entering at
the throat and exiting out the back of the head."

h. Early 1970's interview with Fred Newcomb and Perry Adams for "*Murder from
Within*" (pages 32, 42, 157, 164, 183, and 185)---Texas law prohibited the removal of a body from the state without an autopsy; also: it was the Secret Service
who changed the orders re: the placement of the motorcycles by JFK's limo [see
B.J. Martin, above, as well as 4 H 171 (Curry) and 338 (Lawson); 7 H 579-581;
17 H 605, 624; 18 H 741, 809; 20 H 489; 21 H 571, 768-770; see also 20 H 391
re: cancelled squad car];

i. "*CBS News Inquiry*" *The American Assassins*" 1975;

214

j. *"The Fifth Estate-Dallas and after"* 1977 CBC (interviewed by P.D. Scott!);

k. *"The Killing of President Kennedy"* (1978/1983) [full length version of *"Declassified: The Plot to Kill President Kennedy"* (1978/1988)]: Curry said that, from the direction of the blood and the brain matter, one shot had to have come from the front;

l. 4/22/80 issue of *"The Continuing Inquiry"* newsletter: interview with Gary Mack re: *"The Stop-And-Go Motorcade"*;

m. *"Murder in Dealey Plaza"* by James Fetzer (2000), pages 11, 18, 25-26, 32, 34, 42-43, 59, 83, 101-103, 117, 155, 161, 169, 172, 220, 416, 418, 419, 361-368, 404

n. *"JFK Absolute Proof"* by Robert Groden (2013): see page 154- Curry is pictured with a nice summary of his statements

298) Dallas Sheriff James Eric "Bill" Decker, rode in the lead car in the motorcade (deceased 8/29/70):

a. 12 H 42-52 / testimony;

b. 19 H 458: Decker's report---"As I heard the first retort [sic], I looked back over my shoulder and saw what appeared to me to be a spray of water come out of the rear seat of the President's car...We arrived within minutes at the Emergency entrance to Parkland Hospital where I got out of the car and stood at the side of the Presidential automobile while the President was removed from the automobile and placed on a stretcher carriage and taken into the emergency room..."

c. 23 H 913---"Have my office move all available men out of my office into the railroad yard to try to determine what happened in there and hold everything secure until Homicide and other investigators should get there."

d. Other WC references: too numerous to list (see *"Referenced Index Guide to the Warren Commission"* by Walt Brown, 1995, pp. 50-51 and 295)

e. Decker's report dated 11/22/63 as contained in CD 3 [LBJ Library]---"...I assisted with the removal of the President onto the hospital carriage. I also was present when the Governor was removed from the car."

f. *"Crossfire"* by Jim Marrs (1989), p. 14---"On hearing the first burst of firing, Sheriff Decker glanced back and thought he saw a bullet bouncing off the street pavement." [**Missed shot/ pavement:** DPD *Stavis Ellis* (12 HSCA 23; *"No More Silence"* by Larry Sneed, page 145), *Virgie Baker* (7 H 507, 515), *Royce Skelton* (6 H 236-238+19 H 496), *Austin Miller* (19 II 485 [see above]), *Jack Franzen* (17 H 840), *Mrs. Franzen* (24 H 525), *Harry Holmes* (7 H 290-292), and Secret Service agent *Warren Taylor* (18 H 782); ALSO: *James Tague* (7 H 552-558); **MANHOLE COVER/ TURF:** DPD *J.W. Foster* (6 H 252+"No More Silence" by Larry Sneed, pp. 212-213+Mark Oakes' videotaped interview), *Hugh Betzner* (24 H 200), 24 H 540, *Wayne and Edna Hartman* (FBI report dated 7/10/64+"Crossfire", pp. 315-316+videotaped interview with Mark Oakes 1991+"Who's Who in the JFK Assassination", p. 175),Clemon Earl Johnson ("No More Silence" by Larry

Sneed, p. 82), Newsman Harry Cabluck ("Crossfire", p. 315), DPD D.V. Harkness ("No More Silence" by Larry Sneed, p. 207), DPD Carl Day ("No More Silence" by Larry Sneed, p. 235), Jean Hill (6 H 221 [see above]), Deputy Sheriff Roger Craig (19 H 524+"Two Men In Dallas" video 1976), Deputy Sheriff Buddy Walthers (7 H 546+19 H 518+"High Treason", p. 131+Mark Oakes' letter from Walthers' widow Dorothy+"No More Silence", p.509+Al Maddox' 7/12/96 interview with Mark Oakes)+11/23/63 "Fort Worth Star-Telegram"+11/24/63 "Dallas Morning News"+12/21/63 "New Republic": story by Richard Dudman (all 3: see "Crossfire", p. 315)+"JFK Assassination File" by Curry, p. 57+"POTP", pp. 496-498] According-ing to Duffy and Ricci in "A Complete Book of Facts" (p. 156), "Newspaper reports the afternoon of the shooting quoted Decker as saying that after he heard the first shot, he thought he saw a bullet bounce off the pavement."

g. "Who's Who in the JFK Assassination" by Michael Benson (1993), page 107---provides many of the multiple sources of info. re: Decker that can be obtained from various other books;

h. "Murder in Dealey Plaza" by James Fetzer (2000), pages 23, 26, 36, 94, 161

299) DPD Harold R. ("H.R.", "Harry") Freeman, one of the lead motorcycle officers in the motorcade:

a. [See Kinney and Ellis above]

b. WC references: 7 H 28; 19 H 134; 20 H 489;

c. 4/21/71 interview with Gil Toff for "Murder from Within" [see also "Best Evidence", pp.370-371n] ---saw a bullet hole in the windshield at Parkland Hospital;

d. "Murder in Dealey Plaza" by James Fetzer (2000), page 139

300) DPD Bobby Joe Dale, one of two rear mid motorcade motorcycle officers:

a. WC references: 19 H 134; 20 H 489;

b. 1978 Texas News re: acoustical tests for HSCA;

c. "No More Silence" by Larry Sneed (1998), pp. 132-141+photos--- [pp. 135-136]"...the President was on the gurney beside the car, and they were wheeling him in. At that time, it was obvious that nobody could have survived a wound like that...Blood and matter was everywhere inside the car including a bone fragment which was oblong shaped, probably an inch to an inch and a half long by three-quarters of an inch wide. As I turned it over and looked at it, I determined that it came from some part of the forehead because there was hair on it, which appeared to be near the hairline. There were other fragments around, but that was the largest piece that grabbed my attention. What stood out in my mind was that there was makeup up to the hairline. Apparently he had used makeup for the cameras to knock down the glare. It was fairly distinct where it stopped and the wrap of skin took up. Other than that, nobody messed with anything inside the car in any manner, shape, or form. Nobody said, "Clean this up!" We then put the top up and secured it."

d. *"Murder in Dealey Plaza"* by James Fetzer (2000), page 120

301) DPD James W. ("J.W.") Courson, one of two mid motorcade motorcycle officers:

a. WC references 19 H 134; 20 H 489;

b. DPD James C. Bowles' manuscript *"The Kennedy Assassination Tapes"* (see also "POTP", p. 614);

c. *"Presidential Motorcade Schematic Listing"* by Todd Wayne Vaughan (1993), p. 24;

d. *"No More Silence"* by Larry Sneed (1998), pp. 127-131+photos: [pp. 129-130] "The driver immediately got out into the center lane with me on his left rear and another officer on the right. Mrs. Kennedy had, by that time, gotten back down in the seat and was holding the President's head in her lap. I was able to see that his head was horribly mangled. Skull, brain, and blood material was all along the seat... Flowers were scattered all around the car... Two other officers and I helped take the President out of the car and put him onto the stretcher. From what I was able to see of the wound, the damage seemed to be in the right rear of his head, but it was hard to tell because there was so much blood. The back part of the skull seemed to be laying over the forehead. I didn't actually see an exit wound since I saw only the back part of his head." See also *"JFK Absolute Proof"* by Robert Groden (2013): see page 154- this statement is summarized here

[Note: Jim Courson's brother, **Detective Bill Courson** from the Dallas County Sheriff's Department, was also interviewed by Larry Sneed: see *"No More Silence"*, pp. 481-506+photos; Bill Courson died in 1990. From page 505: "In my opinion, and in the opinion of several others around here, the Secret Service made a bunch of fools of themselves in the whole assassination, especially when they confiscated evidence and tainted it by breaking the chain of evidence. I think if Oswald had lived that they would never have convicted him of killing President Kennedy."]

e. *"Murder in Dealey Plaza"* by James Fetzer (2000), pages 120, 140

302) DPD William G. ("W.G.", "Bill") Lumpkin, one of the five lead motorcycle officers in the motorcade:

a. WC references: 19 H 134; 20 H 489;

b. 2/26/87 interview with Richard Trask ("POTP", pp. 234-235);

c. *"Who's Who in the JFK Assassination"* by Michael Benson (1993), pp. 261-262;

d. *"Presidential Motorcade Schematic Listing"* by Todd Wayne Vaughan (1993), p.4;

e. *"No More Silence"* by Larry Sneed (1998), pp. 154-161+photos--- [p. 158] "...I didn't see much of the President other than he was just slumped down and that he had been shot, and that his brains had been blown out. I must have seen that somewhere along the way... his brains were blown out... We knew that he was dead."

303) DPD Hollis B. "H.B." McClain, one of the two forward mid motorcade motorcycle officers:

a. WC references: 19 H 134; 20 H 489;

b. Texas News 1978 re: acoustical testing/ HSCA testimony---McClain denied that his mike was the one stuck open after hearing the tapes with the media

c. HSCA Report 75, 487, 492-493;

d. *"Who's Who in the JFK Assassination"* by Michael Benson (1993), page 270, "TKOAP" by Robert Groden (1993), p. 172, and "POTP" by Richard Trask (1994), pages 132, 208, 209, 306, 400, 418, 425, 444, 469, 480, and 616---useful summary of his HSCA testimony, post-HSCA beliefs, and various sources;

e. Mark Oakes' *"Eyewitness Video Tape III"* (1998)---"helped get Mrs. Kennedy out of the car"; nothing about the wounds, per se; "I feel like that there's somebody on that railroad track shot him a second time."

f. *"No More Silence"* by Larry Sneed (1998), pp. 162-168+photos: [p. 164] "I figured at the time that the wound was fatal. Part of the skull was laying on the floorboard. Blood and brain material was splattered all over as if a ripe watermelon had been dropped. It was a pretty gory scene."

g. *"Murder in Dealey Plaza"* by James Fetzer (2000), page 30

304) Secret Service (PRS) Agent Glen A. Bennett, rode in Secret Service follow-up car in motorcade (deceased 1994):

a. 24 H 541-542: includes Bennett's alleged contemporaneous handwritten notes from 11/22/63---"... I heard a noise that immediately reminded me of a firecracker. Immediately, upon hearing the supposed firecracker, looked at the Boss's [JFK's] car. At this exact time I saw a shot that hit the Boss about *four inches down from the right shoulder*; a second shoot [sic] followed immediately and hit the right rear high [sic] of the Boss's head."(Emphasis added) [**Back wound**] Although *the autopsy photo* ["*Best Evidence*", autopsy photo 5], *the death certificate signed by Dr. Burkley* [see above], FBI Exhibit 60 (*JFK's shirt*) ["*Best Evidence*", photo 18; 17 H 25-26], FBI Exhibit 59 (*JFK's jacket*) ["*Best Evidence*", photo17], the autopsy face sheet (17 H 45; "*Postmortem*", p.310:"verified" by Dr. Burkley), the Sibert & O'Neill report (see above), Secret Service Agent Clint Hill's report (18 H 744-745), and the testimonies of Secret Service agents' Hill (2 H 143), Bill Greer (2 H 127 and RIF#180-10099-10491: 2/28/78 HSCA interview), and Roy Kellerman (2 H 93), not to mention the 1/27/64 WC executive session transcript (Groden's "TKOAP", p. 118) and Nurse Diana Bowron's recent statements ("*Killing The Truth*", p. 183), corroborate Bennett within an inch or two, Phil Willis' photo #5 (21 H 770), the Hugh Betzner photo ("*Mortal Error*", photo 14 blow-up), the Zapruder film ("*Image of an Assassination*" video 1998: sprocket hole area), and the James Altgens' photo (21 H 781-782) depict Bennett looking AWAY from Kennedy.;

b. 18 H 760: Bennett's typed report dated 11/23/63---"...I heard what sounded like a firecracker. I immediately looked from the right/ crowd/ physical area/ and looked towards the President who was seated in the right rear seat of his limousine [sic] open convertible. *At the moment I looked at the back of the President I heard another firecracker noise and saw the shot hit the President about four inches down from the right shoulder.* A second shot followed immediately and hit the right rear high [sic] of the President's head...We peered towards the rear and particularly the right side of the area." (Emphasis added);

c. 18 H 682: Bennett's report regarding the Secret Service drinking incident of 11/21-11/22/63---Bennett was one of the four agents on the follow-up car who drank alcohol against strict Secret Service regulations (18 H 665; the other three agents were Clint Hill [18 H 685], John Ready [18 H 690], and Paul Landis [18 H 687]);

d. Other WC references: WR 48, 111; 2 H 69, 96, 134, 153; 5 H 452-453; 17 H 631; 18 H 679, 722, 724, 733, 734, 735, 737, 738, 739, 741, 746, 747, 752, 755, 758, 769, 770, 780, 783, 810, 811, 812, 813;

e. 1/30/78 HSCA interview (RIF#180-10082-10452)---"He remembers hearing what he hoped was a firecracker. He then heard another noise and saw what appeared to be *a nick in the back of President Kennedy's coat below the shoulder. He thought the President had been hit in the back.* Glen Bennett stated that he believes the first and second shots were close together and then a longer pause before the third shot...Bennett stated that he does not recall any agents reacting before the third shot...Bennett stated that he believes he saw the nick in the President's coat after the second shot." (Emphasis added);

f. July 1998 article by the author in "*JFK/ Deep Politics Quarterly*" journal entitled "Anatomy of a Threat"

g. "*Murder In Dealey Plaza*" by James Fetzer (2000), pages 26, 37, 60, 122, 167

305) Secret Service Agent (ATSAIC) Emory P. Roberts, commander of the follow-up car in the motorcade (deceased 1973):

a. 18 H 739: report dated 11/22/63---"About 1 minute later at 12:30 p.m. two or three shots were fired, at which time I saw the President lean over on Mrs. Kennedy. I knew he was hit. Just as the first or second shot was fired [Clint] Hill ran from follow-up car to President's car-jumped aboard and placed himself over Mrs. Kennedy and the President. Upon seeing the President shot, I radioed Lawson to escort us to the nearest hospital fast but at a safe speed. During the downtown motorcade [Main St.] the streets were lined with people, however, in the area where the shots rang out, the crowd was very sparse, in fact only a few people [?]. It is estimated that were [sic] were traveling about 20-25 miles an hour at the time of the shooting [actually, 8-11 mph maximum], and it is believed that the follow-up car was approx. 25 feet behind the President's car [actually about 5 feet!]. I could not determine from what direction the shots came, but felt they had come from the right side. I immediately asked everyone on car to look to see if they could determine where the shots came from-no one [?] seemed to know." [Emphasis added];

b. 18 H 733-738: report dated 11/29/63---"First of three shots fired, at which time I saw the President lean toward Mrs. Kennedy. I do not know if it was the next shot or third shot that hit the President in the head, but I saw what appeared to be a small explosion on the right side of the President's head, saw blood, at which time the President fell further to his left."; "I had in mind Vice President Johnson's safety, as well as the President's, if he was not already dead." [Emphasis added-see below];

c. 18 H 807: report dated 4/10/64 regarding 11/18/63 Tampa motorcade;

d. 18 H 679: report dated 4/28/64 regarding the drinking incident;

e. Other WC references: WR 51; 2 H 68, 96, 134, 149, 152; 5 H 562, 565; 7 H 475; 18 H 682, 722, 724, 726, 728, 741, 746, 747, 749, 750, 752, 755, 756, 758, 760, 762, 763, 765, 769, 778, 779, 783, 803, 806, 810, 811, 812, 813, 815;

f. 12/4/64 and 4/26/65 interviews with William Manchester ("The Death of a President", numerous): [p. 155] "Emory Roberts recognized Oswald's first shot as a shot." [p. 165] "Indeed, the first realist was Agent Emory Roberts, a graying, round-shouldered former Baltimore County policeman who made a tough but necessary [?] switch in allegiance while Kennedy's heart was still beating. From his seat beside Kinney, Roberts had seen the last shot strike Kennedy's skull. He was certain the wound was mortal, and he had assessed the implications at once." [Emphasis added];

g. 8/6/91 letter to Vince Palamara from Howard Donahue ("Mortal Error")---"As for Roberts, he was a cop in Towson [MD] (where I live) and I knew him slightly when I was in High School. He graduated from Towson High 9 years before I did."

Please also see, in entirety, Vince Palamara's article entitled "The Strange Actions (and Inaction) of Agent Emory Roberts", October 1996 "JFK Deep Politics Quarterly" journal:

h. "Murder In Dealey Plaza" by James Fetzer (2000), pages 26, 39, 43-44, 46, 59, 60, 78, 155, 159, 161-163, 166-172

i. "J. Edgar Hoover: The Father of The Cold War" by R. Andrew Kiel (2000), pages 308-309

306) Secret Service Agent George Warren Hickey, Jr., rode in follow-up car in motorcade (AR-15) (deceased 2011):

a. 18 H 765: report dated 11/22/63---"...I heard what seemed to me that a firecracker exploded to the right and rear. I stood partially up and turned to the rear to see if I could observe anything. Nothing was observed and I turned around and looked at the President's car. The President was slumped to the left in the car and I observed him come up. I heard what appeared to be two shots and it seemed as if the right side of his head was hit and his hair flew forward. I then reached down, picked up the AR15, cocked and loaded it and stood part way up in the car and looked about."; "...I assisted Agent Kinney to put the plastic top on 100-X. We were then told by Roy Kellerman to take the cars to the plane and stand by. I drove 100-X to the plane, loaded it in company with Agent Kinney..."

b. 18 H 761-764: report dated 11/30/63---"After a very short distance I heard a loud report which sounded like a firecracker. It appeared to come from the right and rear and *seemed to me to be at ground level* [Thomas Atkins, in Camera Car 1, thought the same thing: see "POTP", p. 386]. I stood up and looked to my right and rear in an attempt to identify it. Nothing caught my attention except people shouting and cheering. A disturbance in 679X [the follow-up car] caused me to look forward toward the President's car. Perhaps 2 or 3 seconds elapsed from the time I looked to the rear and then looked at the President. He was slumped forward and to his left, and was straightening up to an almost erect sitting position as I turned and looked. At the moment he was almost sitting erect *I heard two reports* which I thought were shots and that appeared to me *completely different in sound* than the first report and were in *such rapid succession* that there seemed to be *practically no time element between them*. It looked to me as if the President was struck in the right upper rear of his head. *The first shot of the second two seemed as if it missed because the hair on the right side of his head flew forward and there didn't seem to be any impact against his head. The last shot seemed to hit his head* and cause a noise at the point of impact which made him fall forward and to his left again. *Possibly four or five seconds elapsed from the first report and the last.*" [Emphasis added];

c. Other WC references: WR 51; 2 H 69, 134; 5 H 143-144; 17 H 607, 608, 625, 626, 630, 632; 18 H 679, 722, 724, 730, 734, 735, 739, 741, 746, 752, 758, 760, 768, 810, 811;

d. "*Mortal Error*" by Bonar Meninger (1992): author(s) allege that Hickey, by 'accident', shot JFK in the head [see the author's article in the May 1992 "*Third Decade*": not only does the Bronson film debunk the notion that Hickey's gun was fired, but Hugh Betzner, in a 11/28/67 letter to Researcher Richard E. Sprague, wrote that the gun "was not fired." ("POTP", p. 162). In addition, in Secret Service Agent Tim McIntyre's 11/29/63 report, he wrote, "no shots were fired by any agent." (18 H 746-747, below)];

e. Hickey, with the help of attorney's Mark Zaid and Jim Lesar, sued St. Martin's Press in April 1995 over "*Mortal Error*", but the case was ultimately dismissed in Sept. 1997 because the suit was brought long after Maryland's one-year statute of limitations for defamation cases.

f. "*Murder in Dealey Plaza*" by James Fetzer (2000), pages 19, 20, 24, 26, 43, 135, 167, 343, 429

307) Secret Service Agent William "Tim" McIntyre, rode on running board of follow-up car (behind Hill):

a. 18 H 748: report dated 11/22/63---"I heard three shots fired and observing the President, noticed that he had been struck by at least one bullet, I thought in the head...I attempted to locate the origin of the shots, but was unable to do so."

b. 18 H 746-747: report dated 11/29/63---"The Presidential vehicle was approximately 200 feet from the underpass when the first shot was fired, followed in quick succession by two more. I would estimate that all three shots were fired within five seconds. After the second shot, I looked at the President and witnesses his being struck in the head by the third and last shot...None of us could determine the origin of the shots, and no shots were fired by any agent."

c. Other WC references: 2 H 68, 96, 134-136; 17 H 595, 597, 607, 614, 615; 18 H 679, 722, 724, 733, 734, 735, 738, 739, 741, 752, 758, 810, 811, 812, 813, 815;

d. 1/31/78 HSCA interview (RIF#180-10082-10454)---"As they were approaching the overpass, McIntyre heard the first report, which he described as "very loud." He said that he had no doubt that it was a shot. There was a pause and then 2 more shots in succession. McIntyre stated that at the first two shots, he was scanning the area to try to determine where they were coming from. He stated that the President was directly in his vision when the third shot was fired and he saw the President struck in the head. He remembers saying to Jack Ready, "What the hell was that?" He feels certain that Clint Hill left the running board and ran to the limousine before the third shot was fired. He stated that Greer, driver of the Presidential limousine, accelerated after the third shot. At that time, he judged the three shots had been fired in about 6 or 7 seconds. There was no way to tell if more than one person was firing at the motorcade...He remembers at a later date Agent Dick Johnson [sic] told him that he picked up a bullet from a stretcher. Johnson didn't say which stretcher but McIntyre got the impression it was from the President's stretcher."

e. *"The Dark Side of Camelot"* by Seymour Hersh (1997), pp. 240-241+photo---NOTHING about Dallas!

f. *"Dangerous World: The Kennedy Years"* (12/4/97 ABC);

g. ABC News 1/28/98;

h. *"Murder in Dealey Plaza"* by James Fetzer (2000), pages 27, 46, 60, 122, 167

i. 2005 interview with Vince Palamara

308) Secret Service Agent John D. "Jack" Ready, rode on right-front running board of follow-up car (deceased 2/24/2014)

a. 18 H 750: first report dated 11/22/63 (7:25 p.m.)---"At about 12:30 p.m. I heard what sounded like firecrackers going off from my post on the right front running board. *The president's car slowed,* someone in the follow-up car stated he was shot, and I left to run to the President's car. At that time I was recalled to the follow-up car [no reason given] and took the right front seat aside ATSAIC Roberts, and proceeded to a hospital several miles distant. The shooting occurred as we were approaching the Thornton Freeway, *traveling about 20-25 miles per hour in a slight incline. There appeared to be no spectators on the right side of the roadway [?].* After the initial shot I attempted to locate the area from where they had come from but was not able to. It appeared that the shots came from my right-rear side." [Emphasis added];

b.   18 H 749: second report dated 11/22/63---"At about 12:30 p.m. we began the approach to the Thornton Freeway *traveling about 20-25 MPH* in a slight incline. *I was about 25-30 feet from President Kennedy* who was located in the right rear seat. I heard what appeared to be firecrackers going off from my position. I immediately turned to my right rear trying to locate the source but was not able to determine the exact location. At this time *the U.S. Secret Service follow-up car seemed to slow* and I heard someone from inside this car say: "he's shot". I left the follow-up car in the direction of the President's car but was recalled by ATSAIC Emory Roberts (Secret Service) as the cars increased their speeds." [Emphasis added];

c.   18 H 690: report dated 12/8/63 regarding the drinking incident;

d.   18 H 808: report dated 4/11/64 regarding the Tampa motorcade;

e.   Other WC references: WR 48, 51; 2 H 68, 96, 134-135; 5 H 452-453; 17 H 595, 597, 607, 614, 615; 18 H 679, 722, 724, 733, 734, 737, 738, 739, 741, 746, 747, 752, 753, 754, 758, 763, 777, 810, 811, 812, 813, 815;

f.   3/1/78 HSCA interview (RIF# 180-10071-10165)---"He thought the first shot was a firecracker thrown from behind them. He said that the second and third shots were closer in time than the first and second shots. He heard someone say either, "He's hit," or "He's shot," but doesn't remember when it was said, relative to the second or third shot. Ready stated that he jumped off of the running board to go to the President's vehicle but was called back by Agent in Charge Emory Roberts. He had been watching the right side and was not aware of Clint Hill running to the Presidential limousine."

g.   *"Mortal Error"* by Bonar Meninger (1992), p. 234---Ready "declined to discuss the matter"

h.   *"Murder in Dealey Plaza"* by James Fetzer (2000), pages 26, 39, 122, 155, 160, 167, 168, 169

i.   *"J. Edgar Hoover: The Father of the Cold War"* by R. Andrew Kiel (2000), page 308

j.   2005 interview with Vince Palamara

309) Thomas Maurer Atkins, Navy White House photographer, rode in Camera Car 1 in motorcade (deceased 8/24/2011):

a.   Shot the film *"The Last Two Days"*, culled from his films from the Texas trip of 11/21-11/22/63.

b. 3/1/77 tabloid publication "*Midnight*": article by **Robert Sibley**, a civilian who worked at NPC and was hired by Atkins (see also "POTP", pp. 385-386, "*Cross-fire*", pp. 16-17, and "*Who's Who in the JFK Assassination*", p. 19)-"The shots came from below and off to the right side from where I was… I never thought the shots came from above. They did not sound like shots coming from anything higher than street level." [See Hickey, above]; interestingly, **Leonard Pullin**, a civilian employee of the U.S. Navy who helped in the filming of Atkins' "*The Last Two Days*," was killed in a single-car accident in 1967 ("*Crossfire*", p. 561, and "*JFK: The Dead Witnesses*", p. 43. For his part, Gerald Posner states that Pullin was "a cameraman, not a reporter, and never claimed to have any special information": see "*Case Closed*", p. 496)

c. 3/19/86 interview and 3/2/89 correspondence with Richard Trask ("POTP", numerous, esp. Chapter 15 [see also "*That Day In Dallas*" by Richard Trask, pp. 10, 15, 32-34, 52, 55, and 70]): [p. 386] "What Atkins does recall quite clearly is that as his car was traveling down Houston Street towards the Texas School Book Depository the "shots sounded in front of me. I didn't get the sensation that they were from up high. It sounded like in the crowd at my level. I had not even seen the grassy knoll at that point. If they were coming from anywhere, they were coming from that turn. If they had come from the grassy knoll, I don't think they would have been near as loud, because I think the buildings there tended to throw the sound at us."; [p. 388, based off Trask's 3/19/86 interview] "*And to see pictures of the autopsy and what the bullet had done to the hair*…those are things that just stick out in your memory." [Emphasis added; this was said to Trask over two years before some of the autopsy pictures began appearing in books---did Atkins see the photos, possibly at NPC with fellow Navy man and WH photographer Robert Knudsen, during the weekend of the assassination?]

d. "*Murder in Dealey Plaza*" by James Fetzer (2000), page 34

VI

MISC. EYEWITNESSES

310) Deputy Sheriff Jack W. Faulkner (deceased Oct. 1996):

a.   Report dated 11/22/63 (19 H 511)---"...I asked a woman if they had hit the President, and she told me that he was dead, that he had been shot thru the head. I asked her where the shorts [sic] came from, and she pointed toward the concrete arcade on the east side of Elm St., just west of Houston St... we talked to [TSBD] office workers who told us that they were looking out of the third floor window when the shots were fired from the street near the concrete arcade..."

b.   Other WC references: 19 H 466, 514;

c.   "*No More Silence*" by Larry Sneed (1998), pp. 215-223+photos--- [p.216] "As we were crossing Elm Street, [A.D.] McCurley picked up a white piece of bone near the north curb. He asked me, "Do you suppose that could be part of his skull?" I said, "There's no blood on it," and he put it down. Later, we got to thinking, and somebody said your skull doesn't necessarily have to be touching something that's bloody. We went back and looked for it later but never found it. To this day, I believe it was a piece of John Kennedy's skull."

311) Phil Willis (deceased):

a.   7 H 492-497 / testimony;

b.   WC references: WR 112; 7 H 352; 15 H 695-697; 20 H 183; 21 H 765-773 (12 Willis' photos);

c.   "*Photographic Whitewash*" by Harold Weisberg (1967), p. 178---letter to Weisberg.

d.   Prosecution witness in Jim Garrison's trial of Clay Shaw (see "*Destiny Betrayed: JFK, Cuba, and the Garrison Case*" by James DiEugenio, p. 289);

e.   HSCA interview;

f.   "*Speak-Up America: JFK Assassination Inquiry*" NBC 1980;

g.   "*The Men Who Killed Kennedy*" 1988 [see also "High Treason", p. 454]: "I'm very dead certain at least one shot came from the front."

h.   "*USA Today Program: Opening of the TSBD Assassination Museum*" 2/20/89;

i.   *"Who's Who in the JFK Assassination"* by Michael Benson (1993), p. 483---good summary of sources re: Willis;

j.   *"JFK: The Case for Conspiracy"* video 1993 [see also Groden's "TKOAP", p. 86: captioned photo]: "It took the back of his head off [indicating]."

k.   *"Pictures of the Pain"* by Richard Trask (1994), pp. 167-182 (chapter 5) [see also *"Photographic Memory"* by Richard Trask (1996), pp. 59-63]: includes information gleaned from Willis' letter to Trask dated 6/29/84 and an interview with Willis from 11/22/85; "No one will ever convince us that the last shot did not come form the right front, from the knoll area."

l.   l*"Murder In Dealey Plaza"* by James Fetzer (2000), pages 32, 42, 50, 122, 174

m.   *"JFK Absolute Proof"* by Robert Groden (2013): see page 149- Willis is pictured with a nice summary of his statements

312) Marilyn Willis, Phil's wife:

a.   Testified with husband Phil at Clay Shaw trial.

b.   HSCA interview;

c.   *"The Men Who Killed Kennedy"* 1988---"The head shot seemed to come from the right front. It seemed to strike him here [indicating right temple/forehead area], his head went back, and all the brain matter went out the back of the head, it was like a red halo."

d.   *"Geraldo"*, 11/18/91---two shooters, shots from two directions;

e.   *"JFK: The Case for Conspiracy"* video 1993 [see also Groden's "TKOAP", p. 87]: "A red 'halo.' Matter [was] coming out the back of his head [indicating]."

f.   Interviewed on A&E's *"Biography: Lee Harvey Oswald"* 11/21/95---doesn't say much due to editing.

g.   *"Murder in Dealey Plaza"* by James Fetzer (2000), pages 123, 174

h.   *"JFK Absolute Proof"* by Robert Groden (2013): see page 149- Willis is pictured with a nice summary of her statements

313) Linda Kay Willis, one of two daughters:

a.   7 H 498-499 / testimony;

b.   *"The Men Who Killed Kennedy"* 1988---"the back of his head blew off...it doesn't make sense to be hit from the rear and still have your face intact."

c.   *"Geraldo"*, 11/18/91---agreed with mother that there were two shooters and the shots came from two directions.

d.   *"Who's Who in the JFK Assassination"* by Michael Benson (1993), pp. 482-483---good summary of sources re: Linda Willis;

e.   Interviewed on A&E's *"Biography: Lee Harvey Oswald"* 11/21/95---doesn't say much due to editing.

314) Rosemary Willis, one of two daughters:

a. WC reference: 7 H 496;

b. *"The Dallas Times-Herald"*, 6/3/79 [see also *"Case Closed"* by Gerald Posner, pp. 321-322, and *"Case Open"* by Harold Weisberg, pp. 11-14, 25-30, 34-37;

c. *"San Francisco Examiner"*, 6/5/79---believed that other shots, particularly the headshot, were fired from elsewhere, possibly from a silencer.

d. *"Conspiracy"* by Anthony Summers, p. 49;

e. *"Conspiracy of One"* by Jim Moore (1990), p. 118;

315) Beverly Oliver (Massagee):

a. 1964 film shown on *"Reel Wild Cinema"* 7/15/97 USA Network [clips from this "stag" film appear in *"Who Killed JFK: The Final Chapter?"* 11/19/93 CBS];

b. *"The Men Who Killed Kennedy"* 1988/1991/1995 [see also *"High Treason"*, p. 461]: saw "the back of his head come off."

c. Technical adviser to *"JFK"* 1991---cameo? [See *"JFK: The Book of the Film"*, pp. 119-121 and footnotes];

d. Mark Oakes Eyewitness Video 1991;

e. *"Beyond JFK: The Question of Conspiracy"* (1991/1992);

f. *"Mack VS. Oliver"* 1993;

g. *"Who Killed JFK: The Final Chapter?"* 11/19/93 CBS;

h. *"Who's Who in the JFK Assassination"* by Michael Benson (1993), pp. 323-324---good summary/ sources on Oliver.

i. *"JFK: The Case for Conspiracy"* 1993/1994 Groden [see also Groden's *"TKOAP"*, p. 86: captioned photo]: "The whole back of his head went flying out the back of the car [indicating]."

j. Her book *"Nightmare in Dallas"* (1994);

k. Mark Oakes' video *"On the Trail of the Mystery FBI Man"* (w/ Al Maddox);

l. *"Treachery in Dallas"* by Walt Brown (1995), pp. 190-192;

m. *Vince Palamara video 11/22/97;*

n. *"Murder in Dealey Plaza"* by James Fetzer (2000), pages 45, 174

o. *"JFK Absolute Proof"* by Robert Groden (2013): see page 149- Oliver is pictured with a nice summary of her statements

316) Ed Hoffman (deceased):

a. *"The Men Who Killed Kennedy"* 1988/1991/1995 [see also *"High Treason"*, pp.

462-463]: saw two men behind picket fence atop the grassy knoll, one of which fired upon JFK.

b.   A.S.K. conference 11/91;

c.   "*Beyond JFK: The Question of Conspiracy*" (1991/1992);

d.   "*48 Hours*" CBS 2/92;

e.   "*The Jim Garrison Tapes*" 1992 [daughter Mary Hoffman Sawyer acts as his interpreter here].

f.   "*The Search for the Truth*" 1992 AIC.

g.   "*Who Killed JFK: The Final Chapter?*" 11/19/93 CBS.

h.   "*Who's Who in the JFK Assassination*" by Michael Benson (1993), p. 192---good summary/ sources on Hoffman.

i.   "*JFK: Breaking the Silence*" by Bill Sloan (1993), pp. 10-49 (chapter one): very detailed information on Hoffman.

j.   "*JFK: The Case for Conspiracy*" 1993/1994 Groden [see also Groden's "TKOAP", p. 87: captioned photo]--"The rear of his head was gone, blasted outward [indicating]."

k.   Olathe, KS symposium 10/94 [see "Dallas '63", Vol. 1, No.4, pp. 27-28];

l.   JFK/ Lancer conference 11/96;

m.   JFK/ Lancer conference 11/97;

n.   Bill Law video 11/22/97;

o.   His manuscript "*Eyewitness*" (1997/ updated);

p.   "*Murder in Dealey Plaza*" by James Fetzer (2000), pages 45, 46, 174

q.   "*JFK Absolute Proof*" by Robert Groden (2013): see page 149- Hoffman is pictured with a nice summary of his statements

317) Vincent E. Drain, FBI Special Agent:

a.   WC references: numerous (see "*Referenced Index Guide to the Warren Commission*" by Walt Brown, p. 54);

b.   "*The Day Kennedy Was Shot*" by Jim Bishop, pp. 188-189, 467, 543, 614, 636, 641-643, 663-664;

c.   "*Who's Who in the JFK Assassination*" by Michael Benson (1993), pp. 117-118---good summary/ sources on Drain, includes Drain's 1984 comments to Henry Hurt ("*Reasonable Doubt*", p. 109).

d.   "*With Malice: Lee Harvey Oswald and the Murder of Officer J.D. Tippit*" by Dale K. Myers (1998), pp. 641-642;

e.   "*No More Silence*" by Larry Sneed (1998), pp. 245-262+photo--- [p. 246] "When I arrived in the trauma room, the doctors were working with President Kennedy.

They were trying to do what they could to stop the gurgling sound he was making by performing a tracheotomy on him. Despite the fact, as I later learned, that he was dead, his body reflexes were still working. I wasn't up close to the body, but I could still see fairly well the large amount of blood from the head wound. The head was badly damaged from the lower right base across the top extending across the top of the ear. It appeared to me as though the bullet traveled upward and had taken off the right portion of his skull. It may have been the security officer or one of the other officers who gave me a portion of the skull, which was about the size of a teacup, much larger than a silver dollar. Apparently the explosion had jerked it because the hair was still on it. I carried that back to Washington later that night and turned it over to the FBI laboratory."

f. *"Murder in Dealey Plaza"* by James Fetzer (2000), page 116

g. *"JFK Absolute Proof"* by Robert Groden (2013): see page 154- a nice summary of his statements

[Original FBI and Secret Service conclusions: all three shots hit within the limousine (CD1, p. 1; CD87, SS235, p. 1; "Six Seconds In Dallas", p. 64; "Reasonable Doubt", p. 132; "Whitewash II: the FBI-Secret Service Coverup" by Harold Weisberg, pages 168, 243 and 248)]

318) James "Ike" Altgens, AP photographer (deceased 12/12/95):

a. 7 H 515-525 / testimony;

b. Other WC references: 16 H 584, 965; 17 H 93; 22 H 790-792;

c. *"The Trial of Lee Harvey Oswald"* 1964 [Altgens appears as a witness, but not as himself];

d. Part 2 of *"CBS News Inquiry: The Warren Report"* 6/26/67;

e. 6/2/64 FBI interview (see *"Photographic Whitewash"* by Harold Weisberg, pp. 202-206): "He said the bullet struck President Kennedy on the right side of his head and the impact knocked the President forward. Altgens stated pieces of flesh, blood, and bones appeared to fly from the right side of the President's head and pass in front of Mrs. Kennedy to the left of the Presidential limousine."

f. C-Span 11/20/93;

g. All 3 of Richard Trask's books: *"Pictures of the Pain"* (1994), pp. 307-324 (chapter 13), *"Photographic Memory"* (1996), pp. 13-19, and *"That Day in Dallas"* (1998), pp. 57-76 (chapter 2)---includes information gleaned from interviews with (11/21/85, 11/16/91, 10/23/92) and letters (3/31/84, 4/21/84, 6/23/84, 6/21/86, 12/19/91, 8/11/93) from Altgens;

h. *"No More Silence"* by Larry Sneed (1998), pp. 41-59+photo: [pp. 49-50] "The tissue, perhaps bone, a lot of fragments, all came my way. It came in my direction because I was standing right by the curb area on the south side of Elm Street which means that it came across Jackie Kennedy, perhaps fifteen feet from the limousine, some of this, of course, falling in the car, some out of the car. But the majority of the mass that was coming from his head came directly like a straight shot out my way on to the left in a straight line. When he fell over into her lap, the blood was on the left side of his face. There was no blood on the right hand side which suggested to me that the wound was more to the left than it was to the right."

i. "*Murder in Dealey Plaza*" by James Fetzer (2000), pages 28, 34, 35, 123, 152, 259

319)-320) William Eugene and (Frances) Gayle Newman:

a. a) WFAA/ ABC 11/22/63 [see 1983 rebroadcast "*The Kennedy Tapes*" for unedited portions]: "...a gunshot, apparently from behind us, hit the President in the side of the temple [indicating]."

[Above clip familiar/ repeated: Mark Lane "*Rush To Judgment*" film

(1967/1988), "*The Two Kennedys*" (1976), "*JFK: The Day the Nation Cried*"

(1988), "*The Jim Garrison Tapes*" (1992), "*Beyond JFK: The Question Of*

Conspiracy" (1991/1992), etc.];

b. Complete Tom Alyea film from 11/22/63 (silent)---Newman is shown pointing emphatically at his right temple.

c. 19 H 490 / 24 H 219: Bill Newman's 11/22/63 Sheriff Dept. interview report---"...he was hit in the side of the head. Then he fell back...I thought the shot had come from the garden directly behind me, that was on an elevation from where I was as I was right on the curb. I do not recall looking toward the Texas School Book Depository. I looked back in the vicinity of the garden."

d. 22 H 842-843: Bill Newmans' 11/24/63 FBI interview report---"He said the President was hit on the right side of the head with the third shot and he heard the thud when the bullet struck the President."

e. 19 H 488 / 24 H 218: Gayle Newman's 11/22/63 Sheriff Dept. interview report---"I saw blood all over the side of his head."

f. 22 H 842: Gayle Newman's 11/24/63 FBI interview report---"...the President had been hit in the head..."

g. William only: 1966 interview with Josiah Thompson ("*Six Seconds In Dallas*", p. 126; see also "*Reasonable Doubt*" by Henry Hurt, p. 118)---"I thought the shot was fired from directly behind where we were standing."

h. Both Bill and Gayle testified in the Clay Shaw trial; in fact, Bill was the first witness called by Jim Garrison [see Groden's "TKOAP", p. 142];

i. William only: "*On Trial: Lee Harvey Oswald*" 1986 Showtime;

j. William & Gayle: "*JFK: The Day the Nation Cried*" (1988);

k. William & Gayle: "*USA Today Program: Opening of TSBD Assassination Museum*" 2/20/89;

l. William & Gayle: "*The Men Who Killed Kennedy*" 1991/1995;

m. William & Gayle: Mark Oakes EyeWitness Video 1991;

n. William only: Portrayed by actor Vincent D'Onofrio in the Oliver Stone movie "*JFK*" (1991) [see also pages 12 and 582 of "*JFK: The Book of the Film*"];

o. "*JFK: Breaking the Silence*" by Bill Sloan (1993), pp. 168-174 (chapter 8);

p. "*Who's Who in the JFK Assassination*" by Michael Benson (1993), pp. 310-311--- good summary/ sources on the Newmans.

q. William only: Bill Law video 11/22/97;

r. William & Gayle: "*48 Hours*" (7/9/98) CBS [then and now];

s. William only: "*No More Silence*" by Larry Sneed (1998), pp. 94-101+photo;

t. William only: "*Murder in Dealey Plaza*" by James Fetzer (2000), pages 125, 148, 172, and 341.

u. "*JFK Absolute Proof*" by Robert Groden (2013): see page 149- Both are pictured with a nice summary of their statements

321) Postal Inspector Harry D. Holmes (deceased 10/89):

a. 7 H 289-308, 525-530 / testimony;

b. Other WC references: WR 121, 181, 201, 312; 4 H 228-229; 7 H 155, 256, 266, 590, 592; 13 H 4, 25-26; 15 H 151; 20 H 177-180; 24 H 488-492;

c. "*Murder from Within*" by Fred Newcomb and Perry Adams, p. 213 (based off an early 1970's interview): "A postal inspector [Holmes] picked up a piece of skull from the Elm St. pavement. He said it was as "...big as the end of my finger..." Furthermore, it was one of many: "...there was just pieces of skull and bone and corruption all over the place..." He later discarded it. [!!!]";

d. "*No More Silence*" by Larry Sneed (1998), pp. 351-371+photo--- [p. 352] "... there was just a cone of blood and corruption that went up right in the back of his head and neck. I thought it was red paper on a firecracker. It looked like a fire-cracker lit up which looks like little bits of red paper as it goes up. But in reality it was his skull and brains and everything else that went up perhaps as much as six or eight feet. Just like that!"

e. "*Murder in Dealey Plaza*" by James Fetzer (2000), pages 46, 124, 172

f. "*JFK Absolute Proof*" by Robert Groden (2013): see page 154- a nice summary of his statements

322) Deputy Sheriff Al Maddox:

a. Mark Oakes Eyewitness Video 1991;

b. "*The Kennedy Assassinations-Coincidence or Conspiracy?*" 7/7/92;

c. Oakes' "*On the Trail of the Mystery FBI Man*" (w/ Beverly Oliver);

d. Mark Oakes "*Eyewitness Video III*" 1998---Regarding Deputy Sheriff Buddy Walthers: "I believe he showed me the bullet" [the one found near the manhole cover on Elm].

e. "*No More Silence*" by Larry Sneed (1998), pp. 507-517+photo--- [p. 509] "...I also saw human tissue lying in the street which was being wiped and cleaned up at the time. That was right about where the President was said to have been hit. I also saw one of the motorcycle officers who was splattered with blood."

323) Norman Mitchel Similas:

a. "*The New York Times*", 11/23/63---"I could see a hole in the President's left temple and his head and hair were bathed in blood."

b. "*Photographic Whitewash*" by Harold Weisberg (1967), pp. 81-94, 97, 212, 214-222, 224-235, 237-240---includes the 7/15/64 "*Liberty*" magazine article and several FBI reports on Similas;

c. "*Who's Who in the JFK Assassination*" by Michael Benson (1993), page 419---good summary/ sources on Similas.

d. "*Pictures of the Pain*" by Richard Trask (1994), pp. 594-599;

e. "*Murder In Dealey Plaza*" by James Fetzer (2000), pages 59, 126, 152, 259

324) Alan Smith:

a. "*Chicago Tribune*", 11/23/63, p. 9 [see also "*Murder from Within*", p. 71]: "...The car was ten feet from me when a bullet hit the President in the forehead...the car went about five feet and stopped." [See Dr. Seldin, DPD Chaney, and Bill Newman, above; "*Triangle of Fire*" author Bob Goodman claimed to be Alan Smith during a 1992 interview with Ian Griggs. Goodman does claim to be an eyewitness in his book---on page 3; he states, "One of the bullets hit the President in his forehead."];

b. "*Murder in Dealey Plaza*" by James Fetzer (2000), pages 123, 342

325) DPD Joseph R. "Joe" Cody:

a. WC references: 13 H 189-190; 14 H 33, 295, 558; 15 H 616; 23 H 344;

b. "*Geraldo*", 11/23/88;

c. '*Who's Who in the JFK Assassination*" by Michael Benson (1993), p. 82;

d. "*The Search for Lee Harvey Oswald*" by Robert Groden (1995), p. 176;

e. "*With Malice: Lee Harvey Oswald and the Murder of Officer J.D. Tippit*" by Dale Myers (1998), p. 335;

f. "*No More Silence*" by Larry Sneed (1998), pp. 467-480+photo--- [p.467] "...we jumped in our car and arrived at the scene where Kennedy was shot and killed in just three or four minutes. By that time, it was probably ten minutes after the shooting. While we were there, *I searched the plaza and found a bone lying in the gutter that apparently came out of the back of the President's head.*" [Emphasis added];

g. "*JFK Absolute Proof*" by Robert Groden (2013): see page 154- a nice summary of his statements.

326) Robert E. Schorlemer, M.D.

a. "I was a senior medical student making rounds in the E.R. (at Parkland Hospital) with second-year surgery resident, Dr. James Carrico, to evaluate who was to be admitted from the night-shift holdovers. We were moving from one stall to another when we heard banging of doors from the triage station at the front of the ER. Shortly thereafter, we heard screaming from the front asking for more stretchers, and right after that Gov. Connally was pushed through the hall door on a gurney. He was wearing a gray silk suit with alligator shoes and was moaning and gasping for air.

Red Duke, the chief resident in surgery manning the ER, jumped up from the nurses' station, and we all moved into ER operating room #1 to take care of him. I opened his shirt to see a chest wound on his right side sucking air. Red directed that a Vaseline gauze pad be placed over the wound to help seal the pneumothorax that was produced by this until they could get a chest tube placed. I did this.

At that point, Jim Carrico said, "Let's go to the next room to get ready for the next case coming in."

As we walked out of the room, President Kennedy was wheeled into the hallway separating the two rooms. In my disbelief, I figured that this had to be his double, as no one could believe that the president could be placed in such jeopardy. As one could see, half of the calivarium of the skull had been blown away with the underlying brain exposed and the flap produced lying behind his head. Some agonal movements were being made, and Jim directed that I get the IV started while he tried to intubate him. His comment was, "Boy, I'm lucky to have been able to intubate him because the trachea was severed by one of the bullets."

At this time two Secret Service agents entered the room cursing and yelling. They asked who I was, since I had removed my newly cleaned and pressed white jacket worn by all medical students at the time. I didn't want to get any stains on it at the time. (Now it would have been a collector's item.) When they found out I was a lowly medical student, they kicked me out of the room. I then called for the chief of the surgery and neurosurgery resident and Dr. Kemp Clark, head of the neurosurgery department.

Jackie, who had come in with the stretcher carrying President Kennedy, stood outside the room in the hall separating the two ER operating rooms. She remained there, until they removed Kennedy after pronouncing him dead. Even though the Secret Service agents removed me from the room, they did not cordon the area off enough to keep another medical student... from coming around from the prep and cleaning area to come up to Jackie and attempt to console her.

233

I thought this rather strange that no one was paying attention to her at the time other than a complete stranger. He had, previous to being a medical student, been an evangelistic singer.

It's amazing that (my) memory is unchanged from the day this happened. I don't have trouble remembering any of the details.

Robert E. Schorlemer, M.D.

San Antonio, Texas"

a. *"JFK Absolute Proof"* by Robert Groden (2013): see page 153- Dr. Schorlemer is pictured with a nice summary of his statements

327) Nurse Phyllis Hall:

a. *Sixth Floor Museum* oral history: A nurse in the outpatient clinic at Parkland Memorial Hospital in 1963, Hall was in Trauma Room One during the treatment of President Kennedy. Shortly before the assassination, Hall assisted with the care of Marina Oswald during her second pregnancy. Recorded December 16, 2010, February 7, 2011, March 9, June 5, and December 13, 2012, and February 22 and June 12, 2013.

b. *Mirror UK* 11/10/13: "[JFK's] pupils were dilated and there was a gaping exit wound in his throat... Mr. Kennedy had such a thick head of hair, and few people noticed the gaping wound to his skull. The bullet had ripped it clean away. His brain was severely damaged and the blood loss was huge... I could see a bullet lodged between his ear and his shoulder. It was pointed at its tip and showed no signs of damage. I remember looking at it – there was no blunting of the bullet or scarring around the shell from where it had been fired. I'd had a great deal of experience working with gunshot wounds but I had never seen anything like this before. It was about one-and-a-half inches long – nothing like the bullets that were later produced. It was taken away but never have I seen it presented in evidence or heard what happened to it. It remains a mystery... I truly believe no man could have carried out the attack without some sort of help, and after seeing the mystery bullet in Mr. Kennedy's head I feel there is something far deeper to his death than we the public know." [Sandra Scott: "I was personally acquainted with Phyllis Hall, as I worked with her now deceased husband, Dave Hall, at the time. I knew her to be an absolutely honest person, and I remember her husband speaking about his wife's involvement with President Kennedy when he was first brought to Parkland. What she is saying now, is exactly what I heard 50 years ago."]

c. *"JFK Absolute Proof"* by Robert Groden (2013): see page 153- Nurse Hall is pictured with a nice summary of her statements

VII

VARIOUS SOURCES USED

(IN NO PARTICULAR ORDER)

1) *"High Treason"* by Robert J. Groden and Harrison Edward Livingstone (NOV. 1990 BERKLEY PAPERBACK EDITION [sometimes abbreviated HT]);

2) *"The Death of a President"* by William Manchester (FIRST PERENNIAL LIBRARY EDITION, 1988 [PAPERBACK]);

3) *"The Day Kennedy Was Shot"* by Jim Bishop (FIRST HARPER PERENNIAL EDITION, 1992 [PAPERBACK]);

4) *The Warren Report* (GPO EDITION, 1964 [888 PAGES]);

5) *26 Volumes of Hearings and Exhibits*, 1964;

6) *"Best Evidence"* by David Lifton (CARROLL & GRAF PAPERBACK EDITION, 1988 [INC. AUTOPSY PHOTOS]) [often abbreviated as "BE"].

7) *"Conspiracy"* by Anthony Summers (FIRST PARAGON HOUSE PAPERBACK EDITION 1989);

8) *"The Killing of a President"* by Robert Groden (1993/ hardcover) [often abbreviated as "TKOAP"];

9) *"Killing the Truth"* by Harrison Edward Livingstone (1993);

10) *"Killing Kennedy"* by Harrison Edward Livingstone [author's initials sometimes abbreviated as H.E.L.] (1995);

11) *"Cause of Death"* by Cyril Wecht, M.D., J.D., with Mark Curriden and Benjamin Wecht (FIRST ONYX PRINTING, NOVEMBER 1994 [PAPERBACK]);

12) *"A Complete Book of Facts"* by James P. Duffy and Vincent L. Ricci (1992);

13) *"Who's Who in the JFK Assassination"* by Michael Benson (1993);

14) *"Post Mortem"* by Harold Weisberg (1975);

15) *"High Treason 2"* by Harrison Edward Livingstone (1992);

16) *"Assassination Science"* by James Fetzer (1998);

17) *"Case Closed"* by Gerald Posner (1993);

18) *"JFK: Conspiracy of Silence"* by Charles A. Crenshaw, M.D. with Jens Hansen and J. Gary Shaw (1992) [*later renamed "Trauma Room One" (2001)* and *"JFK Has Been Shot"* (2013)];

19) *"Treachery in Dallas"* by Walt Brown (1995);

20) *"Bloody Treason"* by Noel Twyman (1997);

21) *HSCA Report and Volumes* **(1979)**

22) *"Crossfire"* by Jim Marrs (1989);

23) *"Reasonable Doubt"* by Henry Hurt (1985);

24) *"Destiny Betrayed: JFK, Cuba, and the Garrison Case"* by James DiEugenio (1992/2012);

25) *"JFK: The Book of the Film"* by Oliver Stone and Zachary Sklar (1992);

26) *"The Search for Lee Harvey Oswald"* by Robert Groden (1995);

27) *"Mortal Error"* by Bonar Menninger (1992/2013);

28) *"Breach of Faith"* by William P. Truels, M.D., M.S. (1996 SECOND EDITION);

29) *"Survivor's Guilt: The Secret Service and the Failure to Protect President Kennedy"* by Vince Palamara (2013);

30) *"JFK: Breaking the Silence"* by Bill Sloan (1993) [later renamed *"The Kennedy Conspiracy"* (2012)];

31) *"JFK: For A New Generation"* by Conover Hunt (1996);

32) *"The Man Who Knew Too Much"* by Dick Russell (1992);

33) *"Between The Signal and the Noise"* by Roger Bruce Feinman (1993);

34) *"The Way We Were"* by Robert MacNeil (1988);

35) **COPA 1994 conference video**: Dr. Gary Aguilar, Kathleen Cunningham, R.N., Dr. Randy Robertson, Wallace Milam, Andy Purdy (HSCA) and Mark Flanagan (HSCA);

36) **COPA 1995 conference videos**: Dr. Gary Aguilar, Kathleen Cunningham, R.N., Dr. Randy Robertson, Dr. David Mantik, Andy Purdy (HSCA), Dr. Cyril Wecht (HSCA), and Dr. Michael Baden (HSCA);

37) **COPA 1996 conference video**: Art Smith, Dr. Gary Aguilar, Dr. Randy Robertson, Dr. David Mantik;

38) *"Best Evidence: The Research Video"* (1980/ 1990) w/ Rike, O'Connor, Custer, and David;

39) *"JFK: The Case for Conspiracy"* video (1993) w/ Salyer, Crenshaw, Peters,

Dulany, O'Neill, McClelland, Bell, etc. [includes excerpts from KRON program below].

40) *"JFK: An Unsolved Murder"*, KRON, 11/18/88 w/ Rike, O'Connor, Custer, David, Riebe, Jones, McClelland, Bell, Carrico, Jenkins, etc.

41) *"Nova"*, 11/15/88 w/ Dulany, Peters, McClelland, Jenkins, Bell, Tomlinson, and Shaw [includes excerpts from *"Best Evidence"* video above].

42) **11/22/91 video of Jerrol Custer [and Tom Wilson] filmed by Vince Palamara (for** *"High Treason 2"*/**Harry Livingstone)** [see "High Treason 2", pages 210, 212, 213, 221, and 626 (4 references), as well as "Killing the Truth", pages 266 re: Wilson, 582, 675 and 742];

43) **3/15-3/16/98 video of Jerrol Custer filmed by Vince Palamara (for JFK Lancer).**

44) *"JFK: The Assassination, The Cover-up, and Beyond"* video 1994 by Prof. James Fetzer;

45) **11/22/97 video of Aubrey Rike filmed by Vince Palamara;**

46) **Midwest Symposium, 4/93: Medical Debate** w/ Wallace Milam, David Lifton, Dr. Gary Aguilar, Dr. Cyril Wecht, Roger Bruce Feinman, Dr. David Mantik, etc.;

47) *"Witness VS. Research: Questioning the Facts"* 1992 w/ Francis X. O'Neill, Evica;

48) Various segments from *"The Men Who Killed Kennedy"* (1988/1991/1995) w/ Peters, McClelland, O'Connor, David re: Pitzer;

49) **Various programs/ videos re: Dr. Charles Crenshaw:** *"20/20"* 4/92 w/ Baxter, **The Third Decade Conference, Chicago, IL 6/92**, *etc.*

50) *"Hard Copy"* 5/90 w/ Rike, O'Connor, McClelland;

51) *"Kennedy in Texas"* video (1984) w/ Perry from 11/23/63 (also Huber);

52) Donald Rebentisch on *"The Fifth Estate"* (1981/ 1983) CBC;

53) Paul O'Connor on *"On Trial: Lee Harvey Oswald"* 1986 Showtime;

54) Dr. Marion Jenkins on *"20/20"* 11/93;

55) Dr. McClelland on *"The Jim Garrison Tapes"* video 1992;

56) **WFAA/ ABC video 11/22-11/24/63** w/ Shaw, Shires, McClelland, Jones, Huber, Rike, McGuire, etc.;

57) Elizabeth Wright-Good on **Mark Oakes second Eyewitness Video** (1994);

58) *Audio tapes* of **Dr. Gary Aguilar's 3/30/94 interviews** of J. Thornton Boswell and James J. Humes;

59) **Air Force One radio transmissions for 11/22/63**: *audiotapes* and transcripts;

60) **"Pictures of the Pain"** by Richard Trask (1994) [often abbreviated as "POTP"].

61) **"Presidential Motorcade Schematic Listing November 22, 1963"** by Todd Wayne Vaughan (1993);

62) **"JFK: The Dead Witnesses"** by Craig Roberts and John Armstrong (1995);

63) **"Texas State Journal of Medicine"**, **January 1964, Vol. 60, pp. 61-74;**

64) **"CBS News Inquiry: The Warren Report"**, **Parts 1-4, 6/25-6/28/67;**

65) **"Reasonable Doubt"** video (1988);

66) **"JFK Assassination File"** (1969) by DPD Chief Jesse Curry;

67) **JAMA, May 27, 1992-Vol 267, No. 20: "JFK's Death---the plain truth from the MDs who did the autopsy"** by Dennis L. Brea (interview with James J. Humes and "J" Thornton Boswell);

68) **JAMA May 27, 1992: "JFK's Death, Part II, Dallas Mds Recall Their Memories";**

69) **"Six Seconds in Dallas"** by Josiah Thompson (1967);

70) **"Speak-Up America: JFK Assassination Inquiry"** **NBC 1980;**

71) **Boston Globe article 6/21/81.**

72) **"A Hero for Our Time"** by Ralph Martin (1983);

73) **"Four Days in November"** **(1964, David Wolper);**

74) **"Who Killed JFK: The Final Chapter?"** **(11/19/93) CBS;**

75) **"JFK" movie by Oliver Stone (1991);**

76) **"Murder From Within"** by Fred Newcomb and Perry Adams (1974/2011);

77) **"After Action Report/ Summary,"** **Gen. Wehle's Office, Military District of Washington (MDW), 11/22/63:** *attached* **Memorandum for the Record dated 11/27/63;**

78) **"Where were you when President Kennedy was shot?"** by Abigail ("Dear Abby") Van Buren (1993);

79) **"That Day in Dallas"** by Richard Trask (1998);

80) **"Selections from Whitewash"** (1994) by Harold Weisberg;

81) **"Final Report of the Assassination Records Review Board"** (1998);

82) **"Deep Politics and the Death of JFK"** by Peter Dale Scott (1993);

83) **"The Warren Omission"** by Walt Brown (1996);

84) *"Cover-Up"* by Stewart Galanor (1998);

85) *"With Malice: Lee Harvey Oswald and the Murder of Officer J.D. Tippit"* by Dale K. Myers (1998/2013);

86) *"An Annotated Film. TV, and Videography 1963-1992"* by Anthony Frewin (1993);

87) *"Referenced Index Guide to the Warren Commission"* by Walt Brown (1995);

88) *"Cover-Up"* by Gary Shaw and Larry Ray Harris (1976);

89) *"Nightmare in Dallas"* by Beverly Oliver with Coke Buchanan (1994);

90) *"No More Silence"* by Larry Sneed (1998/2002);

91) *"Conspiracy of One"* by Jim Moore (1990);

92) *"Case Open"* by Harold Weisberg (1994);

93) *"Photographic Memory"* by Richard Trask (1996);

94) *"Photographic Whitewash"* by Harold Weisberg (1967);

95) *"High Treason III"* by Harrison Edward Livingstone (1998 edition of *"High Treason"*);

96) *"The Dark Side of Camelot"* by Seymour Hersh (1997);

97) *"Eyewitness Video III"* by Mark Oakes (1998);

98) *"Who Killed JFK?"* by Carl Oglesby (1992);

99) *"Triangle of Fire"* by Bob Goodman (1993);

100) *"Whitewash II: the FBI-Secret Service Coverup"* by Harold Weisberg (1966);

101) *"The People VS. Lee Harvey Oswald"* by Walt Brown (1992);

102) *"Murder in Dealey Plaza"* by James Fetzer (2000)

103) *"In the Eye of History: Disclosures in The JFK Assassination Medical Evidence"* by William Law (2004)

104) *"J. Edgar Hoover: The Father of the Cold War"* by R. Andrew Kiel (2000)

105) *"The Men Who Killed Kennedy"* (2003) DVD

106) *"Encyclopedia of the JFK Assassination"* by Michael Benson (2002)

107) *"The Radical Right and the Murder of President John F. Kennedy"* by Harrison Edward Livingstone (2004)

108) *"Inside the ARRB"* by Douglas Horne (2009) [all ARRB references can be found in this valuable 5 volume series]

109) *"JFK Absolute Proof"* by Robert Groden (2013)

110) *"The Kennedy Half Century"* by Larry Sabato (2013)

111) *"The Kennedy Detail"* by Gerald Blaine and Lisa McCubbin (2010)

112) *"Mrs. Kennedy and Me"* by Clint Hill and Lisa McCubbin (2012)

113) *"Five Days in November"* by Clint Hill and Lisa McCubbin (2013)

SPECIAL THANKS TO: Amanda Palamara, Brad Parker, Wallace Milam, Dr. Gary Aguilar, Bill Law, Dr. Adolph Giesecke, Russ McLean, Dr. David Mantik, Malcolm Blount, Bill Drenas, Joanne Braun, Ed Sherry, Larry Sneed, Stewart Galanor, Jan Stevens, Walt Brown, Robert Groden, David Lifton, and Harry Livingstone. Also, Dr. Randy Robertson and Kathleen Cunningham provided some valuable insights via their conference presentations.

AUTHOR (<u>MEDICAL</u>) INTERVIEWS/ CORRESPONDENCE LISTING:
[Not included are attempted interviews/contacts: these are duly noted throughout the text i.e. "Unanswered letter from Vince Palamara 1998". In addition, this list does <u>not</u> include many of the author's Secret Service/ related interviews- see the author's first book Survivor's Guilt: The Secret Service and the Failure to Protect President Kennedy]

I. PARKLAND

1. <u>Dr. Charles Crenshaw (deceased);</u>
2. Dr. Malcolm Perry (deceased)
3. Dr. Ronald Coy Jones;
4. Dr. Paul Peters (deceased);
5. Dr. Donald Seldin;
6. Dr. Donald T. Curtis;
7. Aubrey Rike (deceased);
8. Milton T. Wright *;
9. MRS. Hurchel Jacks*;
10. <u>Dr. Robert N. McClelland;</u>
11. <u>Nurse Patricia B. Gustafson (Hutton);</u>
12. Dr. Adolph Giesecke (deceased);
13. DPD Stavis Ellis*;
14. Mrs. Billie Martinets;
15. <u>Dr. William Risk;</u>
16. Dr. William Osborne;
17. <u>Dr. Donald Jackson;</u>
18. <u>Dr. Boris Porto, son of Dr. Lito Porto;</u>
19. <u>Dr. Earl F. Rose (deceased);</u>

II. C-130

1. Vincent Gullo;
2. Sam Kinney *(deceased);

III. Methodist Hospital (re: Harper fragment)

1. Dr. Gerard Noteboom;
2. William A. Harper;

IV. Bethesda

1. Chester Boyers;
2. Richard Lipsey;
3. Jerrol Custer (deceased);
4. John T. Stringer, Jr.;
5. James W. Sibert (deceased);
6. MRS. Layton Ledbetter;
7. Don Rebentisch;
8. Dr. James J. Humes (deceased);
9. Paul K. O'Connor (deceased);
10. Jan Gail "Nick" Rudnicki;

V. Limousine (White House garage)

1. Cortlandt Cunningham;

VI.* MISC. MOTORCADE OCCUPANTS:

1. George Whitmeyer, Jr. the son of Lt. Col. George Whitmeyer (deceased);
2. DPD Samuel Q. Bellah (deceased);
3. DPD Marion Baker;
4. Gary Beckworth, son of Congressman Lindley Beckworth (deceased);
5. Henry Burroughs (deceased);